WHO IS AFRAID OF THE STATE?

CANADA IN A WORLD OF MULTIPLE CENTRES OF POWER

Edited by Gordon Smith and Daniel Wolfish

Is government becoming less powerful? Is it in retreat vis-à-vis a proliferation of non-governmental agencies, multinational corporations, and international organizations? The essays in this collection argue that – contrary to some private-sector populists – the state is in the best position to lead in making policy in a rapidly changing world and should retain and refine this responsibility. Examining the interaction of government, international organizations, civil society, and the private sector, the contributors show that government, far from being stagnant, is in a constant state of transformation and revitalization. It may work to prepare citizens for changes that often seem inevitable, and sometimes it challenges, even resists, the directions or modes of such change. It remains an important – perhaps the most crucial – actor in the governance process.

(The Trends Project Series)

GORDON SMITH is executive director of the Centre for Global Studies, University of Victoria, and chairs the board of the International Development Research Centre. Until 1997, he served as deputy minister in the Department of Foreign Affairs and as the prime minister's personal representative for G7/G8 summits, as well as ambassador to NATO and the EU.

DANIEL WOLFISH started his career in government as an associate at the Policy Research Initiative in Ottawa and as a co-editor of the policy research magazine *Horizons*. He is currently a strategic priorities analyst for the Department of Fisheries and Oceans.

POLICY RESEARCH: THE TRENDS PROJECT SERIES

The Trends Project Series is a result of the government of Canada's Policy Research Initiative, an undertaking that seeks to strengthen the government of Canada's policy capacity and ensure that policy development benefits from the work of researchers and academics. The Policy Research Secretariat, in co-operation with the Social Sciences and Humanities Research Council, developed a new model for academics and government to collaborate on policy research. Teams of academics examined the forces that are driving change in Canada and identified the potential implications for public policy. This collaboration came to be known as the Trends Project. Under the project, academics, research institutes, and government officials worked in partnership to build a better knowledge base on longer-term issues to support policy development and identify knowledge gaps requiring further research. The Trends Project will result in the following books:

Gordon Smith and Daniel Wolfish, editors,
Who Is Afraid of the State? Canada in a World of Multiple Centres of Power

Edward A. Parson, editor,
Governing the Environment: Persistent Challenges, Uncertain Innovations

Danielle Juteau, editor,
Social Differentiation: Patterns and Processes

George Hoberg, editor,
Capacity for Choice: Canada in a New North America

Neil Nevitte, editor,
Value Change and Governance in Canada

David Cheal, editor,
Aging and Demographic Change in Canadian Context

WHO IS AFRAID OF THE STATE?

Canada in a World of Multiple Centres of Power

Edited by Gordon Smith and Daniel Wolfish

UNIVERSITY OF TORONTO PRESS
Toronto Buffalo London

Toronto Buffalo London
Printed in Canada

ISBN 0-8020-8388-9

Printed on acid-free paper

National Library of Canada Cataloguing in Publication Data

Main entry under title:

Who is afraid of the state? : Canada in a world of multiple centres of power

(Trends series)
Includes bibliographical references.
ISBN 0-8020-8388-9

1. Canada – Politics and government. 2. Political planning – Canada.
3. Canada – Foreign relations – 1945– . 4. Power (Social sciences).
5. International relations. I. Smith, Gordon S. II. Wolfish, Daniel.
III. Series: Trends series (Toronto, Ont.).

JL75.W56 2001 320.971 C00-933121-2

University of Toronto Press acknowledges the financial assistance to its publishing program of the Canada Council for the Arts and the Ontario Arts Council.

University of Toronto Press acknowledges the financial support for its publishing activities of the Government of Canada through the Book Publishing Industry Development Program (BPIDP).

Contents

Figures and Tables

Figures

Tables

Preface

Exchanging ideas, perspectives, frameworks, and data between academics and government is at once necessary for the development of innovative and effective public policy and increasingly difficult in time of constant change. The Trends Project, a collaborative effort of the Policy Research Secretariat and the Social Sciences and Humanities Research Council, was conceived as a means of addressing this challenge by providing a new model for academics and government to collaborate on policy research and for supporting policy development.

Three goals lie at the heart of the Policy Research Secretariat and its Trends Project:

- to develop a future-oriented research agenda
- to enhance the policy-research capacity of both the academic community and government
- to facilitate a change of culture in both government and the academic community

In the past, the federal government has usually commissioned research to address government-identified gaps in knowledge and the federal granting councils have funded academic-led research. Under the Trends Project, academics, think tanks, and government officials worked in partnership to identify the knowledge gaps requiring further research. The objective of this collaboration was not to engage in problem-solving research, but rather to identify what we do and do not know and to understand how we know it. The research undertaken by research undertaken by the Trends Project teams looked forward to the medium to long term rather than addressing immediate policy concerns.

The makeup of the teams themselves was unique. The Project brought together some of Canada's leading academics to head eight teams made up of over fifty researchers from universities across the country. Participating researchers were selected through a call for proposals administered by the Social Sciences and Humanities Research Council. By creating multidisciplinary teams consisting of participants from across Canada, the Trends Project succeeded in bringing together people who would normally not interact with one another. The result of this multidisciplinary and cross-Canada approach has been a greater depth and breadth of understanding of the emergent policy pressures that Canada is likely to confront in the coming years.

The Trends Project was also innovative because it provided a means for academics to have their ideas and research circulated widely throughout government. The overall product was not simply research papers, but also the process of continual collaboration between government and academic communities. The resultant research papers were presented on several occasions at workshops and conferences across the country, where Canadian researchers and government officials provided insight and feedback. Commentaries and research excerpts have been featured regularly in *Horizons*, the Policy Research Initiative's newsletter. *Horizons* targets a broad policy audience of over 8100 people throughout the Canadian policy research community, both inside and outside government.

The second annual National Policy Research Conference in November 1999 offered an opportunity for researchers to showcase their work to over 800 policy developers and experts in the federal and provincial governments. Finally, each of the papers published under the Trends Project underwent anonymous peer review.

Bringing government and academic communities together on an ongoing basis exposed both parties to each other's research needs, perspectives, and constraints. The Trends Project is one part of a larger effort to build a Canada-wide policy research capacity. It is a model that we would like to build on in the future.

Laura A. Chapman
Executive Director
Policy Research Initiative
Ottawa, Ontario
August 2000

Acknowledgments

This volume is genuinely a group effort and would not have been possible without the co-operation of a number of people and organizations. At the Policy Research Secretariat in Ottawa, Margaret Moore provided leadership and support throughout the Multiple Centres of Power phase of the Trends Project. In addition to organizing two workshops, she provided valuable assistance to the editors and team members, and we thank her. We are grateful also to Michael Carley, consulting editor on the Trends Project for the Policy Research Secretariat. His comments on various drafts of the Introduction and Conclusion to this volume and his advice on editing its chapters proved invaluable. We would also like to thank Alexander Wake and Ehab Shanti; without them, this book could not have been completed. We wish to extend our thanks as well to Michele Wingelman and Jane Purdue at the Centre for Global Studies for time they spent organizing workshops, copyediting text, compiling the bibliography, and preparing this volume. Finally, we thank Claire Cutler, Rodney Dobell, Brian Job, Andy Knight, John Langford, Michael M'Gonigle, Robert Walker, Michael Webb, and Mark Zacher for participating in the original workshop held in Victoria in May 1999 and for reviewing the work of the contributing authors.

Contributors

Julien Bauer is professor of political science at the Université du Québec à Montréal (UQAM). He is a member of the executive and a past chair of the Institute of Public Administration of Greater Montreal. His current research interests include the Canadian political system, religion and politics, minorities, and the Middle East. His latest books include *Le Système politique canadien* (1998) and *Politique et religion* (1999), Presses Universitaires de France, Collection Que sais-je ?

Stephen Clarkson has been teaching political economy at the University of Toronto, his alma mater, since 1964. He has a BA from Toronto, an MA from Oxford (Rhodes scholar), and a doctorate from the Sorbonne. His research focus has shifted from his original interest in the relationship between the USSR and India to his present work on that between the United States and Canada. He spent the 1980s researching and co-writing the award-winning, two-volume biography *Trudeau and Our Times*. Now enjoying both a Killam and a Woodrow Wilson fellowship, he is studying the impact of globalization (WTO) and continentalism (NAFTA) on the Canadian state.

Ronald Crelinsten is professor of criminology at the University of Ottawa. He is currently visiting professor in the Department of Political Science and Public Administration and the Department of International Relations at the Middle East Technical University in Ankara, Turkey. His recent books include *The Politics of Pain: Torturers and Their Masters* (1995) and *Western Responses to Terrorism* (1993).

Robert M. Cutler is research fellow in the Institute of European and Russian Studies at Carleton University. He has been a professor and research fellow also at other major universities in the United States, France, Switzerland, and Russia. His articles have been published in the *Global Governance, International Affairs* (London), *International Organization, International Studies Quarterly,* and *World Politics,* among others. He contributes as well to the print and broadcast mass media.

Vincent Della Sala is an associate professor of political science and director of the Centre for European Politics and Society at Carleton University. His teaching and research interests focus on comparative political economy and European politics. He has published work on the impact of integration and globalization on national state structures, on European integration, and on citizenship and constitutionalism.

Philippe Le Prestre is a professor in the Department of Political Science and at the Institute of environmental sciences of the Université de Québec à Montréal (UQAM), where he specializes in international environmental politics and foreign policy analysis and heads the Global Ecopolitics Observatory. Between 1995 and 1999, he chaired the Environmental Studies Section of the International Studies Association. Le Prestre is the author of *Ecopolitique internationale* (1997) and *The World Bank and the Environmental Challenge* (1989). He also edited *Protecting the Ozone Layer* (1998) and *Role Quests in the Post–Cold War Era* (1997).

Gordon Smith spent his career in the Canadian government, where his last position was as deputy minister of foreign affairs and the prime minister's personal representative for the G7/G8 summits. On retiring from government, Smith became director of the Centre for Global Studies at the University of Victoria. He is also chair of the International Development Research Centre (IDRC), chair of the International Network on Bamboo and Rattan (INBAR), and director of the Canadian Global Change Program. He recently wrote a report entitled *Altered States: Globalization, Sovereignty and Governance.* He has a PhD in political science from MIT.

Robert Wolfe, a former Canadian foreign service officer, is a professor in the School of Policy Studies at Queen's University. His recent publications include *Farm Wars: The Political Economy of Agriculture and the*

International Trade Regime (1998), 'Why the WTO Is Not (Yet) the Antidote for Globaphobia,' *International Journal* (spring 1999), and, as editor, *Diplomatic Missions: The Ambassador in Canadian Foreign Policy* (1998). His current research includes projects on the challenges to global governance posed by concerns about food safety, and on democracy and the trading system.

Daniel Wolfish has research interests that include global governance and international security. Until recently, he was the program co-ordinator for the Centre for Global Studies at the University of Victoria. He is now an associate at the Policy Research Secretariat, where he works on issues related to the Canadian–U.S. border. He is also the co-editor of *Horizons*, the Policy Research Secretariat's policy research magazine.

Acronyms

CBD	Convention on Biological Diversity
CCD	Convention to Combat Desertification
CCS	Climate Change Secretariat (Canada)
CITES	Convention on International Trade in Endangered Species
CMS	Convention on Migratory Species
CoP	conference of the parties
EEC	European Economic Community
ECSC	European Coal and Steel Community
EP	European Parliament
EU	European Union
FAO	Food and Agriculture Organization
GATT	General Agreement on Tariffs and Trade
IGO	intergovernmental organization
IEA	International Environmental Agreement
IFF	Intergovernmental Forum on Forests
ILO	International Labour Organization
IMO	International Maritime Organisation
IPI	international parliamentary institution
IPU	Inter-Parliamentary Union
IPF	Intergovernmental Panel on Forests
ITTF	Interagency Task Force on Tropical Forests
ITTO	International Tropical Timber Organization
IUCN	World Conservation Union
LRTAP	long-range transport of air pollutants

NAFTA	North American Free Trade Agreement
NGO	non-governmental organization
OECD	Organization for Economic Co-operation and Development
POP	persistent organic pollutant
SCBD	Secretariat of the Convention on Biological Diversity
SBSTA	Subsidiary Body on Scientific and Technical Advice (UNFCCC)
SBSTTA	Subsidiary Body on Scientific, Technical and Technological Advice
TNC	transnational corporation
UNECE	United Nations Economic Commission for Europe
UNEP	United Nations Environment Programme
UNFCCC	UN Framework Convention on Climate Change
WHC	World Heritage Convention
WMD	weapon of mass destruction
WTO	World Trade Organization

WHO IS AFRAID OF THE STATE?

CANADA IN A WORLD OF MULTIPLE CENTRES OF POWER

1. Introduction: Conceptualizing Multiple Centres of Power

Gordon Smith and Daniel Wolfish

Moving Together, Moving Apart

For a decade we have been living in an atmosphere of political transformation. The Soviet retreat from Eastern Europe, the fall of the Berlin Wall, and the eventual collapse of the Soviet Union set off this period of political change on a global scale. Scholars and those seeking to influence or to make public policy have grappled with what was optimistically called the new world order. It was in this spirit of looming change and a new world order that scholars such as Francis Fukuyama, Samuel Huntington, and James Rosenau proposed their sometimes controversial ideas on what the future of world politics would look like.[1]

In addition to the political upheavals taking place in Eastern Europe and the Soviet Union, commentators noticed other factors at work contributing to a fundamental change in international politics and in the domestic affairs of states. In particular, scholars observed that massive global social and economic forces, often referred to as 'globalization and interdependence,' were changing the way in which states, societies, and individuals interacted.[2] Observers of world politics also noticed that international actors other than states, such as non-governmental organizations (NGOs) and multinational corporations, were beginning to have significant influence on politics and on policy formulation, implementation, and evaluation.[3] Some scholars have even labelled the burgeoning academic literature explaining this trend 'global governance theory.'[4] Many policy makers and scholars now believe that we have entered a new period in world politics in which there are multiple centres of power and authority and that we need to understand this new world in order for us to prepare for the future.

The Canadian government felt a sense of urgency to understand this new multicentric world. The clerk of the Privy Council (the senior civil servant) organized deputy ministers to think about how the world was changing. Gordon Smith, one of the deputy ministers, is co-editor of this volume. The process included formation of two committees at the level of assistant deputy minister and establishment of the Policy Research Initiative (PRI). The PRI has engaged the academic community in an effort to understand the changes under way in the world and their implications for policy. This volume is a product of that initiative.

In *Canada 2005: Global Challenges and Opportunities*, the interim report of the Assistant Deputy Ministers' Sub-Committee on Global Challenges and Opportunities (hereafter ADMs' subcommittee) noted: 'We are increasingly having to deal with a world that, in new ways which we have yet to fully comprehend and at a speed with often seems frightening, is both moving together and moving apart.'[5] The report goes on to note that 'we can expect the next decade to pose significant challenges for our regulatory regimes and governing institutions' and that power has become more diffuse by shifting in several directions – outwards to provinces and local governments, laterally to the private sector and nongovernmental actors, and extraterritorially to regional and international organizations.[6] In effect, government was no longer seen as the sole institution of governance. The challenge for Canada over the next few years will be to evaluate this multicentric world; to examine the formal and informal systems by which its citizens variously manage their affairs, exercise their rights and obligations, and mediate their differences, both at home and abroad, and to decide how to interact with this new reality.

The chapters in this volume speak to the challenge posed by a world of multiple centres of power. Each assesses the phenomenon itself and outlines its implications for the policy process in Canada and, more fundamentally, for governance both in Canada and elsewhere. This volume examines the implications of the emergence of multiple centres of power on the political, policy and governance processes. It not only seeks to determine the effects on the institutions and workings of government, but also identifies the new actors now engaged in governance. The chapters together provide a rich understanding of multiple centres of powers, for each individual chapter provides a unique perspective on the causes and attributes of this phenomenon. All argue that the state and its governance structures will continue to play a crucial role in setting rules as well as in making and implementing policy, both domestically and in the international arena. The authors also all agree that states will need to engage NGOs, businesses, and individuals in the governance process.

In this chapter, we seek to explain the scope and utility of the ideas offered by the contributors to this volume. The richness of this volume stems from the discussion and varied opinions presented in the individual chapters and the editors and contributors do not necessarily agree with each other on all the issues examined. For this reason, the reader should see these chapters as part of an ongoing debate, not as a definitive account. This chapter begins by offering three definitions of the concept of multiple centres of power and noting how the authors in this book employ the concept. It then discusses the four major themes that thread through the chapters – the future of the state, the causes of change, managing transnational and global issues, and the meaning of democracy, accountability, and the rule of law in a changing world. Finally, it outlines the contents of this volume.

Three Definitions

The term 'multiple centres of power' is a fuzzy concept that, without elaboration, describes very little. The images that it evokes can vary, depending on how one defines 'centre' and 'power.' For the purpose of this book, 'multiple centres of power' refers to one of three possible definitions, varying with understandings of 'centre' and 'power.'

The first definition – which is implicit in Clarkson (chapter 5) and Le Prestre (chapter 7) – refers to the existence of three or more states that together exercise a preponderance of economic and military power in the international system. In the past, these powerful states were referred to as 'superpowers' or 'great powers.' A multicentric world stands in contrast to the Cold War era, which was characterized by two powerful states.

The second definition – accepted by all our authors except Wolfe (chapter 8) – refers to the emergence of new political participants such as NGOs and multinational corporations that either partake in or have a great impact on policy and governance. Governments are one, perhaps the most powerful, of many participants in national and international politics.

The third definition – used only by Wolfe – is more abstract. It refers not to the distribution of military and economic power or to the arrival of new participants, but rather to the multiple sources of authority that exist today in our political, economic, and social lives. States and national governments are authoritative, but they do not have a monopoly on authority. In a multicentric world, authority comes from the inter-subjective consensus that arises from continued human interaction.

The distinction between the first two definitions is analogous to that which Robert Gilpin makes between a change within the international system and a wholesale transformation of the international system itself.[7] The third definition conceives of multiple centres of power as a plurality of sources of authority as opposed to a variety of powerful actors. We look now at how our contributors understand and apply these definitions.

Definition 1: Systemic Change in a Post–Cold War World

The first definition of multiple centres of power takes a conventional approach to what constitutes a centre and what constitutes power. According to Kenneth Waltz, international politics consists of the interaction of undifferentiated unitary actors pursuing power in the international system.[8] International politics accordingly is characterized by the distribution of capabilities across states interacting in the system. For Waltz, no other actors in the international system require analysis or consideration other than states; states are the primary political actors. Moreover, Waltz went so far as to suggest that only great powers really matter. For Waltz, a centre is synonymous with a state, and 'power' refers to the capability of states to pursue their goals in international politics. Multiple centres of power, then, stands in contrast to the bipolar system typical of the Cold War era. Such a shift, which Gilpin calls systemic change, requires a concomitant alteration in the strategies that states use to pursue their goals.[9] This definition of multiple centres of power therefore leads one to consider policy research questions relating to international political instability and national security and on their implications for Canada's armed forces, its strategic alliances, its military and technological capabilities, its international economic and political partnerships, and so on.

When the ADMs' subcommittee issued *Canada 2005*, it considered this type of change a major component of multiple centres of power, if not the most significant international force affecting Canadian interests over the medium term. In particular, the subcommittee understood the concept as referring almost entirely to economic and military power, the essential components of 'hard' power.[10] *Canada 2005* noted particularly the emergence of Asia as a 'third pillar of the world economy and a region that is playing a significant and distinctive role in the councils of the world. The rise of Asia exemplifies the new reality of the millennium – in terms of economic power, a new security balance, the global environmental equation and even the 'values' that underlie the workings of multilateral institutions ... This is a new reality to which we Canadians, like others, will have to adapt and respond.'[11] The report noted the rise of Asia as an economic and military power, the growing influence of the European Union, the emergence of markets in Latin America, and the transition of Russia as key components of a multicentric world. The appearance of new international powers, one could argue, places new constraints on Canada's capacity to pursue its national objectives in the world.

This definition of multiple centres of power does not comprise the departure point for any of the chapters in this volume, although it does play an underlying role in two of them. Both Stephen Clarkson (chapter 5) and Philippe Le Prestre (chapter 7) address this theme when they note that Canada has always prefered a rules-based international order. According to Clarkson, Canada should engage in the new global conjecture by developing coalitions of like-minded states and transnational actors in order to help counterbalance the overwhelming power of its neighbour the United States, the continental and global hegemon in global decision making. Le Prestre, in his discussion of the international system of convention governance, notes that this form of global and regional governance is more capable of adapting to a world in which there is a change in the distribution of power across states. Traditional intergovernmental organizations (IGOs) have difficulty adapting when the international system undergoes systemic change because such a change also precipitates a new structure of interests. Le Prestre argues that systems of convention governance are more flexible – they can easily modify their internal structure as needed, and they reflect the international distribution of power in a single issue-area covered by the convention. Thus such arrangements can help overcome the gap between the structure of the IGO and the distribution of power.

Definition 2: New Actors, New Governance?

The second definition of multiple centres of power challenges conventional international relations theory on what constitutes a centre and what constitutes power. Those who subscribe to this definition argue that political power is no longer concentrated in the central governments of nation-states as has historically been the case. They believe that capabilities, responsibilities, and sometimes even decision-making authority have desolved to international organizations, to sub-state actors, and to non-state actors such as NGOs, firms, powerful individuals, and central banks.[12] The arrival of these new actors is synonymous with what Gilpin calls systems change, and these new players, whether they be domestic, transnational, or international in their activities, supplant the traditional dominant role of the state, which itself may be becoming an increasingly anachronistic institution.[13]

In her assessment of multiple centres of power, Jessica Tuchman Mathews speaks of a power shift, arguing that 'the end of the Cold War has brought about not a mere adjustment among states but a novel redistribution of power among states, markets, and civil society. National governments are not simply losing autonomy in a globalizing economy, they are sharing powers – including political, social, and security roles at the core of sovereignty – with business, with international organizations.'[14]

Vincent Della Sala (chapter 4) outlines best this new approach when he describes it as a concern for the notion of governance. The emphasis here is not simply on institutions of governing but on the processes and the range of actors involved in making decisions that determine collective goods. It reflects a growing multiplicity of sites and levels of decision making, and it stems from the view that there remains a need for some form of regulation of social, economic, and political life, although the instruments of regulation may be changing. Governance in a multicentric world implies that the state no longer enjoys the monopoly that it once had in decision making in areas that govern the public good and collective action. There now exists a set of domestic and international actors – some working collaboratively and others competing with the state and each other. In short, power has shifted in various directions away from the state.

This understanding of multiple centres of power suggests that we are no longer well served by the notion that states and national governments are the essential actors in politics. We have become so accustomed to treating these entities as the foundations of politics that we continually fall back on them when contemplating the prospects for future governance. Perhaps we need a new set of concepts and analytical approaches.

This definition leads us to ask a different set of policy questions. For example, how can governments in Canada manage a process of policy consultation involving the provinces, NGOs, and individuals while meeting its international commitments, which often require specific and timely action? How have multiple centres of power affected democratic and political accountability in Canada? How can Canada, in partnership with other countries, best manage the emergence of transnational and global challenges, including provision for human security, global environmental change, transnational organized crime, and the spread of infectious diseases? These questions are addressed in this volume.

There is no doubt that the ADM's subcommittee recognized the role of new political actors, in addition to acknowledging the international redistribution of hard power, when it issued *Canada 2005*. 'Over the past few years most industrialized countries, including Canada, have seen a profound shift of power away from central governments. The once uncontested authority of states and central governments is being challenged by the rise of non-governmental actors and by the development of international organizations and arrangements that seek to hold all nation-states accountable to certain standards of behaviour.'[15] The subcommittee noted that responsibilities and decision making in Canada have become more widely dispersed both within the country to provincial and municipal governments and internationally to international organizations and convention secretariats. Moreover, *Canada 2005* posits that power and even decision making have been shifting away from governments to NGOs and the private sector.

With the exception of Robert Wolfe's chapter 8, all the contributors to the book adopt this understanding of multiple centres of power. Bauer and Le Prestre (chapter 2) provide the most comprehensive assessment of the contention that governance today involves new actors and that power has shifted 'upward' and 'outward.' In particular, they investigate the state's relationship to IGOs, NGOs, and multinational enterprises. They argue that the desire of the state to minimize external uncertainties may, paradoxically, have reduced its autonomy and that its legitimacy may no longer be exclusive. The state must now share legitimacy with other actors that sometimes become its partners.

Concerned with whether power has shifted to international regimes, Le Prestre (chapter 7) assesses the impact of convention governance and convention secretariats on states' capacity to act independently. He contrasts convention secretariats with traditional IGOs and questions the degree to which power has shifted.

Ronald D. Crelinsten (chapter 3) examines how power has shifted outward from the state to NGOs and the private sector. He argues that states coexist and interact with a multicentric world in which NGOs, multinational corporations, and individuals exercise considerable power. We should, he argues, view the state not as a unitary actor in the international system, but rather as a networked component that if necessary forms relationships with NGOs and individuals in other countries to pursue international and even national policies.[16]

In his assessment of how financial power has shifted outward from the state, Vincent Della Sala (chapter 4) notes that the growing importance of bond rating agencies such as Moody's Investors Service and Standard and Poor's Rating Service in debates about fiscal policies is an indication that market forces outside territorial boundaries are curtailing the freedom of manoeuvre for state action. Stephen Clarkson (chapter 5) notes that the federal state contains competing institutions. For instance, 'the Bank of Canada's obdurate governor John Crow, demonstrated his de facto autonomy from the Canadian government as a power centre in the early 1990s by pushing interest rates up unmercifully.' Both authors warn that this shift of power creates the risk that markets and state agencies may be regulating social and economic life without considering state-defined policy goals such as creating employment or protecting the environment.

In his discussion of how power has dispersed downward and upward, Clarkson constructs a five-level model of governance that encompasses municipal, provincial, state, regional/continental, and international levels. Similarly, Della Sala assesses the emergence of continental and sub-state levels of governance when he examines the impact of the European Union on governance in Italy. Going beyond a simple assessment of the theoretical literature, both Clarkson and Della Sala present evidence by examining how Canada and Italy, respectively, are embedded in a multicentric world. Their investigations lead them, however, to different conclusions. Clarkson notes how continental arrangements such as the North American Free Trade Agreement (NAFTA) and international organizations, such as the World Trade Organization (WTO), act as external institutions that curtail the capability and autonomy of the Canadian federal government. Della Sala, in contrast, observes that continental arrangements in Europe, as embodied in the European Union (EU), have constrained the autonomy of the Italian government vis-à-vis the Italian regions and the EU government.

The idea that the world has charged from state-centric to multicentric is contentious. It implies some form of systems change and that states will soon no longer be, if they still are, the dominant participants in politics. This approach also drives us to explain the state's loss of autonomy and its retreat, erosion, or transformation.[17] A number of factors may explain this change, many of which fall under the rubric of globalization.[18] However, the effects of globalization are not uniform across the world.[19] A case can be made that it has had a greater impact on industrialized democratic countries than on developing ones and thus that the state's decline is peculiar to North America and Europe.

One may even question the degree to which power is dispersed across states, NGOs, and multinational enterprises internationally. One cannot dispute that the United States today is the most influential state power in the international system. The absence of U.S. participation significantly weakens major global initiatives such as the international ban on landmines and the International Criminal Court. In addition, many of the world's most influential international NGOs are based in the United States, depend on money from the American government, and comprise mainly U.S. members. Similarly, many of the largest multinational corporations have their global headquarters in the United States, depend on the American market and American stockholders, and are staffed by U.S. citizens. In this sense, perhaps we are living in an age not of multiple centres of power, but of U.S. dominance.[20]

One could also argue, as Robert Wolfe does (chapter 8), that we have always lived in a multicentric world. The political problem 'may not be a changing world, but our assumptions, now exposed as fictions. The actors of interest today are not new, but we literally could not see them within a Westphalian worldview.' That worldview makes the assumption that the state is the most important political participant in the international system and that it is the sole source of political legitimacy in domestic affairs. By accepting that understanding of the world, we overlook other sources of authority, such as religious institutions, which have had tremendous influence on both state and individual behaviour for centuries. Similarly, the market has been a major source of authority since the advent of capitalism, and multinational corporations have wielded significant power for over a century.

Definition 3: Challenging a State-Centric Worldview

Robert Wolfe, in chapter 8, uses the third meaning of multiple centres of power. For him, the centre is not a political participant but rather a source of power; and 'power' is synonymous not with 'capability,' but with 'authority.' Thus he concerns himself not with new actors but rather with the various sources of authority that affect political behaviour. States are only one of many sources of authority, only one of many organizations through which the dynamics of politics and governance take shape. This is similar to James Rosenau's image of the world, 'instead of initially positing a world dominated by states and national governments,' instead 'builds on the premise that the world is comprised of spheres of authority that are not necessarily consistent with the division of territorial space and are subject to considerable flux.'[21]

Such sources of authority are different from actors who demand compliance when exercising authority – in other words, authority is not a possession of actors, nor embedded in roles. Authority is relational: its existence can be observed only when it is both exercised and followed. Whether it is effective and/or enduring depends on the response of those to whom its exercise is directed. If they are responsive, then authority can be said to be operative; if they are not, then authority is absent.

'Authority' refers to a normative order or set of informal and formal legitimate rules. These rules are generated by individuals and groups – whether they be firms, NGOs, or ethnic groups, for instance – as they gather and interact. This interaction produces what Wolfe calls '*intersubjective, consensual understandings*' of what constitutes legitimate and proper behaviour. Many formal and informal avenues for agreement on these norms exist. They may evolve into formal, codified laws or unwritten customary rules. Practices and norms established by custom have an evolutionary quality and thus often appear to be spontaneous developments. This appearance, however, obscures their nature as purposeful actions that over time acquire legitimacy. Informal rules and practices reflect a common approach to problems; they are focal points around which behaviour converges.

'Multiple centres of power' refers, then, in Wolfe's view, to the variety of sources of authority present today. The existence of alternative sources of authority takes on great significance. In a recent publication, Claire Cutler examines different issues in which the private sector took the lead in establishing norms, rules, and institutions that guide the behaviour of actors and affect the opportunities available to them. She emphasized that the traditional focus of state sovereignty that dominates theoretical and practical discussions of international affairs is inadequate for explaining the full contours of contemporary global life.[22]

Similarly, Wolfe argues that the state is only one of many sources of normative order; he encourages us to see law and authority as derivatives not only of states, but of other sources as well, including the private sector. He disagrees with those who assert that politics in advanced industrial societies has been based on the premises that the state is the repository of political authority and governance of social and economic life and that legitimate authority in liberal democracy is expressed through its formal political institutions. Wolfe would argue that this approach puts the state at the centre of the analysis and neglects other consensual normative systems that confer authority. It follows from his discussion that political, economic, and social life can be governed by law without being governed by the state. When we look beyond the state centric approach, we can see that power and authority can be generated as people come together for various purposes.

This definition of multiple centres of power leads us to pose a different set of policy research questions from those posed under our other two definitions. It recasts the policy problem away from worrying about the state's diminished capacity to examining issues concerning its co-ordination with other spheres of authoritative. Moreover, the Canadian federal government should see itself not as leading the co-ordination effort in Canada, but as a participant. To explain this policy problem, Wolfe invokes a metaphor: Ottawa should see itself as playing in rather than conducting an orchestra.

Wolfe's discussion encourages us to be critical of the ADM subcommittee's *Canada 2005*. The report did note the existence of various sources of authority, but it recognized them only in the context of the retreat of state: 'For several hundred years the nation-state has been perceived, at least in the western world, as the primary unit for security, economic and social policy. Other levels of government and civil society have been largely defined in terms of national boundaries and seen as existing in a subordinate or symbiotic relationship with national governments.' Wolfe would argue that the document's characterization of multiple centres of power and of the problems facing Canada is unhelpful for policy making and policy research. It misrepresents the state, which has neither transferred nor relinquished power, authority, or sovereignty. The state was never as capable as the authors of *Canada 2005* would have us assume, nor is it as incapable as they now suppose.

We hope that the chapters in this volume will contribute to ongoing discussions of change and authority in world politics: they assess the phenomenon of multiple centres of power, and they outline its implications for the policy process and, more fundamentally, for the process of governance. Taken together, they provide insight into how multiple centres of power will affect the future role of the state, the quality of democracy and political accountability, and the management of transnational issues.

Four Central Themes

Accepting the idea that we live in a multicentric world – regardless of whether we define the term as a redistribution of power across states, as the arrival of new actors that rival the state, or as recognition of new sources of authority – requires us to think differently about the world and Canada's place in it. Hence the contributors have examined four basic questions that governments in Canada should consider when preparing for the medium-term future.

- What are the position and the role of the state, given that today we have an array of actors, institutions, and/or sources of authority?
- If fundamental global political change is underway, with the seeming retreat of the state a central feature, what are the causes of this transformation?
- How do we manage the growing number of transnational and global problems, some of which have serious implications for human well-being and are gaining priority on the agendas of governments?
- What are the implications of a multicentric world for democracy, accountability, and the rule of law?

Let us look briefly at each in turn.

Future Role of the State

Three premises – that the state is the sole repository of political authority, that the state is the pivotal institution in the governance of social and economic life, and that authority is expressed through state institutions – are at the heart of major debates in the study of politics and international relations. As far back as 1977, Hedley Bull wrote, 'It is often argued today' 'that the states system is in decline, that it is giving place, or will give place, to some fundamentally different form of universal political organization. What evidence is there that between now and the end of the century the states system is likely to be replaced by one or anther of the alternatives?'[23] Susan Strange echoed Bull's question nearly twenty years later 'By the closing years of the twentieth century, the major debate in international studies is a new one. It is between those scholars who think that, even after the end of the Cold War, very little has changed, and those who are convinced a great deal has changed. Since the thesis of this book belongs to the latter camp, and *since the fundamental argument is really about the role of states in the international system*, serious consideration has be given to the views of those who maintain that, in essence, there has been and still is, continuity in the international system, from its inception.'[24]

The contributors to this volume concur that those observers and government officials who argue that the state is in retreat and becoming anachronistic overstate their case. Most agree that the state plays, and will continue to play in the near future, a significant role in governance. They disagree, however, on the future role of the state. Clarkson (chapter 5) is sceptical about the retreat of the state in Canada. While he concedes that further responsibilities have devolved to the provinces, he notes that the federal government has exercised considerable power to produce this devolution. Furthermore when Ottawa strove to balance its budget by cutting back federal functions, it demonstrated its strength by taking steps that many entrenched interests bitterly resisted, including the provinces.

By examining how states interact in the international arena, Le Prestre (chapter 7) confirms that the state maintains its primacy. He argues that, since the Rio Conference on the Environment in 1992, the system of convention governance represents attempts by states to regain control of the role and functions that intergovernmental organizations can play in the international system. Convention governance helps states maintain and even strengthen the fundamental prerequisites of effective state action while facilitating progress towards collective goals. It helps states to maintain their influence internationally, whereas intergovernmental organizations can develop their own sets of interests beyond that of the state.

In contrast, the other authors note that the state has evolved, although it is not necessarily in retreat. Robert M. Cutler (chapter 6) points out that while international parliamentary institutions (IPIs) provide a forum where states may continue to assert themselves, they also heighten the potential role of NGOs in managing transnational issues. Moreover, IPIs encourage states to strengthen then legislative branch of government in matters of international politics; it is only in IPIs among all international organizations, that the legislative branch of governments participate, not the executive. Cutler argues that if the state's role continues to be significant, it is necessary to rethink who or what 'the state' is in world politics. In this context, Cutler shows why the term 'world society' is sometimes preferable to the term 'system of states.'

Julién Bauer and Philippe Le Prestre (chapter 2) demonstrate the durability and constant transformation of the state. States are, they argue, always changing and facing new challenges. If our era is more significant than past eras, it is because states confront important and inevitable challenges to the fundamental attributes that define them. Seeming new constraints that lead to a basic questioning of the state may prove largely subjective or even reflect states' efforts to reassert their decision-making autonomy and legitimacy. If we reason from the fundamental attributes of the state, we see that states' desire to minimize external uncertainties may have reduced their autonomy, their legitimacy is no longer exclusive, and that their capacity to act has increased in some areas and diminished in others.

While recognizing that the state has transformed in response to the proliferation of new political actors and the pressures of globalization, Bauer and Le Prestre argue that it still has a crucial role in governance. It plays the role of intermediary between NGOs, corporations, and other states acting beyond its own borders and between NGOs, corporations, and citizens acting domestically. It is the only institution that possesses a general knowledge of the problems and interests of all parties involved and that is capable of identifying, negotiating, and enforcing solutions. In a multicentric world, the state plays the role of the intermediary.

Della Sala (chapter 4) also puts forth arguments detailing the transformation of the state. Certain parts of the state – the executive, for example – have been strengthened by the same pressures that may be weakening state capacity overall. It can also be argued that while the state gives up responsibilities and capacity in some areas, it may have enhanced its capacity in others. Della Sala suggests that as the state gives up responsibilities it becomes 'hollow.' In order for a 'hollowing out' to take place, the state needs to become less accommodating and accessible to a wide range of social and political demands. Moreover, in transferring powers to transnational bodies, the state has to demonstrate that it is capable of enforcing agreements that it makes with its new partners – in other words, that it still has power.

The Causes of Transformation[25]

If one agrees that we are experiencing unprecedented transformation, then the next logical question would be to ask about its causes. This line of inquiry, it seems, has generated an industry of research and publishing,[26] most of which can be considered as part of the wider debate on globalization and interdependence.[27] This is not the place to provide a survey of the literature on globalization and interdependence; suffice it to note that Bauer and Le Prestre (chapter 2), Crelinsten (chapter 3), and Della Sala (chapter 4) make significant contributions to this discussion. Beyond this, however, Bauer and Le Prestre, Crelinsten, and Clarkson (chapter 5) note the impact of ideology, particularly the ascent of neoliberalism, on the role of the state. Essentially they argue that multiple centres of power emerged as a result of the Canadian government's ideological shift in the 1980s away from social-democratic principles to neoliberalism and its accompanying commitment to limiting the activities of government in economic and social life. Della Sala provides an analysis of the neoliberal policies that have predominated over the past decade, arguing that it was these policies that have weakened governments' capacities to act autonomously in the face of international market forces. Bauer and Le Prestre, in agreement with Della Sala, suggest that this ideological shift may also contribute to a decline in states' legitimacy.

Clarkson believes that this condition is not necessarily permanent. Just as neoliberalism motivated the shrinking of state functions, the rise of an alternative ideology could reverse this trend. Given the seeming inability of the neoliberal model to respond to public demands for public health and education accessible to all, the pendulum may be poised to swing back towards a state less reluctant to exercise its power to regulate the market and to provide civil society with the services that it desires. Although it may have lost considerable authority and legitimacy, the federal government in Canada may try to reassert itself in ways that it had earlier abandoned and to reclaim some of the authority and legitimacy that it had previously alienated. In short, the potential for further change remains.

Managing Transnational Problems

The academic literature concerning the management of transnational issues has until recently been dominated by discussions of the obstacles and the incentives for the growth of interdependence[28] and interstate co-operation.[29] Over the past ten years, however, an infusion of new ideas and observations has enriched this discussion, bringing to light such factors as the importance of technical experts and NGOs in the negotiation and implementation of international treaties.[30] At the same time, the concerns of world leaders have changed in the light of growing concerns about climate change and the environment, transnational organized crime, the spread of infectious diseases, the use of genetically modified organisms, poverty, and other problems. Issues that were once of domestic concern have become transnational, if not global, in nature, requiring a concerted effort for their management. The question of interest is no longer why states succeed or fail to co-operate – this question offers little help to policy makers on how to respond to the realities of a multicentric world. Instead, scholars have begun to ask about how and with whom governments ought to manage transnational relations. In some ways, they encourage us to look at public policy from a more transnational, even global, perspective.[31] It is on these questions that Le Prestre, Crelinsten, Cutler, and Wolfe make their contributions to this book.

Le Prestre (chapter 7) compares convention secretariats and systems of convention governance that have proliferated since the Rio Conference on the Environment of 1992 to traditional intergovernmental organizations (IGOs). In his assessment, convention governance provides a more effective way for national governments to manage transnational and global problems such as environmental change. As international agreements and processes increasingly drive Canada's environmental agenda, convention governance can assist it in maintaining or strengthening the means of effective state action while facilitating progress towards international collective goals. Secretariats are issue-specific, mission-oriented organizations that are more responsive to needs and requirements of the regimes that they maintain than are traditional IGOs. Convention governance is in certain circumstances, better able to pursue specific objectives in a world of multiple 'stakeholders,' overlapping issues, and states attempting to regain some independent initiative. Le Prestre argues that their focus, accountability and flexibility can make them attractive alternatives to IGOs.

While Le Prestre concentrates on state-to-state relations, Cutler and Crelinsten propose a framework for relations between state and civil society in the management of transnational issues. The intersection between civil society and the state in a democracy, Cutler (chapter 6) argues, is the elected legislature. IPIs offer a possible place for civil society to interact with national governments in the management of transnational issues. In his framework, which he calls 'complex world society,' Cutler shows how IPIs enable transnational civil society groups to aggregate their interests unrestricted by the rules of national politics. He points out that the establishment of some of the most recent IPIs actually arises from bottom–up networking by NGOs. But if IPIs encourage the growth and development of NGOs, offering them a site for lobbying, informing, and consulting, then they also provide states with a forum for 'interfacing' with NGOs and transnational social movements.

Crelinsten (chapter 3) encourages us to do away with our old, rudimentary understanding of the state as a unitary actor. He argues that it would be more productive to see the state as a set of networked components interacting with each other and with civil society. In a multicentric world, states interact with other centres of power, sometimes in concert, sometimes in opposition. Moreover, civil society itself is a transnational or global phenomenon in which there is no distinction between national and global politics. Management of transnational issues and policy making in a multicentric world therefore rely much less on regulation and (re)distribution and much more on exhortation, persuasion, and management of state partners. Power is exercised by directing and integrating the decision making and actions of non-state partners in the governance process. In this case, the government plays a management function.

Wolfe (chapter 8), in his investigation of the norms and spheres of authority that structure international trade, attempts to explain how Canada and other countries can operate in a rules based system in which they may have overlapping and indeed conflictual international obligations and standards. One could believe that such a world may force governments to choose to ignore their commitments to certain international regimes while respecting others. For Wolfe, this kind of world is not problematic. Governments do not necessarily have to harmonize rules across regimes and issue-areas. Wolfe argues that different norms and rules may be authoritative at different points in time. The challenge is to understand and reconcile differences, ensuring that the players can proceed with some degree of predictability. Countries do not need the same laws, or even harmonized laws; they need recognizable rules that structure activity and the divergent interests of many states.

Democracy, Accountability, and the Rule of Law

While questions about the future of the state, the causes of transformation, and the management of transnational issues have occupied a central place in the academic literature for some time, the same cannot be said about the efficacy of accountable and democratic governance in a multicentric world. It was not long ago that leading scholars contributed to a volume on governance in the international system in which they hardly considered democracy and accountability.[32] Today, however, questions of who should govern and what forms of governance are most appropriate in a multicentric world, both nationally and internationally, have become central features of academic discussions.[33]

The advent of multiple centres of power has produced a striking paradox. At the moment in history when more and more countries are championing the idea of democracy, the efficacy of democracy appears open to question. The observer of politics can identify four challenges to accountability and democratic governance. First, globalization has transformed the state, in many cases strengthening the executive while weakening the legislatures.[34] Second, there is a growing incongruence between national boundaries within which democracies operate and the geographical organization of much of human economic and social activity. As substantial aspects of human activity become progressively organized on a regional or global level, the fate of democracy, and in particular of the independent democratic nation-state, is fraught with uncertainty. Third, inter-state structures designed to manage transnational and global issues are seldom accountable to citizens. Finally, new centres of power such as NGOs and transnational corporations

(TNCs) are seldom accountable to their members or shareholders, let alone to others who may be affected by their activities, and yet they are increasingly exercising power, and perhaps authority, in the international system. Whatever the precise challenges, to democracy, they are all based on the recognition that the nature and quality of democracy within a particular community and the nature and quality of democratic relations among communities are interconnected and that new legal and organizational mechanisms must be created if democracy is to flourish. While it may be premature to suggest a crisis in democracy, the time has come to raise questions about accountability and democratic governance in a multicentric world.

The theme of legitimacy, democratic governance, and the rule of law threads its way through the chapters of this book. There is broad agreement among the authors that globalization and the emergence of new powerful non-state actors can serve to undermine the legitimacy of national governments. Della Sala is among the most concerned. In a multicentric world, he argues, states play an increasingly marginal role in the economic and social life of their societies, leading to a hollowing out of the state. In order for a hollowing out to take place, the state needs to become less accommodating and accessible to a wide range of social and political forces likely to resist economic liberalization. Moreover, in transferring power to transnational bodies, the state has to demonstrate it is capable of enforcing agreements it makes with its new partners. This often means concentrating decision-making power in structures and processes that are less penetrable by groups in society favouring an alternative way of regulating social and political life.

Crelinsten (chapter 3) argues that, in response to a multicentric world, states are redefining governance in such a way as to circumvent the issue of legitimacy and public accountability while maintaining control over the burgeoning alliances and partnerships with the private sector and civil society. As governments withdraw from regular management of social and economic life and 'offload' some of their responsibilities to the private sector, the notion of the public good and the role of the state as protector of citizens' rights seem to fall through the cracks between the state and its partners. New actors participating in policy making and governance do not necessarily share the same notion of accountability. Partnering with non-state actors can create ambiguities and uncertainties about who is accountable for decisions taken and policies adopted.

Looking at relations among states, Cutler (chapter 6) suggests that IPIs provide one antidote to the problems of democratic governance and accountability. He points to the real and growing significance of IPIs in the governance of transnational regions, especially in such matters as energy, the environment, and sustainable development. These institutions have a good track record as a forum for consultation among different components of world society, particularly among NGOs and the private sector. Cutler sees IPIs as a possible nexus for governmental, non-governmental, and intergovernmental organizations that would be responsive to local needs, accountable to citizens, and effective at dealing with transnational issues.

Wolfe (chapter 8), however, encourages us not to rush to reproduce this IPI-style nexus in all international organizations. In his discussion of the World Trade Organization (WTO), he argues that current efforts aimed at improving the accessibility of the WTO may not lead to such an outcome. If NGOs are not part of the collective life of an institution – and there is no sense in which they are part of the WTO in its current guise – then making decisions 'transparent' could be futile. The WTO is not equipped to think in public. It has a characteristic mode of operation that was not meant to accommodate non-state actors. To admit them without a fundamental rethinking and then renegotiation of all the WTO's existing agreements might actually make the organization less democratic and more rigid rather than the reverse.

In short, the author suggests that the world today consists of multiple normative orders, none of which is paramount. If we maintain Westphalian assumptions about the international normative order, then we see the state at the apex and law and order as derivatives of the state. However, the state, it could be argued, is only one of many sources of normative order. Life can be governed by law without being state-governed. When we question the state centred approach, we can see that power and authority can multiply as people come together for various purposes. We must accept this ambiguity and work within it.

Outline of the Book

This book address two central questions:[35] What are the changes taking place throughout the world concerning the location and diffusion of power and authority? What are the implications – for governance and for policy making – of a world characterized by multiple centres of power?

The two chapters of part I deal with the causes and trends of the diffusion of power. Bauer and Le Prestre's (chapter 2) begins the discussion by examining the argument that globalization and changing identity are forcing a redefinition of national and international authority away from the traditional state system. Crelinsten's discussion (chapter 3) builds on this idea by analysing the impact of globalization, decentralization, and privatization on the ability of states to conduct policy and on the extent to which governance can adhere to democratic principles in a multicentric world.

The next two chapters, part II, consider the state and how it operates in a multicentric world by presenting empirical studies. Using the case of Italy in an integrating Europe, Della Sala (chapter 4) argues that there is pressure for become less accessible and permeable to social and political demands if it is to meet the challenges of multi-level governance. Clarkson (chapter 5), looking at multi-level governance in Canada, argues that the shift in belief from social-democratic to neoliberal principles has supported the transfer of power to the market and undermined the capacity of the federal government to act autonomously.

The three chapters in part III present multiple centres of power from an international perspective. Cutler (chapter 6) presents IPIs as a possible nexus between government, non-governmental, and inter-governmental actors. Le Prestre (chapter 7) calls our attention to the strengths and weaknesses of the system of convention governance in the management of global and transnational issues. Lastly, Wolfe (chapter 8), analyses the WTO to demonstrate to us that we live in a world consisting of many formal and informal normative orders. His focus on normative orders and authority presents us with a refreshingly novel discussion of multiple centres of power.

Chapter 9 attempts highlight the implications of multiple centres of power for decision making and governance. It argues that states have retained a central role in regulating our lives.

NOTES

We would like to thank Mark Schacter who, on behalf of the Institute on Governance, provided a summary report of the Workshop 'Trends: Multiple Centres of Power' held in Victoria in May 1999; his report helped us prepare this text. We would also like to thank Michael Carley, and Alexander Wake and Michele Wingelman, for their help in preparing this chapter.

1 Samuel Huntington, 'The Clash of Civilizations?' *Foreign Affairs* 72, no. 3 (Summer 1993): 22–49; Francis Fukuyama, 'The End of History,' *National Interest*, 16 (Summer 1989): 3–18; and James Rosenau, *Turbulence in World Politics: A Theory of Change and Continuity* (Princeton NJ: Princeton University Press, 1990).

2 Robert Keohane and Joseph Nye, 'Power and Interdependence in the Information Age,' *Foreign Affairs* 77, no. 5 (September / October 1998): 81–94; Peter Drucker, 'The Global Economy and the Nation-State,' *Foreign Affairs* 76, no. 5 (September / October 1997): 159–71; James Rosenau, *Along the Domestic–Foreign Frontier: Exploring Governance in a Turbulent World* (Cambridge: Cambridge University Press, 1997); and David Held et al., *Global Transformations: Politics, Economics, and Culture* (Stanford, Calif.: Stanford University Press, 1999).

3 Susan Strange, *The Retreat of the State: The Diffusion of Power in the World Economy* (Cambridge: Cambridge University Press, 1996); James Rosenau, *Along the Domestic–Foreign Frontier*, 273–401; and P.J. Simmons, 'Learning to Live with NGOs,' *Foreign Policy* (Fall 1998): 21–33.

4 Martin Hewson and Timothy Sinclair, 'The Emergence of Global Governance Theory,' in Martin Hewson and Timothy Sinclair, eds., *Approaches to Global Governance Theory* (Albany: State University of New York, 1999), 3–22.

5 The Assistant Deputy Minister Sub-Committee for Global Challenges and Opportunities, *Canada 2005, Draft Interim Report: Global Challenges and Opportunities* (Ottawa, 2, February, 1997), 'The International Context.'

6 Ibid.

7 Robert Gilpin, *War and Change in World Politics* (Cambridge: Cambridge University Press, 1981), 39–44; see also James Rosenau, 'Governance, Order, and Change in World Politics,' in James Rosenau and Ernst-Otto Czempiel, eds., *Governance without Government: Order and Change in World Politics*, (Cambridge: Cambridge University Press, 1992), 1–29.

8 Kenneth Waltz, *Theory of International Politics* (Berkeley; University of California Press, 1979).

9 Robert Gilpin, *War and Change in World Politics*, 42–43.

10 The distinction between 'hard' and 'soft' power was first made by Joseph Nye. See Joseph Nye, 'Soft Power,' *Foreign Policy* (Fall 1990): 153–71.

11 ADM Sub-Committee, *Canada 2005*, 13.

12 On this latter point, James Rosenau refers to these actors as sovereignty-free actors. See Rosenau, *Turbulence in World Politics*; see also Strange, *Retreat of the State*.

13 Gilpin, *War and Change in World Politics*, 41–2; for a different description of

change see Hewson and Sinclair, 'The Emergence of Global Governance Theory,' 5–19.

14 Jessica Tuchman Matthews, 'Power Shift,' *Foreign Affairs* 76, no. 1 (January/February 1997): 50.

15 The ADM Sub-Committee, 'Governance,' 1.

16 For an account of this effort, see Phil Stewart, 'Brazil's Home for Child Offenders Sparks Anger,' *Globe and Mail* (9 September 1999), A5A.

17 This is certainly an underlying assumption contained in many of the leading works on the subject. See Rosenau, *Turbulence in World Politics*; Strange, *The Retreat of the State*; Paul Hirst, *From Statism to Pluralism* (London: UCL Press, 1997); Kenichi Ohmae, *The End of the Nation State: The Rise of Regional Economies* (New York: Free Press, 1995).

18 Manual Castells, *The Power of Identity* (Oxford: Blackwell Publishers, 1997); and Held et al., *Global Transformations*.

19 William Coleman and Geoffrey Underhill, eds., *Regionalism and Global Economic Integration: Europe, Asia, and the Americas* (New York: Routledge, 1998); and A.S. Bhalla, ed., *Globalization, Growth, and Marginalization* (New York: St Martin's Press, 1998).

20 We thank Michael Carley for bring this argument to our attention.

21 James Rosenau, 'Toward an Ontology of Global Governance,' in Hewson and Sinclair, eds., *Approaches to Global Governance Theory*, 295.

22 Claire Cutler et al., 'Private Authority and International Affairs,' in Cutler et al., eds., *Private Authority and International Affairs* (Albany: State University of New York Press, 1999) 4; and Claire Cutler, 'Locating Authority in the Global Political Economy,' *International Studies Quearterly* 43, no. 1 (March 1999): 59–82.

23 Hedley Bull, *The Anarchical Society: A Study of Order in World Politics* (London: Macmillan Press, 1977), 225–307.

24 Strange, *The Retreat of the State*, 66 (emphasis added).

25 Globalization comprised one of the research teams of the Policy Research Initiative's Trends Project.

26 See, for example, Held et al., *Global Transformations*; and Rosenau, *Turbulence in World Politics*.

27 For a discussion on the difference between these two similar terms, see Wolfgang Reinicke, *Global Public Policy: Governing without Government* (Washington, DC: United States Institute for Peace Press, 1998), 4–7 and 59–62.

28 On interdependence, see Robert Keohane and Joseph Nye, *Power and Interdependence* (Glenview, Ill.: Scott, Foresman and Company, 1989); David Baldwin, 'Interdependence and Power: A Conceptual Analysis,' *Interna-*

tional Organization 34 (1989): 471–506; and Kjell Goldmann and Gunnar Sjostedt, eds., *Power, Capabilities, Interdependence: Problems in the Study of International Influence* (New York: Sage 1979).

29 On co-operation see, for example, Stephen Krasner, ed., *International Regimes* (Ithaca, NY: Cornell University Press, 1983). For a survey of the literature, see also Andreas Hasenclever et al., *Theories of International Regimes* (Cambridge: Cambridge University Press, 1997).

30 On the role of technical experts, see Peter Haas, 'Do Regimes Matter? Epistemic Communities and Mediterranean Pollution Control,' *International Organization* 43 (1989): 377–403. On the role of NGOs, see Simmons, 'Learning to Live with NGOs,' 21–33; Ramesh Thakur and William Maley, 'The Ottawa Convention on Landmines: A Landmark Humanitarian Treaty in Arms Control?' *Global Governance* 5, no. 3 (July–September 1999): 273–302; and Thomas Weiss and Leon Gordenker, ed., *NGOs, the UN, and Global Governance* (Bouldner, Col.: Lynne Rienner, 1996).

31 Reinicke, *Global Public Policy*; and Daniel Morales-Gomez, ed., *Transnational Social Policies* (Ottawa: International Development Research Centre, 1999).

32 Rosenau and Czempiel, ed., *Governance without Government.*

33 See, for example, Daniele Archibugi et al., eds., *Re-imaging Political Community: Studies in Cosmopolitan Democracy* (Cambridge: Polity Press, 1998); David Held, *Democracy and the Global Order: From the Modern State to Cosmopolitan Governance* (Cambridge: Polity Press, 1995); Rosenau, *Along the Domestic–Foreign Frontier.*

34 Della Sala raises this question in chapter 4 in this volume.

35 We would like to thank Mark Schacter for helping us to understand this.

Part One

Multiple Centres of Power

2. *Ménage à trois*: The State between Civil Society and the International System

Julien Bauer and Philippe Le Prestre

It is common today to talk about the weakening of the state: to view it as an entity caught between the international system and domestic forces, between emerging transnational and supranational forces, and between national institutions and social groups that limit its internal autonomy and its international flexibility.[1] This is a phenomenon that has previously been labelled 'interdependence.' The apparent triumph of an anti-statist neoliberal ideology, the desire for regional economic consolidation,[2] the globalization of the economy,[3] communications[4] and environmental issues,[5] cultural standardization,[6] the emergence of global civil society[7] and identity groups,[8] and the desire for social or religious independence[9] arguably exacerbate the disintegration of the state.

This situation, we are told, is giving rise to states that are 'impotent' abroad and 'blocked' at home, thereby resulting in a delegitimization of the public servant,[10] the nation-states' increasing vulnerability to social pressures from lower levels of government, its growing difficulty in articulating collective societal projects, its loss of sovereignty, and the merging of internal and external policies,[11] leading to the end of its monopoly on diplomacy and the growth of its concomitant obligations to negotiate the implementation of international commitments.

The announcement of the demise of the state, however, is premature, and the power of its competitors often exaggerated. Some observers, without denouncing this trend, attempt to reaffirm the necessity of the state. Others challenge the initial analysis. If the state's action has become more complex, is that equivalent to saying that it has lost autonomy? Are we witnessing not the death of the state, but its transformation? Is the state subject to pressures that paralyse it or restrict its freedom to act, or is it capable of building itself a new type of manoeuvrability that allows it to maintain its autonomy, redefine its role, and disseminate its political preferences on the international stage?

We argue that the state still retains some latitude and decision-making power. Far from leading to its death, the proliferation of new players could reinforce its position. Technical agreements with supranational and internal institutions do not necessarily weaken the state. Sometimes they allow it to continue making general public decisions and to leave their concrete application to other levels of government. On the international stage, the state offers an indispensable link between domestic and external actors. It is the only player that has general knowledge of the problems and interests of all the 'stakeholders' and that is capable of identifying, negotiating, and enforcing a solution acceptable to all and thus of holding onto a domain in which it is free to act. In other words, the diffusion of power increases the state's capacity to play the role of referee and mediator among actors, both within and outside national boundaries.

In this chapter, the first section isolates the sources of challenges to the state. The second section offers a critical assessment of the significance of these challenges. The third looks at a few analytical and methodological problems. The final section suggests avenues for further research and suggests that the very challenges that confront the state may also represent opportunities.

Challenges to the State

The state, we are told, is challenged by a multitude of factors ranging from the international system to civil society, from economic pressures to the demands of identity groups, from new threats (such as terrorism or environmental degradation) to the new power of multinationals, from intergovernmental to NGOs. We review these challenges under four headings: globalization, identity, ideology, and actors.

First, globalization – a contested concept itself – stems from the idea that the world is a single market whose rules are imposed on states. The economic dimension is predominant here, but other global processes, such as the standardization of cultural benchmarks, harmonization of technical or humanitarian standards, communication and environmental problems, are also important.

The rise of identity groups poses a second challenge to the state. Whether these identities are ethnic, linguistic, or religious in origin, they undermine both the state's internal legitimacy and its external margin of manoeuvre; they explode the myth of the nation-state. At the juncture of economic and identity trends lies regionalism, which is in competition with the centralized state. Globalization and identity become two dimensions of the third challenge – ideological questioning of the state. Whereas for dozens of years Marxism played the role of ideological critic of the state, today it is neoliberalism that is increasingly serving that function. Fourth, the state must confront the ever-growing role of multinational corporations and of intergovernmental and non-governmental organizations, which are also undermining its foundations.

Globalization

Economic Aspects

Few authors question the increased importance that the financial markets have acquired in the affairs of states.[12] This role results from the intensification of trade between rich countries, the explosion of foreign investment, and the speed of capital movement.[13] This new situation forces states to give preference to the economic dimension of their activities and to redefine the national interest in terms of the interests of multinational corporations (MNCs). In this regard, the argument goes, chapter 11 of the North American Free Trade Agreement (NAFTA), which is intended to protect against any reduction of profit opportunities arising from the adoption of social or environmental measures that did not exist at the time of the initial investment, illustrates the submission of the state and society to the standards and interests of private companies.

For many authors, the emergence of MNCs on the international stage appears to force states to redefine their role. Increasingly, governments find themselves in the position of supplicants with respect to firms, many of which are quick to threaten to relocate in order to obtain satisfaction – a threat that in some cases has actually been carried out.[14] This situation compels governments to take into account the internationalization of production when developing their national economic policy and to anticipate the reactions of the business world when making decisions affecting the economic sphere – for example, tabling of the budget and setting of wage policy.

The internationalization of production, as opposed to simple creation of foreign subsidiaries, reduces the amount of pressure that a state can place on the behaviour of these firms and forces it to adjust the definition of collective interest to these firms' definition of their own interest. In many cases, diplomacy may find itself subsumed by commercial imperatives.

Judged increasingly by the yardstick of its economic power, the state is presented as being caught in the meshes of the world monetary establishment – as subject to the 'rules of the marketplace' and therefore to strict limitations on its activities. One result is that one could transfer the speeches of finance ministers, from one country to another without adjusting to the basic arguments. The market thus seems to be exerting strong pressure on the mode of existence of states, on the perception of the state, and on the definition of the public interest as something limited to its economic dimension. In giving free rein to the economy, globalization risks being considered the *de facto* cause of a substantial loss of sovereignty. But if economic constraint comes from outside national borders – in the form of pressure from the international financial community – another challenge to states has its roots within their borders in the ever-growing cultural and/or identity disparity that exists between citizens.

Culture

Although immigration is not a new phenomenon, large and diverse population movements have affected host countries. Regardless of whether these movements are a characteristic or a cause of globalization, societies are increasingly required to deal with foreign cultures within their borders. For example, in 1996 over 17 per cent of the people living in Canada were not born here. Close to 9 per cent speak a language other than English or French. Consequently, Canada – for which immigration is crucial – has to listen to the demands proceeding from its various constituent ethnic groups. In this debate, it is individuals' perception of cultures different from their own that most often influences one's decisions. The state has to make a choice between ethnocentrism and partial or absolute relativism. The debate on relativism is not just an anthropological issue but has a direct impact on the state's role in society, as evidenced by debates over dress codes. Such examples include veils in schools and Sikhs wearing their traditional garb in the Royal Canadian Mounted Police and the Legion.

Harmonization of Standards

With the enhanced position of international organizations on the world stage, the explosion of communications, and the growing importance of non-governmental organizations (NGOs) in national and international political debates, we can expect international society to move towards harmonization of the norms governing relations between the state and civil society. This would be a consequence of globalization that would be reflected in a universal conception of standards. The study of human rights has much to teach us in this regard.

It seems increasingly difficult for states to ignore world opinion on human rights issues.[15] Who has forgotten the extraordinary impact of the events in Beijing's Tienanmen Square in 1989? They were covered by all the world's media and shocked people of all origins, cultures, and languages. When a state changes its approach to dealing with such problems – for example, Argentina and the Soviet Union – to a method more like that of a Western democratic one, we generally consider this significant moral progress. In contrast, when the situation deteriorates (Algeria, the former Yugoslavia), we denounce the 'return to barbarism.'[16]

This situation gives states less room to manoeuvre, forcing them to redefine their relations with civil society. Moral universalism tends to become the unavoidable standard that has to be respected if one does not want to be an outcast of the international community. However, it would be incorrect to think that there is no logic behind the emergence of universal norms. In fact, the standards that are most likely to be imposed meet two criteria: they are inclusive, and they are not imposed by force.

Inclusive standards have more chance of being accepted by states because they are not discriminatory.[17] Such is the case with human rights. Even if certain states proclaim a distinctive identity that is supposed to justify different treatment, pressures from the international community are defining a general trend that states are finding difficult to resist.

Paradoxically, the absence of military threat or use of armed force facilitates the harmonization of standards. If states are obliged to comply with these standards, it is thanks to joint pressure from national groups and the international community, which has various means of making its views understood, including resolutions and international trade restrictions.[18]

Communication

We are in fact far removed from the time when a state could manage its internal affairs sheltered from the eyes of the international community. The propagation of information is one of the characteristics of globalization. Information has become difficult for states to control, which makes the notion of political borders increasingly obsolete. One of the factors explaining the implosion of the Soviet Union is the sense of frustration of its populace as it became aware – thanks to the communication media – of the ever-growing gap separating it from the affluence of the West.[19] New information and communication technology affects states by challenging the structure of their domestic political institutions and their management of the economy.

When states control all the communication media available to their citizens, political authorities can rest easy. But with greater access to the outside world, people are able to realize the shortcomings of their own governments and, in certain cases, the oppression they suffer. Hence their demands are no longer based on impressions, but on existing or emerging norms in the international community. Citizens compare their lot not to that of their parents, but to that of their neighbours. Governments that do not fulfil the aspirations of their citizens face increasing pressure. In some cases, economic and social aspirations can lead to political demands regarding the structure of the existing regime. Beyond the type of regime, globalization is forcing states to review the nature of the economy.

Information exchange and international migration have in fact made certain traditional forms of management anachronistic. States that were established on a different ideological basis from most Western states now have to approximate some form of liberal economic management. These states, such as China or Cuba, are not renouncing their economic philosophy outright. They are, however, offering certain 'facilities' – that is, exemptions from national economic legislation either in certain geographical regions (China) or economic sectors (Cuba). States can no longer remain entirely divorced from the policy development and implementation practices common in Europe and North America. Thanks to new forms of communication, the absence of material goods can be attributed to a government's mismanagement of the economy, thus placing its legitimacy under pressure. In short, domestic political agendas are increasingly determined by action taking place beyond the political boundary of the state.

Environment

The emergence of global environmental problems is often interpreted as demonstrating the interdependence of modern states and, consequently, both their growing vulnerability to the actions of other states and their inability to face these threats alone. In other words, threats and solutions are collective in nature. At first sight, environmental problems would seem to challenge two fundamental aspects of the state – sovereignty and autonomy – while also affecting a third – the consolidation of state legitimacy.

The ecological interdependence of societies weakens the state's control over society, limits its autonomy, and diminishes its capacity to predict the consequences of its actions. The national and international environmental agenda is the product not of government decisions, but of thousands of exchanges at all levels – state, sub-state, and societal. A multitude of players participate in ecopolitics.

Consequently, there is no single, universally accepted definition of a national interest. In fact, one can speak not of a single national interest but only of multiple conceptions of it, both national and transnational in origin. For example, the tendency of states to compel one another, as in the case of the Montreal Protocol of 1987, to comply with certain agreements under the threat of direct or indirect trade sanctions suggests that the national interest has an international component. What then are the implications of membership in international organizations for both state sovereignty and the national interest?

With the increase in the number of states, the communication revolution, and the emergence of transboundary and global issues, the modern age has given birth to two contradictory trends – on the one hand, the triumph of the state as a mode of political organization and the effort of many governments to consolidate the state; and on the other hand, the limited capacity of the state to respond to the aspirations of its citizens, to protect itself from outside influences, to control the consequences of its actions, and to deal with the combined effects of its actions on the integrity of the biosphere. At the same time as the scope of sovereignty widens in some areas – for example, through the extension of claims over natural resources – the state's capacity to exercise it in others is undermined.

In the context of environmental protection, the exercise of this sovereignty is called into question by various forces, including: first, the principle of transborder responsibility; second, the responsibility that states assume to comply with international norms, which may restrict their actions; third, the contested development of the concept of the common heritage of humankind, which aims to legitimize not only the exclusion of some states from certain territories and their inability to exercise traditional sovereign rights, but also the right of all states to share in the exploitation of those same resources; and fourth, the difficulties that governments experience in exercising state sovereignty.

Twenty-five years ago, when the international community began to recognize the salience of environmental problems, the state was perceived as providing the solution to these problems and as offering the only effective means of preventing environmental degradation by forcing individuals and companies to change their harmful behaviour. Richard Falk[20] and William Ophuls[21] were putting their hopes in a supranational authority – benevolent for the former, authoritarian for the latter.

This central role of the state is now in question. Non-governmental organizations (NGOs) advocate decentralized management of environmental problems. Neoliberals argue that there are economic instruments that can be useful in changing the behaviour of both firms and individuals. Intergovernmental organizations (IGOs) claim that they alone are able to resolve global problems. Bilateral development agencies and international NGOs promote aid policies designed both to strengthen the role of local communities and to facilitate the emergence of local organizations, both of which trends lead to decentralized decision making. No longer seen as the solution, the state is now understood to be part of the problem. Once the primary means of promoting the national interest, the state today can be seen as impeding the pursuit of the common good, particularly by ethnic, religious, or linguistic minorities living within the national boundaries.

Identity

The concept of state sovereignty, born with the Treaty of Westphalia (1648), granted the monarch the right to impose his or her religion on his subjects and, at the same time, recognized the right to exile of those refusing to convert.[22] The political philosophy underlying state sovereignty was further elaborated during the French Revolution with the advent of the concept of the nation-state, which values a homogeneous population, at least in terms of religion and language. This model can be found not only in centralized states (such as France) but also in federal states (such as Canada), which provide local powers to subnational administrative units.

The awakening of national sentiment had two types of consequences. First, it made certain peoples living in a number of sovereign jurisdictions aware that they comprised a national entity entitled to its own state – for example, Germany and Italy. Second, it prompted a desire by minorities to secede from the sovereign jurisdictions to which they belonged and to form their own states – for example, in Austria-Hungary. Following the Second World War, decolonization saw the entry of over a hundred new states onto the international stage.

Minorities quickly became subjects of international concern insofar as there was a possibility that they might call into question existing territorial boundaries and create international conflicts. That is why article 27 of the International Covenant on Civil and Political Rights (1966) states, 'In those States in which ethnic, religious or linguistic minorities exist, persons belonging to such minorities shall not be denied the right, in community with the other members of their group, to enjoy their own culture, to profess and practise their own religion, or to use their own language.' The criteria adopted are ethnicity, language, religion, and regionalism. Let us see how they might today pose a challenge to the state.

Ethnicity

Ethnicity is not a new phenomenon in the history of states. The Ottoman Empire had institutionalized the existence of minorities. Through the millet system, it granted special status to Christian and Jewish religious minorities.[23] None the less members of minorities remained marginal in the empire: they were not allowed political power, and the principle of inequality, on which the millet system was based, would make it unacceptable in contemporary democratic societies.

In this vein, it would be naïve not to take into account the interest that 'each state has in creating its own mythology of origins, to create an ideal to which all citizens can refer.'[24] This situation leads some authors to question the very idea of ethnicity, claiming that it is an artificial construct fabricated by states to elicit the support of their citizens.[25] Without entering the debate on the relevance of such a theory, we must acknowledge that the presence of ethnic groups is a regular pretext for the inflaming of nationalist passions. There is no lack of examples of conflicts between one or more ethnic groups that pose a threat to the state. In the former Yugoslavia, four states are claiming ethnic legitimacy with the consent of the international community. To them we can add the Basque, Berber, Corsican, Kurdish, Ogoni, Palestinian and Tibetan peoples, to name but a few. So, it is not surprising that ethnicity is often considered an obstacle to peace. Demands for status equal to that of the dominant ethnic group can lead to calls for special status within the state and even to the demand for political autonomy. The proliferation of international treaties recognizing the existence and rights of ethnic groups is forcing the signatory states to respect their commitments. Even if, under article 27 of the International Convention on Civil and Political Rights, the states themselves are the sole arbiters of whether their behaviour towards their own minorities is in compliance with their international commitments, minorities always have the option of denouncing the way in which they are treated before the United Nations Human Rights Commission.

The same applies to indigenous peoples. As they arrived before the majority (hence 'aboriginal'), they are governed by specific laws. In Canada, Aboriginal rights are recognized in section 25 of the Canadian Charter of Rights and Freedoms. Yet the behaviour of the Canadian state towards its Aboriginal peoples has recently been the object of international denunciation. Although the state is often forced to deal with challenges posed by identity groups, the state itself may create a sense of community among a minority or aboriginal group. In this case, it is not the ethnic groups that pose a problem for the state, but the reverse. States thus face a dilemma: either they try to assimilate ethnic groups, at the risk of being accused of not respecting their cultural heritage, or they encourage and promote ethnic affiliation, at the risk of creating among ethnic communities an inclination to reject state institutions.

Language

The problem of ethnicity is often related to that of language. In most cases, one of the specific cultural features of ethnic groups is the possession and use of a language different from that used by the majority. Language is an instrument of communication that permits social exchange. On one hand, it can form an integral part of a nation's cultural heritage, so that knowledge of it becomes indispensable to anyone who wishes to develop a sense of membership; on the other hand, language can be regarded as just one of the many attributes of a people – a matter of personal choice rather than a yardstick for measuring an individual's integration or non-integration. In most states, however, language constitutes a 'paramount issue because it is not solely a cultural asset that serves as a medium of communication and information, but above all a symbolic resource that signifies the primordial unity of the group.'[26]

Can we then regard language as one of the foundations of political communities? The reality seems more complex. Let us cite a few examples that illustrate why language is not always sufficient to form a nation: Catholic Irish speak English but did/do not feel part of the British nation (different religions); the Serbs and Croats speak the same language but do not form a nation (different ethnic origins); the Alsatians, whose language is Germanic, feel more French than German. So it is clear that language is not always the dominant factor at the origin of conflicts.[27]

However, it would also be wrong to minimize the importance of language issues, which can call into question state sovereignty. The recent official recognition of regional languages within the European Union is forcing its members to respect minority languages within their borders. Consequently, France, which previously prohibited instruction of regional languages, must now permit it. The recognition of regional languages limits the sovereignty of states but poses no challenge to their role, much less to their existence. The French minister of education continues to manage school programs. So what we see in France is a redefinition of the centralizing philosophy of the state and, at best, a partial infringement of its sovereignty.

The situation may be altogether different elsewhere. For Canada, linguistic issues have a contextual significance that differs from most other countries. Here language has remained the only vestige of a distinction between two groups, with religion and judicial systems becoming less important. Because it is more emotional, more central in people's lives, and more of a driving political force, language continues to be central to Quebec's challenge to the Canadian state. The official Canadian policy of bilingualism is a response to this historical duality. The Canadian and Quebec political authorities are thus obliged to pass language laws and to intervene at the request of groups in civil society.

In different circumstances, some U.S. states, which had never before thought about language policy, must now adopt one, be it to declare English the official language or to offer public services, including education, in other languages.

Religion

Religion seems to be a universal factor of national integration.[28] It is relevant both for monotheistic faiths such as Christianity, Judaism and Islam, for polytheistic faiths such as Hinduism and Shinto, and for non-theistic systems, such as Buddhism and Confucianism. It can be particularly important for stateless, oppressed peoples.

Do religions have an influence on international politics? Both its admirers and opponents see the Vatican as *sui generis*, with the pope at once head of the Catholic church and head of the sovereign state of the Holy See. Its official relations with other states – via concordats and, since the late 1970s, conventions, which are less solemn but serve a similar purpose – have no equivalent in any other religion. Concordats and conventions reflect the Holy See's power over the policies of national churches. This recognized right poses a challenge to the primacy of the sovereign state within its borders.[29] Examples of the Vatican's influence on national and international policy include the nomination of bishops and the more or less rapid adjustment of the boundary lines of dioceses to those of international borders.

Very different is the activity of the World Council of Churches (WCC). There we can see an encounter between churches that are subject to state governments, such as the Russian Orthodox church in Soviet times, and Western Protestant churches, which are independent of government authorities. The result has been the adoption of positions condemning the capitalist and imperialist northern states, condemnations of Israel, and silence on the internal and international policies of the Soviet Union – including its violation of the religious rights of Christians – and on the policies of Third World dictatorships.

The WCC has thus served as a sounding board for certain ideas that Moscow wished to disseminate in Western countries. Since the disappearance of the Soviet Union, the WCC has remained faithful to its ideology, critical of Western democracies and apologetic for 'left-wing' dictatorships.[30] Repeated by its member churches, which include the elites in power (the evangelical churches – often poor, black, and theologically conservative – are underrepresented in the WCC), the predominant political discourse of the WCC has more chance of influencing political decision makers than one church would have acting alone. This is the result not of coercion but of political lobbying to influence the policy process.

The Islamic Conference, created in 1969, could be seen as imposing constraints on Muslim states. It includes all states with Muslim majorities, including secular Turkey, and all states with mixed populations where Muslims constitute the upper classes and control the levers of state power – for example, Sudan and Nigeria. It includes two European states, Albania and Bosnia. Is membership a political choice or an obligation that is imposed? The question is particularly important, since this body does not confine itself to general goals pertaining to religious solidarity, economic and social co-operation, and anti-colonialism. Its charter also mentions 'support for the struggle of all Muslim peoples, for their dignity, their independence and their national rights.' This concept introduces something new to international politics – the declared right to intervene in the domestic affairs of a state that has a Muslim minority in revolt against the central authority. This is the case in Philippines, where Muslim groups have launched guerrilla operations against Manila.

If we are to believe the declarations of the Islamic Conference and the fears of its detractors, the role of states could well be challenged by the conference in the name of the *Ummah* – the transnational Muslim community. The mere threat of condemnation or intervention by a group of more than fifty states on three continents would impose a policy line on its member states and limit the choices of other states.

Despite everything that distinguishes the activities of the Vatican, the WCC, and the Islamic Conference, they all reflect the trend of increasingly strong religious influence on governments, which can extend to the point of imposing decisions on the authorities of particular countries.

Other religious groups have influence but do not necessarily call the state into question. For example, the Baptist World Alliance and Armenian, Jewish, and Orthodox Christian groups intervene in favour of fellow believers experiencing distress in other countries, but in doing so they behave like a classical lobby group; they are not a threat to the state. To most Orthodox Christians, certain religious affiliations can be seen as explaining political alignments such as: the 'sacred union' supposedly existing between Catholics and Protestants against the Serb Orthodox, which motion is supported by the Russian, Greek, and Romanian Orthodox. Historically based religious affinities can help explain reactions of public opinion, but we know of no author who sees a political determinant in these religious nebulae.

Different from the established religions are the religious movements that pose security problems for states. The Islamic movements are compelling states, primarily the Arabic and Muslim states, to intensify their machinery of repression. For Marx Juergensmeyer,[31] the challenge to the state stems not so much from the fundamentalists – a catch-all term with little political meaning – as from what he calls the 'religious nationalists,' who deliberately combine political interests with a religious discourse. They see secular nationalism as devoid of values; only religious nationalism might restore meaning to life in society by introducing a new political order based on religion and not overly concerned with either democracy or human rights. Religious nationalists would include not only the various Islamic movements but also the Hindu and Sikh militant groups. Speaking on behalf of the nation and its religious beliefs, these movements lay claim to superior legitimacy, to the moral authority to keep states in line and to the use violence to achieve their ends.

Democratic states are confronted not only by religions with a dependent affiliation to a spiritual centre outside the states' borders, but also by those that question their roles from within the national society itself. For example, when Quakers and Jehovah's Witnesses refuse to use any form of violence, even in time of war, they are not merely objecting to having to participate in the military effort; they are also objecting to the use of force by the state.[32]

More subtle is what Thiemann calls the 'dilemma for democracy' – the competition between religion and the state in determining public and social norms.[33] Should the religious values of the majority of Americans determine the moral framework for legal decisions? This raises ethical questions: Is abortion simply a legal problem or a moral or societal problem? Given that legal texts, from the U.S. constitution to the Canadian Charter of Rights and Freedoms, do not deal with the rights or absence of rights of the fetus, what criteria should guide the state's responses to these new problems? The very fact that religions and churches are stepping in to try to impose their views or influence public decisions in the name of a superior legitimacy calls into question the state's power to make decisions based on what it perceives to be the public interest. What is being challenged is not only the legitimacy of the state, but also its autonomy.

Regionalism

The emergence of economic regions that do not correspond to state boundaries now seems to be an established fact. Whether these regions overlap with different states or lie within one state is of little importance; in both cases, these regions are capable of entering into commercial agreements without the government's intervention. The German state of Baden-Württemberg 'has signed several hundred agreements with other regions and entities. And what, if any, control does [Berlin] exercise over this activity?'[34] Thus the emergence of economic regions within states calls into question the economic relevance of the national state. This problem is accentuated by citizens' identification with these regions.[35]

This desire for autonomy often accompanies the emergence of economic regions or is made possible by a specific economic situation.[36] According to Ohmae,[37] the nation-state is no longer able to guarantee the economic prosperity of the entire country. For instance, in the signing of economic agreements it has become more of a hindrance than a help. The reason is simple: the idea of national interest is itself obsolete, for it is based on a representation of the economy as something oriented around the resources to be found within the national territory. This implies that protection of these resources constitutes the purpose of the nation-state.[38] Today, however, the economy is determined not by the exploitation of resources but by the transfer and acquisition of knowledge and skills. The nation-state's protection no longer serves any purpose because it inhibits acquisition of that knowledge and those skills.[39]

The size, physical resources, and population of a country are no longer the factors that determine its economic prosperity. Hong Kong, Singapore, and many others are major players in the world economy, despite their limited territory, population, and natural resources.[40] Ohmae criticizes states for continuing to entertain what he calls 'the illusion of resources,'[41] with all that it implies about protection, when the real engines of economic expansion are regions.

In the industrialized world, the state is not even a factor of social or economic integration any more. Newhouse too suggests that inhabitants of regions identify not with the central state but with a region that generates wealth and symbolizes success.[42]

In North America, the economic relations of the entire Pacific coast are such that many inhabitants of British Columbia no longer identify themselves only with their province or country, but also with this vast, economically dynamic entity. Without exaggerating the political impact of this phenomenon in Canada, it could raise doubts as to the role of the federal state in the construction of a pan-Canadian identity. From this standpoint, the federal government would become manager of interprovincial relations, even a mere 'mailbox.' This situation is not particular to Canada. Newhouse gives the example of Germany: 'Today's Germans exist comfortably within their federal structure;

many, if not most of them, feel as if they are living once again as Thuringians, Bavarians, Westphalians, and so on.'[43] In addition to Germany, economic regions can be found in most industrialized countries, including France, Italy, Spain, and the United Kingdom. Some regions are also claiming a national or transnational cultural or historical identity and distinctiveness – for example, the Basque country, Catalonia, Catalonia-Roussillon, northern Italy, and Rhone–Alpes–Piedmont.

Thus the challenge to the state's role, and even to its right to pass legislation in certain sectors of regional importance, seems very strong. When two regions in two different countries are capable of coming to an agreement without recourse to their respective states, and for the greater good of all, why complicate things with national legislation? What legitimacy does the state have to intervene if the inhabitants of these two bordering regions share more in common than they do with the citizens of their respective countries? Accordingly, economic regions are emerging that could well, with time, become important political entities that rival the state as the major form of collective political action: 'The question many Europeans are asking is whether regions are gradually supplanting central states as sources of political authority and custodians of public policy.'[44]

Ohmae sees regions in industrialized countries increasingly defined by the economic activity and success that distinguish them from the rest of the country to which they belong. Newhouse, in contrast, sees regions as primarily cultural entities that represent more of a threat than a step forward. There is a connection here to the traditional regional political demands that have arisen in Europe and elsewhere over the past thirty years in reaction to the modernization of states and that could become significant again in a new context of globalization. But are regions making progress because they have to make up for a state less and less able to perform its traditional functions, or are they trying to assert new interests? These different foundations (economic or cultural) of the increasing power of regions have different political consequences. Economic logic leads regions to ask for autonomy in decision making in the name of efficiency, while cultural logic leads to the pursuit of independence in the name of identity.

Ideology

Economic globalization and identity challenge the state; this challenge is itself sustained by ideologies that can acquire the status of what

David Apter calls 'modern myths.'[45] Ideas, as in the case of Friedmann's theories from the 1970s, can even be used by national leaders to challenge the nature and role of the state.[46]

Is this challenge to the state by politicians themselves the result of a new ideology, the application of a ready-made model, or a reaction to an economy in transformation? For his part, Spulber emphasizes the ideological role of liberal political/economic theory. He sees the challenge as coming from outside the state; but public servants, using fashionable economic or political theories, may eventually renounce their own capacity to make decisions. Other observers stress the role of economic transformations and development, as opposed to an ideology that serves to justify political action. Yet even in this case, systematic reference to a political theory as a panacea for all the problems that economic, social, or other types of change pose for the state can lead to a questioning of the state, of its functions (economic intervention), of its legitimacy (inability to respond to its citizens' aspirations), or of its sovereignty. Such references often take on the value of an ideology. When faced with an external challenge, the state may bring itself even further into question through its own decisions and the adoption of an ideological direction.

The welfare state has been dethroned by a neoliberal ideology aimed at keeping state intervention to a minimum in an economy regulated by the laws of the marketplace. Many view this paradigm shift as the result of the inability of states to manage effectively the economic problems of the 1970s and 1980s, such as inflation, zero growth, high unemployment, and large budget deficits.[47] Incapable of resolving these problems, and having trouble responding to calls for protection from social groups, the industrialized nations were no longer able to keep their actions in line with the principles on which they based their authority. A new model was then adopted, grounded in the idea of giving an enhanced role to the private sector as an economic regulator and remodelling management of the state to resemble that of private enterprise. This assault on the state became a leitmotif 'shared by all political parties, both conservatives and professed social democrats.'[48]

Privatization, the causes of which are at once historical, empirical, and ideological,[49] has encouraged governments to abandon regulatory intervention and accept the 'rules' of the market. The predominant notion of the inevitable growth of the state has given way to the ubiquitous ideology of privatization.[50] This idea became attractive because it allowed the state to cut its expenditures while increasing its short-term revenues, thereby affording it the tools to reduce its debt or meet its obligations. In this sense, it does not call into question the role of the state.

However, privatization was not implemented in every country in the same way. Feigenbaum and Henig[51] identify three types of privatization – systemic, pragmatic, and tactical. Systemic privatization refers to a government's attempt to transform society, as, for example, in post-Communist Eastern Europe and in Margaret Thatcher's United Kingdom. In the United States, where public ownership is not as widespread as in other countries of the Organization for Economic Co-operation and Development, privatization has focused on two main themes: economic deregulation and reduction of the state's role and intervention in citizens' lives.[52]

Pragmatic privatization derives not from ideological motivations but from economic concerns, based on cost–benefit analyses. In this category appear most of the municipal privatizations in the United States, the sale of the companies of the Institute for Industrial Reconstruction (an Italian conglomerate), and the creation of certificates of investment in French public firms. In Canada, this trend has found expression in many federal and provincial policies concerned with privatization and the stabilization of public finances undertaken by governments since the mid-1980s.

Finally, tactical privatization is a response to short-term political goals. The platform of the *cohabitation* government in France in 1986–8 is a good example, since it proved a way of offering a clear alternative to the electoral strategy of the Socialists, who had already adopted most of the neoliberal economic agenda. Many developing countries have also used tactical privatization in order to demonstrate to international backers that they have converted to market principles.[53]

Has the implementation of privatization, whatever its form, really reduced the role of the state? The current neoliberal ideology would suggest such an interpretation. However, from a liberal standpoint, the state must assume a minimum number of functions. According to Richard Falk,[54] it essentially fills three roles: guarantor of the physical security of people and their property, facilitator of economic growth, and liberator and emancipator of civil society. Falk gives the examples of the international convention to eliminate anti-personnel landmines and the creation of the International Criminal Court. Their sponsors, including Canada, have replaced the Westphalian vision of the superior interest of the state with the vision of an international civil society that imposes certain constraints on the state.

But not everyone has such a minimalist view of the state. Zaki Laïdi,[55] for example, assigns the state a wide variety of functions. In addition to its duty to offer protection against external enemies and internal instability, the state must also distribute public goods and redistribute wealth. This, at least, was the case in Europe, where 'the redistributive effect of the European-style tax system and social benefits in reducing the extent of social inequities has been two to three times greater than for their North American counterparts.'[56] Above all, the state is an important generator of meaning, the sole transmitter of a blueprint for society.[57] According to Krasner,[58] the state will be stronger for being less susceptible to pressures from society.

Neoliberal ideology has inspired federal and provincial policies in Canada predicated on the premise that the economy is too serious a matter to be left in the hands of the state. This has led to privatization, stringent stricter social policies, the quest for 'zero' deficits, and the 'downsizing' of the public service. Based on a neoliberal analysis of the cost of the state, the federal Treasury Board suggested reorganization of government intervention. But to ward off challenges to the system, it declared that overlaps were not really a problem because situations differed.[59]

A distinction must be made, however, between ensuring sound management, which does not call into question the state's role, and making the reduction of the state's role a new standard, regardless of the situation of the public finances. The process of privatization, while retaining the government's responsibility for regulation, calls into doubt only certain functions of the state. But the neoliberal doctrine of privatization-cum-deregulation challenges the very role of the state as guarantor of the common good.

The Actors

Globalization and the evolution of the international system encourage action by other players who claim a legitimate role in national and international governance. These players, such as intergovernmental organizations (IGOs), non-governmental organizations (NGOs), and multinational corporations (MNCs), are not new. However, as the political, ideological, and technological context of their activities has changed, they have come to play a larger role in the formation and implementation of national and international policy. Many other participants, such as regions and networks, are emerging. To what extent do these players challenge the state's autonomy, legitimacy, and sphere of action?

Intergovernmental Organizations (IGOs)

The proliferation of states, the enhanced role of the state in society since the Second World War, the emergence of global problems, and the improvement of communication technologies have facilitated and made necessary increased dialogue and co-operation among states. In this context, IGOs reduce the amount of uncertainty that states face (for example, by increasing the volume of information and making the behaviour of other states more predictable) and increase their capacity for diplomacy.

To what extent can IGOs compete with the state? Some observers see them as the embryos of future world institutions, variously citing the following five factors:

- the supranational characteristics, with laws and decisions in some cases directly enforceable by national courts, replacing existing national laws – as, for example, in the European Union
- their influence on a country's domestic policy or imposition of certain decisions – as with the International Monetary Fund and World Bank
- their influence on the international agenda – for example, with the United Nations Environment Program and depletion of the ozone layer[60]
- their capacity to play states off against one another so as to impose their preferences
- their creation and promotion of transnational networks (which include NGOs, national administrative units, and other IGOs)

Lack of direct access to national corporations has prompted certain IGOs to develop close ties with NGOs, which are often better able to monitor implementation of certain commitments and inform the IGO concerned.

IGOs can also serve as intermediaries between players in society – for example, between industry and NGOs – or influence the latter while bypassing the state. All that the state need do then is adjust to this *fait accompli*, possibly claiming post facto monitoring or inspection rights. This aspect seems to be largely overlooked in the academic literature but deserves attention because it is likely to become more important.

Non-governmental organizations (NGOs)

The modern era has seen an explosion in the number of international associations and NGOs, which has risen from 2,470 in 1970, to 4,700 in 1983, to over 5,000 in 1995. More than five hundred such bodies had advisory status to the UN Economic and Social Council (ECOSOC) in 1995, compared with 90 in 1949.[61] This number continues to increase.

Some NGOs are very powerful and possess substantial financial resources and armies of lawyers, experts, and lobbyists. Some have millions of members; others, an operating budget that exceeds the resources available to many states or certain IGOs working in the same field. Still others have scientific expertise that is lacking in most of the poorer states.

Two related trends have developed since the beginning of the 1980s. The first is the formation of national and international coalitions among a great many organizations, mobilizing around a specific issue. The second is the mobilization of local populations, especially indigenous ones. NGOs have adopted the liberal critique of the centralizing state and promote the virtues of decentralizing decision making and resources. They have laid claim to greater legitimacy than the state by virtue of their motivation to work for justice and the common good, their knowledge of the local community and their 'political impartiality.'

There are five main factors that explain this general growth of NGOs and their international mobilization:

- the development of communication media
- the increasing number of common problems and fields of action in the industrialized nations
- the development of citizen movements dedicated to local action
- the desire of certain governments to develop local intermediaries for their intervention
- NGOs' ability to offer additional avenues of political mobilization in countries where political expression is limited

Although they are highly visible, NGOs' influence varies depending on the issue, the tactics, and the forums for their action. NGOs are active in generating demands and ensuring that issues are placed on the agenda of national and international policy makers. Generally, they greatly facilitate distribution of information – a crucial function for many developing countries. Certain nations lacking in significant diplomatic resources rely on NGO-organized information sessions about current negotiations. The proliferation of tiny states makes many of them dependent on the external expertise and resources provided by other more powerful states, IGOs, and NGOs and makes it easier for NGOs to be heard. Paradoxically, the much-decried principle of sovereignty becomes an asset when an NGO manages to 'capture' a state. The NGO thus gains access to meetings previously closed to it – and that remain closed to other NGO – and obtains the same vote as a powerful state.[62]

In dealing with local shortages, national and international development assistance agencies are relying more and more on local or transnational NGOs for the delivery and management of many projects. In 1985, donors provided U.S.$1.1 billion in aid through local NGOs (compared with U.S.$100 million in 1975). In 1987, governments contributions to NGOs made up about 5 per cent of total development assistance.

NGOs can supervise projects in areas inaccessible to international organizations or monitor states' compliance with their international commitments. Their role goes beyond influencing stages of the public policy process. They can also act as liaison between IGOs and governments, as mediators between and consultants to states (scientific NGOs in particular are closely associated with the negotiation process), or as lobby groups pressing for new fields or new policies. Their capacity to promote their message simultaneously at the international, governmental and social levels adds to their potential influence. Finally, some authors[63] go further, focusing on the emergence of a sphere of political action parallel to that of the state, where NGOs and industry come to an agreement on certain policies or behaviour outside the bounds of the state. In other words, governance, as it applies solutions to environmental problems, is no longer the sole prerogative of the state.

These examples notwithstanding, the actual significance of NGOs in the structure of international co-operation remains ambiguous. Relevant assessments are often based on data supplied by these organizations themselves, which may tend to conclude that all progress observed is related to their activities. Whereas many states feel that NGOs should concentrate on collection and dissemination of information, some NGOs themselves would like to move beyond their watchdog role. They are demanding the right to have a say in decisions, to examine IGOs' activities, to have access to negotiations and documents produced by IGOs, and to take legal action on behalf of the environment.

The Private Sector

It is doubtless the private sector that has aroused both the greatest fears and hopes with regard to the possible weakening or even future disappearance of the state. States' concerns about multinational corporations (MNCs) are nothing new. The 1960s and 1970s saw the publication of many studies critical of their power. These concerns even received institutional sanction – for example, in the creation of a United Nations office for the study of MNCs. But today's debate is different, since its context is different. The UN office has been abolished. Neoliberal ideology brings new legitimacy to the actions of MNCs and their transnational ideology. Globalization has provided them with resources for renewed expansion. Like the NGOs, the private sector is laying claim to legitimate participation in international policy formulation and, in the view of some authors, is placing new constraints on the autonomy of states that threaten their very existence or at least their capacity to carry out their traditional functions.[64]

Industry has tended to be very active in IGOs and in international negotiations aimed at regulating its modes of production or the nature of its products, even if it has usually preferred to advance its interests at the national level. Today, however, we are witnessing a broadening of the international political action of industry. Sometimes industry's greater presence is the result of its conviction that traditional territorial divisions between states are an obstacle to resolving common problems. For instance, in 1996 fifty-seven European insurance companies issued a statement indicating their belief that climate change would increase the frequency of natural disasters (storms, droughts) and calling for a program for fast and substantial reduction of emissions.[65]

But states themselves and IGOs are now allowing industry a more extensive role in certain sectors, for at least three reasons. First, these firms generate more than half of the world's economic activity (production, administration, or distribution of goods and services). Second, they are responsible for some of the problems now facing states (for example, in the environmental field, through their use, sale, or manufacture of hazardous products and their large-scale exploitation of natural resources). Third, they are party to the solutions being adopted by the international community to deal with global problems.[66]

According to Strange,[67] the structural changes to the world economy that are driving the internationalization of production have forced states to enter the competitive ring and take account of corporations in their relations with other states. The state's role is being modified and brought closer to a neomercantilist model; the MNCs have an economic arsenal that states need in order to win their share of the world market (technology, fast access to capital, and major markets).

Implications

Reflection on 'the state of the state' usually centres on its capacity for control, its authority, and its actual power. Conclusions about its future thus depend on the analysis of its ability or inability to exercise such control[68] in the face of the rise to power of other players or the emergence of other sources of power more difficult to control.

The uncertainty regarding the definition of power provides for a rather unproductive basis for reflection. This is complicated by many factors such as the debatable relevance of power analyses, which often overestimate the power lost by the state, the equally debatable overemphasis on the role of the state vis-à-vis other actors, and the conflation of questions about the power of the state writ large and about the relative loss of power of specific governments. In other words, what is the subject of analysis? Is it the loss of power or authority of the state in general or of *certain* states? Or do other transformations challenge the very foundations of the state as a 'vehicle of meaning' or a preferred instrument for the pursuit of the common good?

One must not confuse the state's resources with its capacity to use them in pursuit of a collective goal. To constitute 'challenges,' the aspects described in this section have to affect three attributes of the state – its autonomy, its legitimacy, and its capacity for action – and one characteristic of its context – the degree of uncertainty that the state is facing. By 'autonomy' we mean the capacity of decision makers to resist pressure from the international system or civil society – that is, to define a national interest different from that of specific groups or external players. At the international level, this notion takes the form of the concept of sovereignty. 'Legitimacy' is based on the concurrence between the actions of the state and the principles that it affirms. It affects the state's ability to encourage citizens, groups, and other players in the international system to accept its authority. 'Capacity for action' simply means possession of the resources to pursue the fundamental objectives of the state and the society on which it is founded. Finally, 'degree of uncertainty' refers to decision makers' ability to estimate the probability attached to the behaviour of the other players in the system and to assess the consequences of their own actions.

Susan Strange's conception of the state's loss of authority over its citizens and their activities is much like our own. However, she sees this situation as the product of a loss of power. She sees[69] the retreat of the state not in terms of its diminishing presence in society (in the area of regulation, for example) but in its increasing inability to assume its traditional functions: to uphold law and order, defend the territory against foreign acts of violence, guarantee the currency and the economy, and enforce the equity of contractual transactions. These changes reveal the limitations of the state's capacity for action. In what ways do they also pose a challenge to its autonomy and legitimacy, and in what ways do they increase the degree of uncertainty that it faces?

Loss of Autonomy

The argument that globalization weakens the state is based largely on the notion that it substantially restricts the state's freedom of action and its sovereignty. The state is becoming less capable of deciding for itself the choices that it has to make. The rules of the World Trade Organization are, it is alleged, becoming tyrannical; the state is subject to blackmail from multinationals or ratings firms. High finance weaves ties that the state cannot break without risk. Key decisions are no longer made in the nation's capital, or in any other capital, but by a multitude of independent players pursuing narrow, limited goals.

Strange thus puts the emphasis on structural power – that is, the capacity to influence the rules that govern states' decisions. This capacity is no longer the sole prerogative of the state. There are multiple authorities, and hence multiple legitimacies. Certain players have the capability of developing rules of conduct among themselves to which states will have to adapt – as we saw above, for example, with regard to international shipping.[70]

Delegitimization

If the state is becoming weaker, its detractors will say, it is because it has lost its legitimacy. Not only is the state no longer capable of meeting its citizens' expectations, but it is itself an obstacle to their realization. Since the democratic state can no longer base its legitimacy on charisma, tradition, or efficiency, the authority of the market is replacing that of the state.

This political or economic incapacity will provoke increasing demands on or attempts to bypass the state, which pressure may give rise to the public feeling that the state is no longer the necessary vehicle for the promotion of the common good. Similarly, theorists of integration and interdependence have pointed to loss of legitimacy as the precursor of a surpassing (via integration) or a bypassing (via interdependence) of the state.

The Commission on Global Governance[71] notes that institutions lacking in legitimacy are rarely effective over the long term. Standards are a major foundation of legitimacy. They constrain the exercise of state power or magnify the messages of internal groups and the effectiveness of their pressure.[72]

Zaki Laïdi, for example, stresses the delegitimization of the state. Domestically, this affects the state as the vehicle of common meaning and as the instrument of effective collective action. It is quite conceivable to have a state that is both strongly present (via its spending) and experiencing a loss of legitimacy. Or the state may simply become indifferent to emerging functions and problems. What is most problematic for Laïdi is the future of politics: the capacity to define and pursue a collective project.

At the international level, the state is losing its role as mediator between the domestic and the foreign. Globalization, which externalizes endogenous issues and internalizes exogenous ones, has weakened this function because the international arena no longer comprises diplomatic and strategic issues alone but includes economic, social and environmental ones.

We may question those who argue that the state is suffering from a decline in legitimacy. They assume not only that the state must have legitimacy, but that legitimacy is an attribute that cannot be shared. We saw above that a new dimension of relations between corporations and the state is the formers' enhanced legitimacy as full-fledged players and partners of the state in the resolution of socioeconomic problems. This shift has increased the legitimacy of negotiations between the state and corporations. The pessimists will conclude that there has been a *relative* loss of the state's legitimacy. Those who are pessimistic about the ethnic phenomenon, who perceive it as a challenge to the state's legitimacy and hence a danger, advance the same argument.

But is it not also possible that legitimacy can be shared? For example, we know that Canada sees no contradiction between a new Canadian's political obligation to his or her adopted country and his or her attachment to and identification with an ethnocultural community.[73] If that is the case, under what conditions? How? With what consequences? On what bases will individuals choose between competing legitimacies? The last question becomes very important with the proliferation of sources of legitimacy.

There are also some major methodological difficulties. How does one measure the degree of legitimacy of a state without succumbing to circular logic? When can the state be said to lose its legitimacy? Is that loss uniform or uneven? Does this legitimacy increase in certain sectors or in the context of certain roles, but decrease in others? With what consequences? What are the foundations of this legitimacy, and can they be transformed?

Finally, the existing challenge to the state's legitimacy does not mean that this process is either inevitable or unidirectional. The state can rebuild a different legitimacy. To what extent is there a demand for the state as a potential source of new legitimacy?[74]

Degree of Uncertainty

The magnitude of the uncertainty facing the state is manifested in four ways.[75] First, it may relate to the nature and extent of internal and external changes – i.e., uncertainty about the system's operation. Second, it may concern the impact of those changes on a given policy, reflecting lack of information about the nature of causal relationships. These two types of uncertainty affect the state's ability to assess the nature and quantity of the resources at its disposal for the pursuit of its fundamental objectives. Third, uncertainty may characterize the behaviour of other players with respect to a given policy – in other words, uncertainty about all the preferences or strategies valued by other players. Finally, uncertainty may relate to the consequences of the state's decisions – that is, it may reflect an inability to predict the results of the state's action.

Thus these four types of uncertainty affect the analysis. Whereas uncertainty regarding the actions of other players has always been a factor, the other three types have acquired new importance in the context of globalization and the increasing number of players laying claim to a role in public governance. The effect of this sea change is to reduce the state's capacity to calculate its interests and define the common interest. These uncertainties are sources of new insecurities; each is related to the relative loss of the three attributes described above, and each has different dimensions.[76]

Critiques of the Dominant Discourse

The neoliberal discourse that is accentuating a perception of a decline of the state – or, to use Evans's expression,[77] an eclipse of the state – is far from being confirmed. On the contrary, even if the state's actions appear at times to take new directions, it seems to be, just as at present, autonomous and legitimate. We organize the arguments that take this approach under two headings: the centrality of the state vis-à-vis new players – MNCs, IGOs, NGOs, regions, ethnic groups, and religions – and the transformation of the role of the state. The neoliberal discourse holds that the state is in decline. We join certain authors in believing that the state is in fact capable of adapting and continues to play a central role.

Centrality of the State vis-à-vis New Players

Multinational Corporations (MNCs)

Walter[78] attacks the idea that multinational corporations' increased capabilities to impose their preferences call into question the state's autonomy. He criticizes that theory of globalization which holds that states have lost their power to tax, to manage domestic affairs and to promulgate capital-restrictive regulations. In fact, MNCs often fail in their attempts to have host states adopt investment regulations that would allow them flexibility.[79] States still retain their authority to impose operating parameters on them, thus limiting their freedom of action. Walter bases his thesis on three observations.

First, the general trend to liberalization has not prevented many developing countries from regulating the operations of MNCs, limiting foreign ownership, and even protecting certain strategic sectors. The introduction of such regulations has not curbed the expansion of foreign direct investment (FDI) in these countries. The case of China is particularly striking here. Even though it is the leading recipient of FDI among developing countries, it has the least liberal regime in this regard. Walter even notes an inverse relation between the liberality of the investment system of developing countries and the geographical significance of FDI, with the notable exception of Argentina and Mexico.

Second, if the restraints put in place by the Association of South East Asian Nations (ASEAN) have not prevented those countries from receiving an increasing share of FDI, it is partly because MNCs have difficulty acting in concert.[80] If one of them decides not to invest in

China, another will take advantage of that vast market. The only rule observed by the MNCs is competition, not solidarity.

Third, MNCs still have to act in a context set by the state and exercise traditional pressure on their home governments. For Walter, this constitutes a weakness, for in a world where capital is truly mobile they should not have to use such methods. In the United States, for example, MNCs have pressed the federal government to get host countries to liberalize their investment regulations. This pressure has been strong enough to force the U.S. government into a series of initiatives, yet results seem to be rather disappointing for the MNCs.

Although the proposed Multilateral Agreement on Investment (MAI) had been perceived as a potential victory for the MNCs, the member states of the OECD, including the United States, had made provisions to retain the right to regulate the key activities of MNCs within their national jurisdictions, particularly in such matters as taxation. What is more, contrary to the wishes of its own business community, the U.S. government intended to maintain its extraterritorial legislation, such as the Helms–Burton Act. Other OECD members have demanded numerous exceptions to the basic principles of the MAI, and Canada has called for a 'notwithstanding clause' for the cultural industry.

Far from being totally subject to the powerful MNCs, states still retain the authority to impose parameters regulating their activities, at least as regards foreign investment. Nor is it clear that states have redefined their national interest on the simple basis of the preferences of these corporations.

Dombrowski,[81] too, challenges the notion that states are in the process of beating a retreat from financial markets. He believes that they have largely determined the size and operation of world financial markets. Many specialists concur with Polanyi[82] in regarding the liberalization of financial services as a solution to certain national dilemmas; they feel that states have opted for globalization to resolve certain domestic problems.

This sort of policy, which Ian Clark sees as deliberate,[83] none the less poses new problems for the state, which has to manoeuvre between globalization and fragmentation.[84] Implementation of liberalization policies has led states to create new regulations.[85] His analysis of the regulation of financial services and telecommunication initiated in the 1980s chiefly by the United Kingdom and Japan, but also by France, the United States, and Germany, leads him to conclude that liberalization leads not to deregulation automatically but rather to 're-regulation,' which differs from one country to another.

These studies bring three paradoxes to the fore: first, a movement designed to reduce regulation has succeeded only in increasing it; second, a movement driven by global forces has reinforced national differences; and third, a movement designed to push back the state has been led by the state itself. In the same vein, Rodrik also questions the so-called automatic link between liberalization and the decline of the state.[86] In particular, he demonstrates a positive correlation between the proportion of international trade in a country's gross national product (GNP) and the share of government spending in its gross domestic product (GDP). Such spending serves to reduce risk in economies exposed to greater liberalization. Twenty years ago, David Cameron was already demonstrating this correlation between liberalization and state intervention. Rodrik[87] has refined this analysis by studying total government consumer spending in one hundred countries. His work supports Vogel's findings of a direct relationship between liberalization and intervention. It is also consistent with the more empirical work by Katzenstein in the mid-1980s on the strategy of smaller European states such as Austria, the Netherlands, and Sweden, which had no trouble combining liberalization policies with compensatory mechanisms such as capital programs, industry subsidies, and tax transfers.[88]

This phenomenon is no surprise to Pierre de Senarclens, who emphasizes the primacy of politics: 'For the moment, only the state can guarantee political and legal order, without which there is no profitable investment, no sustainable production, no sustained consumption. Companies and markets, therefore, cannot scoff at national regulations, unless there exist supranational entities that take over from the states.'[89] But can IGOs and NGOs play this role? To what extent do they pose a challenge to the state in the exercise of its traditional functions?

Intergovernmental Organizations (IGOs)

While certain sectors, notably the environment, provide some evidence of the autonomy of international organizations, analytical difficulties persist. How can the interest of the organization and that of states be separated? Any policy pursued by an IGO will at least benefit one or several states that support it. To what extent can IGOs be said to have a global and no longer a national definition of interests? Can an IGO elude the control of states if those states have decided to reduce its freedom of action? In many cases, an IGO will have some latitude simply because certain issues are of secondary political importance to the dominant states. To argue therefore that IGOs can induce certain behaviour or an evolution of international policy that would not have happened without them does not mean that those organizations can impose policies on states that do not want them.

Despite examples of notable influence, IGOs continue to face major obstacles to becoming full-fledged international actors with their own autonomy and legitimacy beyond that of the state. Those commentators who question the autonomy of IGOs tend to raise the following points:

- With a few exceptions, most IGOs are not financially independent.
- The United Nations' attempts to develop independent access to financial resources have always met with fierce opposition.
- International secretariats are often feeble compared with the expertise available to certain states.
- The status of independent international public servants remains illusory, in practice, at least at the United Nations, since few senior officials have made a career outside their respective national administrations.
- Decisions are made by a coalition of governments, and no IGO can impose a decision if its members reject it.

While IGOs have definite influence on the generation of demands, 'agenda setting,' and policy development, their influence on the formulation of decisions is less clear. These two phases often involve different processes. Once a problem is put on the agenda, its resolution depends on political negotiations among states. Still, IGOs may substantially influence the nature of solutions adopted if states accept their definition of the problem.

Like states, IGOs operate in a political universe where the arts of persuasion, compromise, and coalition building are necessary if they are to advance their preferences and interests. But their influence depends on their ability to obtain resources – funding, political support, and expertise – independent of states. Most IGOs appear to be more the objects, or even the instruments, of international relations than players whose activities compete with those of states.

Furthermore, while IGOs have played or can play a considerable role in promoting the common good, they can also act as a barrier to it. For example, UN agencies have made themselves largely the mouthpieces for the concerns of southern countries uneasy about the emergence of environmental values. The World Meteorological Organization needed more than a decade after the World Climate Conference of 1979 to expand its domain from immediate weather prediction to studying the dynamics of long-term climates. Other organizations have sought to minimize environmental concerns because of their ideology or their technology or because they felt threatened.

Finally, as Paul Taylor has reminded us, IGOs have been deeply involved in the process of legitimizing and creating states and civil societies. The United Nations is doubtless the most striking example. It is engaged in the creation of an international society that *includes* states. If we look at institutions in the broad sense, and not at IGOs, there too, despite the prevalent discourse, the literature on international systems does not find them replacing states as primary actors in international relations. Their nature, characteristics, and functions will change in concert with the evolving sovereignty that they are helping to bring about.

Non-governmental Organizations

Faced with this process of evolution, many environmental and human rights activists have decried the concept of sovereignty, presenting it as the main obstacle to any progress towards the common good. But the same NGOs that often criticize the state as an obstacle to protection of individual integrity or of ecosystems on which humanity's survival depends use it to promote unilateral measures and indeed to extend them to other countries. Very often it is the particular exercise of sovereignty rather than the concept itself that they call into question. Far from challenging the state, NGOs depend on its good will, autonomy and capacity for action.[90]

NGOs still function only in the interstices of the state system. It is the states that define their capacity for action by protecting the right of association, giving them access to their territory and society, or supporting their initiatives. That states often view this arrangement as advantageous does not mean that this development is inevitable or that it works to their own detriment. NGOs have been able to gain access to some international negotiations, but they attend informal or working meetings only at the discretion of the organizers and commission chairs. Yet this is where the critical discussions take place.

In most cases, the success of certain NGOs – especially the more activist ones – depends on their alliance with certain states or with the secretariat of an international organization. American environmental NGOs have been able to influence the development of the World Bank's environmental policy thanks to their ability to harness the budgetary and media clout of the U.S. Congress and the support of a few countries that sit on the board of directors of the World Bank, including Canada. When NGOs do not have the support of one or more powerful states, their efforts to participate in decision making only serve to shift that process elsewhere.[91]

How internationally representative are NGOs, and how legitimate are their actions? Do they reflect only the views of certain politically dominant cultures and societies or universal aspirations? Are the solutions that they propose ethnocentric? Do they represent anything more than the small elite that heads them? At the international level, can they stand as substitutes for states or local populations?[92]

The impact of NGOs is also very limited by their divisions. The NGO community has great diversity in objectives, size, financial resources, seniority, origins, ideology, political and organizational culture, expertise, access to political power, and legal status. This diversity, and the contradictions that it can entail, can be found in any one state and any one group of NGOs. For example, US environmental NGOs were deeply divided over the merits of NAFTA, so that in 1993 the U.S. Congress was the target of environmental lobbyists advancing opposed opinions. At the international level, NGOs are either the product of the state in which they originated or the reflection of society. The numerous issues and perspectives that divide states will therefore divide NGOs as well. Conflicts can arise within NGOs regarding the best tactics to be employed. In 1995, the Sierra Club of British Columbia came out against attempts to boycott lumber exports to the United States that were initiated by the Sierra Club of California; and Greenpeace Quebec was profoundly shocked by the tactical alliance between Greenpeace USA and the Cree Indians of Hudson Bay against the Grande Baleine hydroelectric dam. NGOs from the South bitterly denounced the priorities and tactics of those in the North when the latter postulated the existence of harmonious interests. As Tariq Banuri points out,[93] whether they are from the North or from the South, NGOs tend to consider their own experience as definitive, not just for themselves but for others as well. Given the self-righteousness of many activists, dialogue between NGOs has not always been easy.

Relations between NGOs and state authorities also vary from one country and one NGOs to the next. While certain countries associate them in policy formulation and implementation in some fields or involve them in international negotiations, others keep them at a distance. Some states are openly hostile to NGOs and do not accept their claim of representing society, or they suspect them of transmitting foreign values or interests contrary to the national interest. The proliferation of NGOs and the role that certain countries give them as conduits of development assistance can prompt strong negative reactions from officials who fear that they may drain off development aid, perhaps even for the sole purpose of their own survival. Certain states therefore require that their activities – and their books – be transparent.

NGOs are not always the product of the spontaneous mobilization of groups of citizens. Some countries have created NGO networks from scratch in order to short-circuit existing groups, establish a useful consultation process, or facilitate implementation of national policies. Similarly, at the international level, the obligation to promote the participation of concerned groups in its activities has forced the Global Environment Facility Black Sea Program, based in Istanbul, to encourage the formation of NGOs and create networks where none existed before.[94]

On the international stage, therefore, it is states that use NGOs as diplomatic and policy instruments. States also control NGOs' access to the political process.[95] NGOs augment and complement the states' capabilities (for example, in research), relay their policies, and increase their political and diplomatic options.

Still, NGOs can be significant international players. The phenomenon is an ambiguous one. NGOs are at once dependent on and supportive of the state, but they also represent an affirmation of society, which may question the state's *monopoly* on legitimacy. What is new here is not so much the affirmation of a competing legitimacy in times of crisis (such as the 'revolutions' in Eastern Europe in the late 1980s), but the posting in normal times of a parallel legitimacy, with which the state should be required to come to terms.

Regions

Can regions, as Ohmae[96] and Newhouse[97] have argued, compete with the state? These largely deterministic theses also are open to question. Do regions impose themselves on states, or are they the states' instrument and creation? For instance, to what extent are they the product of state policies of industrialization and devolution or of a stable international political environment? What significance should we give to the concept of 'natural economic zones' in a context of globalization, and why should these economic (as opposed to historical or cultural) foundations govern existing political arrangements? To what extent are impulses towards regional autonomy the product of favourable circumstances, such as sustained growth? It is in times of crisis that we should assess the significance of these entities. Are they better positioned to respond to such challenges, or are they obliged to defer to the central state in order to overcome them? Why would they be able to make better use of the resources of the world economy than the central state, as Ohmae maintains?

Neither Ohmae nor Newhouse actually calls the state into question; they simply pose the problem in terms of levels of government. The central issue is not simply the future and capacities of the states that we know (the autonomy problem), but the challenge to the very concept of the state as supreme instrument of a collective desire for security (the legitimacy problem).

Ethnic Groups

What about ethnicity? Current events seem to provide ample demonstration of substantial suspicion towards the state, at least in its current form. However, it is useful to distinguish between ethnic groups that accept the status quo and those that want change, between those that are peaceful and those that use violence.

Deep-rooted ethnic identities and a mutual desire to separate can lead to a peaceful challenge to the state. This is the exceptional case of the division of the Czechoslovak state into two entities, the Czech and Slovak republics. When the sovereignty of the state is challenged by guerrilla activities to which the central authority responds with force, the international community now sometimes feels called on to step in. The Balkans provide an example of this situation: state-encouraged ethnic antagonisms led to the breakup of Yugoslavia, an explosion of successor states and civil and international wars, and finally massive intervention by the North Atlantic Treaty Organization. The reality of ethnic conflict is bringing about a new type of relation between states. In Africa, the Organization of African Unity (OAU), which stands for the inviolability of the post-colonial borders, has had to bow to a *fait accompli* and recognize a new ethnic state, Eritrea, even though twenty years earlier it had opposed the independence of Biafra. Ethnicity combined with violence and foreign intervention can bring about territorial changes.

Ethnic identities in democratic societies can give rise to a redistribution of state powers. It is not a matter of suppressing the state or of creating a new one, but of providing new modes of operation within the state. Scotland and Catalonia are examples of power adjustment negotiated between a state and a segment of its population. Instead of a challenge, we believe it more correct here to speak of a modulation of authority.

An ethnic identity in a democratic society that does not recognize the concept of ethnicity can result in cosmetic changes with a regionalist flavour, with no serious challenge being posed to the central government. For example, the recent creation of a Corsican regional assembly is more a symbolic response to a demand that is itself largely symbolic than a drastic change to the nature of the French state and the way in which it operates.

The combination of an unstable state, violence on both sides (by the ethnic groups and the central authority), and the inability of foreign players to promote a peaceful solution that respects minority rights can produce a challenge not just to a state but to the norms of the international political system. The international system does not supervise the change; it endures it. Stable states, moderate demands by ethnic groups, and the absence of foreign interference call into question the state's modes of operation more than they do the state itself.

Religion

Religion, perceived by many as a factor that can weaken the state, is a component of national identity, particularly for oppressed peoples. Jews, Poles, Irish, and Hindus provide historical evidence of this role. In modern states, especially those whose legitimacy is fragile, it can act as a catalyst for opposition, if not to the state then at least to the political regime. Examples are legion. In Poland, in the face of a self-professed Marxist regime with close ties to Moscow, the opposition in the early 1980s essentially took a religious form. The Catholic church provided *Solidarnoşç* within an ideological framework, a network of institutions, and international recognition.[98] The reservations of some Hong Kong inhabitants to rejoining China were expressed in a demonstration of 40,000 Buddhists in July 1997. In Iran it was a religious discourse and the use of the mosques that enabled the Ayatollah Khomeini to overthrow the Shah. In Algeria, the Islamic Salvation Front is using Islam in its attempt to gain power.

But we often tend to forget that states themselves use religion to impose their authority. Wahhabism is less a militant religious movement within Islam than a state religion justifying the monarchy of the House of Saud and hence Saudi Arabia. It is the state that has decided that a non-Muslim cannot be a Saudi citizen.[99]

Islam is an example of the ambiguity of religion. It can undermine regimes from the inside, through pressure and sometimes violence, and from the outside through the intervention of the Islamic Conference. Certain fundamentalist Islamic movements can attack the legitimacy of and even assassinate political leaders (Egypt and Anwar Sadat, Syria, and so on), but states in turn use Islam to discredit their opponents. Saddam Hussein, whose Baath party is officially pan-Arab but non-denominational, uses religious symbols in his televised addresses to the nation. Yasser Arafat's Palestinian Authority makes massive use of Muslim religious symbols. Islam can serve simultaneously as a front for incumbent regimes – to attack authority is to attack religion – and as motivation for those who want to overthrow those regimes – to obey the political authority is to disobey God.[100]

If Islam can be turned to the state's benefit in domestic politics, why not at the international level? We have seen above that one of the founders of the Islamic Conference is secular Turkey. Does this mean that Turkish foreign policy is influenced by the Islamic Conference? Of course not. At its December 1997 meeting in Teheran, delegates criticized Turkey for its increasingly close ties with Israel. Süleyman Demirel, the Turkish president, reacted by walking out of the gathering; then, in a demonstration of how little importance a member state can attach to the conference's declarations, he announced the holding of naval manoeuvres with Israel and the United States.

Even more contrary to the popular notion of Islam's irresistible power to impose a policy line on Muslim states is the case of the six ex-Soviet Islamic republics. Having used religion to defend their national identities against Moscow, these six should logically have succumbed to Islamism. In fact, they are maintaining a remarkable balance between Muslim Iran, secular Turkey, and Israel, which they consider a model of economic and social development.[101] Like states with Christian majorities, despite all their differences, the Muslim states can adapt to religious realities without submitting to them.

The Islamic 'threat' would therefore seem exaggerated. Other religions face similar situations. For instance, the expression 'Vatican Europe' suggests the emergence of a Europe dominated by the catholic Church. It may be true that the church has a historic claim to another kind of sovereignty, even using the threat of excommunication (a direct intervention in the state's affairs via a measure regarded as extreme by the faithful) until the twentieth century. Such was the case for the French legislators who voted for the separation of Church and State in 1905. It had abandoned such threats by the beginning of the Second World War, and since the Vatican Synod of 1985, it has recognized 'the legitimate autonomy of temporal realities,' including the state. Furthermore, decisions with political repercussions, such as the appointment of bishops, are usually made with the consent of the state.[102]

So is religion a factor of state destabilization or stability? Domestically, in democratic societies, religion may oblige states to take account of the religious dimension of social life, but in so doing it recognizes the legitimacy of the state's decision-making authority. In non-democratic societies, religion can serve as a rallying point for those who challenge either the state (militant religious minorities) or its policies (Algeria, Iran, Poland, and so on). On its own, it is difficult to see religion creating an opposition to the state. The religious dimension of fall of the Communist power in Poland and of the Shah in Iran must not overshadow the fact that religion was only one of many aspects of the rift between state and society. At the international level, religious pressure can create problems for states, but it cannot impose policy on them. In other words, states that are weak, discredited, or held together by fragile consensus can be vulnerable to attacks by religions; but states that are stable and enjoy a broad consensus view religions as neither threats to their legitimacy nor even political competitors. Rather, they are considered pressure groups that attempt to influence government policy. However, this observation leaves open the question not of the state's capacity for action or its autonomy, but of its significance. Can the state remain the forum for development of a truly unifying vision of society in the face of such forces of fragmentation?

Transformation of the State: The Role of Economic Globalization

If the state is far from declining, its functions are also far from static. They remodel themselves along with the transformation of the state's roles.

To benefit from the presence of TNCs, for examples, states must enter into competition with other states. At that point, it becomes irrelevant to compare states in terms of their strengths or weaknesses.

Rather the crucial variables are their capacity to adapt to external change and the speed with which they take account of the actions of other states. Their diplomacy becomes increasingly concerned with interstate economic competition and must take into account the role that TNCs play in it.

Linda Weiss analyses states' capacity to adapt instead of measuring their weakness.[103] She considers their ability to formulate and introduce new industrial policies a major advantage in international competition. Over long periods, states have demonstrated great capacity to adapt to change and to manage national and international relations, including those with the business community. This ability has led not to decline but to reinforcement of their 'infrastructural' capacities and generally to their abandonment of their 'despotic' powers.[104]

In the late 1970s, Peter Katzenstein was already looking at states' strategies in foreign economic policy in relation to the internationalization of industrial and financial capital.[105] A comparative analysis of six industrialized countries convinced him that states were using different strategies to deal with the consequences of interdependence. They derived such strategies from their own historical and structural characteristics, with the enhanced presence of the state in society as the end result. Today the state is going through a new phase of transformation: its adaptation to the context of globalization.

The state's role in fostering economic development remains very strong, if we are to judge from by Linda Weiss three observations.[106] First, states are not losing their capacity for action, they are adapting. The strongly industrialized countries continue to create policies designed to co-ordinate change. Second, the powerful states are more 'midwives' than victims of internationalization. Japan, Singapore, South Korea, and Taiwan are examples of states that have acted as catalysts for corporate internationalization strategies. For example, Japan has offered a wide range of incentives for overseas investment, for the conclusion of technological alliances between national and foreign firms, and for relocation of production networks. State intervention is becoming a condition of successful internationalization. The states that are strongest at the national level will thus be capable of adapting and of helping firms adjust more efficiently to the external environment. The government of Singapore, for instance, has pushed local firms to invest abroad, thereby promoting the (international) regionalization of its economy. Despite the financial troubles of 1997 in Asia, Weiss notes that 'the fundamentals of these coordinated economies remain strong –

especially compared with the uncoordinated market economies of Anglo–America.'[107] In East Asia, states retain substantial capacity in such crucial sectors as savings and investment, which are necessary to sustain growth.

Third, State power is being reconstituted around the consolidation of national and international ties, notably in trade and investment. States are relying less on their own resources, but are aiming for a dominant role in the creation of coalitions of states (for example, the European Union, the North American Free Trade Agreement, and asia–Pacific Economic Co-operation) and of national alliances between the state and corporations. Unlike Hirst and Thompson,[108] Weiss does not believe that the proliferation of national and international coalitions means that the state is losing its authority to more powerful players. On the contrary: the contemporary states that are constantly looking for power-sharing arrangements are seeking a space in which they can become the active centre and hence the catalyst.

As Thomson and Arnaud have pointed out,[109] the acceleration of transborder flows and the full development of the market are largely dependent on an institutional arrangement that is allowed and guaranteed by the state. According to Helleiner,[110] the fiscal deregulation that triggered the enormous expansion of the financial markets was the product of a desire to change systems, the terms and conditions of which were negotiated by the states. Evans goes further, seeing in the intensity of the state's involvement the key to successful integration in the world economy.[111] The best example is Singapore, which has been able to achieve an open market while maintaining the power of its bureaucracy. For MNCs, the absence of the state's involvement is not necessarily an advantage. Evans points out that it may be in their interest to have states guarantee some measure of protection for their profits, especially in the case of intangible assets such as intellectual property. One example is the support granted the pharmaceutical industry by the Canadian government, notably in 1993 by extending protection of patent drugs to twenty years instead of ten.

Reducing the state's capacity for intervention is not necessarily the best way to increase opportunities for individual profit and may heighten the risks of social explosion when it is the social safety net that comes under the knife. Thus the danger is not that states may become marginal institutions; rather, their intervention may come to be limited to promoting economic interests and guaranteeing 'social peace' – that is, to serving a more repressive function.

For Evans,[112] the only way to avoid this tendency is to develop a synergy between the state and civil society, for he regards NGOs as potential allies that are less ambivalent than the business elite about recognizing the value of public institutions. This idea enjoys far from unanimous support when the role of civil society tends to be approached more as a substitute for, rather than a complement to, public institutions. But, Evans feels, it would be unrealistic to think that a relationship between the strength of state institutions and the dynamism of NGOs can have no impact. He reminds us that the crisis of the state in Latin America has led to a degeneration of civil society, with community organization and civic commitment giving way to a kind of fragmentation. Under certain conditions, the fate of society might be intimately linked to the capacity of the public sector to support itself.

Zaki Laïdi[113] deplores the general ignorance about the evolution of the state's role, which cannot be judged solely on the basis of its functions. It is not because its functions are changing that the state itself is in the process of disappearing. In fact, each major transformation of the state has been preceded by a period portending its disappearance. For example, it was during the glory days of the liberal ideology, in the nineteenth century, that the idea of the social welfare state developed. But the state is no longer above the market. It has abandoned many of its functions as producer of goods and services. Sectors formerly protected by the state have become subject to competition, and the state's role in the allocation of the world's resources, particularly development assistance, has been eroded to the benefit of private investment. Finally, by becoming 'dependent on the markets to finance their deficits, the states came under the control of those markets.'[114]

The state, then, while facing economic pressures to submit to the laws of the marketplace, is also called on to maintain its role of social regulator. This social demand is concerned above all with the state's 'exercise of its *regalian* functions: police, justice and security.'[115] Its ability to control its borders is important in this context. Social demand from society also has to do with the ageing of the population, which in Europe has led to a significant increase in expenditures on social coverage. Laïdi also notes a rise in 'compensation demands' related to the effects of market liberalization (employment assistance, protection against unemployment) and the emergence of new demands stemming from globalization (technology development, research assistance). Finally, the state also faces 'demand for meaning': its ability to 'inform society about the issues of the future' remains indispensable.[116]

In other words, the state continues to be the focal point for defining a blueprint for society. In that sense it retains its full legitimacy.

Spulber too notes that, despite two decades of challenges, the state is still very much present, though in different forms.[117] Western states have certainly abandoned part of their functions to the private sector, but this privatization has occurred mainly in sectors already subject to market forces. Like Laïdi, he maintains that economic uncertainties and transformations in the world's production system are working together to facilitate greater state intervention. The state is thus continually redefining itself in various spheres of activity. This redefinition does not necessarily mean that the state will be any less strong politically.[118]

Similarly, Dombrowski argues that not only have states not abandoned their economic, political, and social responsibilities, they have also recognized the need to work in partnership with private stakeholders, or at least with a better understanding of market imperatives, in order to realize their public policy objectives.[119] The emerging role of states is to deal with market globalization on the basis of negotiation with the various public and private players concerned, so as to pursue the collective interest.

The state is reacting and adapting. The environmental sector offers a striking example of an effort to regain national sovereignty, and indeed to assert it more extensively, which has been expressed in four ways:[120] first, reaffirmation of the sacrosanct character of national sovereignty and of the right to develop natural resources on the sole basis of national priorities; second, the will of certain states to make this sovereignty effective by controlling the entirety of their territory; third, extension of the geographical bounds of state territorial sovereignty to the oceans and space; and fourth, broadening of the concept of sovereignty – for example, to genetic materials.

In some cases, environmental problems and trends in the international system can combine to reinforce the state's role. For instance, the negotiations between the European Union (EU) and Poland on the latter's entry into the EU have forced the Polish government to assume direct control over activities related to food production, environmental contamination, and pollution. Poland's desire for membership is causing its government to strengthen its environmental laws and policies and hence the weight of the state within society.

We should approach the discourse on the inevitable decline of the state with a good deal of caution. Many analyses show that the state continues to hold a central place, especially in economic matters. However, its role has been transformed. New imperatives are impelling it into the role of regulator of the economic environment and partner of the private sector, sometimes to the detriment of its social functions, but above all at the expense of its function as a direct producer of goods and services. When we focus on measuring the state's capacity for action, as opposed to its size, we have to acknowledge that, far from disappearing, it is demonstrating immense capacity to adapt to the new realities, and even to direct them. Furthermore, it retains its ability to withstand pressure from the international system and civil society by imposing its own definition of the national interest, even if that definition might differ from the one preferred by specific groups or external players. It is maintaining its legitimacy to the extent that it is also capable of bringing citizens, groups, and other international players to accept its right to make these choices. We can see that support for the neoliberal ideology that was initially meant to accentuate the decline of the state is now emerging as a means for the state to regain autonomy and legitimacy. By reorienting itself to become more of a regulator than a producer, the state has given itself the flexibility that allows it to consolidate its authority in its chosen sectors.

Analytical and Methodological Problems

Even a very partial review of the literature on the state's place and role in changing national and international systems raises a number of methodological concerns that should affect any discussion of the political implications of these studies. Indeed these concerns limit our capacity to generalize from their conclusions. The quandaries involve ambiguities in concepts, problems of measurement, and uncertainty of inference.

Concepts

This chapter deals mostly with independent variables – the phenomena or players that could affect certain attributes of the state. The diversity of variables is illustrative of the amount of imprecision in this field of study. Each author chooses the variable that he or she prefers and analyses it alone, without developing any strategy for comparing variables (globalization, communication, identities, new players, and so on).

The choice of the independent variable remains arbitrary, but the definition of the independent and dependent variables varies considerably. The political vocabulary used reflects diverse realities and often has different meanings in different languages. For example, the concepts of decentralization and deconcentration, which in French are clearly differentiated in political science, are more interchangeable in English. Even a seemingly precise concept may be perceived and interpreted differently under the influence of experience. That which is slightly decentralized in Canada is considered extremely so in France; the notion of indigenous rights is incomprehensible in France, with its Jacobin tradition; the idea of education being the responsibility of the provinces and not the central government seems an aberration to certain French people; the concept of multiculturalism – a 'fundamental characteristic of the Canadian identity,'[121] – has a completely different meaning in the United States.

Some authors speak of the reduction of the state, others of its disappearance, and still others of its transformation. The content of these concepts is highly uncertain. In theory, the matter would seem perfectly clear: if one argues that the state is disappearing, it often means that a certain form of power and political and social organization is being eliminated. Of course, things are not that simple. Depending on the case, one may mean variously that the democratic state is disappearing, but there are other types of state; that the *Canadian* state is disappearing; or that the Canadian *state* is disappearing, or the Canadian state *as it exists today,* or the central federal state. One may postulate this disappearance and say that the concept of 'state' is devoid of meaning, for no such thing exists any longer as a concrete entity.

This word 'state' is in fact used in reference to three different aspects: its legitimacy and purposes (is a state that no longer serves its purposes still legitimate?); its roles and functions (a change of role does not imply a lessening of its legitimacy); or its structures (political organization, such as the division of powers – different levels of government, public, parapublic, or 'peripublic' service).

For the state's legitimacy to be called into doubt, there must be a competing source of legitimacy that might replace it. Revolutionary legitimacy, fashionable in certain circles in the 1960s and 1970s, has passed. Religions or ideologies have succeeded at most in questioning the legitimacy of certain regimes (the Shah's Iran), not that of the state (as a mode of social organization). Liberal hardliners are challenging not the legitimacy of the state but its functions and structures that encroach on the market.

Might the questioning of the state's legitimacy stem from a process initiated by the state itself? One may suppose that a state that abdicates its responsibilities, makes no use of its rights to enforce security, or leaves decision-making authority to others who are not supervised would become an empty shell that no longer meets the minimum expectations of society; only then would it see its legitimacy challenged. This would constitute a suicide of the state, with no legitimate alternative ready to take over.

The roles and functions of the state follow different paradigms. All authors agree that the notions of justice, equity, and well-being, both at the domestic and international levels, make up the core of the state's responsibilities. Management of the economy is also accepted by almost all specialists, whether that management is light-handed (liberal style) or more coercive (Keynesian style). What is being questioned is the state's role as the dominant economic player, engaged in the production and sale of goods and services and providing a social safety net for the public. 'The electorates and a number of key groups, some with right-wing ties, continue to think that intervention is a duty of the state.'[122]

Closely related to its roles and functions is the distribution of power within the state. Authors see the state's limits as varying considerably. Some focus almost exclusively on the central state: the ministers and head of the executive (prime minister or president) and the central administrations (government secretariat, treasury board, departments). Others, whose numbers are growing, talk of 'governance' – a combination of political and administrative institutions and their interrelations.

The structural issue leads to the following question: in Canada, does 'state' refer solely to the 'federal state,' with a single centre, or to the 'federated state,' with its eleven centres of power? In the first case, any transfer of power from the centre to the periphery (decentralization) calls the state into question by reducing its role. In the second case, the state's authority changes location, resulting in a modification of structures but not of the roles and functions of the state. Whether the training of the workforce is managed by Ottawa or Quebec is a matter of structure, of distribution of power; it does not affect the role of the state. The same applies for the four Ottawa–Quebec agreements on immigration. The creation of Nunavut makes changes to structures and domestic borders, but that a public decision is made in Ottawa, Yellowknife, or Iqaluit, however intriguing the constitutional issue, poses no challenge to either the legitimacy or the functions of the state. Similarly, the regions of France – a new intermediary level between the central state and the *départements*, which enjoy relative autonomy – represent a radical change to traditions and habits but not to the 'public' role in society. A shift of decision-making authority within a state does not necessarily call the state itself into question.

If the very concept of the state presents problems, then what of the recent phenomenon of 'globalization'? This fashionable term has two connotations: it can express a direction or a demand, or it can refer to a situation over which we have no choice. While globalization is now a recognized phenomenon, defining it remains difficult. That globalization is a *fact* does not make the *concept* any clearer. What do we mean, exactly, by it? Or is it simply used to refer to a dominant ideological discourse?

The concept has yet to receive an authoritative definition. Certain elements can be found in all definitions, but the correlations between these elements tend to vary considerably. Globalization is an empirical notion that remains insufficiently formalized to be authoritative. It can just as easily lead to analyses designed to assert its scientific legitimacy or to serve as an ideological excuse to justify or criticize the disengagement of the state. Riccardo Petrella, for example, sees it as nothing more than a justificatory discourse,[123] used as a justifying ideology, and not an objective concept: a choice, not an inevitability.

It would seem more relevant to consider the *image* that decision makers have of globalization and of the constraints that it might impose on the state's action. The nature and effects of globalization exist largely in the minds of the elites; there is nothing inevitable about its dimensions and its consequences. What are the factors that have facilitated the adoption of such a mental construct? Are the resulting representations homogeneous? What are the elements that reinforce these images or psychological convictions? How do we explain the transition from an observation (globalization) to action (the responses to globalization)?

Measurement

More pernicious still is the influence of the existing data on the meaning of concepts. One 'proof' of the reduction of the state's role might be the decrease in the number of its public servants and its budget; another, privatization of public companies. But services provided to the population, whether directly by the state or indirectly by other players (as long as they conform to the standards set by the state), are also a component of state governance. Similarly, privatization of public airlines does not prevent states from regulating air transport or negotiating landing rights with other states. Insofar as certain public oil companies represent the interests of the domestic oil lobby more than anything else (Compagnie française des pétroles, Elf-Aquitaine, and Total in France, British Petroleum in the United Kingdom; and so on), one may wonder how their privatization would pose a challenge to the state. Is it better to have a private corporation or a 'state within the state,'? ask Cassese and Wright.[124]

Privatization not accompanied by deregulation in a system where the state continues to define the terms and conditions for implementing the general interest, or where the state still has a strong influence on those terms and conditions, has no effect on the state's legitimacy or capacities, much less on its autonomy, but only on its structures. The volume of regulation (and so, conversely, of deregulation), which is widely used in the literature, is not a good indicator of the state's authority, since that regulation may be the product of its weakness and a futile reaction to the importance of other players, or it may not be enforced (as in many developing countries). It is also useful, in a comparative context, to select *equivalent* indicators rather than seeking identical indicators, since the same term may denote phenomena, behaviour, and meanings that differ widely from one country to the next.[125]

Finally, the arguments of many scholars – Spulber and Strange being exceptions[126] – are empirically weak. They often rely on impressions; the perceptions of citizens and decision makers may differ from the interpretations presented; and the analysts assert rather than demonstrate causal relations.

Problems of Inference

An initial problem relates to the temporal parameters of analyses of the state's changing activities, which often invite the reader to transform a specific situation into a trend. Before concluding that the state has disappeared or weakened, we must adopt a long-term perspective that takes account of its capacity to adapt. Similar problems arose in the 1970s with the emerging theories of interdependence, the forerunner of globalization. Broader and better-researched analyses have since demonstrated that, far from leading to loss of state control, interdependence has often reinforced such control.

A second problem, related to the previous one but more fundamental, is the omnipresent circular reasoning displayed in the tendency to find that the state has disappeared or weakened because of its abandonment of its traditional postwar roles or because it no longer fills certain functions valued by a given author. This presupposition colours selection and interpretation of data. Perhaps the state can change roles (or functions) without losing its authority or its legitimacy.

Confronted with the proliferation and diversity of dependent variables, with the imprecision of concepts, and with the absence of a yardstick, we have to get back to what is important: the attributes of the state and the degree of uncertainty that it faces. These attributes or concerns – legitimacy, autonomy, and capacities for action – are not original, but they help us distinguish between the fundamental and the superficial. This is not the first time that the state has had to adapt to new circumstances. It is the speed and scope of change, as well as its roots in civil society and in the international system, that create the impression that the state is on the defensive. This impression of its being under siege also stems from the strategies that it has adopted in its efforts to adapt to these new conditions.

Conclusion: Implications and Avenues for Research

There are a number of generally accepted ideas that influence the ways in which both practitioners and analysts perceive the state, for it is the target of widespread questioning, proceeding from society and from the international system, the end result of which could be its disappearance. This questioning might be fundamental, targeting the legitimacy of the state, or partial, targeting its degree of autonomy, its flexibility, its means of action, and the degree of uncertainty that it faces.

In reality, states retain genuine latitude and definite decision-making power. Far from ushering in the death of the state, the proliferation of new players could in fact reinforce its position. The technical agreements with supranational and infranational institutions do not necessarily weaken the state. At times they permit it to continue making general public choices, leaving their concrete applications to other levels of government. On the international stage, the state is an essential link between internal and external players.

Environmental issues bear witness to a proliferation of power centres and would seem to cast doubt on the power of the state. Environmental issues, especially when associated with claims by indigenous peoples, reveal this potential marginalization of the state or the strait-jacket in which it may find itself. In Canada, the role of the provinces, indigenous peoples' use of international institutions (treaties, organizations, systems), and the foreign support that they are receiving should logically diminish the state's capacity for action. However, the state could legitimately claim and assume distinct responsibilities there. Only it has general knowledge of the problems and interests of all the parties involved and is capable of identifying, negotiating and enforcing a solution acceptable to all components in society. In other words, the distribution of powers increases its ability to play the role of arbiter and unavoidable intermediary between 'stakeholders' both within and outside the state.

Another sector receiving particular attention is the rise of religious movements. Here again, their entry into politics is often interpreted as a new constraint (for examples, the roles of the religious parties in Israel and of the Islamic movements in the Arab states of the Near East). It would also affect other states such as Canada, which might see their diplomatic flexibility reduced and at times even be confronted with assertions of a right of cultural interference (organization of religion, wearing of the chador, and so on), thereby complicating domestic policies. But does the emergence of these movements mean that the state has lost its margin of manoeuvre here as well?

In the case of Canada, can the state be said to be under threat of disappearance, can its legitimacy be said to be in question? The supporters of globalization and of ethnic, linguistic, or regional identity chant in unison, whether in joy or in sorrow, the approaching end of the Canadian state. The provinces like to distinguish between 'national' politics, in which they play a major role, and 'federal' politics, in which Ottawa is clearly in charge. However, the prediction of the death of the Canadian state seems premature.

The only threat to the state, to its legitimacy and operation, would stem from the secession of Quebec. An independent Quebec would inevitably mean loss of Canadian sovereignty over about a quarter of its land mass and population. Would a Canada that has lost its legitimacy in Quebec remain legitimate for other Canadians – would it still be credible? With the exception of this extreme case, the complex and often contradictory demands from segments of society (Aboriginal peoples,

Quebec, the west) have less to do with the state's legitimacy than with its operation – the way in which power is distributed within the system. Every claimant group is torn in two directions. The Aboriginal peoples want not just the state's protection and the maintenance of transfer payments, but extensive autonomy that would allow them to maintain their traditions and break free from the fundamental laws of the country. Québécois are undecided between different forms of relations with Canada and, to use the expression of comedian Yvon Deschamps, would not be averse to seeing 'an independent Quebec in a united Canada.' Western Canadian regionalists complain of being excluded from power, yet many vote for the opposition. As long as there are calls for a 'new order' within the system – a new division of powers that is, for all intents and purposes, a decentralization – these may pose a challenge to Ottawa's autonomy relative to the other political players, and to its means of action and control, but not to its legitimacy.

The creation of Nunavut and Bill C-49 grant very broad powers of land management to band councils. Is this legislation the product of irresistible pressure from society – in this case, Aboriginal peoples – or of the federal state's desire to divest itself of a portfolio that is difficult to manage both politically and administratively? The phasing out of the Department of Indian Affairs and its progressive replacement by a territory (a future eleventh province) and statutes to increase the power of the bands are the result not of obligations, but of a choice made by the state. Complaints by Aboriginal women of the possible negative effects of Bill C-49 on their rights, particularly in divorce cases, show that the state could have passed legislation without granting full powers to the band councils. This choice is consistent with a corporatist conception whereby Canadian political leaders and Aboriginal peoples enter into agreements that supersede individual rights.

Similarly, the agreement of April 1997 between Ottawa and Quebec transferring responsibility for workforce training from the federal to the provincial level affects not the legitimacy of the federal state but the terms and conditions of state interventions between two levels of government. The preparatory discussions, which went on for more than thirty years, have resulted in a new division of responsibilities – one that is now being demanded by other provinces such as British Columbia. This has no repercussions for the state's legitimacy, or its sovereignty, or the possible vision of its role: the issue is mainly the control of a source of patronage. These are adjustments, not challenges.[127]

Might it be the external challenges that truly call into question, if not the legitimacy of the Canadian state, at least its sovereignty? Nearly 80 per cent of the trade between the United States and Canada is comprised of the internal trade of American multinationals.[128] To limit this U.S. economic dominance, Canada created the Foreign Investment Review Agency (FIRA) to differentiate between welcome and unwelcome foreign investment – a policy that has yielded only limited results. The North American Free Trade Agreement, in contrast, would seem to constitute the revenge of the transnationals – a victory for economic regionalization. But this is an agreement negotiated between states: it is states that have laid down the new trade rules, which certainly curb their theoretical capacity for action but also reduce the uncertainty that they face; it is the two federal states (Washington and Ottawa) that negotiated, not the U.S. states or the Canadian provinces. In short, the role of the states has not been reduced for the benefit of the economy: the economic aspect has been taken into account in formulating the national interest.

Canada's participation, as a member of NATO, in the 1999 war against Serbia on behalf of the Kosovars would appear a perfect example of an externally imposed decision. This decision was made without a vote in Parliament and without analysis of its consequences. 'We are part of a team and we have to respect its decisions,' said Prime Minister Jean Chrétien. Was this decision the reflection of intense pressure on Canada from NATO and the United States, a deliberate choice to let others decide Canada's national interests in this area, or an internal political strategy designed to deflect criticism in the event of excessive loss of life? Is the Canadian state caught between pressures from society and from the international system, with no choice but to give in, or does this attitude simply reflect certain perceptions filtered through an ideology critical of the state that happens to mesh with a political design by Canada's leaders? The answer is far from clear. The pressures may be real, but they can also serve as a smokescreen, or justify a redistribution of power.

The Canadian federal budget offers a good example of how 'globalization' can serve as a political front. Is the balancing of public finances, debt reduction, and their corollaries (downsizing of the public service, stricter rules for employment insurance, reduction of fiscal health transfers, and so on) *imposed* by globalization, or would they inevitably have become, sooner or later, the policy of the Canadian government, regardless of the party in power? Have states set their finances in order only in the last few years? It seems to us more realistic to see the emphasis on globalization, and in the Canadian case on the ratings assigned to Canada by foreign rating firms, as a means of diverting public discontent. External forces about which nothing can be done are blamed, rather than the politicians responsible. The external pressures are indeed there, but the strategies for responding to them are a matter of political choice.

This argument that the international system should define Canadian political choices can be found in other areas as well. As a signatory to the international convention of 1951 and the protocol of 1967 on refugees, the Canadian state is obliged to accept refugees. For several years now, it has been interpreting article 34 of the convention on the definition of refugees ('being persecuted for reasons of race, religion, nationality, membership of a particular social group or political opinion') as also covering women who are victims of *de jure* or *de facto* discrimination – an approach that considerably expands the concept of refugee. This exclusively Canadian interpretation is the result not of international pressures but of domestic pressures, where every political problem is seen through the prism of a male and female approach. The fact of Canada's deciding on a policy and claiming that it follows from its international obligations is a good example of a smokescreen to mask the true origin of decisions.

Canada, like other states, exists in a context that is more complex than before, but this does not mean that it has lost its capacity for action. The idea that the state's role must be first and foremost economic, then social, and finally political is not something that has been imposed: it has been *adopted* by the state. As early as 1975, the Canada Public Service Commission hired masters of business administration rather than masters of public administration and preferred economists to political scientists. In short, it was preparing the ground for a challenge to the state *from within*. If management of the state is to follow the model of private management, if the business approach is valued more than the public interest, should we be surprised that public servants have trouble justifying their role and that of the state? Exposed to criticism from politicians wishing to downsize the public service, and often trained to respect the market as a source of authority, these public servants would be challenged. But was it inevitable? Is it not advisable, now that the public service is starting to recruit again, to provide for some presence of the 'soft' social sciences (political science, sociology) and not exclusively the 'hard' ones (economics, finance)? In short, is it not necessary to analyse the image of the public service and the type of training required of public servants?

Certain new constraints that would seem to pose fundamental challenges to the state may in fact be largely subjective or may even reflect an attempt by the state to assert or regain its decision-making autonomy, its legitimacy, and its capacity for action. This particular dimension – namely, the image that senior officials and politicians have of the nature of the constraints facing Canada and the flexibility that is available to them – seems to us a crucial matter for investigation.[129]

If we look at the fundamental attributes of the state, we can see that the state's desire to reduce external uncertainties may have reduced its autonomy, that its legitimacy is no longer exclusive, and that its capacity for action has increased in some areas and decreased in others. But the state is not disappearing; it is transforming itself.

In this context, it is possible to identify five avenues for research concerned with factors that directly affect the role of the state in Canada:

- the role of the Canadian public administration as a source of stability and model of largely consensual management, in a political context where there are tensions between groups (Aboriginal peoples, Quebec, the west) and between parties (essential in a democracy)
- redefinitions of the role of public servants: upgrading of their education, retraining, conception of the public good
- opinions: belief systems of senior officials regarding the role of the state relative to globalization and society and their influence on the nature and choice of the state's options
- the state and participation: relations between the state and organized groups (environmental, multicultural, employers, and so on) and their effect on the state's legitimacy and effectiveness.
- the adaptation strategies of states: factors that influence the choice of a particular strategy and the consequences of these choices for the autonomy of the state and its ability to pursue its fundamental objectives[130]

The politics of the future will centre on the achievement of these sometimes contradictory objectives. These attempts at adaptation take place sometimes alone, but usually collectively. They may aim to defend a traditional sphere of action or to assert new ones. How are constraints to be transformed into opportunities? Is it not the state's role to establish an architecture of authority that is flexible and changing, that can address the shortcomings of governance? To what extent will this role be the product of a choice and of a clear definition of the interests of the state and of the common good? If neither the state nor the other players can now claim a legitimate monopoly on the definition and pursuit of the common good, on what bases will it be built?

NOTES

1 The authors wish to thank doctoral political science students Céline Métivier, Sébastien Müssi, and Pierre Troin for their contributions to an earlier version of this text.
2 Joyce Hoebing et al., eds; *NAFTA and Sovereignty: Tradeoffs for Canada, Mexico, and the United States* (Washington, DC: Center for Strategic and International Studies, 1997).
3 François Chesnais, *La mondialisation du capital* (Paris: Syros, 1997); Susan Strange, *The Retreat of the State: The Diffusion of Power in the World Economy* (New York: Cambridge University Press, 1997).
4 Paul Mathias, *La cité internet* (Paris: Presses de Sciences Po, 1997).
5 Philippe Le Prestre, *Ecopolitique internationale* (Montreal: Guérin, 1997).
6 Paul Ariès, *Les fils de McDo: La McDonaldisation du monde* (Paris: L'Harmattan, 1997).
7 Ronnie D. Lipschutz, *Global Civil Society and Global Environmental Governance* (Albany: SUNY, 1996).
8 Karen Barkey and Mark von Hagen, eds., *After Empire: Multi-Ethnic Societies and Nation-Building* (Boulder, Col.: Westview, 1997).
9 John P. Entelis, ed., *Islam, Democracy, and the State in North Africa* (Bloomington: Indiana University Press, 1997).
10 Jean-Luc Bodiguel and Luc Rouban, *Le fonctionnaire détrôné, l'État au risque de la modernisation* (Paris: Presses de Sciences Po, 1991).
11 James N. Rosenau, *Along the Domestic–Foreign Frontier: Exploring Governance in a Turbulent World* (Cambridge: Cambridge University Press, 1997).
12 Peter Dombrowski, 'Haute Finance and High Theory: Recent Scholarship on Global Financial Relations,' *Mershon International Studies Review* 42 (1998): 1–28.
13 Chesnais, *La mondialisation du capital*.
14 Susan Strange, 'States, Firms and Diplomacy,' *International Affairs* 68 (1992): 1–15.
15 Thomas G. Weiss and Girat Chopra, 'Sovereignty Is No Longer Sacrosanct: Codifying Humanitarian Intervention,' *Ethics and International Affairs* 6 (1992): 95–118.

16 Alain Finkelkraut, *La défaite de la pensée* (Paris: Gallimard, 1987).
17 Jack Donnelly, 'Human Rights: A New Standard of Civilization?' *International Affairs* 74 (1998): 1–23.
18 Jeffrey Checkel, 'International Norms and Domestic Politics,' *International Relations* 3 (1997): 473–96.
19 Strange, 'States, Firms and Diplomacy.'
20 Richard Falk, *This Endangered Planet* (New York: Random House, 1971).
21 William Ophuls, *Ecology and the Politics of Scarcity* (San Francisco: W. Freeman, 1977).
22 Julien Bauer, *Politique et religion* (Paris: PUF, Que sais-je?, 1999), 46.
23 Ibid., 54.
24 Dominique Schnapper, *La relation à l'autre. Au coeur de la pensée sociologique* (Paris : Gallimard, 1998), 248 (translation).
25 Jean-François Bayart, *L'illusion identitaire* (Paris: Fayard, 1996).
26 A. Dieckhoff, *L'invention d'une nation: Israël et la modernité politique* (Paris: Gallimard, 1993), 126 (translation).
27 The case of Algeria also seems to have many things to teach us. Following independence, the Algerian state very quickly began an Arabization campaign (referred to as pan-Arabism) that has caused many problems for the Berber community, which has long been French-speaking. A current demand of the Muslim fundamentalists that has been acted on by the Algerian state – the imposition of Arabic to the detriment of French – parallels a struggle between militant Islam and the moderate Islam of the Berbers. For the Algerian state, Arabic is a means of weakening the Berbers' position within the society. In this case language becomes one of the instruments for combating an ethnic minority.
28 Bauer, *Politique et religion*, 40–5.
29 Don Baker, 'World Religion and National States: Competing Claims in East Asia,' in Rudolf Hoeber and James Piscatori, eds., *Transnational Religion and Fading States* (Westview Press, 1997).
30 Bauer, *Politique et religion*, 93–9.
31 Marx Jurgensmeyer, *The New Cold War? Religious Nationalism Confronts the Secular State* (Berkeley: University of California Press, 1993).
32 Bauer, *Politique et religion*, 88–9.
33 Ronald S. Thiemann, *Religion in Public Life: A Dilemma for Democracy* (Washington, DC: Georgetown University Press, 1996).
34 John Newhouse, *Europe Adrift* (New York: Pantheon Books, 1997), 24.
35 Kenichi Ohmae, *The End of the Nation State: The Rise of Regional Economies* (New York: Free Press, 1995).
36 Ibid., 63.
37 Ohmae, *The End of the Nation State.*

38 Ibid.
39 Ibid., 96.
40 Ibid., 81.
41 Ibid., 61.
42 Newhouse, *Europe Adrift*, 63.
43 Ibid., 34.
44 Ibid., 71.
45 Apter, *Pour l'État, contre l'État*, p. 255.
46 According to Spulber, 'the political and ideological upheaval brought about by Margaret Thatcher in Britain and by Ronald Reagan in the United States in the late 1970s and early 1980s aimed at liquidating the so-called post-war settlement in the first country and the Roosevelt era consensus in the second ... The new leaders intended to redefine the role of the state, reduce its functions, and bring to an end what they perceived as the era of overcentralized, bureaucratic, and interventionist governments.' Nicolas Spulber, *Redefining the State: Privatization and Welfare Reform in Industrial and Transitional Economies* (Cambridge: Cambridge University Press, 1997), 135.
47 Joel Krieger, *Reagan, Thatcher and the Politics of Economic Adjustment* (New York: Oxford University Press, 1986), and Joel D. Wolfe, 'Reorganizing Interest Representation: A Political Analysis of Privatization in Britain,' in Joel Wolfe and R. Foglesong, eds., *The Politics of Economic Adjustment* (New York: Oxford University Press, 1996).
48 Michel Chossudovsky, 'La Souveraineté des créanciers,' in Sylvie Paquerot ed., *L'État aux orties? Mondialisation de l'économie et rôle de l'État*. (Montreal: Écosociété, 1996), 63 (translation).
49 Christian Saint-Étienne, 'De l'État bureaucratique à l'État incitateur et coordonateur,' in René Lenoir and Jacques Lesourne, eds., *Où va l'État? La souveraineté économique et politique en question*, eds., (Paris: Le Monde, 1992), 321.
50 Harvey B. Feigenbaum and Jeffrey R. Henig, 'Privatization and Political Theory,' *Journal of International Affairs* 50, no. 2 (1997): 338–55; Philip Morgan, ed., *Privatization and the Welfare State: Implications for Consumers and the Workforce* (Adershot: Dartmouth, 1995).
51 Feigenbaum and J. Henig, 'Privatization and Political Theory.'
52 OECD, *Policies for Industrial Development and Competitiveness* (Paris: OECD, 1998).
53 However, the structural adjustment programs imposed by the IMF and the World Bank are an example more of systemic than of tactical privatization.
54 Richard Falk, paper delivered at the annual meeting of the International Studies Association (Washington, DC, February 1999).

55 Zaki Laïdi, *Malaise dans la mondialisation* (Paris: Textuel, 1997).
56 Jérome Vignon, 'La cohésion économique et sociale,' in Zaki Laïdi, ed., *Géopolitique du sens* (Paris: Desclée de Brouwer, 1998), 86 (translation).
57 Laïdi, *Malaise dans la mondialisation.*
58 Stephen D. Krasner, *Defending the National Interest: Raw Materials Investments and U.S. Foreign Policy* (Princeton, NJ: Princeton University Press, 1978).
59 Ian D. Clark, Secretary of the Treasury Board of Canada, 21 November 1991.
60 Le Prestre, *Écopolitique internationale.*
61 For the 1949 data, see Spiro 1995: 51; for 1995, ECOSOC E/1995/INF/5 (20 September 1995).
62 For example, Nauru systematically hands over its seat at meetings of the London Dumping Convention to two American militants, one of them a professor at a California university specializing in the marine environment. Of course such 'capture' occurs in other NGOs, particularly those representing the interests of specific industries. For instance, the American delegation at meetings of the International Telecommunication Union (ITU) has been rechristened the ' Motorola delegation.'
63 Lipschutz, *Global Civil Society and Global Environmental Governance* and Paul Wapner, 'Governance in Global Civil Society,' in Oran Young, ed., *Global Governance: Drawing Insights from the Environmental Experience* (Cambridge, Mass.: MIT Press, 1997).
64 Strange, 'States, Firms and Diplomacy.'
65 *Globe and Mail* (27 July 1996), A1.
66 Nazli Choucri, ed., *Global Accord: Environmental Challenges and International Responses* (Cambridge, Mass.: MIT Press, 1993).
67 Strange, 'States, Firms and Diplomacy.'
68 Strange, *The Retreat of the State.*
69 Ibid., xii.
70 Idem, 'Who Runs World Shipping?' *International Affairs* (1976).
71 Commission on Global Governance, 1995, 66.
72 Jack Donnelly, 'Human Rights.'
73 As we know, other states or societies see this as a major contradiction and source of internal instability.
74 Laïdi, *Géopolitique du sens.*
75 Philippe Le Prestre, 'Strategies of Adaptation to Environmental Insecurities,' in Steve Lonergan, ed., *Environmental Change, Adaptation, and Security* (Dordrecht: Kluwer Academic Publishers, 1999), 57–74.
76 Ibid.

77 Peter Evans, 'The Eclipse of the State? Reflections on Stateness in an Era of Globalization,' *World Politics*, 50 (October 1997): 62–87.
78 Andrew Walter, 'Do They Really Rule the World ?' in *New Political Economy* 3, no. 2 (July 1998): 288–92.
79 Ibid., and Strange, 'States, Firms and Diplomacy.'
80 The behaviour of the oil companies had already provided a striking example of this in the 1960s and 1970s.
81 Dombrowski, 'Haute Finance and High Theory.'
82 Karl Polanyi, *The Great Transformation* (Boston: Beacon, 1944).
83 Ian Clark, *Globalization and Fragmentation* (Oxford: Oxford University Press, 1997).
84 See also Hidemi Suganami, 'Overview: A Note on Some Recent Writings on International Relations and Organizations,' *International Affairs* 74, no. 4 (October 1998): 903–10.
85 Steven K. Vogel, *Freer Markets, More Rules: Regulatory Reform in Advanced Industrial Countries* (Ithaca, NY: Cornell University Press, 1996).
86 Dani Rodrik, 'Why Do More Open Economies Have Bigger Governments?' *Journal of Political Economy*, 106, no. 5 (1998): 997–1032.
87 Ibid.
88 Ibid.
89 Pierre de Senarclens, *Mondialisation, souveraineté et théories des relations internationales* (Paris: Armand Colin, 1998) (translation).
90 Le Prestre, *Écopolitique internationale.*
91 Ibid.
92 For example, in 1991 the National Resources Defense Council (NRDC) claimed, without the permission of the population concerned, to represent the interests of the little equatorial tribe of the Huaorani during negotiations with the U.S. oil company Conoco regarding prospecting rights on their territory, even though the tribe was represented by its own organization. See Joe Kane, 'Letter from the Amazon: With Spears from All Sides,' *New Yorker* (27 September 1993): 54–79.
93 Tariq Banuri, 'The Landscape of Diplomatic Conflict,' in Wolfgang Sachs, ed., *Global Ecology: A New Arena of Political Conflict* (London: Zed Books, 1993): 49–67.
94 Martin Sampson, 'The Global Environmental Facility / Black Sea Environmental Program: Part Way Into Year 2,' paper presented at the Congress of the International Studies Association San Diego, April 1996.
95 Kal Raustiala, 'States, NGOs and International Environmental Institutions,' *International Studies Quarterly* 41 (1997): 719–40.
96 Ohmae, *The End of the Nation State.*

97 Newhouse, *Europe Adrift*.
98 Ralph Della Cara, 'Religious Resource Networks: Roman Catholic Philanthropy in Central and East Europe,' in Rudolf Hoeber and James Piscatori, eds., *Transnational Religion and Fadind States*, (Westview Press, 1997).
99 Joseph Nevo, 'Religion and National Identity in Saudi Arabia,' *Middle Eastern Studies* 34, no. 3 (1998): 34–53.
100 Bauer, *Politique et religion*, 107.
101 Ibid., 103.
102 Ibid., 98.
103 Linda Weiss, *The Myth of the Powerless State* (Ithaca, NY: Cornell University Press, 1998).
104 Ibid.
105 Peter J. Katzenstein, ed., *Between Power and Plenty: Foreign Economic Policies of Advanced Industrial States* (Madison: University of Wisconsin Press, 1978).
106 Weiss, *The Myth of the Powerless State*.
107 Ibid., 218.
108 Paul Hirst and Grahame Thompson, *Globalization in Question* (Cambridge: Cambridge University Press, 1996).
109 Janice E. Thomson, 'State Sovereignty in International Relations: Bridging the Gap between Theory and Empirical Search,' *International Studies Quarterly* 39 (1995): 213–19; André-Jean Arnaud, 'De la régulation par le droit à l'heure de la globalisation. Quelques observations critiques,' *Droit et société* 11 (1997).
110 Eric Helleiner, *States and the Re-emergence of Global Finance: From Bretton Woods to the 1990s* (Ithaca, NY: Cornell University Press, 1994).
111 Evans, 'The Eclipse of the State?'
112 Ibid.
113 Laïdi, *Géopolitique du sens*.
114 Ibid., 95 (translation).
115 Ibid., 96 (translation).
116 Ibid., 100 (translation).
117 Spulber, *Redefining the State*.
118 Jean Coussy, for example, argues that the minimal state can also be a strong state. See Jean Coussy, 'Les ruses de l'État minimum,' in Jean-François Bayart ed., *La réinvention du capitalisme* (Paris: Karthala, 1994), 216, and Bonnie Campbell, 'Reconceptualisation de l'État au Sud – participation démocratique ou managéralisme populiste,' 170.
119 Dombroski, 'Haute Finance and High Theory.'
120 Le Prestre, *Écopolitique internationale*.

121 Department of Multiculturalism and Citizenship Act, 1990, s. 3.6.

122 Sabimo Cassese and Vincent Wright, *La recomposition de l'État en Europe* (Paris: La Découverte, 1996), 12 (translation).

123 Ricardo Petrella, *Écueils de la mondalisation. Urgence d'un nouveau contrat social* (Montreal: Fides, 1997), 7.

124 Cassese and Wright, *La recomposition de l'État en Europe*.

125 J.W. Van Deth, 'Comparative Politics and the Decline of the Nation-State in Western Europe,' *European Journal of Political Research* 27 (1995).

126 Spulber, *Redefining the State*; Strange, 'States, Firms and Diplomacy.'

127 Julien Bauer, *Le système politique canadien* (Paris: PUF, Que sais-je?, 1998), 118–19.

128 Ibid., 27.

129 Élie Cohen, *La tentation héxagonale. La souveraineté à l'heure de la mondialisation* (Paris: Fayard, 1996), 410–11.

130 Le Prestre, 'Strategies of Adaptation to Environmental Insecurities.'

3. Policy Making in a Multicentric World: The Impact of Globalization, Privatization, and Decentralization on Democratic Governance

Ronald D. Crelinsten

Challenges to Policy Research: Complexity and the Collapse of Distinctions

At the policy research conference 'Creating Linkages,' held in Ottawa in October 1998, the clerk of the Privy Council and secretary to the cabinet, Jocelyn Bourgon, spoke of the challenges that the public service's policy research community currently faces. Issues have become more complex in that they are both more global, requiring co-ordinated and simultaneous action on international, national, and local levels, and more horizontal, requiring what she called a 'whole of government approach.'[1] The policy process has also become more complicated, necessitating 'an integrated approach among governments at all levels,' as well as 'a longer lead time, a multidisciplinary approach, teamwork among departments and among governments, and strong alliances with other partners in society.' These partners include not only the broader policy community and a complex network of international forums, but also individual citizens who increasingly expect to be involved in the policy process.[2]

This chapter examines the impact of globalization, decentralization, and privatization on the ability of states to conduct policy across a wide variety of domains, placing special emphasis on issues of security, human rights, and criminal justice and on the relationship between economic and social policy. The chapter focuses primarily on the theme of governance. In doing so, it explores the extent to which governance can adhere to democratic principles in a world of multiple centres of power, where the state is but one voice among many, and the forms and distributions of power have changed significantly. It is one thing to keep a watch on government. It is quite another to keep a watch on a multiplicity of actors, some of whom may hold radically differing values and pursue very different goals from whatever government is in power at a particular time – even if such actors are partners–in–governance. It is also an open question whether devolving responsibility to other centres of decision making and action means giving up power to determine outcomes.

To explain the dynamics involved in multicentric governance, I examine two literatures. One deals with the nature of the state in the post–Cold War era, while the other concerns the nature of policy making and the policy process. The former derives primarily from international relations theory; the latter, from policy analysis and public management studies. In trying to understand globalization, these two literatures are coming together, resulting in the bridging of disciplines. Academic research that is most relevant to the question of multiple centres of power has clearly begun to transcend disciplinary boundaries; transdisciplinary research is fast becoming the norm.[3] By moving across the boundaries that separate these two literatures and the disciplines that contribute to them I hope to expose heuristic research questions on democratic governance in a changing world.

The central theme of this chapter is that policy making in a multicentric world is driven by two major ideological trends. The first is related to neoliberalism and its economic imperative and can be termed 'marketization' or 'commodification.' Here, government services are commodified and marketed as products to be consumed not by citizens but by clients or customers. The literature on policy studies in a globalized world highlights this trend, with evidence coming from a wide variety of issue-areas from criminal justice to welfare. International relations theory, development studies, the impact of economic neoliberalism on Third World countries, and the political economy literature have also highlighted this trend.

The second ideological trend can be called securitization,[4] which redefines the entire spectrum of policy domains as an array of security problems. Issues as wide ranging as migration, environmental degradation, organized crime, and drug trafficking become part of the mandate of security services seeking to find new enemies in the wake of the Cold War. Distinctions between external and internal security, peacetime and wartime, police and military, and crime and war break down.

International relations theory on the impact of globalization on the international system of states has dealt with this trend, as has a great deal of the literature on international security and policing, including my own work on counterterrorism.[5]

Both these trends involve struggles over meaning, values, norms, and practices. Their predominance reflects in part the exercise of state power – not the 'hard' power of military domination and police repression, but the 'soft' power of exhortation, consultation, partnership, and restructuring. I argue here that, at least in certain policy domains, the state may not really be losing autonomy or power, but rather redefining governance in such a way as to circumvent issues of legitimacy, public responsibility, and accountability, while maintaining control over the burgeoning alliances and partnerships with the private sector and society at large. In other domains, the state may be giving up autonomy to the supranational level in order to maintain legitimacy or control at home. Commodification-marketization and securitization can help states to achieve these complex goals, either directly or indirectly. I focus on the possibilities – or lack of them – for achieving accountability, openness, and legitimacy in the exercise of these new forms of power and governance.

In the first part of this chapter, I survey some of the current thinking on the role of the state and its place in the global structure. My aim there is to describe some of the conceptual models that scholars have put forward to try and characterize how the state fits into a multicentric world. Because such debates have taken place in a variety of schools of thought, I do not intend to get into the details of such debates.[6] Instead, I try and capture the mix of concepts and models that characterize current thinking and attempt to integrate them in some coherent way. In the second part, I turn to the literature on policy making and democratic governance. Finally, I propose a research agenda that addresses both literatures.

The State of the State[7]

The primacy of economic considerations in a number of policy issues, as reflected in the theme of marketization-commodification, is consistent with much of the literature on the emergence of a global economy that limits the ability of states to control transnational flows of production and exchange. A range of metaphors and models have been proposed to describe the place of the state in this world. Stephen Krasner has suggested the metaphor of tectonic plates, as opposed to the billiard-ball image of traditional realist thought. The latter image conceives the state as a unitary actor on the world stage that bumps up against other unitary actors, entering into alliances or cooperating within international regimes. The former model portrays international regimes as determined by states' self-interest. With time, the regimes take on a life of their own – until the disparity between self-interest/exercise-of-power and regime persistence leads to a readjustment (an earthquake). 'One plate can be envisioned as the distribution of power among states, the other as regimes and related behaviour and outcomes.'[8]

Mark Zacher describes a 'fundamental transformation from a system of highly autonomous states [billiard balls] to one where states are increasingly enmeshed in a network of interdependencies and regimes.'[9] The word 'enmeshed' suggests that states are parts of larger wholes, whether conceived as networks or as webs. While states are one kind of entity within these networks, others exist as well: transnational corporations (TNCs), intergovernmental organizations (IGOs), non-governmental organizations (NGOs), and a host of transnational actors ranging from international terrorists and Mafias to private cartels.[10] While traditional realist thought conceives the state as unitary, many of these other models portray the state as porous and part of a series of entities, embedded one within the other within the other – what Yale Ferguson and Richard Mansbach, for example, refer to as 'nesting.'[11]

Much of the debate about the nature of the state and its place in the world order has been cast in 'either/or' terms: the state is in retreat, withering away, hollowing out, or the state is still the centre of the world order and its interests are primary in determining outcomes. One finds books entitled *Bringing the State Back In*, followed by others entitled *Bringing Transnational Relations Back In*.[12] The title of William McNeill's review of Ferguson and Mansbach's book, *Polities*, captures the flavour of this debate;[13] 'Territorial States Buried Too Soon' takes the two authors to task for ignoring the importance of military force and the primacy of states.[14] For the purposes of this chapter, I adopt James Rosenau's *fragmegrative* model, which rejects this polarization of opinion and sees a state-centric world existing side by side with a multicentric one. This bifurcation means that alongside the traditional state-centric world there has emerged a multicentric world involving a wide range of actors at local, regional, national, international, and global levels, in which increasingly skilled, organized, mobilized, and mobile individuals participate across levels and transnationally. This bifurcated global structure introduces turbulence and complexity into world politics.[15]

A distinctive feature of Rosenau's model is that the traditional world of states is not replaced by a new one of multiple centres of power, but rather it coexists and interacts with this multicentric world. State actors participate in both worlds, moving back and forth between international summits and meetings and regional conferences. Similarly, non-state actors increasingly interact with the state-centric world through participation in multilateral events such as United Nations conferences, as well as public consultation, town hall meetings, and lobbying by what Margaret Keck and Kathryn Sikkink call 'transnational advocacy networks.'[16] Some of the impact of these non-state actors on government policy is channelled through the mass media, of course, and some is the indirect product of migration and the emergence of diaspora communities.[17] The result of these electronic and migratory trends is the promulgation and diffusion of an alternative set of norms and principles to realist notions of national and international security – for example, promotion of human rights, environmental protection, human security, and global governance.

This complex movement back and forth between the state-centric and multicentric worlds results in a 'complex and endless array of feedback loops,'[18] and contradictions, ambiguities, and uncertainties have become the norm: 'Territory and boundaries are still important, but attachments to them are weakening. Domestic and foreign affairs still seem like separate domains, but the line between them is transgressed with increasing frequency. The international system is less commanding, but it is still powerful. States are changing, but they are not disappearing. State sovereignty has eroded, but it is still vigorously asserted. Governments are weaker, but they still possess considerable resources and they can still throw their weight around ... The United Nations is asked to take on more assignments and not supplied with the funds to carry them out ... Citizens are both more active and more cynical. Borders still keep out intruders, but they are also increasingly porous.'[19]

It is these contradictions and the simultaneous operation of conflicting processes that form the central features of Rosenau's model. The term 'fragmegration' – the simultaneous operation of fragmentation and integration – is an attempt to capture this feature in a single word.

Rosenau is certainly not the only scholar to describe and attempt to systematize the profound changes occurring in world politics since the end of the Cold War. He insists, however, that prefixing a label with 'post' – as in 'post–Cold War' or 'postmodern' or even his earlier term, 'postinternational'[20] – recasts the present in terms of the past and fails to suggest a truly new era. 'The emergent epoch is marked by accelerating processes in which global spaces are moving into local places and local repercussions are occurring on a global scale.'[21]

International Regimes

While other chapters look more closely at regimes,[22] any discussion of the role of states in a multicentric world must deal with the subject. Some of the debate over regime theory has provided useful models that complement those mentioned above. Susan Strange's alternative to regime theory consists of 'trying to draw a map of interlocking, overlapping bargains' – bargains that are made between partners with very different types of power and vulnerability to risk, not all of them states. These bargaining maps, she argues, 'will ... reveal the domestic roots of international arrangements.'[23] According to Strange, this conceptualization leads to research questions over, for example, who gets what and what values are represented 'in terms of order and stability, wealth and efficiency, justice and freedom; and in terms of all the opposite qualities – insecurity and risk, poverty and waste, inequity and constraint.'[24]

Despite her criticism of regime theory, Strange's notion of a map of interlocking and overlapping bargains lying underneath the surface of international regimes is a useful way of depicting the complex nexus of international regimes in which states are enmeshed (to use Zacher's term) with other actors.[25] Her criticism of regime theory as too state-centric and static, as well as too focused on the United States, can be addressed by opening up the study of regimes to those transnational actors that she identifies, as well as by trying to decipher the key bargains underlying the regimes. What she calls a 'new realism' that focuses on the power of markets and transnational actors such as cartels, insurance companies, and auditors can be assimilated into a more complex approach to regimes that is consistent with Rosenau's 'fragmegrative' model. This would entail conceiving of regimes as being applicable to many levels of analysis: the international, the transnational, the national, and even the sub-national. A key research project would then be to draw bargaining maps at each of these levels of analysis and even across levels.

Take, for example, the problem of maintaining national standards in the context of decentralization. 'Downloading' power from central to regional and local governments – in Canada, from Ottawa to the provinces and municipalities – can expose those sub-national governments to international norms. While this endeavour may initially produce 'a patchwork of standards – some of which conform to Canada's international commitments and others which do not,'[26] it may also help over the long run to create a more homogeneous pattern. Ironically, this would result not from any pressure from the federal government, but from independent pressure on individual sub-national governments from international regimes. Janice Thomson calls this 'convergence,' rather than 'harmonization.'[27] Of course, if federal policy is already in line with international norms, then federal pressure could simply be an additional voice that is consistent with the international one. A research project could be conducted on trying to apply regime theory to the sub-national level and doing case studies on, for example, provincial policy initiatives to see if they are sometimes influenced by international norms.

The idea that political leaders can be socialized by international or even national norms could explain why newly elected leaders from parties with more radical ideas, such as the (now-defunct) Refah Party in Turkey or the BJP in India, will often moderate their views once in power. At the international level, Martha Finnemore argues: 'states are embedded in dense networks of transnational and international social relations that shape their perceptions of the world and their role in that world. States are socialized to want certain things by the international society in which they and the people in them live.'[28] If one accepts the concept of nesting referred to above, then the permutations of this teaching process across levels of government can be considerable, from a trickle-down version that proceeds via national governments to sub-national ones, to a more direct link between the international and the sub-national levels.

Legal pluralism provides a further framework for considering how regimes may overlap and how the state fits in with the interlocking patterns of norms across different levels. According to Roderick Macdonald, 'legal pluralists posit a multiplicity of legal orders in every society. Different social milieux ... give citizens the occasion to create and negotiate their own normative standards ... and their own institutions to reinforce or apply these standards. Even the simplest legal regimes are constituted by a plurality of decision-making institutions, distributive criteria and cultural traditions ... Different legal regimes are in constant interaction, mutually influencing the emergence of each other's rules, processes and institutions. The structures and trajectories of interaction ... between these multiple legal orders are varied and unpredictable.[29]

If we link this idea to Strange's bargaining maps that underlie international regimes, the more visible and formal rules, processes, and institutions of such regimes would then reflect less visible and more informal bargaining processes, where gains, losses, and compromises differ for each constellation of bargainers. These bargaining processes in turn would reflect the specific cultural traditions, distributive criteria, and decision-making rules that emerge from the values and goals of each bargaining party.

Macdonald also suggests that the concept of plurality can be extended to disciplines other than law. The reified *state*, the reified *market*, the reified *law* mask the complexity of human agency and interaction that generates the social, political, and economic phenomena that led to these concepts in the first place. Multiplicity and complexity are the order of the day, and understanding the relationships between overlapping systems of norms, rules, and values that will almost certainly multiply in a multicentric world would help policy makers better understand their environment. Developing research strategies to deal with these overlapping systems obviously presents unique challenges.

Case Studies of Regime Formation and Failure

One research strategy is to conduct case studies on how particular regimes came about or how attempts to create particular regimes failed. Realists argue that the success of regime formation is dependent on the interests of powerful, hegemonic states. Neoliberals, in contrast, argue that mutual interests are more important.[30] In the case of piracy, criminologist William Chambliss shows how it was only when powerful states were seriously harmed by piracy that they agreed to do something about it. Until then, piracy was a useful alternative to war.[31] The parallel with contemporary state-sponsored terrorism and transnational organized crime is striking. States can still condemn international terrorism, transnational organized crime, drug trafficking, arms trafficking, or the dumping of toxic waste as threats to peace and security, since their laws usually proscribe such activities or they are signatories to international conventions that forbid them. Yet when they see such acts as a less risky alternative to more direct confrontation, such as war, or as a boon to economic development or to the maintenance of competitiveness in international markets, then many states choose to provide all kinds of assistance to transnational groups. This is consistent with the realist view of international regimes; national interest will usually be the sticking point on which such regimes will falter or fail. Whether at the international, national, sub-national, or institutional level, the conflicting goals of states, jurisdictions, organizations, governmental departments and agencies will always be a key variable in determining the extent to which co-operation and regimes succeed or not.

The degree to which today's growing interdependence alters the fundamental nature of national interest is another key area for research. The changing conceptions of security, for example, could mean a better international climate for security regimes. But the debate over NATO's airstrikes of 1999 against the former Yugoslavia/Serbia suggest that many still see regional and national interests as driving the decision as to whether, when, and where to intervene in conflicts. Whether the strikes represent the regional interests of NATO or the demise of the principle of non-intervention and the strengthening of humanitarian intervention and human rights norms is a question for research. International co-operation in the fight against terrorism, in particular the rule to extradite or prosecute, has certainly fallen victim time and again to national interest.[32] The debate concerning whether evolving human rights norms are universal or Western is another important area crying out for research.[33] Roderick Macdonald points out that 'the theory of legal pluralism raises the hypothesis that non conforming behaviour in any particular regime is not simply a failure of enforcement or civil disobedience. It may be the reflection of an alternative conception of legal normativity.'[34] In other words, there may be other overlapping norms that induce non-compliance other than that of pure self-interest.

Janice Thomson has explored the question of why certain transnational practices are delegitimized internationally and why some are not.[35] She examines six transnational practices: the drug trade (opium and cocaine), terrorism (piracy and privateering), alcohol consumption, the arms trade, mercenarism, and tobacco (smoking) and looks at whether the issue was placed on the international regulatory agenda and if so whether international regulation resulted. The results of her inquiry only partially support her original hypothesis that strong states will push for international regulation of those activities that threaten it and block control of those that benefit it. In some cases, such as piracy and privateering, the interests of the most powerful states did indeed play a decisive role. In others, it did not, and in one (the arms trade), non-state actors were decisive. As for Mark Zacher and Brent Sutton's comparative analysis of transportation and communication regimes, they uncovered more evidence for a neoliberal interpretation of regime formation and maintenance than for a neorealist one, although they did find that some regime norms were based on mutual interests in state autonomy, a neorealist concern.[36]

While the above studies look at international regimes that on the whole are the work of states, Margaret Keck and Kathryn Sikkink examine cases involving a range of state and non-state actors. The result is an analysis that comes close to integrating the approaches of Susan Strange and Roderick Macdonald. Keck and Sikkink's research highlights the importance of norms and values, how they are changed or maintained and how they resist change.[37] Relating norms to practices, they suggest that practice should be conceived not only as 'that which is done,' but also as 'the act of doing something repeatedly.' This allows them to 'imagine norms whose practice over time has become so automatic that they gain a taken-for-granted quality, in which practices and standards become so routinized as to be taken almost as laws of nature.'[38] If they are viewed in this way, then 'normative change is inherently disruptive or difficult because it requires actors to question this routinized practice and contemplate new practices.'[39]

This is the challenge taken up, for example, by penal abolitionists, who argue that the practice of using imprisonment to deal with a whole variety of social problems is so ingrained that only abolishing prisons would make alternative practices conceivable to the majority of people. Similarly, the predominance of the 'war on drugs,' particularly in the United States, has made it difficult for states such as Canada to reorient drug policy from a military model towards a public health model.[40] The inherent difficulty of questioning practices that are so routinized is directly related to the establishment and maintenance of international regimes in areas such as human rights, environmental protection, and prevention of violence against women. Many international regimes are perceived to be inimical to local custom and values. Keck and Sikkink show that the way an issue is framed can determine whether a campaign for a control regime will succeed. For example, contemporary campaigns to ban female genital mutilation were initially resisted by many groups where the practice was prevalent, until it was reframed as part of a broader campaign against violence towards women. Only then did charges of cultural imperialism and racism dissipate and the campaign gain broad legitimacy.[41]

Much of the tension over norms and practices involves non-Western states resisting the imposition of what they see as Western rather than universal values. The best-known field for such resistance involves human rights, where many Third World countries accuse advocacy groups of cultural imperialism. A striking example occurs in the area of social and labour standards in the Third World. Some states there have resisted European attempts to include social clauses in free trade agreements, seeing them as a guise for economic protectionism that threatens their competitiveness, which is based in part on lower wages and weaker labour standards.[42]

There can be other variations as well. Canadian and western European resistance to U.S. pressure to allow their cultural industries to compete openly in the world market is in part a function of different values, norms, and practices in these countries. Similarly, certain European countries, in particular the Netherlands and Switzerland, resist U.S. approaches to drug enforcement, preferring a medical model,[43] while France, Italy, and Spain resisted adopting the U.S. practice of using undercover operations to combat the drug trade, despite partnerships between their law enforcement agencies and the U.S. Drug Enforcement Administration (DEA).[44]

Central to Keck and Sikkink's analysis is what they call 'the boomerang pattern of influence,' whereby 'domestic NGOs bypass their state and directly search out international allies to try to bring pressure on their states from outside.'[45] Typically those external allies are other NGOs, who then put pressure on their own states, and sometimes an IGO, to apply pressure on the original state. In this way, reaching abroad to non-state actors who in turn encourage other states to become involved helps transcend a domestic political blockage.

State Actors as Network Components: The Challenge of Double Roles

Margaret Keck and Kathryn Sikkink's cases are designed to study transnational advocacy networks. Consistent with Rosenau's bifurcated world structure, such networks include both state and non-state actors. This raises the important question of whether state actors, when involved in such networks, are functioning always as state actors per se or rather as actors reflecting other norms and values than those which they officially represent. This is reminiscent of Macdonald's legal pluralism and his contention that failure to adhere to one system of norms may reflect loyalty to another one that is less visible simply because it is not defined by a state. Keck and Sikkink characterize state actors as network components that 'bring to international relations identities and goals that are not purely derived from their structural position in a world of states – and that may even be constituted by relationships established with citizens of other states.'[46] They suggest that there may be contradictions between these identities and goals and the traditional systemic roles of these states.

The concept of state actors as network components is an interesting way of conceiving the link between the state and transnational advocacy networks or an emerging global civil society. The challenge for states such as Canada is to ensure that their state actors are part of transnational networks, IGOs, and international NGOs that can affect other states. But there are dangers, as Keck and Sikkink suggest when they speak of contradictions between identities and goals held by state actors involved in transnational networks. When former Chilean dictator Augusto Pinochet's defence lawyers found out that one of the judges in the British House of Lords who voted for their client's extradition to Spain was active in Amnesty International, they launched an appeal that was upheld in December 1998. Here, a state actor – a judge in the House of Lords – lost authority precisely because he was a network component. This suggests that membership or participation in transnational advocacy networks can sometimes undermine the authority of a state actor in his or her capacity as state actor, rather than bolster it.[47]

Knowledge can be power. But it can also be interpreted as bias. For this reason, Robert Keohane and Joseph Nye argue that 'to be credible, ... information must be produced through a process that is in accordance with professional norms and characterized by transparency and procedural fairness.'[48] As NGOs such as Amnesty International and Greenpeace become more involved in partnerships with states and international institutions, their credibility and that of the information that they provide will increasingly depend on whether they are perceived to be open and accountable. The same is true for states. 'If governments and NGOs are to take advantage of the information revolution, they will have to establish reputations for credibility amid the white noise of the information revolution.'[49] The problems of double agents, undercover agents and conflict of interest in government are all well known.[50] In a multicentric world, more and more individuals will assume multiple roles and allegiances. The same will be true for policy makers and policy analysts. Research on how norms and values change or resist change and how individual actors juggle different and sometimes-conflicting identities will help policy makers understand how specific regimes play out in a multicentric world.

Global Civil Society

In the discussion above of regimes and of the kinds of actors involved in the bargaining that underlies their formation, I have looked mostly at interstate, state–regime, or, in some cases, state–non-state interaction. There is a body of literature that deals with the level of individual citizens, suggesting that they are increasingly identifying with a society that transcends state boundaries. Ronnie Lipschutz, for example, defines 'global civil society' as 'self-conscious constructions of networks of knowledge and action, by decentred, local actors, that cross the reified boundaries of space as if they were not there.'[51] The actors are decentred because their focus is global, yet they are local because they act within their own locality to inculcate global norms – think globally, act locally.

The concept of legal pluralism could then be operable here too, with a citizen's value system varying according to the level of identification at which he or she operates in a particular policy debate. The level of identification could be ethnic, territorial, national, or even global, or it could represent more narrowly defined interests such as victims of crime, milk producers, or small business. In some cases, as often happens with women's, environmental, and human rights groups, different interests may even converge on particular issues. As a result, the concept of citizen involvement in a multicentric world is an ambiguous one, which raises questions about the nature of sovereignty, the interests being served by participation in the policy process, and the capacity of a state that solicits citizens' participation to accommodate their views.

The concept of global civil society and a global citizenry that acts locally to promote global norms and values is consistent with the breakdown in the distinction between domestic and foreign affairs that is often identified as a feature of the current policy environment. The idea that individuals have a legitimate right to engage in international affairs was eloquently articulated by Michel Foucault and other French intellectuals as long ago as 1981. The French newspaper *Le Monde* published the following appeal by a French trade union concerning the Polish government's crackdown on the Solidarity trade union and the invocation of martial law in December 1981. Foucault and many of his associates also signed the appeal:

> Faithful to the spirit of Solidarnosc, in which trade unionists and intellectuals worked and struggled to free themselves from the hold of totalitarianism, [the signatories] declare that it is not enough to denounce the coup in Poland. Above all, we must immediately associate ourselves with the combat of the Polish people by combining intellectual criticism and social struggle, as Solidarity has done ... No, this is not an internal Polish affair.
>
> Invocations of the principle of non-interference must not lead to non-assistance. It is clear that the coup occurred as a result of pressure from the Soviet Union. We will not resign ourselves to it. Let us stop thinking about the situation in Poland purely in terms of geostrategic constraints, of state-to-state or bloc-to-bloc relations, which leads to human rights, the rights of peoples, the action of public opinion and international solidarity being seen as negligible quantities. We cannot accept a definitive partition of Europe which refuses Poland and other countries under Soviet domination a democratic future.[52]

Here we see a sign of what has become a new discourse that moves beyond state-to-state or bloc-to-bloc relations to include non-state actors.

Similarly, in July 1984, Foucault and some friends from the NGO *Médecins du Monde* attended an international congress on piracy at the United Nations' Offices in Geneva. Foucault made the following impromptu address at the congress. Stating that he and his friends were there as private individuals, he went on:

> Then who mandated us? No one. And it is precisely that which gives us the right to speak. It seems to me that we have to bear in mind three principles ...
>
> There is such a thing as international citizenship which has its rights, which has its duties and which implies a commitment to rise up against any abuse of power, whoever its author, whoever the victims. After all,

> we are all governed [*nous sommes tous des gouvernés*] and, by that token, our fates are bound up together.
>
> Because they claim to look after the happiness of societies, governments arrogate to themselves the right to draw up profit-and-loss accounts for the human misery which their decisions provoke, or which their negligence causes. One of the duties of international citizenship is to reveal human misery to the eyes and ears of government, as it is not true that they are not responsible for it. Human misery must never be the silent residue of politics. It founds an absolute right to rise up and to address those who hold power.
>
> We must reject the division of labour we are so often offered: it is up to individuals to become indignant and to talk; it is up to governments to think and to act ... Amnesty International, Terre des Hommes and Médecins du Monde are the initiatives which have created this new right: the right of private individuals to intervene effectively in the order of international policies and strategies. The will of individuals must be inscribed in a reality over which governments wish to have a monopoly, a monopoly which we must wrest away from them, gradually and day by day.[53]

Here, in this address as a private, though world-renowned, individual at an international congress at the United Nations, Foucault articulates a kind of manifesto for the international citizen that presages the rise of the non-state actor and the NGO. The division of labour that he rejects is the old order; the new order is to create a new division of labour, a new form of governance that includes concerned citizens.

I say more below about the problems of partnership and the forms of government–society relationships that have developed under the new philosophy of *offloading* from government to the private sector and civil society. Suffice it to say at this point that governments themselves have since rejected the division of labour that Foucault decries. Private citizens and communities are being asked to think and to act for themselves, or in partnership with government. Whether this sea change has really resulted in wresting away a government monopoly on policy formulation and implementation is a question I return to below. However, Foucault would probably have been surprised that the monopoly was, at least at face value, given up voluntarily by government.

Foucault's dramatic rhetoric about citizens rising up and addressing those in power suggests that government–society relations are necessarily conflictual. Clearly, the philosophy of partnership espoused by Jocelyn Bourgon and others is not. Yet many theorists and scholars writing about the kinds of interaction and bargaining that underlie regime formation note that such processes are indeed marked by conflict and confrontation. For Margaret Keck and Kathryn Sikkink, sociological theories such as world polity theory, which posit the passive diffusion of global norms, 'ignore the issues of agency and political opportunity that we find central for understanding the evolution of new international institutions and relationships.'[54] Their own research findings, they argue, do not support the idea that a global civil society is emerging. Rather, they speak of a 'transnational civil society as an arena of struggle, a fragmented and contested area.'[55]

In a multicentric world, struggles over meaning and policy can be expected to predominate. Just as legal pluralism postulates the interaction of norms, so transnational advocacy networks highlight the struggles over definition that characterize many policy debates. Yet Keck and Sikkink do hold out hope for the integration of the different approaches. 'Perhaps some understanding of "thresholds" might help integrate our work with that of world polity theorists.'[56] From a policy perspective, the idea of thresholds suggests that the policy process will be quite different when there is consensus over norms and practices than when there is conflict. This is not a new insight, since policy analysis has always recognized the potential conflict inherent in setting agendas and in identifying and defining problems. In a multicentric world, however, the scope and intensity of such conflicts over meaning increase dramatically and introduce a greater level of complexity to the policy process. One of the key findings of the Policy Research Initiative's social cohesion network is that 'a cohesive society is not one where conflict is absent.'[57] They identify 'the strength and success of [Canada's] governance structures – formal, informal, domestic and international, public, private, non-governmental, and voluntary' – as the determining variable in predicting how these inevitable conflicts will affect Canadian society in the medium to long term. It is the panoply of governance structures created by globalization, decentralization, and privatization that are central to any research project designed to explain policy making in a multicentric world. It is to this topic that I now turn.

Policy Making in a Multicentric World

Democratic Governance in a World of Multiple Centres of Power

K.J. Holsti, in reviewing two recent books on international society, asks: 'If one of the tasks of international theory is to make a complex world more intelligible, how can we keep piling up more variables and contexts without making things less intelligible?'[58] This is indeed a formidable challenge, and it is equally relevant for policy research, especially if we take complexity and multiplicity seriously. Policy making in Canada faces enormous challenges across a wide variety of dimensions. Any survey of recent news stories reveals three common themes: first, the centrality of economic factors in defining the limits of any particular policy initiative; second, the increasing mistrust of government by citizens; and third, the increasing disparity between public expectations and government's ability to respond to them.

The first theme reflects much of the literature on the retreat of the state in the face of economic globalization. The need to remain competitive in a global market becomes a justification for states to reduce the size of government, rein in social programs, and pursue new markets for their goods and services, even if this means downplaying defence of human rights and protection of the environment. The second and third themes also appear to revolve around economics. Keith Banting, for example, provides data from 1995 that reveal a wide gap between what the general public most values and what elites and decision makers value most.[59] While the latter groups ranked competitiveness and minimal government highest (ranked first and third, respectively), the former ranked these lowest (twentieth and twenty-second out of twenty-two, respectively). The top three-ranked items by the general public – freedom, clean environment, and healthy population – placed seventh, tenth, and ninth, respectively, for the decision makers.

The challenges that Jocelyn Bourgon outlined in Ottawa in 1998 (cited at the opening of this chapter) are particularly salient in the tension between social and economic policy. While she stated that 'there are no distinctions anymore between economic and social policies,' Keith Banting has shown that 'the internationalization of the policy process at élite levels is increasing the distance between government and the domestic social-policy community to which government also belongs.'[60] He suggests that 'in a world of tightened international constraints, there is a danger that public consultations will heighten, not reduce, cynicism about the responsiveness of our political institutions.'[61] This is consistent with Leslie Pal's observation, in his discussion of consultation and partnering,[62] that 'with consultations, the challenge is balancing public demands with the realities of hard decisions.'[63] If public consultation is not to be seen as a cynical public relations ploy, how then do policy makers deal with public reaction to initiatives that do not take into account the positions that they put forward – even if the decisions taken reflect hard realities of resource constraints and loss of economic sovereignty?

The tension between fiscal and economic policy on the one hand and a whole range of social policy domains on the other hand clearly renders the harmonization of government policy across economic and social domains extremely problematic. When we say that there is no longer any distinction between social and economic policy, are we really simply accepting the fact that economic considerations are setting the social policy agenda? Consider, for example, the disparity in resources and resulting influence in the policy process between producer interest groups and public interest groups.[64] The former are better connected with government, are consulted by government regularly, and have much better resources for promoting their policy preferences, especially in the economic domain. The latter are not as well connected with government and, though consulted with increasing frequency (in line with Bourgon's emphasis on partnerships and alliances), they have fewer resources, are dependent on fiscally constrained government funding, and do not always speak with one voice. In Canada, such groups have become even more fragmented under the impact of globalization and the internationalization of the social policy process.[65] As a result of these differences in motivation, resources, and internal structure, the impact of these groups on the policy process also diverges. While producer groups have considerable influence on the later stages of the policy process, particularly implementation, public interest groups have their greatest influence on the earlier stages, such as agenda setting and problem definition, particularly in social policy.

These differences in influence are mirrored within the federal government itself, where the traditional tension between the Department of Finance and those departments in charge of social programs has been affected by changes in the economic field wrought by globalization. 'The fiscal and economic problems of the last decade have clearly strengthened the hand of the Department of Finance, making it the dominant social-policy department in the federal government.'[66] Finance is also favoured in Canadian representation in international bodies, such as the Organization for Economic Cooperation and Development (OECD).[67] The Department of Human Resources Development, however, is 'trying to insert itself more vigorously into international networks'[68] and is devoting more resources to preparing for international meetings and projects, including contributing to the OECD's analytical studies.

Here we see how the international arena can provide new opportunities for government departments responsible for policy domains that are traditionally viewed as strictly domestic, particularly social policy. This shows once again how the distinction between domestic and foreign policy and between domestic politics and international affairs has increasingly blurred. This blurring makes it harder to discern how particular domestic constituents come to be marginalized by 'harmonizing' of national policy and how individual states can be disadvantaged by emerging international norms and regimes.[69] It also masks the continuing power of the United States to influence the agenda of international institutions and to set the tone and the agenda in a variety of domains.[70]

Downloading, Offloading, Privatization

By reducing budget deficits in response to the pressures arising from economic globalization and the need to be competitive in a global market, states have voluntarily 'downloaded' obligations to sub-national levels of government, 'offloaded' responsibilities to the private sector and to civil society, and 'privatized' many government industries and services. When coupled with the all-of-government approach referred to by Jocelyn Bourgon, where policy making must proceed horizontally across a spectrum of domains, such decentralizing trends can affect overall governance in several ways. Sometimes governance can proceed in a concerted, co-ordinated fashion, but sometimes conflicting and counterproductive approaches undermine both effectiveness and coherence.

An example of this latter trend can be seen in the contradiction between fiscal policies that emphasize cost efficiency and criminal justice policies that demand harsher penalties, particularly with respect to narcotics. Strict enforcement and harsher penalties result in increased prison populations and generate pressure for construction of more prisons, which cost money. The solution then becomes privatization, whereby delivery of prison services, including construction and running of prisons, is turned over to the private sector. The profit motive behind the running of private prisons supplants government responsibility for the welfare of prisoners and accountability for what happens to them.[71]

Another problematic area is the control of hate propaganda and child pornography on the internet. A criminal justice approach emphasizes the use of criminal law to prosecute those who disseminate hate and/or child pornography electronically through the internet. This method necessitates creation of specialized police units that search the internet for sites propagating hate and pornography and that prepare investigations for eventual prosecution. The result has been raids on homes and offices, seizure of computer hard- and software, and pressure on internet service providers to monitor and limit access to internet chat rooms, e-mail services, and web sites.

In their fight against internet-based hate and pornography, law enforcement agencies have insisted on the right to circumvent encryption technologies. Similarly, security intelligence agencies argue that circumventing encryption would help them in the fight against computer hackers, organized crime, and information terrorism.[72] The demand by state agencies for technology to circumvent encryption has generated conflict with two types of interest groups: business groups that want to use the internet for financial transactions and rely on encryption to protect their data and groups that see encryption as a valuable tool to protect the privacy rights of internet users. That a producer group and a public interest group both contest encryption-circumvention technology for law enforcement does not mean that there is increasing convergence between such groups in general. The two groups have very different motives, and it is likely that the concerns of business are more influential than those of privacy groups, although research would be required to test this assumption. The result is that government is finding it very difficult to achieve any kind of consensus on the issue.

A contrasting approach to the criminal justice one is that of Ken McVay,[73] who runs the privately operated Nizkor Project's web site, which is used to challenge Holocaust deniers and hate propagandists on the internet. He links Holocaust denial and hate sites directly with his site and asks the webmasters of those sites to link their sites with his. A committed free speech activist, McVay does not agree with the criminal justice approach but prefers to engage hate propagandists directly and to counter their propaganda with factual explanations. Here, we see a contrast between a state-run approach and an individual citizen's, where the solution is sought within society and not in state regulation.[74]

In some policy domains entirely new forms of governance have emerged. For example, David Garland suggests that a 'responsibilization' strategy has emerged in the United Kingdom in criminal justice: 'This involves the central government seeking to act upon crime not in a direct fashion through state agencies ... but instead by acting indirectly, seeking to activate action on the part of non-state agencies and organizations ... Its primary concern is to devolve responsibility for crime prevention on to agencies, organizations and individuals which are quite outside the state and to persuade them to act appropriately.'[75] The key aspects of this strategy are partnership with non-state actors, co-operation across state agencies, and involvement of citizens – many of the same ideas put forth by Bourgon in her 1998 speech. The ideas reflect the general tendency of government to download and offload government functions. Whether this constitutes the transfer of power is another question.

Garland, for example, rejects the notion that responsibilization simply offloads state functions through the privatization of crime control. Instead, he characterizes it as 'a new form of governance-at-a-distance ... a new mode of exercising power.' He offers a much more intricate description of the situation than simple erosion of sovereignty: 'The state does not diminish or become merely a nightwatchman. On the contrary, it retains all its traditional functions ... and, in addition, takes on a new set of co-ordinating and activating roles, which, in time, develop into new structures of support, funding, information exchange or co-operation, [leaving] the centralized state machine more powerful than before, with an extended capacity for action and influence. At the same time, however, this strategy serves to erode the notion of the state as the public's representative and primary protector.'[76]

An increase in responsibility does not necessarily mean an increase in power. Power, like sovereignty, can be conceived of in a variety of ways. Karen Litfin has suggested that sovereignty can be divided into sub-dimensions: she proposes autonomy, control, and legitimacy, while others add territoriality. In environmental policy, states make bargains that affect these sub-dimensions differently. Autonomy may decrease, but control increase; legitimacy may be sacrificed in exchange for more control.[77] Similarly, Garland's description of crime-prevention policy in the United Kingdom (and the United States) implies that the state gives up autonomy and even legitimacy in this area, in order to gain greater control. But far from representing a decrease in state power, this control constitutes a new form of power that relieves the state of any sense of obligation to the public:

> The recurring message of this [responsibilization] approach is that the state alone is not, and cannot effectively be, responsible for preventing and controlling crime [decrease in the state's legitimacy]. Property owners, residents, retailers, manufacturers, town planners, school authorities, transport managers, employers, parents, and individual citizens – all of these must be made to recognize that they too have a responsibility in this regard [decrease in the state's autonomy], and must be persuaded to change their practices in order to reduce criminal opportunities and increase informal controls [increase in a new form of state control, involving the soft power of exhortation and persuasion]. In effect, central government is, in this field of policy as in several others, operating upon the established boundaries which separate the private from the public realm, seeking to renegotiate the question of what is properly a state function and what is not.[78]

It is as if the state has developed a new policy instrument – the promotion of self-regulation – that bridges the traditional gap between private behaviour and state action. This need for government to persuade citizens to change their habits has led, for example, to numerous crime-prevention programs and information campaigns in many industrialized countries: 'Citizens are expected to lock everything behind them, to carry their handbags diagonally around their shoulder, to fit alarm systems, to leave the curtains open and to leave a light on when they go on holiday, to remove their radios from their cars, to use inside pockets in their jackets and to keep their cheques separate from their bank cards; they are also, in some cases, encouraged to participate in or finance neighbourhood-watch schemes. This new focus is closely associated with the development of late modern society as a *risk society*.'[79] The result has been an increase in the role of insurance companies, manufacturers and distributors of alarm systems, and companies that assess and manage risk in what has traditionally been an area of public policy.

This approach to crime control is consistent with the changes in governance and public management practices that Pal outlines in his survey of the altered policy environment in industrialized countries.[80] He outlines three main features: smaller governments; the idea that traditional policy instruments no longer work and may even do more harm than good; and a more client-focused, service-oriented system of management. Despite variations from country to country, there is a common emphasis on specific techniques: decentralization of budgeting, performance indicators, performance-related pay, an emphasis on quality and standards, the contractualization of relationships, and evaluation coupled with a concern about value for money.

Pal contrasts this approach with traditional public administration, which is 'couched in an understanding that politics is different from economics: in politics, it is citizens and not merely customers or clients that interact; they interact with an eye to the common public interest and not to personal interests. In democratic politics there has to be a heavy premium on accountability and public debate.'[81] Garland notes the same contrast. 'This new ethos also entails a concern with what might be called "customer relations." State agencies increasingly redefine their mission in terms of serving particular "consumers" (such as victims and their families, or even inmates) and being responsive to their expressed needs, rather than serving the more abstract, top–down notion of the public good.'[82]

This phenomenon of the privatization of public interests is consistent with the primacy of economic concerns over social ones that I discussed above. It does not necessarily mean the offloading of state power to the private sector and civil society, since the state still maintains the power to direct, co-ordinate, influence, and even fund what those sectors do. Instead, the state is offloading responsibility for what used to be a public good which has now become a private commodity that society must acquire itself, often by purchasing it from private-sector actors, who often work in partnership with the state.

So pervasive is this new approach that it even colours the discourse of an academic text such as Pal's.[83] For example, Pal asks the rhetorical question: 'To what extent should government encourage the pursuit of what are basically private interests, such as child care or a university education, through direct services or financial support?'[84] Here we see university education defined as a private interest, even though it is clearly in a state's interest to have highly educated citizens, particularly in a knowledge-based society. Similarly, with the increasing presence of women in the workforce and the continuing tendency for men to remain there rather than to take over household and child-rearing duties, it is again in the state's interest to ensure the availability of adequately trained care-givers and child care facilities to two-income families raising children. The fact that Pal assumes university education and child care to be private interests rather than public goods merely attests to the degree to which the new thinking has permeated policy discourse.

Downloading, offloading, and privatization are central features of a multicentric world, since they engender, by their very nature, new centres of potential power, authority, and influence. As such, they present unique challenges to democratic governance. Much of the impetus of democratic life is directed at the maintenance of clear distinctions between policy domains, the institutions of social control that implement their policies, and the rules of governance that they follow. Avoiding conflict of interest, separation of powers, and balancing of the exercise of power with the rule of law, accountability, and transparency are common goals of democratic governance. In a world where distinctions are breaking down and mandates are blurring into one another, there is cause for concern.[85] Whether sub-national governments or private-sector actors can incorporate democratic norms into their *modi operandi* is a key question for research. If downloading, offloading, and privatization are creating new roles for individuals – as client, consumer, producer, self-regulator – to what extent are any of these new roles compatible with that of citizen?

Partnership

The new management approach to public policy places great emphasis on government partnership, either with the private sector or with civil society. Much of this concern is driven by the dominance of economic considerations in an era of globalization, although securitization also leads to increasing partnerships with private security companies and neighbourhoods. The two trends interact through government downsizing. The case of privatization of prison services and prisons highlights the kinds of problems that can arise when governments offload state responsibilities to the private sector – there is a potential conflict between maximization of profits and protection of the public good. Even when public good is defined as job creation, the use of non-unionized employees deviates from a standard rule of governance in labour policy. However, private companies that get involved in what are traditionally state responsibilities may become exposed to rules of governance that could change the way in which they do business.

In the area of disaster response in the aviation industry, for example, the TWA 800 explosion off Long Island, New York, in 1996 exposed the airline to pressure from victims' families to which it was unaccustomed in a corporate world where secrecy and accountability only to shareholders is the norm.[86] The company learned rather quickly that people were more than commodities. By the time a Swissair flight went down off Peggy's Cove, Nova Scotia, in the autumn of 1998, that airline's handling of grieving relatives showed that the industry had changed its ways of responding to disasters. The fact that two women who lost relatives in air disasters were appointed members of U.S. Vice-President Al Gore's Commission on Aviation Safety and Security attests to the increasing involvement of citizens in the policy process. Whether this change translates into increased power remains an open question. One of the two women was extremely critical of the commission's final recommendations, and, although her dissent was published as an annex to the report, her objections were not taken into consideration.

It is quite likely that transnational private enterprises will begin to exhibit signs of convergence in crisis response similar to what Janice Thomson found for international control of transnational practices (see above, pp. 95, 97–8) and comparable to what I posited for sub-national governments exposed to international norms (p. 95). What are the trade-offs and bargains between states and private companies when they engage in partnerships? If, for example, private companies become partners with governments in the growing number of humanitarian aid missions, the question of profits versus the public good will certainly arise.[87] Research into how such private–public arrangements are funded might reveal interesting ways to deal with the potential strain on public money. Could an airline get permission to fly to additional cities in a country or to use certain favoured air routes in exchange for bearing the cost of such international missions? Similar questions arise with the increasing use of private armies by developing countries and failed states. The suggestion has been made that such armies can become involved in peacekeeping operations.[88] If this ever happens, we must ask how private interests can be reconciled with the international community's interest in maintaining peace and security.

The increasing involvement of the private sector, civil society, and individual citizens in a variety of policy domains reflects not only the decreasing autonomy or legitimacy of government, but also the skill revolution posited by James Rosenau.[89] With governments' declining capacity or willingness to deal with all kinds of social problems and their increased partnering with the private sector and civil society to develop and implement policy initiatives, though usually under the guidance of government, these new partners will develop skills normally restricted to the political elite. Airline companies, private security firms, and other private-sector actors will not only develop skills and expertise that help governments deal with a variety of issues, but they will also have to develop procedures and structures more consistent with democratic governance than with the closed world of private profit and competition.

The same can be said for interest groups. Many of these groups possess expertise that governments find invaluable in developing their policies.[90] Public consultation has become the new mantra in public management, as governments reach out to society for help in dealing with public problems.[91] Such groups will find that the more they are involved, the more they will be subjected to the type of scrutiny usually reserved for government. As a result, they will have to pay more attention to accountability and openness, as well as ensuring the reliability of their information sources. What Robert Keohane and Joseph Nye call 'the politics of credibility' will become a much more important part of policy making in a multicentric world, especially in areas such as the environment, human rights, and telecommunications.[92]

A whole new set of interest groups armed with knowledge of computers and information technology has begun to influence emerging policy pertaining to electronic commerce, privacy, copyright protection, and crime control, while a variety of scientific networks have become influential in environmental policy. In the latter case, Karen Litfin warns that 'we should be wary of promoting science as a universalistic source of authority on the brink of replacing state authority,' since states often tailor scientific information to their own interests and scientists are rarely disinterested themselves. Yet she does argue that 'the politics of science is engendering new norms of legitimation and relations of authority beyond state-based politics.'[93] The net result will be that public interest groups, like private-sector and producer interest groups, will have to pay more attention to rules of democratic governance than they may have done in the past.

Whether or not the increasing involvement of non-state actors in the policy process translates into real power beyond the ability to influence agenda setting and problem definition, such as the ability to shape policy design and implementation, remains to be seen. In international environmental policy, for example, Kal Raustiala argues that: 'NGO inclusion does not come at the expense of state power or centrality. The participation of NGOs enhances the ability, in both technocratic and political terms, of states to regulate through the treaty process. As states in concert have expanded and coordinated their regulatory powers in recent decades they have incorporated NGOs; the terms of NGO participation reflect the resources and skills of NGOs as well as the political and technocratic incentives of states. Thus, the expansion of the substantive domain of international regulation has been accompanied by an expanded participatory system which, while strengthening the role of private actors, simultaneously tempers and legitimizes the arrogation of new state powers through new international accords.'[94]

Power shifts are not necessarily 'zero-sum' games, as implied, for example, by responsibilization, whereby the state arrogates to itself a new form of power while divesting itself of responsibility, accountability, and even legitimacy. New partners can develop new power, authority, or influence in the exercise of their new responsibilities – a process perhaps akin to Martha Finnemore's socialization processes (see above, p. 95). While this does not take place necessarily at the expense of state power or in contradiction to it, problems related to accountability, transparency, and democratic governance can still arise. Furthermore, partnership with government does not automatically result in more power or influence along with offloaded responsibilities, as I discuss below.

The Dark Side of Partnering

One of the driving forces behind the responsibilization strategy described by Garland in the criminal justice domain was the desire to reduce government costs by creating governance-at-a-distance. Complementing this trend is what he calls a punitive countertendency that takes the form of law enforcement policies such as new powers of imprisonment, the trying of juveniles in adult court, as is done in Canada, and the 'three strikes and you're out' laws in some U.S. states. Such policies 'frequently involve a knowing and cynical manipulation of the symbols of state power and of the emotions of fear and insecurity which give these symbols their potency.'[95] They are typically developed during times of general insecurity engendered in part by a widely perceived failure on the part of the state to provide economic security to specific social groups.

The result is a disparity between the administrative and the political side of the policy process. The actions of politicians, which are directed at the electorate, are inconsistent with the actions of bureaucrats, whose criteria are 'the rational and efficient pursuit of policy goals,' in line with the new style of public management.[96] On the one hand, there is an emotional discourse of securitization and its complement, insecuritization, or the creation of insecurities through, for example, moral panics, scapegoating and fear-mongering. The message is that society is faced with serious threats that require government intervention. On the other hand, there is a rational discourse of marketization and commodification that foists responsibility for dealing with these threats onto the private sector and the public at large.

Why does this disparity in tone and message exist? One answer lies in a partner that has become a favourite of criminal justice policy–makers in the United Kingdom, the United States, and Canada. One of the consumers in the new management model is victims of crime and their families, who now play an important role in the criminal justice process, particularly in sentencing. The result has been a marriage between the punitive discourse of traumatized victims seeking justice and the law-and-order discourse of politicians seeking votes, both consistent with securitization and insecuritization. The policy result, which reflects marketization and commodification, has been the rise of incapacitation. Offenders who are identified as dangerous to society are warehoused in overcrowded prisons. Success of criminal justice policies is now measured in terms of internal organizational goals rather than of such social goals as reducing crime rates or rehabilitating offenders: 'The new performance indicators tend to measure outputs rather than outcomes, what the organization does, rather than what, if anything, it achieves.'[97]

According to a former crown prosecutor in Canada, privileging victims in the criminal process has dangerous consequences, creating a contradiction between the traditional goals of a criminal trial and the punitive goals of victims.[98] Yet these narrow, punitive goals allow politicians to claim that their policies reflect public opinion even though they in fact stem from broader ideological concerns related to securitization that simply happen to be consistent with those victims' concerns. The performance indicators mentioned above allow the government to claim that it is doing something about dangerous offenders, while shedding responsibility for longer-term social goals, such as crime reduction and rehabilitation. These wider goals then become marketable commodities that the public must acquire from the private sector or through self-regulation.

Another disparity has already been pointed out in drug enforcement and prison construction. The U.S. approach to drug enforcement has had considerable influence on Canadian drug policy. In 1986, for example, shortly after Ronald Reagan announced the new war on drugs, Prime Minister Brian Mulroney announced that there was a serious drug problem in Canada.[99] Despite protestations to the contrary by the Royal Canadian Mounted Police, drug policy makers in Canada ultimately rejected a public health model advocated by policy experts and reaffirmed a prohibition model consistent with the U.S. approach. These examples highlight the importance of discourse in setting the tone for policy debates. Whether it comes from a powerful interest group or a powerful state, pressure to adopt policies that contradict fiscal goals or other policy goals are likely when emotionally driven discourse prevails. The same can be said for gun control policy in Canada. Despite the philosophy of smaller government and outsourcing to private and civil partners, the horror of the Montréal massacre of 1989 and the effective lobbying of victims' families ultimately led to a policy more consistent with big government.

Another more recent example of emotional discourse driving problem definition and policy formulation is the preoccupation by many security professionals with defence against biological or chemical terrorist attacks, or what is called weapons of mass destruction (WMD) terrorism.[100] In the United States, this obsession has led to an extensive – and expensive – program of emergency preparedness, involving the stockpiling of vaccines and antidotes and the development of training programs for emergency response at local, regional, and national levels, including simulations of sarin attacks against major U.S. cities.[101] While the security and economic discourses can be seen to be contradictory within an all-of-government approach (lack of horizontal consistency), the former discourse actually tends to reinforce the latter, whereby calls to or by the state for more security lead to contracting out and partnering. This pattern suggests that the increasing influence and even power of groups such as crime or disaster victims, security professionals, and law enforcers may be a reflection of the power of states to privilege those groups whose demands are consistent with their own ideological goals.

Research on the kinds of issues that mobilize people and that resonate across a variety of interests and cultures would help identify those issues that are most conducive to marshalling widespread and active support. Margaret Keck and Kathryn Sikkink identify two types of issues most characteristic of transnational advocacy networks: those involving bodily harm to vulnerable individuals and legal equality of opportunity.[102] Both have what they call transnational resonance. The first theme would certainly resonate with many victims' rights groups, anti-gun lobby groups, and anti-paedophilia or anti–child pornography groups, as well as those who suggest that WMD terrorism is the greatest threat to national security. Issues such as abortion, euthanasia, doctor-assisted suicide, genetic engineering of food, and use of hormones in milk and meat could also be linked to bodily harm. The last two issues also relate to economic issues of increasing production and widening markets. Research on how 'focusing events'[103] such as airline crashes, natural disasters, and horrific crimes trigger problem definition and policy initiatives would be relevant here.[104]

In a multicentric world, isolated events can have impacts and repercussions that go far beyond the original source of the event (scope), they can move very rapidly through systems and subsystems (intensity), and they can last as long as several years (duration).[105] This is true of actual events, such as a terrorist attack or a flood of refugees, but also of discourse such as policy statements or threat predictions. Ole Waever argues that by linking a problem to security, one is claiming that extraordinary measures are needed to deal with it, even if they are costly or potentially anti-democratic.[106] In the example of WMD terrorism, security professionals linked WMD to the issue of security and, in doing so, implied that extraordinary measures are necessary to deal with the problem. In time, the discourse was reproduced in the U.S. President's 1999 State of the Union Address and other public addresses,[107] and concrete policy initiatives were announced and implemented. The challenge for policy makers is to avoid the snowballing of crises and the triggering of public reactions or institutional responses that can become problems in themselves, looping back to create escalating chains of reaction. The same applies to any partners that government may wish to enlist for help in the policy process. If such partners employ inflammatory or emotion-laden discourse to argue the facts of the case, then they risk distorting the policy process and triggering outputs and outcomes that conflict with other policy initiatives within the same or different policy domains.

Focusing events and emotional discourse, however, also can serve as tools for getting proposals onto the policy agenda. A lobbyist interviewed by John Kingdon used the metaphor of surfing to capture the idea of waiting for the right moment: 'When you lobby for something, what you have to do is put together your coalition, you have to gear up, you have to get your political forces in line, and then you sit there and wait for the fortuitous event ... As I see it, people who are trying to advocate change are like surfers waiting for the big wave. You get out there, you have to be ready to go, you have to be ready to paddle. If you're not ready to paddle when the big wave comes along, you're not going to ride it in.'[108]

A key area for research would be to analyse how such campaigns work and which variables lead to success and which to failure. The role of the media in these processes should be an important part of such research.[109] While many argue that a 'CNN effect' exists, whereby media images and news coverage can directly influence policy decisions, such as intervention in armed conflicts, increasing evidence suggests that the cause-and-effect relationship is not so obvious or direct.[110] Research on communication flows and networks of influence among different elements of society would help to clarify whether increasing involvement, responsibility, or influence of non-state actors actually translate into their being able to effect specific policy outcomes. Research on how governments and politicians use public opinion or the demands of specific interest groups as a governance tool for justifying ideologically driven policy agendas would help to tease out the parameters of the distribution of power across the state/non-state divide.

Conclusion: Opportunities for Policy Research

In this section, I summarize the implications of the preceding analysis for policy making in a multicentric world and propose a research agenda for exploring the possibilities of democratic governance in a world of multiple centres of power.

The Place of the State in a Multicentric World

State power is not a unitary entity, nor is it exercised in a single fashion. In a multicentric world, it interacts with other centres and forms of power, sometimes in concert, sometimes in contradiction. Often the very exercise of state power is to give some power to other actors, such as 'uploading' to international organizations or 'downloading' to provinces. Sometimes it is more a question of 'offloading' responsibility rather than power itself and governing at a distance. Policy making in a multicentric world is more and more an exercise in bargaining and trade-offs. The number of players involved in these bargains and trade-offs, the levels at which they play in the international system of states, the value systems to which they adhere, and the norms that they follow have also multiplied. For the state, this means that to gain control, it sometimes gives up autonomy or even legitimacy to these other players. In some cases, the state appears to be abdicating its responsibility for protecting the public good and downloading or offloading such responsibility to other levels of government or to the private sector and civil society. This renunciation can have serious consequences for maintaining democratic forms of governance, since these sub-state and non-state actors do not necessarily share the same notion of public good as do states that are responsible for the well-being of their citizens.

The uploading of responsibility for much national policy to intergovernmental organizations and international regimes can counterbalance these intra-state trends. Under these circumstances, downloading can expose sub-national levels of government to international norms and regimes, while offloading opens the private sector to the kinds of demands and scrutiny typical of states, such as the watchdog function of the media and NGOs. As for NGOs, although many of them adhere to and promote norms and values that support human rights and social justice, they do not necessarily function democratically. Some NGOs and lobby groups promote norms and values that implicitly or explicitly deny human rights and social justice or apply them selectively to favoured groups while excluding others.

Research projects designed to study the governance structures of this variety of sub- and non-state actors are needed to determine how democratic they are and, if they are not, what the impediments are to making them more so. National standards will become increasingly difficult to sustain unless new mechanisms and structures of communication and co-operation between state and non-state actors are developed to coordinate and integrate multiple centres of decision making and advocacy. Yet such governance at a distance should adhere to democratic principles, and state power should be exercised for the public good and for all citizens, no matter which partner-in-governance is involved.

The Nature of Policy Making in a Multicentric World

Policy making in a multicentric world relies much less on regulation and (re)distribution and much more on exhortation, persuasion, and management of partners created by downloading, offloading and privatization. All this is consistent with the ideology of commodification and marketization of government services. One result is the emergence of a new form of governance, governance at a distance, in which the state retains considerable power even as it devolves responsibility for many aspects of public policy to the private sector and civil society. The state exercises power by directing and integrating the decision making and actions of non-state partners-in-governance – a kind of management function based on a business model of government as provider of services. In this model, however, the notion of the public good and the role of the state as protector of citizens' rights seem to fall through the cracks between the state and its partners. It is here that the implications for democratic governance come to the fore. Partnering can create ambiguities and uncertainties about who is accountable for decisions taken and policies adopted. Securitization and insecuritization have become vehicles for the state and some of its partners to promote policy initiatives that are anti-democratic or that contradict other policies.

Research can determine possibilities for increasing accountability, transparency of procedure, and credibility of information for the private-sector and non-governmental partners that the state relies on in a multicentric world. Research should also be directed to how the state deals with the increasingly complex and chaotic marketplace of ideas in which policy is formulated. If, as Robert Wolfe argues in chapter 8 below, multiple centres of power are better conceived as multiple sources of authority, then research becomes imperative on how the state deals with values, norms, and practices that vary across states, markets, and legal systems, as well as with the shifting loyalties that citizens can have to these different sources of authority.

Key Research Questions

Throughout this chapter, I have identified key areas where policy research could advance knowledge on the constraints and opportunities for policy making in a world of multiple centres of power. I propose seven themes concerning the impact on democratic governance of globalization, decentralization, and privatization:

- the impact of decentralization and downloading on the maintenance of national standards that conform to international norms, and whether harmonization is possible or desirable in a multicentric world

- the impact of privatization on democratic accountability and the notion of the public good
- the maintenance of democratic governance in the face of powerful lobbies, including foreign governments, that use marketization/commodification and securitization/insecuritization to promote practices that do not maintain a balance between economic growth and social justice
- the potential for democratization of private-sector and civil-society actors, including an analysis of their governance structures
- the impact of governance at a distance on democracy and on governance, including how to make economic liberalization more compatible with social justice
- the role of information technologies in the generation of public debate on important policy issues, including the use by the state or others of focusing events in contentious policy areas
- the relationship between the different roles that people adopt – citizen, client, customer, consumer, producer – and the duties and responsibilities vis-à-vis the state and the public good that are attached to them

These research themes attempt to go beyond the established wisdom that is reflected in the two ideological trends that form the focus of this chapter. They are based on three assumptions: that democratic governance can achieve both economic and social goals; that a balance can be maintained between the imperatives of economic competitiveness and those of social justice; and that national security and social welfare can both be achieved without playing on the insecurities of people. The challenge for the policy community is to find ways of transforming these assumptions into concrete, attainable goals.

NOTES

1 Jocelyn Bourgon, 'Building a Strong Public Policy Capacity,' Address to the Policy Conference, 'Policy Research: Creating Linkages,' Ottawa, 1 October 1998, 3.
2 Ibid., 3–4.
3 To call this kind of research 'multidisciplinary' or 'interdisciplinary' is probably misleading. 'Multi-' is too patchwork and lacks the horizontal integration that Bourgon emphasizes. 'Inter-' is more integrative, even col-

laborative, but lacks the connotation of dynamic movement across boundaries that the prefix 'trans-' captures.

4 Ole Waever coined this term. See, for example, Ole Waever, 'Securitization and Desecuritization,' in Ronnie D. Lipschutz, ed., *On Security* (New York: Columbia University Press, 1995), 46–86.

5 See, for example, Ronald D. Crelinsten, 'The Discourse and Practice of Counter-terrorism in Liberal Democracies,' *Australian Journal of Politics and History* 44, no. 3 (September 1998): 389–413.

6 'Debates pitting those who argue that international politics is a zero–sum game dominated by concerns for security, autonomy, and relative gains against those who believe that institutionalized cooperation can help overcome market failures no longer excite much attention or drive new insights.' K.J. Holsti, 'America Meets the "English School": State Interests in International Society,' *Mershon International Studies Review* 41, no. 2 (1997): 275–80.

7 Subtitle inspired by Susan Strange, *The Retreat of the State: The Diffusion of Power in the World Economy* (Cambridge: Cambridge University Press, 1996), 66.

8 Stephen D. Krasner, 'Regimes and the Limits of Realism: Regimes as Autonomous Variables,' in Krasner, ed., *International Regimes* (Ithaca, NY: Cornell University Press, 1983), 355–68.

9 Mark W. Zacher, 'The Decaying Pillars of the Westphalian Temple: Implications for International Order and Governance,' in James N. Rosenau and Ernst-Otto Czempiel, eds., *Governance without Government: Order and Change in World Politics* (Cambridge: Cambridge University Press, 1992), 58–101.

10 See Strange, *The Retreat of the State.*

11 Yale H. Ferguson and Richard W. Mansbach, *Polities: Authority, Identities, and Change* (Columbia: University of South Carolina Press, 1996), 48, cited in William H. McNeill, 'Territorial States Buried Too Soon,' *Mershon International Studies Review* 41, no. 2 (November 1997): 271. See also Stephen Clarkson, chapter 5, below, for a model that uses the concept of nesting.

12 Peter B. Evans, Dietrich Rueschemeyer, and Theda Skocpol, eds., *Bringing the State Back In* (New York: Cambridge University Press, 1985); Thomas Risse-Kappen, ed., *Bringing Transnational Relations Back In: Non-State Actors, Domestic Structures and International Institutions* (Cambridge: Cambridge University Press, 1995).

13 McNeill, 'Territorial States Buried Too Soon.'

14 Ibid., 271. Robert Keohane and Joseph Nye, in a recent discussion of the information revolution, also strike this theme of the continuing importance

of military force and the power of states. See Robert O. Keohane and Joseph S. Nye, Jr, 'Power and Interdependence in the Information Age,' *Foreign Affairs* 77, no. 5 (September/October 1998): 81–94.

15 James N. Rosenau, *Turbulence in World Politics: A Theory of Change and Continuity* (Princeton, NJ: Princeton University Press, 1990); James N. Rosenau, *Along the Domestic–Foreign Frontier: Exploring Governance in a Turbulent World* (Cambridge: Cambridge University Press, 1997). For other treatments of these developments, see Strange, *The Retreat of the State*; Risse-Kappen, ed., *Bringing Transnational Relations Back In*.

16 Margaret E. Keck and Kathryn Sikkink, *Activists beyond Borders: Advocacy Networks in International Politics* (Ithaca, NY: Cornell University Press, 1998).

17 Arjun Appadurai, *Modernity at Large: Cultural Dimensions of Globalization* (Minneapolis: University of Minnesota Press, 1996).

18 James N. Rosenau, 'The Future of Politics,' presentation to Assembly of the World Academy of Art and Science on the Global Century, Vancouver, 7 November 1998, 8.

19 Ibid., 8–9.

20 James N. Rosenau and Mary Durfee, *Thinking Theory Thoroughly: Coherent Approaches to an Incoherent World* (Boulder, Col.: Westview Press, 1995), 31–56.

21 Rosenau, 'The Future of Politics,' 3. Stephen Clarkson, too, decries the use of *post-* labels in chapter 5, below.

22 See in particular Philippe Le Prestre (chapter 7) and Robert Wolfe (chapter 8) in this book.

23 Susan Strange, 'Cave! hic dragones: A Critique Of Regime Analysis,' in Krasner, ed., *International Regimes*, 337–354.

24 Ibid.

25 In a more recent work, Mark Zacher uses the phrase 'cobwebs of agreements' to describe the international regimes of transportation and communication. See Mark W. Zacher with Brent A. Sutton, *Governing Global Networks: International Regimes for Transportation and Communications* (Cambridge: Cambridge University Press, 1996), 232.

26 Assistant Deputy Ministers' Sub-Committee for Global Challenges and Opportunities, *Canada 2005, Draft Interim Report: Global Challenges and Opportunities* (25 February 1997), chap. 11, available at http://policyresearch.schoolnet.ca/keydocs/global/11governance-e.htm

27 Janice Thomson, 'Explaining the Regulation of Transnational Practices: A State-Building Approach,' in Rosenau and Czempiel, eds., *Governance without Government*, 195–218.

28 Martha Finnemore, *National Interests in International Society* (Ithaca, NY: Cornell University Press, 1996), cited in Keck and Sikkink, *Activists beyond Borders*, 3.
29 Roderick A. Macdonald, 'Metaphors of Multiplicity: Civil Society, Regimes, and Legal Pluralism,' *Arizona Journal of International and Comparative Law* 15, no. 1 (1998): 77. Thanks to Robert Wolfe for bringing Roderick Macdonald's work to my attention.
30 For a lucid discussion of these two viewpoints, see Zacher and Sutton, *Governing Global Networks*, chap. 2.
31 William J. Chambliss, 'State-Organized Crime: The American Society of Criminology, 1988 Presidential Address,' *Criminology* 27, no. 2 (1989): 183–208.
32 Two examples are the expulsion by France of Palestinian terrorist Abu Daoud in 1977 and the expulsion by Italy of Kurdish terrorist Abdullah Öcalan in 1999. See Ronald D. Crelinsten, 'Terrorism and Counter-terrorism in a Multi-centric World: Challenges and Opportunities,' *Terrorism and Political Violence* 11, no. 4 (1999): 170–96; reprinted in Max Taylor and John Horgan, eds., The *Future of Terrorism* (London: Frank Cass, 2000), 170–96.
33 On the cultural relativism debate, see Jack Donnelly, *International Human Rights* (Boulder, Col.: Westview, 1993), 34–8. See also Johan Galtung, *Human Rights in Another Key* (Cambridge: Polity Press, 1994).
34 Macdonald, 'Metaphors of Multiplicity,' 77.
35 Thomson, 'Explaining the Regulation of Transnational Practices.'
36 Mark Zacher and Brent Sutton suggest that the two approaches are not necessarily mutually exclusive: 'Power relations and the use of coercion are important to regimes based on mutual interests.' Zacher and Sutton, *Governing Global Networks*, 232.
37 Keck and Sikkink, *Activists beyond Borders*, 34.
38 Ibid., 35.
39 Ibid.
40 Benedikt Fischer, 'Prohibition as the Art of Political Diplomacy: The Benign Guises of the "War on Drugs" in Canada,' and Patricia G. Erickson and Jennifer Butters, 'The Emerging Harm Reduction Movement: The De-Escalation of the War on Drugs?,' in Eric Jensen and Jurg Gerber, eds., *The New War on Drugs: Symbolic Politics and Criminal Justice Policy* (Cincinnati: Anderson Publishing, 1998), 157–75 and 177–96, respectively.
41 Keck and Sikkink, *Activists beyond Borders*, 197.
42 Bob Deacon with Michelle Hulse and Paul Stubbs, *Global Social Policy: International Organizations and the Future of Welfare* (London: Sage, 1997).
43 Erickson and Butters, 'The Emerging Harm Reduction Movement.'

44 Ethan A. Nadelmann, *Cops across Borders: The Internationalization of US Criminal Law Enforcement* (University Park: Pennsylvania State University Press, 1993), 231.
45 Keck and Sikkink, *Activists beyond Borders*, 12.
46 Ibid., 216.
47 However, if the judge's involvement in Amnesty International had been interpreted as an asset, giving him certain knowledge and awareness not accessible to his colleagues that informed his judgment, then the appeal could have failed.
48 Keohane and Nye, 'Power and Interdependence in the Information Age,' 92.
49 Ibid., 94.
50 For an excellent discussion of the problems faced by undercover agents, see Gary T. Marx, *Undercover: Police Surveillance in America* (Berkeley: University of California Press, 1988).
51 Ronnie D. Lipschutz, 'Reconstructing World Politics: The Emergence of Global Civil Society,' *Millennium* 21 (Winter 1992): 389–420, cited in Karen Litfin, 'Sovereignty in World Ecopolitics,' *Mershon International Studies Review* 41, no. 2 (1997): 176. See also Mary C. Bateson, 'Beyond Sovereignty: An Emerging Global Civilization,' in R.B.J. Walker and S.H. Mendlovitz, eds., *Contending Sovereignties: Redefining Political Community* (Lynne Reinner, 1990), 145–58.
52 *Le Monde* (24 December 1981), cited in David Macey, *The Lives of Michel Foucault: A Biography* (New York: Vintage Books, 1995), 442–3.
53 'Face aux gouvernements, les droits de l'homme,' *Actes: Les cahiers d'action juridique* 54 (Summer 1986): 22; first published in *Libération*, (1 July 1984), cited in Macey, *The Lives of Michel Foucault*, 437–8.
54 Keck and Sikkink, *Activists beyond Borders*, 33.
55 Ibid.
56 Ibid.
57 Policy Research Initiative, 'Sustaining Growth, Human Development, and Social Cohesion in a Global World,' February 1999, 27.
58 K.J. Holsti. 'America Meets the "English School": State Interests in International Society,' 278. The two books reviewed are Martha Finnemore, *National Interests in International Society*, and Rick Fawn and Jeremy Larkins, eds., *International Society after the Cold War* (New York: St. Martin's Press, 1996).
59 Keith G. Banting, 'Social Policy,' in Bruce Doern, Leslie Pal, and Brian Tomlin, eds., *Border Crossings: The Internationalization of Canadian Public Policy*, (Toronto: Oxford University Press, 1996), 39.
60 Ibid., 43.

61 Ibid., 45.

62 Leslie Pal, *Beyond Policy Analysis: Public Issue Management in Turbulent Times* (Scarborough, Ont.: ITP Nelson, 1997), 217–24.

63 Ibid., 217.

64 Bruce Doern and Richard W. Phidd, *Canadian Public Policy: Ideas, Structure, Process*, second edition (Scarborough, Ont.: Nelson Canada, 1992), 66.

65 Banting, 'Social Policy.'

66 Ibid., 40.

67 'Finance is the only department to have one of its own officials posted to the embassy to the OECD; all other departments must rely on officials at the Department of Foreign Affairs and International Trade, who normally have little experience with their issues.' Ibid., 54. However, Bruce Doern and John Kirton suggest that Finance, too, has suffered from budgetary restrictions: 'Even the relatively powerful Finance Department has had to withdraw some of its hard-won finance counsellors from G7 embassies abroad.' See G. Bruce Doern and John Kirton, 'Foreign Policy,' in Doern, Pal and Tomlin, eds., *Border Crossings*, 250.

68 Banting, 'Social Policy,' 42.

69 For a discussion of the impact of economic liberalization and structural adjustment programs on Third World countries and its relationship with democratization, see Mahmood Monshipouri, 'State Prerogatives, Civil Society, and Liberalization,' *Ethics and International Affairs* 11 (1997): 233–51.

70 For examples, see Stephen Clarkson, chapter 5, below, and the chapters on agricultural, telecommunication, investment, and banking and securities policy in Doern, Pal and Tomlin, eds., *Border Crossings*.

71 This description is based on an analysis of such trends in the United States. See David Guimond, 'Prisons of Industry: The History of Private Prisons,' unpublished master's thesis, Department of Criminology, University of Ottawa, 1998.

72 See, for example, Matthew G. Devost, Brian K. Houghton, and Neal Allen Pollard, 'Information Terrorism: Political Violence in the Information Age,' *Terrorism and Political Violence* 9, no. 1 (1997): 72–83. In strict definitional terms, many of these phenomena are really new forms of sabotage, rather than new forms of terrorism, since they rarely impose demands on the targets or other parties.

73 See the Nizkor Project web site, http://www2.nizkor.org/index.html

74 Of course, Ken McVay has his critics, who feel that active engagement with hatemongers will achieve nothing and that such people should be prosecuted and punished.

75 David Garland, 'The Limits of the Sovereign State: Strategies of Crime Con-

trol in Contemporary Society,' *British Journal of Criminology* 36, no. 4 (Autumn 1996): 445–71.

76 Ibid., 454.

77 Litfin, 'Sovereignty in World Ecopolitics,' 169–70.

78 Garland, 'The Limits of the Sovereign State,' 453.

79 Malcolm Anderson, Monica den Boer, Peter Cullen, William Gilmore, Charles Raab, and Neil Walker, *Policing the European Union* (Oxford: Clarendon Press, 1995), 161. For a detailed analysis of how a risk society functions, see Richard V. Ericson and Kevin D. Haggerty, *Policing the Risk Society* (Toronto: University of Toronto Press, 1997).

80 Pal, *Beyond Policy Analysis*, 54–62.

81 Ibid., 61–2.

82 Garland, 'The Limits of the Sovereign State,' 456.

83 For an analysis of university mission statements in the United Kingdom that reflect the new public management approach while still seeking to maintain control and legitimacy, see Ian Connell and Dauriusz Galasinski, 'Academic Mission Statements: An Exercise in Negotiation,' *Discourse and Society* 9, no. 4 (October 1998): 44–61.

84 Pal, *Beyond Policy Analysis*, 55.

85 For a discussion of security, immigration, and counter-terrorism, see Crelinsten, 'The Discourse and Practice of Counter-Terrorism.'

86 Family members were puzzled when TWA officials began asking them about the smoking habits of those they had lost in the explosion, until they realized that such information was intended for use by the company's insurer in order to 'actuarialize' the worth of each passenger. Comments by a panellist at a plenary session on the role of the media in disaster response, International Conference on Aviation Safety and Security in the 21st Century, organized by the White House Commission on Aviation Safety and Security and George Washington University, Washington, DC, January 1997.

87 A few weeks into the refugee crisis in Kosovo in spring 1999, the Pentagon announced that it was contracting out to private airline companies to use 747s to transport humanitarian aid to refugee camps in Albania and Macedonia. Remarks by Ken Bacon during Pentagon press briefing, 3 April 1999, broadcast live on CNN International.

88 David Shearer, 'Outsourcing War,' *Foreign Policy* (Fall 1998): 68–81.

89 See Crelinsten, 'Terrorism and Counter-terrorism in a Multi-centric World.'

90 For a discussion of the role of epistemic communities in global social policy, see Deacon with Hulse and Stubbs, *Global Social Policy*, 197–202.

91 See also Pal, *Beyond Policy Analysis*, 217–21.

92 Keohane and Nye, 'Power and Interdependence in the Information Age,' 89–92.
93 Litfin, 'Sovereignty in World Ecopolitics,' 193–4.
94 Kal Raustiala, 'States, NGOs, and International Environmental Institutions,' *International Studies Quarterly* 41, no. 4 (December 1997): 736.
95 Garland, 'The Limits of the Sovereign State,' 460.
96 Ibid., 459.
97 Ibid., 458.
98 In an interview at the launching of his 1998 book, *Getting Away with Murder,* David Paciocco of the University of Ottawa's Faculty of Law stated, 'We cannot conduct trials with a view to satisfying victims without risking the conviction of the innocent. The victim's suffering is the responsibility of the civil process ... and civil suits.' James Careless, 'Law Professor Gets Used to Fame,' *University of Ottawa Gazette* 11 no. 5 (4 December 1998).
99 Fischer, 'Prohibition as the Art of Political Diplomacy,' 163.
100 For a discussion that relates this discourse to features of a multicentric world, see Crelinsten, 'Terrorism and Counter-terrorism in a Multi-centric World.'
101 Ibid.; Ehud Sprinzak, 'The Great Superterrorism Scare,' *Foreign Policy* (Fall 1998): 110–24.
102 Keck and Sikkink, *Activists beyond Borders*, 204.
103 John W. Kingdon, 'How Do Issues Get on Public Policy Agendas?' W.J. Wilson, ed., *Sociology and the Public Agenda* (Newbury Park, CA: Sage, 1993), 40–50.
104 See Joel Best, ed., *Images of Issues: Typifying Contemporary Social Problems,* second edition (New York: Aldine de Gruyter, 1995).
105 Rosenau, *Turbulence in World Politics*, 298–305.
106 See, for example, Waever, 'Securitization and Desecuritization.' For a rigorous and comprehensive application of this approach to Barry Buzan's broadened framework of security analysis, see Barry Buzan, Ole Waever, and Jaap de Wilde, *Security: A New Framework for Analysis* (Boulder, Col.: Lynne Rienner, 1998), chap. 2.
107 See, for example, 'Remarks by the President on Keeping America Secure for the 21st Century,' National Academy of Sciences, Washington, DC, 22 January 1999, Press Release from the White House, Office of the Press Secretary; downloaded from the White House web site http://www.whitehouse.gov/WH/New/html/19990122-7214.html
108 Kingdon, 'How Do Issues Get on Public Policy Agendas?' 45.
109 For the role of the media in crisis management, see Ronald D. Crelinsten, 'The Impact of Television on Terrorism and Crisis Situations: Implications

for Public Policy,' *Journal of Contingencies and Crisis Management* 2, no. 2 (1994): 61–72; 'Television and Terrorism: Implications for Crisis Management and Policymaking,' *Terrorism and Political Violence* 9, no. 4 (1997): 8–32.

110 See Stephen A. Cambone, *Kodak Moments, Inescapable Momentum, and the World Wide Web: Has the Infocomm Revolution Transformed Diplomacy?* (McLean, Va.: Center for Information Strategy and Policy, 1996); Nik Gowing, 'Media Coverage: Help or Hindrance in Conflict Prevention?' in Stephen Badsey, ed., *The Media and International Security* (London: Frank Cass, 2000), 203–26.

Part Two

The State and Multiple Centres of Power

4. Governance of Politics without a Centre

Vincent Della Sala

Globalization has contributed to an ever-more-apparent paradox in the politics of developed liberal democracies. While there is agreement on the principles and structures of liberal democracy, there is a growing malaise over its central institutions and processes and distrust of its principal participants. This dissatisfaction manifests itself in a number of ways. There are doubts about the capacity of the national state and its actors to manage economic and social relations in an emerging global society and great suspicion concerning agreements reached by political, economic, or social elites, especially over institutional and constitutional matters. This has occurred even though there are no serious alternatives to, and unprecedented acceptance of, liberal democracy and market capitalism.

This chapter argues that this paradox reflects the tensions in a society that no longer has political epicentres. Politics in advanced industrialized societies has been based on a number of premises: that national identity and the national state are the sources of political integration and community; that the state is the repository of political authority and governance of social and economic life; and that legitimate authority in liberal democracy is expressed through formal political institutions, particularly representative assemblies. These premises provide central sites for the generation and mobilization of norms and processes for the governance of society.

The chapter's objectives are two-fold. Its first goal is to engage two strands in the academic literature that deal with the political and social consequences of globalization. One trend is the argument that globalization undermines political authority and the capacity of the state. State actors must remain sensitive not only to how policy choices will be received by the international investment community, but also to how decisions taken beyond state borders generate new demands on them. This pressure has led to a range of characterizations of the state; it is said to be shrinking, becoming competitive, being hollowed out, fragmenting, and so on, with such descriptions all pointing to limited state capacity. The pressures on the national state come not only from external forces, primarily in the form of highly mobile capital, but also from internal forces such as sub-national governments and social movements.

The perception of the erosion of the state's monopoly of political authority has generated another trend: a concern with the notion of governance. The emphasis here is not simply on institutions of governing but on the processes and range of actors involved in making decisions that determine collective goods. It reflects a multiplicity of sites and levels of decision–making. Moreover, it stems from the view that there remains a need for some form of regulation of social, economic, and political life but that the domains and instruments may be changing.

While both strands in the academic literature have opened avenues of research, especially with respect to new actors and arenas where decision making may take place, they remain limited in providing a way to understand the evolution of democratic politics in an era of globalization. While it may appear that the state's authority is diminishing in some areas – for instance, monetary policy – it also is clear that it continues to intervene in many areas of economic and social life. For example, the U.S. anti-trust suits against Microsoft and Intel suggest that the state's retreat from economic life is far from complete. Moreover, the need to provide an economic and social infrastructure to create a competitive environment requires the state to affect outcomes. The literature on state decline and multi-level governance has largely ignored questions about the type of state structures that may emerge and the type of democracy that globalization may generate in an advanced industrialized state such as Canada. Certain parts of the state – for example, the executive – have been strengthened by the same pressures that may be weakening state capacity overall. This chapter argues that in addition to a 'hollowing out' of the state, there has been a 'hardening' of its shell; the displacement of national state authority requires state structures that are less permeable to penetration from interests and demands emanating from society. In turn, a hollow state leads to claims of less inclusive representation in decision making and of a reduced space for policy-making discussion.

The second objective of the chapter is to illustrate the erosion of several of the political epicentres in advanced industrialized societies in the face of globalization, and the consequences that this change may have for the type of democracy that may emerge. It argues that a hollowing out and hardening of the state, even in an environment of multilevel governance, risks being exclusionary and less permeable to groups in society. It illustrates this concept focusing on the impact of European integration – as an instance of multiple centres of power – on Italy. There can be little doubt that there are few better examples of the effects of greater economic integration than those found in the European Union. It has assumed powers in central areas of economic life, such as monetary policy, and has become an important site for governance of most areas of economic and social life. While a great deal of work has looked at the institutions and processes of the European Union, less attention has been given to the impact of integration on member states and societies. In addition, there has been a great deal written about the political changes that have taken place in Italy, much of which traces the transformation of domestic political conditions. However, changes to the structures of government and governance may be the result of some of the consequences of economic integration – namely, a hollowing out of the state and changes to the structures of liberal democracy.

The chapter has two sections. The first examines the literature that discusses the decline of the state. It points out some of the weaknesses of both the proponents of state decline as well as those who argue for the state's adaptability. It shows that the pressures for a hollowing out of the state and the displacement of its authority lead to the loss of political epicentres. The second section examines, as an example of governance of politics without a centre, the case of Italy within an integrated Europe.

Hollow, Less Permeable States

There is no shortage of writing being produced that focuses on a crisis of governing advanced liberal democracies. There is even the occasional admission that these governments might not have the ability that they once had to decide outcomes. Susan Strange emphasizes this change: 'Today it seems as if the heads of governments may be the last to recognize that they and their ministers have lost the authority over national societies and economies that they used to have.'[1] There is a growing sense that the political architecture of the modern era – with its foundations in representational democracy and the territorial sovereignty of national states – no longer has the capacity to claim authority to govern complex societies. Claus Offe is more emphatic than Strange: 'Many of those political agents that were well known to political analysts of earlier times and were taken for granted by them seem to have lost, in the West and the East alike, much of the evidence of their capacity for action.'[2] The sources of these crises are often found in social fragmentation and the force of markets as modes of regulation in a world of highly mobile capital.

Perhaps no other feature of politics has drawn more attention in the recent literature examining crisis or decline than the modern state. Concern about its role in political and social life is not new, as observers have grappled with questions about its usefulness as a conceptual tool for a long time. However, the current debate about the state questions its constitutive elements – territory, population, sovereignty – rather than its relevance in social and political life.

In comparative politics, discussion about the state in the first decades after the Second World War centred on interests. A great deal of the debate dealt with two questions: was it really important to study the state if what mattered were the preferences and interests of individuals? In whose interest did the state rule?[3] In both camps, the state was incidental to the definition of interests or the structures that formed them and on whose behalf the state ruled. The architecture of the state and its various institutional forms was of secondary importance to its role in the articulation and promotion of interests. For observers such as Ralph Miliband and David Easton, whether the state was highly centralized or fragmented, or based on a consensual instead of a majoritarian form of liberal democracy, did not change its nature or its capacity to act on, or on behalf of, interests.

The irony is that the state was being made incidental by observers at a time when the range of state capacity was extending into new areas of economic and social regulation. While comparative politics was debating the relative merits of pluralism and positivist approaches, states throughout the industrialized world were pushing the boundaries for the provision of collective goods and social rights. What was incidental in a large part of the literature was undergoing a significant transformation in expectations of its capacity to affect political, social and economic outcomes.

The positions began to reverse in the 1970s, when scholars noted a crisis of the state as they began to pose questions about state capacity and political authority just as the golden age of postwar capitalism began to decline. No longer incidental, the state was brought back in only to have questions about its relevance raised again.[4] However, the challenges that it faces; come not from conceptual frameworks that choose to minimize the importance of structures but from political and economic changes that question its essential features. As Linda Weiss argues, 'The state is being killed off not so much by the appearance of new perspectives, but by the emergence of allegedly new tendencies in the world at large.'[5] The alleged developments fall under the umbrella of globalization, understood primarily as the transcendence of national boundaries as the basis for commanding sovereignty and defining territorial limits.[6]

There is a school of thought that argues for the diffusion, disintegration, decline, or eventual disappearance of the political authority of the national state. The state's monopoly on political authority in the modern era is being 'eclipsed' by, 'reinvigorated political faith in the efficacy of markets with a combined rediscovery of civil society.'[7] This has led authors such as Susan Strange, Bob Jessop, R.A.W. Rhodes, and James Rosenau to indicate some of the ways in which state authority has seeped, flowed, or drained 'upwards,' 'sideways,' or 'downwards' to other public and private institutions.[8] The sources for this decline are found not simply among the velocity and mobility of capital but in a number of social and economic factors that have disrupted the symmetry of the state's authority with territorial boundaries and weakened individuals' sense of identity with political communities.

There is no dearth of evidence to support the claim made by the decline-of-the-state argument. Authority for collective decisions may be identified in a number of different arenas that a few decades ago would not have merited consideration as a rival to the state. For instance, even the highly centralized European states such as France and Italy created sub-national levels of government in the 1970s and 1980s. At the same time, they were transferring a great deal of authority to the European Union. Governments throughout the Organization for Economic Cooperation and Development (OECD) 'downloaded' a number of responsibilities to 'lower' levels throughout the 1990s. As sub-national governments had to respond to greater demands, they insisted on greater constitutional and jurisdictional powers. Moreover, it was not just constitutional structures such as regional governments that began to assume many of the powers held by the national state.

Recent decades have seen new structures that cross the public and private divides and involve a number of participants, such as non-governmental organizations, that are not recognized in constitutions but have become responsible for a larger share of the delivery of public goods and services.[9]

The steady rise of supranational structures accelerated in the 1990s, with different results among parts of the industrialized world. The decade saw the European Union achieve a single market for most good and services, enshrine the notion of European citizenship in its constitutional process, and launch the single currency for a common financial market. Supranationalists and intergovernmentalists may argue about the nature of the European Union, but it is indisputable that authority for many areas of the public realm, such as agriculture and monetary policy, is increasingly in the hands of structures that rival the state. More important, the recent evolution of the European Union has been a response to the recognition that the territorially defined limits of the state were inadequate in an interdependent global economy.[10] Similar arguments about creating continental authorities as a way of responding to global challenges were put forth in favour of the North American Free Trade Agreement (NAFTA).

It is not only formal supranational political structures such as the European Union that are displacing state authority. The importance of assessments of bond-rating agencies such as Standard and Poor's and Moody's for debates about budgetary politics is an indication that social forces beyond national borders are curtailing the boundaries for state action.[11] As capital has become more mobile, and new instruments have been created to find new ways to use capital, the role of the agencies has grown as they provide a way of assessing risk.[12] Their influence on bond markets, and possibly the cost of financing public expenditures and debt, ensure that decisions by monetary authorities are made with an eye beyond the demands of their citizens. As Robert Boyer and Daniel Drache argue, 'Powerful financial markets monitor many, if not all, aspects of state spending and, therefore, are able to set broad policy goals with respect to employment, social welfare policy, taxation and the like.'[13] They do indicate how the mobility of capital affects decisions made in the name of the public good. It is not just financial markets that may be replacing the authority of national governments. Social movements are increasingly working across borders and assuming greater decision-making responsibilities in areas such as the environment, human and civil rights, famine relief, and international development.

The political authority of the state is not only being displaced 'upwards, sideways and downwards.' In some cases it has disappeared.[14] Political authority is often reconstituted as private authority with the market regulating social and economic life while paying no heed to defined policy goals such as employment or the environment. While many forms of privatization within OECD countries have led to the creation of arm's-length regulatory bodies, especially in previously state-held utilities, other forms have led to less clearly defined public authority. For instance, in the area of telecommunication, states have tried to retain a regulatory role, especially in the firms that they have sold to the private sector. However, technological changes and shake-ups in corporate structures resulting from corporate alliances and mergers make this exercise problematic. The rise of the internet as a form of communication and economic activity highlights the difficulty in locating public and state authority, regardless of the telecommunication regime that may be established.

The proponents of decline are careful to point out that the disappearance of the state is not imminent and that it remains a significant, if not the primary, source of political authority. Many scholars question whether the state, in the face of challenges to its monopoly of authority, has become obsolete. By recognizing the limits on the state's ability to act effectively, they begin to question its legitimacy. While proponents may be right in pointing out this trend, it is less clear what it means for the continued importance of the state. At what point does the state become obsolete? How much political authority must be displaced before the doubts about the legitimacy of the state become significant enough that serious consideration is given to replacing it? Is it possible that these trends will lead simply to a different kind of state that retains the essential ingredients of an ultimate political authority governing a population within a defined territory? For instance, there is some debate about whether this is the future of the European Union. Moreover, the 'downward' move of state authority may be part of a demand for the creation of a state that is currently a sub-national unit, as is the case for Quebec secession.

Paul Hirst makes an interesting and convincing case for the challenge to the authority of the state.[15] It is interesting in that he has serious doubts about many of the arguments made about globalization; and it is convincing because it is based on more than just the economic determinism of globalization proponents such as Kenichi Ohmae and Richard O'Brien.[16] Hirst points to a pluralism of forces in society that have questioned, from both the left and the right of the political spectrum, an interventionist state. His call for a prominent role for associations as another form of governance, alongside the state and market, is intended as a way of ensuring participatory forms of governance.[17] Self-governing associations run largely at the local level by citizens who voluntarily choose them will replace the postwar state, with its emphasis on universality. For instance, health care will not be in the hands of a national health service that provides a set menu of services across a country. Rather, decisions will be made and controlled by self-governing bodies with direct participation of concerned citizens who will make choices such as those between hospital beds and home care. Hirst contends that recent changes in civil society will render intolerable a universal, monolithic state that provides a standard set of goods and services that emanates from the centre.[18]

However, Hirst does not see the state disappearing in the near future, nor does he expect that it will be replaced as the primary source of governance. In fact, the state will retain a number of essential duties, including collecting revenues to pay for the services that will be provided by associations. Taxpayers will, according to Hirst's prescription, be allowed to choose a set number of associations to which the state will direct a portion of their income taxes. The state will serve as an intermediary, channelling funds from citizens to the associations of their choice, but its role in the delivery of most services will stop there.[19]

Hirst provides a compelling argument that illustrates some of the ways in which the authority of the state has been displaced and some of the long-term consequences that may result. However, as with many of the proponents of decline, he does not address the question at which point the state will have lost so many of its responsibilities that there will be questions about its legitimacy. For instance, a state that serves to collect taxes but is not responsible for providing services will have a difficult time in either limiting itself to that role or in maintaining its legitimacy as a revenue collector. Hirst forgets that tax collecting, along with waging war, was one of the functions that helped create the modern state. While there may be a plurality of authorities and forms of governance emerging, with more avenues for participation, citizens may not view all the multiple centres of power equally. If the state is going to continue to be the tax collector, we can assume two outcomes. As it has greater control of the purse strings, citizens will see it as having greater authority. As it is responsible for taking money from individuals but is not seen delivering the services that they feel are important, citizens may question the state's legitimacy. Hirst's argument reveals the tension that those who see the state in decline face when they point out the sources of erosion yet claim that the state will remain a central governing site. He at least makes a case for the type of democracy – associative democracy – that may emerge in a politics without a centre.

It is not just the Realists in the field of international relations who argue that the reports of the decline of the national state are largely overstated. There is a range of scholarship that does not contest the claims made about the challenges to state authority. However, it contends that these arguments present a partial picture that ignores the adaptability of political structures. For instance, one of the assumptions about some of the globalization arguments is that not only is there emerging a global economic order but that this means the eventual disappearance of national diversity in approaches to governing the economy. The volume edited by Robert Wade and Suzanne Berger addresses the continued diversity of national economic models in the face of global capitalism.[20] There is evidence of convergence, not simply in areas such as fiscal, monetary and social policies, but also in production processes. The contributors examine a wide variety of cases, from convergence on monetary policy between France and Germany to the adoption of production and workplace processes made famous in Japan. The extent to which convergence has taken place differs, but the contributions conclude that it is too early to speak of the end of national diversity. This implies that if there is still room to account for national differences, then governments retain the authority to make decisions that will lead to different ways of governing economic and social life.

Few would argue that there has not been any lessening in the differences between the policy choices of industrialized states in the last two decades. Moreover, a great deal of this is the result of a deliberate choice to co-ordinate policy or in some instances, such as the European Union and NAFTA, of structural constraints imposed by choices made with other states. The conceptual issue that remains is how much coordination and decisions making taking place in conjunction with member states is required before convergence occurs, with an attendant loss of state authority? Policy convergence can be fascinating in itself, but it may tell us little about what is happening to the state. A lessening of diversity may be the result just as likely of weakened state authority as of an enhanced state that enters into agreements with other member states.

Policy convergence, however, may be a useful vehicle for looking at state capacity. Much of the state-decline argument assumes that once some authority other than the state assumes responsibility for governance, state capacity in general diminishes. Defining state capacity and its limits is not an easy task. John Ikenberry argues that it refers to 'the differential ability of states to assert control over political outcomes.'[21] But, as Linda Weiss points out, it is impossible to talk about 'generalized state capacity' – one can look only at capacities in specific areas.[22] It is difficult to define the limits of political outcomes over which the state is supposed to assert control. By using a broad definition of state capacity, any argument about decline that focuses on loss of authority in one area will lead to questions about the decline of the state overall. Moreover, it may overlook the possibility that the state may have greater control over some political outcomes once it has had its authority to control other outcomes displaced. This is a different version of a meaner, leaner state having greater authority than one that tries to do all things without having the capacity to affect outcomes. For instance, when a state turns over to the private sector its industrial holdings and the delivery of services, it ceases to be a major employer. As it no longer has to deal with labour as the employer, it may be easier for the state to affect outcomes in areas such as labour market policies and cuts in public spending.

The claim by Weiss that to speak of generalized state capacity is meaningless points out one of the problems that many state-decline arguments face – while states may be giving up authority in some areas, they may have their capacity enhanced in some others. For instance, essentially the same information technology that facilitates the mobility of capital also strengthens surveillance and control of individuals by political authorities. The United States has seen, in the same period of the withdrawal of the state in economic regulation, its prison population reach record levels and the prison industry become a major economic activity. The move to a cashless economy makes available data about individuals' behaviour, choices, and preferences that could make it easier for states to collect taxes. Moreover, while states may be withdrawing from the regulation of some parts of economic life, they are under pressure to expand further into other areas of social life, especially those that were deemed to be in the personal sphere until the postwar period.[23] This is the case with the rise of reproductive technologies, which are forcing states to make decisions about issues such as surrogate parenting and, perhaps in the not-too-distant future, genetic composition.

There also may be pressure for state capacity to be extended to more and more areas of what might be termed a 'risk society.'[24] For instance, growing awareness of the health risks of certain dietary patterns, products, and ways of life has meant that many states are assuming greater responsibility for, at a minimum, warning their citizens of the risks involved. While governments in industrialized countries have been restructuring their health care systems, leading many observers to speculate on diminished capacity, states have faced greater pressures to address widespread concerns about the sources and causes of disease. It is not just HIV/AIDS that has generated widespread interest and demands on governments, but also a range of medical issues from control of donated blood to the potential dangers of hydroelectric lines. In some instances, the state is taking over parts of the risk society. For example, all levels of government throughout Western Europe and North America have entered or expanded forms of legalized gambling, including not just lotteries but state-run casinos.

The limits of generalized state capacity are apparent when we see evidence that the state may be enhancing its capacity to affect outcomes in an increasing number of areas. The question then is whether the displacement of the state's authority in governing the economy constitutes a change of such magnitude that we can begin to consider the state in decline. Weiss argues that this has not happened and that state capacity has been equated incorrectly with intervention in the economy. She does not deny that the state may be curtailed by economic interdependence, but this means not its weakening but loss of effectiveness of certain of its policy instruments, especially in fiscal and monetary policy, which has been limited by capital mobility. However, a different picture emerges if we focus on the transformative capacity of the state – its ability 'to adapt to external shocks and pressures by generating ever-new means of governing the process of industrial change.'[25]

Weiss assumes that the role of the state must be assessed in relative, not absolute, terms. The criteria are its ability to respond to economic change and to help achieve and sustain 'regime goals.'[26] These goals are historically determined and are expressed in a state's institutional architecture. For instance, liberal states such as the United Kingdom and the United States were designed to achieve objectives, such as the protection of property rights, that called for limited state intervention. The state's capacity to generate new means of governing change depends on its ability to co-ordinate productive resources, to be selective, and to enforce rules and modes of behaviour. This does not necessarily mean direct state intervention in regulating the economy; in fact, Weiss is critical of Sweden's economic governance because it has not emphasized the elements of transformative capacity while being interventionist. Using the example of East Asian states, she argues that we can find evidence that the capacity of states to affect outcomes in specific, important areas remains. Moreover, contrary to some of the arguments coming from the globalization camp – that the state is a hindrance to economic development – she claims that its ability to respond to economic change its transformative capacity can facilitate economic growth.[27]

While Weiss's argument points out the limits of looking at state decline in absolute terms, the state adaptation argument faces a number of problems. Although looking at state authority in absolute terms is limited, for conceptual and methodological reasons, it might be equally dangerous to slip into relativism by claiming that states are adapting to changing internal and external conditions. The argument tries to avoid relativism by establishing reference points by which to mark changes. This method raises problems, however. For instance, Weiss finds these reference points in the regime's goals and objectives. Her view assumes a 'big bang' approach to regime formation – a defining moment, at which interests, institutions, and social forces crystallize around a series of clearly defined objectives. It does not take into account the possibility that the objectives of a regime are never quite clear and are often constructed in different ways by different political and social participants. For example, scholars of the U.S. constitution continue to argue over the intentions of its framers, and there continues to be a great debate over Charles Beard's interpretation of the constitution as the product of an emerging commercial class.[28] Moreover, regimes are the product more likely of a gradual evolution than of a big bang, with objectives changing over time and in response to social, economic and political transformations. The reference points for adaptability of states, then, can be interpreted in very relative ways. Descriptions of the regime's goals today may reflect what it is responding to at this time.

A broader problem with adaptability is the question of whether the displacement of political authority in major areas of decision making, especially macroeconomic policy, is offset by an enhanced role for the state in other areas. The assumption of new powers and responsibilities may be not simply adaptive, but a function of decline. In order for the state's role to changes, especially for its authority to move to markets and extra-constitutional institutions, some social forces need to be disarmed or muted. Particular phases of economic liberalization may require state structures that can withstand popular resistance and deal with some of the consequences of emphasizing competitiveness.[29]

The proponents of state resilience are right to point out that the state's authority has grown because its capacity to enforce rules and sanctions is now greater than before. For examples, a number of jurisdictions have approved legislation since the mid-1980s that limits the powers of trade unions to carry out industrial action. This could be seen as evidence of a state adapting to changing circumstances and offsetting the authority that it is losing to markets by asserting control over another part of civil society. Similar arguments may be made about the ways in which many states have found it easier to ignore pressure from social movements such as women's and environmental groups. But the state's insulation from popular movements may not be a sign that it is enhancing its capacity. In order for the state's authority to be displaced – for it to be 'hollowed out – it must become harder for broad sections of society, particularly those that will be harmed by economic liberalization, to obtained access to state structures so as to resist change or to intervene with its consequences.

An illustration of the contrasting evidence of the state's retreating and advancing comes from the reform of income-support programs. Commonly known as 'workfare,' many recent changes have seen the state cutting back on funding and tying social assistance to changes in an individual's behaviour, from having to work to abstention from alcohol. For instance, the Ontario Work Act, 1997, lists a series of mandatory actions as a condition for receiving social assistance. Moreover, it gives investigators police powers that leave no parts of recipients' lives immune to intrusion by government officials intent on finding cases of fraud. The rights of appeal are suspended, as is the requirement to adhere to employment standards for employers of social assistance recipients. The state seems to be enhancing its surveillance and control mechanisms, and it is hard to speak of the retreat of the state when it can now gather information on the drinking habits and sexual partners of some of its citizens. However, these are actions being taken in order to change the perception of social assistance as a social right protected by the state. They emphasizes individual agency rather than collective responsibility carried out by the state. The intrusion is selective and directed at particular groups as part of a broader process aimed at changing the role of the state in providing income support for individuals.

What seems like resilience and adaptability may be a redefinition of the state that sees the state playing an increasingly marginal role in economic and social life. In order for a 'hollowing out' to take place, the state needs to become less accommodating and accessible to a range of social and political groups that are likely to resist economic liberalization. Furthermore, in transferring powers to transnational bodies, the state has to demonstrate that it is capable of enforcing agreements that it makes with its new partners. As we see below, this change often means concentrating decision-making power in structures and processes that are less penetrable to those groups in society that might favour alternative ways of regulating social and political life. This resolution manifests itself in a number of ways from strengthening executives at the expense of legislatures to contracting out policy development to consulting firms.

Towards Multi-level Governance

The arguments of state decline are related to a second strand in the academic literature – growing concern with governing without government, or governance.[30] Elements of such arguments appear in research covering corporate structures and behaviour, international relations, and international development policies.[31] Not surprisingly, they have generated a range of interpretations of what constitutes governance. There is agreement that a style of governing is emerging that blurs the boundaries between public and private authority. As well, they centre on ways of creating order and structuring collective action that do not rest on the authority, and ultimately sanctions, of government structures.[32]

Governance arguments assume a displacement – largely but not exclusively brought about by globalization – of the political authority that rested with the modern state. Its monopoly is now challenged on a number of fronts: by other levels of formal government, by parts of civil society (especially markets), and by regulatory agencies that may be created or recognized by the state but are not part of the state. For instance, the section of *Canada 2005* on governance makes the following claim, under the heading 'Globalization and the Shrinking State': 'Over the past few years, most industrialized countries, including Canada, have seen a profound shift of power away from central governments. The once uncontested authority of states and central governments is being challenged by the rise of non-governmental actors and by the development of international organizations and arrangements that seek to hold all nation-states accountable to certain standards of behaviour.'[33]

Governance, then, implies multiple centres of decision making that govern collective action, since the monopoly once enjoyed by the state has not been assumed by any other single centre. *Canada 2005* assumes a multi-centred world when it states that power is more diffused and that, 'government is no longer seen as the sole or even the primary institution of governance.'[34]

The claim that power is diffused in industrialized societies is not new, and some of the literature on multi-level governance may be just a different interpretation of Madison-style pluralism. Pluralist theorists such as Dahl and Polsby took part in seminal debates in the 1950s and 1960s about the diffusion of power as an essential element of liberal democracy.[35] However, we are now also talking about the role of international organizations and non-governmental actors. Earlier pluralist debates may have identified the diffusion of social power but saw political authority as resting ultimately with formal political and constitutional institutions. Decisions about collective action remained within the confines of the state, and much of the research looked to the ways in which diffused power worked within existing institutions to produce policy outcomes.

In contrast, the governance literature, in announcing the decline of the state and the displacement of authority to multiple centres, is less concerned with structures. Its emphasis is on relationships, processes, networks, and organization of collective action. Governance is not about structures but about practice.[36] It is not that governance arguments do not identify structures involved in decision making; rather they explore the complex web of relationships, and the processes that define them, that develops alongside the diffusion of power. Governance, then, looks to flexibility that often escapes formal government structures, and it is about looking beyond dichotomies that have defined modern politics: public–private, state–society, states–markets.[37]

This leads to one of the major challenges faced by policy makers and scholars of multi-level governance. The move away from institutions of government raises the question of how to balance the flexibility that comes with diffusion with the need for order and structures necessary to ensure transparency and accountability. Formal institutions have clearly identifiable centres; loose, informal, or at least extra-constitutional, networks, make it hard to identify responsibility for decisions that affect people's lives.[38] Quite often, ultimate responsibility resorts back to the most identifiable centre – the state. For instance, citizens still turn to the state to deal with such consequences of globalization as unemployment and regional development, even if authority may rest elsewhere. However, the state does not have the authority to respond like it once did, precisely because the pressures of globalization have hollowed it out.

How then to provide a form of constitutionalism for multiple centres of power that is faithful to the values and processes of postwar liberal democracy? It is not simply a matter of avoiding the procedural shortcomings associated with 'democratic deficits' within polities such as the European Union. More important, it requires new forms of political organization and authority within the confines now undermined by the emergence of multiple centres of power.[39] David Held observes cogently: 'The question is whether politics will be shaped by an explicit, formal constitution or model which might, in principle, be open and contestable, or whether politics will be subject to an unwritten constitution, which is altogether more difficult to invoke as a defence in the face of unaccountable systems of power.'[40] The unwritten constitution may refer not only to the British type, but also to the rules and procedures that shape the multiple sites of authority. This includes what may be called the 'economic constitution' – that is, the rules for the governance of the economy that may not be in a written constitutional text.

Constitutions define and identify the locus of political authority; they lay out the rules and define the centres in any form of governance. The challenge is to try to arrive at this kind of definition when authority is being displaced and diffused and may not reside in any centre. The case of independent central banks is a useful example. One of the requirements for a member's entry into the European Union is new currency (the euro) was an independent central bank, because such a bank was seen to provide a better guarantee against 'loose' monetary policy and inflation and as a first step in the establishment of a European Central Bank, which would eventually govern the euro and the European Union's monetary policy. Any attempt to make central banks accountable to liberal democratic institutions in the conventional sense, especially to elected assemblies, would leave them anything but independent. Monetary policy has shifted to another level, with the commitment that it will not be open and accessible to societal groups. This situation highlights a more general question about governance without identifiable centres: how and who will define the terms of membership and access to these different levels? For instance, a small amount of money can give anyone access to financial markets by buying a few shares in a publicly traded company. Theoretically, this will make him or her a 'stakeholder,' but it does not guarantee equal membership with other shareholders.[41] Moreover, it says little about access to this level of decision making by other, unnamed stakeholders, such as local and distant communities or employees, who are affected by its actions.

The governance literature then has been useful in pointing out the erosion of formal institutions, especially the state, and the new processes that reflect the diffusion of political authority. However, this literature faces two challenges. First, how to constitutionalize – that is, give formal, legal recognition to – processes whose strength rests with flexibility and informality? Relatedly, how to ensure participation in networks that are often based on technical knowledge, as is the case of financial markets? Second, governance arguments have not addressed the continued importance of the state. Because it is hard to constitutionalize the diffusion of the state's authority, the state remains the only identifiable centre in which all political and social groups can participate. Further, the state has to create the conditions and respond to the consequences of diffusion. This while the state is hollowing out it must also provide effective decision making that promotes the economic and social conditions of globalization. The resulting paradox is that the state may seem more effective precisely when it is losing its authority. The governance literature needs to address the state in politics without a centre, because this paradox may cause a questioning of the processes that are changing the state.

Governance of Politics without a Centre: The Case of Italy in the European Union

Italy was one of the founding members of the European Economic Community in the 1950s, and its government and population remain strong proponents of greater economic and political integration in the

European Union (EU). The introduction of the single currency, the euro, has not unleashed concerns in Italy about the loss of sovereignty or dented the level of support for the EU. This is the case even though few other member states have had to impose the level of fiscal austerity that Italian governments imposed in the 1990s. Much has been written about the budgetary measures that governments throughout the EU have pursued to achieve the 'convergence criteria' set in the Maastricht treaty, but what of the consequences of the diffusion of political authority and multi-level governance? As we see first, the new order has hollowed out has the Italian state's authority in governing the economy, producing, second, a new type of state and democratic governance.

Governance of the Economy: Hollowing Out the State

The leaders of the then-twelve-member states of the EU agreed in the Maastricht Treaty on European Union, signed in December 1991, to a three-stage plan to establish a single currency by the end of the decade. The treaty established the procedures and criteria for the creation of a single currency. Member states whose economies had converged sufficiently would gain entry into economic and monetary union. A number of convergence criteria would be used to determine entry, including an inflationary target of 1.5 per cent of the average of the three best-performing economies, long-term interest rates within 2.0 per cent of the average of the best-performing countries, a debt-to-GDP (gross domestic product) ratio of 60 per cent, and a deficit-to-GDP ratio of 3 per cent.

These criteria seemed unobtainable for Italy, as it had a budget deficit of over 10 per cent of GDP, and its public debt had reached over 110 per cent. It might be argued that only an external constraint could allow the Italian government to bring into line internal social and political forces that had the most to lose by the pressures of globalization.[42] Whatever the government's motives, Maasricht soon affected its governing of the economy. The currency crisis that hit the European exchange rate mechanism (ERM) in the summer of 1002, just before the French referendum on Maastricht, forced the Italian lira out of the mechanism. The ensuing devaluation of the lira led to an export boom that lasted for the first half of the decade. It also led to fears of spiralling inflation, with the attendant consequences for monetary, income, and budgetary policies. There was a sense, beginning in the autumn of

1992, that the governing of the economy required drastic measures if public finances and inflation were to be brought under control. The fear was not only that Italy would not be among the initial entrants into the single currency, but that the widespread perception that it could not meet the convergence criteria would cause it irreparable damage in international financial markets.

Two policy responses transformed governing of the Italian economy. First, a series of agreements for wage restraint – an informal one in 1992 and a four-year agreement in July 1993 – established Italy's first incomes policy in the postwar era, based on *concertation* between employers, trade unions, and the government.[43] It came at a time when the classic models of concertation, especially in the Scandinavian countries, started to unravel. More important, the conventional basis for wage restraint was that trade unions would offer concessions on wages in return for promises of job security from employers and a commitment from government to promote employment growth and social policy. One feature of the EU's unwritten economic constitution is that such a trade-off is not negotiable, because the policy priority of governments consists of controlling inflation; as well, employers cannot guarantee employment in a competitive global economy. The concentration made no challenge to keeping inflation under control as the primary policy objective; at least labour would have some say in setting inflationary targets. Finally, in the case of income policy and later with reform of the welfare state and labour markets, key decisions were made not in constitutional structures, but in a new bargaining arena that had no formal basis other than the agreement between social partners and government.

The second major policy initiative after Maastricht came in budgetary politics. The period since September 1992 has been characterized not simply by cuts in the size of the deficit and debt, but by fundamental changes in how government spends.[44] The result has been a transformation of the role of the state in the governance of the economy. By any measure, the changes to Italian public finances from 1992 to 1998 are impressive. Governments introduced changes that amounted to about Can.$400 billion – two-thirds of this through cuts in spending, the rest through tax increases,[45] which produced the immediate effect of Italy gaining entry into the single currency in May 1998. In this period, three budgets were presented by governments run by *technicians* (Giuliano Amato in 1992, Carlo Azeglio Ciampi in 1993, and Lamberto Dini in 1996) – that is, by governments composed of non-elected officials chosen for their technical expertise and not on the basis of representative criteria. This shift was a function not only of a political crisis but of the perception that governance was increasingly a technical, not a political, exercise; indeed, Ciampi and Dini came from the Bank of Italy. As well, there has been a trend to insulating the budgetary process from social demands.[46] For instance, the budget itself has been rationalized, and the number of budgetary items has been reduced from 5,000 to 500.[47] It is much harder for social groups to lobby legislators about specific budget items, and they must now compete against each other to gain access to fewer resources.

More notably, the quest to meet the convergence criteria for public finances led to a hollowing out of state authority in a number of areas of macroeconomic and social policy. First, a series of structural changes transformed the financing of some major areas – in terms of both the amount of money spent and the political salience – of social policy, such as pensions and health care. The case of health care is a good example of 'downloading' of decision making to the regional level of government. The shift from conditional to block grants has shifted decisions such as choosing between hospital beds and child care spaces to regional governments. In addition, the regions are encouraged to promote new arrangements between private and public- sector health care providers and to have *clients* (not citizens or patients) pay a larger share of their health care costs through user fees.[48]

Another example of the changing nature of Italian public spending as both cause and effect of multiple centres of power comes with regional development policy. The issue of regional disparities in income and economic growth between northern and southern Italy has been a feature of Italian political economy since unification in 1860. The postwar experience has not lessened the divide, despite massive spending between the late 1950s and the late 1980s. This came in the form of subsidies, investment by state-held companies such as steel makers, large infrastructure projects, and public-sector employment. This investment did little to narrow income gaps, and structural unemployment – with rates averaging over 20 per cent in the south – showed few signs of easing in the 1990s. Another government response was transfers to individuals through income-maintenance programs. Both these approaches became untenable in a more integrated Europe. Competition regulations within the EU have made it difficult for states to provide direct subsidies, even for regional development, as this is now dictated almost entirely at the EU level. The effort to bring public finances under control has meant that governments have made drastic cuts to programs that transferred money to individuals and public-sector employment.

However, the plight of the southern regions could not be ignored. Recent policies have emphasized processes that would be familiar to the governance writers. The aim has been to develop local networks in specific areas that bring together individuals from trade unions, local banks, local political authorities, retailers and non-governmental organizations. The state is present only as a facilitator while private- sector actors and social partners assume greater responsibility for economic development. One of the central government's roles is to provide technical assistance to prepare bids for EU regional funds.[49]

We can find further evidence of a changing role for the Italian state in economic and social life in the area of privatization. While there is a tendency to underestimate the extent of privatization in Italy in the 1980s, there was a noticeable shift in the 1990s with respect to the discourse about how to deal with state assets.[50] Privatization in the era of the EU convergence criteria has brought about a change in more than just the scale of the firms turned over to the private sector. We begin to see arguments from all parts of the political spectrum for the selling of state assets as part of a strategy to promote competitiveness and entrepreneurship. Banks, insurance companies, and Telecom Italia were sold off in the 1990s.[51] More ambitious plans to sell the electricity and parts of the energy sectors have stalled; however, this has not prevented Italy from leading OECD countries in the amount of money collected from the sale of state firms.[52] The sale of state assets has raised the challenge of how to regulate industries that were once under direct state control. Independent authorities, based on the model of U.S. regulatory agencies, have been established to regulate many privatized industries, so that the state's direct role in governing is now limited.[53] The government now plays an arm's-length role in ensuring that rules that foster competition and competitiveness are implemented and enforced. Objectives that may have been part of state ownership, such as regional development or employment, are today not part of the privatized firm's obligations.

Budgetary politics and privatization are just two instances of a series of policy initiatives that have contributed to the hollowing out of state authority in Italy in a range of macroeconomic and social policy areas. They reflect the diffusion of political power in a number of directions. In some instances, this has been to identifiable sites that are often not accessible to social groups, such as monetary policy, which moved 'upwards' to the EU and the European Central Bank, and responsibilities in health care and social policy, which shifted 'downwards' to regional and local governments. In other cases, authority has been displaced to independent regulatory agencies that govern a range of activities from privacy to the press to telecommunication. Authority has also seeped to new relationships among social partners that are assuming greater responsibility for economic and regional development. The paradox is that this displacement of state authority has required a state that acts in an authoritative and effective manner. This paradox raises questions about the type of state and democracy that may emerge with multiple centres of power.

Democratic Governance in the New Europe: Hardening the State

Much has been written about the ways in which European integration has affected macroeconomic and social policy. As discussion of the Italian case has shown, it has led to a hollowing out of the state as its authority has shifted to the European or regional levels or to markets or to new bodies that cannot be placed easily in either the public or private sectors. Few scholars have examined the ways in which the hollowing out has affected democratic governance. We may gain insight by looking at institutional and constitutional change at the national (Italian) level within an integrated Europe.

There is a perception that economic and monetary union has diminished the scope of constitutional politics in Europe. In arguments similar to those on the decline of ideology of the 1960s, globalization and European integration have generated claims that there are no challenges to the principles and structures of market economies. The only questions to be resolved are *technical* ones concerning ways to free up market forces and concerning who is best qualified to administer agreed-on policies.[54] The popularity of Italy's recent *technocratic* governments is evidence that perhaps some Italians feel that government was best left out of the hands of elected politicians and in the hands of technical experts.[55]

The belief that there are no major differences among political participants on economic and social life and that electoral politics hinders the management of those issues has affected constitutional politics and the nature of the Italian state. Scholars and politicians agree that Italy developed a form of consensual democracy in the postwar period.[56]

The 1948 constitution, drafted by a constituent assembly anxious to avoid a return to dictatorship and aware of the ideological divide in Italian society, did not concentrate too much power in the executive. There was no single epicentre in Italy's constitutional and political architecture which had many entry points for articulating, bargaining, and negotiating political demands.

As a consequence, Italy developed a model of consensual democracy that emphasizes easy access to decision making for a range of social and political participants, often at the expense of decision-making effectiveness. It is here that the debate on institutional reform has been affected by European integration and by the need to carry out major changes to meet the convergence criteria for the euro.[57] Italy's institutional architecture now seems too permeable and accessible. The result is arguments made across the political spectrum for concentrating decision-making power in the executive and for limiting access to decision-making centres.[58] This realignment has already begun without formal constitutional change. For instance, in the budgetary process, a superministry now combines the Treasury and Finance ministries. This was initially proposed by the Amato government in 1992 but rejected; however, when Romano Prodi appointed a super economics minister in 1996, it was hailed as an important step in bringing public finances under control.

European integration has promoted concentration of decision-making authority so as to generate policies that will enhance competitiveness. Institutions whose primary aim is to increase access to decision making appear to inhibit the making of difficult choices that require sacrifices. This perception has led to efforts to concentrate macroeconomic decision making, such as changes to the parliamentary procedures for approving the budget. These have not been sufficient to stem the pressure for major reforms to government structures. A special bicameral committee on constitutional reform had achieved an agreement in 1998 on a semi-presidential regime similar to France's (current) Fifth Republic.[59] Responsibility for political and policy-making direction would rest with the executive. The objective was to shift the balance away from those institutions, especially Parliament, that and more open to popular demands. The smaller parties changes to the electoral system to move it further in a majoritarian direction, have resisted by but the only proposals seriously considered by the bicameral committee would facilitate reduction of the number of parties.

European integration has added pressure for a different form of institutional reform – giving more powers to regional governments. At the start of the 1990s, federalism was marginal to the debate on constitutional change; by mid-decade, it was part of any such discussion. The new emphasis on competitiveness has made large sections of the Italian business community, especially owners of small and medium-sized business, aware that the structure of the Italian state may affect how they compete with their European counterparts.[60] Taxation and the delivery of services are now even more important; and the figures for revenues sent to, and transfers received from, the central state are not just administrative details but business costs and receipts. For the wealthy regions of northern Italy, which are developing close links with regions across the Alps and whose target markets for produced goods lie beyond Italy's borders, the economic rationale for the fiscal transfer of resources to the south is now weaker. Economic integration affects different regions in various ways, and there emerge conflicting political demands that become difficult to reconcile. Having to make decisions about which regions will benefit and which will lose out, much like budgetary decisions in the 1990s, will severely strain the consensual nature of Italian liberal democracy.

The EU's Maastricht convergence criteria also increased pressure to desolve powers to the regions. One of the ways in which the EU's central governments cut public deficits was to transfer decisions to subnational governments without necessarily enhancing their power in areas such as taxation. In Italy, regional governments were forced to make policy decisions – for instance, in the delivery of health services – that would prove unpopular; but they did not control revenue generation. It is not surprising that demands for greater decision-making authority grew as regions received greater responsibilities while facing demands for which they lacked the capacity to respond. But the shifting of powers does not increase popular access to decision making. As we saw in health care, downloading may allow authority to seep outside the public sector or to disappear altogether. There is no guarantee that a citizen will have find it easier to have access to a health association run by private interests than to a permeable state. Part of the reason for shifting powers to the regional level is that it will create a competitive environment between regions seeking to reduce the boundaries of political authority.[61]

While the debate on the strengthening of the executive and shifting powers to the regions has been extensive, there have been few concrete proposals on how to constitutionalize the hollowing out of the state and the diffusion of political authority. While constitutional reform has remained elusive despite being prominent on the political agenda, the basic structures and location of political power have shifted. The creation of a European Central Bank, which will assume most of the levers for monetary policy, raises questions about the transparency and accountability that may not be realized by formal constitutional changes that transfer powers to regional governments. However, it is just the latest stage in a process that Stephen Gill has termed the 'new constitutionalism,' in which more areas of collective decision making are being assumed by non-constitutional structures.[62] These bodies include independent central banks, bond-rating agencies, independent and self-regulating authorities, and non-governmental organizations. As state capacity and authority have shrunk in many areas of social and economic life, there has been a corresponding increase in the authority of structures that do not appear in formal constitutions.

Concluding Remarks

There is little dispute that the structures and processes that defined politics in the modern era face a number of challenges. These have led to a political paradox. On the one hand, state authority has been diffused in a number of directions, making it difficult for it to act authoritatively as its monopoly position is challenged from a number of centres. On the other hand, the state remains a central site for the expression of political and social demands, especially for the growing number of social groups affected by the same processes that are hollowing out the state. These groups are finding it harder to penetrate state structures and to participate in state decision-making processes. This raises the question of what kind of state, and what kind of democracy, may emerge, given multiple centres of power; or more precisely, politics without a centre.

The governance literature has generally taken a positive view of the hollowing out of state authority, suggesting that multi-level governance provides many more access points for political demands. The blurring of dichotomies may indeed give individuals and groups greater access to decision making. However, many of the new centres of power are immune to demands of transparency, accountability, and access. The case of the hollowing out of the Italian state in an integrated Europe suggests that the competitive nature of multiple centres makes it difficult to sustain a consensual model of democracy. The resources that were once used for trade-offs and to mobilize consent are no longer available. The lack of a clear political epicentre allows for an exit strategy for many social forces, but it also means that many groups in society that have no such option are faced with a state that is limiting access to them and has less capacity to respond to their demands.

The Italian experience provides some lessons for Canada. First, hollowing out of the political authority of the state raises questions about its continued political legitimacy. One may wonder to what extent citizens in Quebec or elsewhere would continue to support a state whose capacity seems to be limited to intrusion and repression, while their political leaders admit the state's inability to provide collective goods such as health care and regional development. Second, and related to legitimacy, multiple centres of power will lead to questions about the accountability, transparency, and accessibility of decisions that affect citizens' lives. Canadians are being told that it is pressures of international financial markets that have led to measures such as cuts in health care and education, but they have no way of holding those markets accountable. Trying to create continental structures to address the asymmetry between the source of decisions and political jurisdiction will have limited effect if those structures are not readily accessible to those whom they govern. Third, the European experience has pointed out the need for new ways of thinking about the principles of how we govern ourselves and about what sort of institutions best realize our democratic objectives. Shifting political authority to many sites, thus ending the monopoly of the state, has raised the problem of how to create institutions and procedures that ensure transparency, accountability, and access for citizens. These are questions that Canadians may ask themselves as more decisions are displaced to the continental level, to the provinces, and to financial markets.

The challenge ahead is how to arrive at a politics without a centre that can continue to provide flexibility and innovation but that also guarantees access and accountability. This may mean exploring ways in which to adapt democratic structures and processes, which are based on formal institutions, and on conventional dichotomies of public and private, states and markets. Hence the need to develop a new political and constitutional architecture for politics without a centre. Will the lack of an identifiable centre lead only to confusion, to general exclusion from political authority, and to access for only a privileged few? The European case has not provided reasons to be hopeful.

NOTES

I would like to thank Poland Lai, Philippe Le Prestre, Miriam Smith, and the other members of the Multiple Centres of Power team for their helpful comments, including Gordon Smith, Ronald Crelisten, Robert Wolfe, Robert Cutler, Stephen Clarkson, Julien Bauer, and Daniel Wolfish, who met in May 1999 to discuss these papers.

1 Susan Strange, *The Retreat of the State: The Diffusion of Power in the World Economy* (Cambridge: Cambridge University Press, 1996), 3.

2 Claus Offe, *Modernity and the State: East, West* (Cambridge, Mass.: MIT Press, 1996), vii.

3 David Easton, *A Framework for Political Analysis* (Englewood Cliffs, NJ: Prentice-Hall, 1965); Ralph Miliband, *The State in Capitalist Society* (London: Weidenfeld, 1969).

4 Peter Evans, Dietrich Reuschemeyer, and Theda Skocpol, *Bringing the State Back In* (Cambridge: Cambridge University Press, 1985).

5 Linda Weiss, *The Myth of the Powerless State* (Ithaca, NY: Cornell University Press, 1998), 2.

6 Manual Castells, *The Power of Identity* (Oxford: Blackwell Publishers, 1997), chap. 5.

7 Peter Evans, 'The Eclipse of the State? Reflection on the Stateness in an Era of Globalization,' *World Politics* 50, no. 1 (October 1997): 62–3.

8 Bob Jessop, 'Towards a Schumpeterian Workfare State?' *Studies in Political Economy* 40 (Spring 1993): 7–39; R.A.W. Rhodes, 'The Hollowing Out of the British State,' *Political Quarterly* 65, no. 2 (April 1994): 138–51; James Rosenau, 'The Future of Politics,' Paper presented at the conference 'The Global Century,' Vancouver, 4–7 November 1998; Susan Strange, 'The Defective State,' *Daedulus* 124, no. 2 (Spring 1995): 55–75.

9 John Freeman, ed., *Democracy and Markets: The Politics of Mixed Economies* (Ithaca, NY: Cornell University Press, 1989).

10 Gary Marks, ed., *Governance in the European Union* (London: Sage, 1996).

11 An indication of the importance of the bond rating agencies is the report that officials at Canada's Department of Finance tried to ensure that parts of the nation's public debt were downgraded so as to neutralize public opposition to budgetary cuts. See Linda McQuaig, *Shooting the Hippo: Death by Deficit and Other Canadian Myths* (Toronto: Viking, 1995).

12 For a discussion of the role of bond rating agencies, see Timothy J. Sinclair, 'Passing Judgement: Credit Rating Processes as Regulatory Mechanisms of Governance in the Emerging World Order,' *Review of International Political Economy* 1, no. 1 (Spring 1994): 133–59.

13 Robert Boyer and Daniel Drache, 'Introduction,' in Robert Boyer and Daniel Drache, eds., *States against Markets: The Limits of Globalization* (London: Routledge, 1996), 2–3.
14 Strange, 'The Defective State,' 56.
15 Paul Hirst, *From Statism to Pluralism* (London: UCL Press, 1997).
16 Paul Hirst and Grahame Thompson, *Globalization in Question: The International Economy and the Possibilities of Governance* (Cambridge: Polity Press, 1996); Kenichi Ohmae, *The End of the Nation State; The Rise of Regional Economies* (New York: Free Press, 1995); Richard O'Brien, *Global Financial Integration: The End of Geography* (London: Royal Institute of International Affairs, 1992).
17 Paul Hirst, *Associative Democracy* (Amherst: University of Massachusetts Press, 1994).
18 Hirst, *From Statism to Pluralism*, 29.
19 Ibid., 32–40.
20 Robert Wade and Suzanne Berger, *National Diversity and Global Capitalism* (Ithaca, NY: Cornell University Press, 1996).
21 John Ikenberry, 'The Irony of State Strength: Comparative Responses to the Oil Shocks in the 1970s,' *International Organization* 40, no. 1 (Winter 1986): 106.
22 Weiss, *The Myth of the Powerless State*, 4.
23 Michael Mann, 'Has Globalization Ended the Rise and Rise of the Nation-State?' *Review of International Political Economy* 4, no. 3 (Autumn 1997): 472–96.
24 Jane Franklin, ed., *The Politics of Risk Society* (Cambridge: Polity Press, 1998).
25 Weiss, *The Myth of the Powerless State*, 4.
26 Ibid., 22–3.
27 Ibid., chap. 4.
28 Charles Beard, *An Economic Interpretation of the Constitution of the United States* (New York: Macmillan, 1935).
29 Andrew Gamble, *The Free State and the Strong Economy* (Basingstoke: Macmillan, 1994).
30 James Rosenau and Ernst Czempiel, eds., *Governance without Government: Order and Change in World Politics* (Cambridge: Cambridge University Press, 1992).
31 UNDP, *Reconceptualising Governance*, Discussion Paper No. 2 (New York: UNDP, 1997); Morten Balling et al., eds., *Corporate Governance, Financial Markets and Global Convergence* (Dordecht: Kluwer, 1998).
32 Gerry Stoker, 'Governance as Theory: Five Propositions,' *International Social Science Journal* 155 (March 1998): 17–18.

33 Assistant Deputy Minister's Sub-Committee for Global Challenges and Opportunities, *Canada 2005: Global Challenges and Opportunities* (Ottawa, 25 February 1997), chap. 11, p. 1.
34 Ibid.
35 Robert Dahl, *Who Governs? Democratic Power in an American City* (New Haven, Conn.: Yale University Press, 1961); Nelson Polsby, *Community Power and Political Theory* (New Haven, Conn.: Yale University Press, 1963).
36 Bob Jessop, 'The Rise of Governance and the Risks of Failure: The Case Of Economic Development,' *International Social Science Journal* 155 (March 1998): 29–32.
37 Renate Mayntz, 'Governing Failures and the Problem of Governability: Some Comments on a Theoretical Framework,' in Jan Kooiman, ed., *Modern Governance*, (London: Sage, 1993), 10–11.
38 Andrew Dunsire, 'Modes of Governance,' in Jan Kooiman, ed., *Modern Governance*, 22–3.
39 Antje Weiner and Vincent Della Sala, 'Constitution-Making and Citizenship Practice: Bridging the Democracy Gap in the EU?' *Journal of Common Market Studies* 35, no. 4 (December 1997): 595–614.
40 David Held, 'Democracy: From City-States to a Cosmopolitan Order?,' *Political Studies* 40, special issue (1992): 37.
41 As the Italian merchant banker Enrico Cuccia is reported to have said, 'We weigh shares, we don't count them.'
42 Kenneth Dyson and Kevin Featherstone, 'Italy and EMU as a "Vincolo Esterno": Empowering the Technocrats, Transforming the State,' *South European Politics and Society* 1, no. 2 (Autumn 1996): 279–99.
43 Marino Regini and Ida Regalia, 'Italia anni '90: Rinasce la concertazione,' IRES Lombardia, *Collana discussioni* (January 1996): 1–19.
44 Franco Reviglio, *Come siamo entrati in Europa* (Milan: UTET, 1998).
45 Camera dei Deputati, XIII Legislatura, *Atti Parlamentari*, Documento di programmazione economico e finanziaria, 1999–2001, Doc. LVII, n. 3, 18 April 1998.
46 Vincent Della Sala, 'Hollowing Out and Hardening the State: European Integration and the Italian Economy,' in Martin Bull and Martin Rhodes, eds., *Crisis and Transition in Italian Politics*, (London: Frank Cass, 1997).
47 Camera dei Deputati. XIII Legislatura, *Atti Parlamentari*, Documento di programmazione economico e finanziaria, 1999–2001, Doc. LVII, n. 2, 31 May 1997, 69.
48 Ibid., 77.
49 Camera dei Deputati, XIII Legislatura, Servizio Studi, Documentazione e ricerca, *I patti territoriali* (Rome, June 1998).

50 Ministero del Tesoro, Le Commissioni di Studi del Ministero del Tesoro, *Pensioni, privatizzazioni e spesa pubblica* (Rome: Istituto Poligrafico dello Stato, 1993); Sabino Cassese, 'Deregulation and Privatization in Italy,' in M. Moran and T. Prosser, eds., *Privatization and Regulatory Change in Europe* (Buckingham: Open University Press, 1994).

51 Camera dei Deputati, XIII Legislatura, *Atti Parlamentari,* Relazione sulle operazioni di cessione delle partecipazioni in societa controllate direttamento o indirettamento dallo stato (Rome, 6 August 1998).

52 Simone Bemporad and Oscar Giannino, 'Storia di un'illusione italiana: come e perche banche e aziende rimangono di stato,' *Liberal,* 16 July 1998, 11–15.

53 Giulio Amato et al., *Regulazione e garanzia del pluralismo: le autorita' amministrative indipendenti* (Milan: Giuffre, 1997).

54 For instance, see Censis, *Inventare una societa' neo-competitiva* (Milan: Franco Angeli, 1994).

55 This is not unique to Italy if one thinks of the growing appeal of the 'outsider' in a number of industrialized democracies or of political agendas that emphasize 'common sense.'

56 Sergio Fabbrini, *Quale democrazia?* (Rome: Laterza, 1994).

57 Reviglio, Come siamo entrati in Europa, 13.

58 Bruno Dente, 'Politica, istituzioni e deficit pubblico,' *Stato e mercato,* no. 33 (December 1991), 339–70.

59 Commissione parlamentare per le riforme costituzionali, 'Progetto di legge costituzionale approvato il 30 giugno 1997' (Atto Camera 3931 – Atto Senato 2583).

60 For instance, see Industry Minister Alberto Clo before a parliamentary committee in Camera dei Deputati, XII Legislatura, *Atti Parlamentari,* Decima Commissione, 9 February 1995, 206–8.

61 Camera dei Deputati, XIII Legislatura, *Atti Parlamentari,* Documento di programmazione economico e finanziaria, 1999–2001, Doc. LVII, n. 3, 18 April 1998.

62 Stephen Gill, 'The Emerging World Order and European Change: The Political Economy of European Union,' in Ralph Miliband and Leo Panitch, eds., *Socialist Register* (London: Merlin Press, 1992).

5. The Multi-centred State: Canadian Government under Globalizing Pressures

Stephen Clarkson

Keynes is dead! Fordism is finished! Income disparities are increasing![1] Society is polarized! Corporate capitalism has carried off a silent coup![2] The nation-state has been dismantled![3] and shrunk![4]

In the light of these dire diagnoses, citizens everywhere are experiencing high levels of anxiety concerning the social cohesion, economic performance, and political viability of their state structures. In Asia, the devastating combination of currency crises and government austerity imposed by the International Monetary Fund has shaken these newly industrializing states' capacity to promote their interests. In the far more stable context created by the European Union, its fifteen member states share a nagging concern about their continuing capacity to function once they lose their monetary policy autonomy and then admit another ten applicants.

Located somewhere in between these extremes of externally determined dysfunctionality and self-imposed truncation, Canadians are beset with doubts about the capacity of their political system to perform its expected functions. They are so bombarded by disconnected bursts of political and economic information that they have difficulty understanding the whole: a plethora of individual analyses does not automatically generate an overall synthesis. When it comes to comprehending the specific entity once known as the nation-state, the dilemma is understandable, for there is no longer just one state to be comprehended. In our postmodern, globalized situation, stateness exists on many levels, and governance functions are performed not only on these public levels but in the marketplace and in society, both within nations and transnationally, because power has been fragmented and reconstituted in many different centres.

To explore the nature of the multi-centred state in the Canadian case under conditions of centrifugal fragmentation and international integration is an ambitious undertaking. This chapter takes up the challenge by attempting an exercise in triangulation. *Chronologically,* it asks how the Canadian state has evolved into a five-tier model over the years since the social-democratic paradigm held sway during the prime ministerships of Lester Pearson and Pierre Trudeau (1963–1984), till the neoliberal prime ministerships of Brian Mulroney and Jean Chrétien (1984–200?). *Functionally,* it identifies the ways in which the state's performance of its principal tasks has altered over this same quarter-century. *Structurally,* it argues that these functions have been performed in a state structure with a disaggregated but interconnected and interactive architecture that operates on five levels, from the traditional local (municipal) and sub-national (provincial) tiers through the federal and on to the more recently established continental and global levels.[5] The chapter's three sections look at the five-level structure of governance, at the Canadian state's economic role, and at the activities of what I term the 'civil state.'

The Canadian State: A Multi-level Structure

Not all these five levels of governance can be properly described as governments. In Canada only the federal and provincial levels have formal constitutional standing, municipalities remaining the colony-like creatures of their provinces. At the continental and global levels, governance structures are more like works in progress than well established institutions. However, there has been sufficient institution building at these latter levels that governance functions with the quality of stateness are performed to some degree at each tier in the model.[6] This section briefly elaborates this five-tier model, so that we can next see how its chief state functions are activated through a dialectical linking of the many components of this multi-layered, increasingly decentred state.

The Federal State

The federal state started its shift towards neoliberal governance some two years before the election of Brian Mulroney and has been realizing this never openly declared mandate ever since. As many scholars have shown, a prime characteristic of the neoliberal state is to have 'downloaded' functions to 'lower' levels of governance and 'uploaded' authority to the global and continental tiers. In addition to this vertical devolution, the state has 'offloaded' functions to the marketplace by privatizing crown corporations and deregulating sectors that it used to supervise strictly.[7] Paradoxically, these apparent losses of power have occurred because the federal state has displayed considerable strength. It strove for many years to balance its budgets by taking steps that many entrenched interests, including the provinces, bitterly resisted, and it imposed structural reforms, which favoured market outcomes constraining both itself and civil society. In 1989 the government used its treaty power to help create a new continental regime of accumulation in which it has been an enthusiastically self-restraining participant. Successive federal governments cut and reinvented social programs, reducing citizens' protection from the greater perils of the deregulated market. In each of these cases, Ottawa exerted discipline over the provinces, which were forced to face new difficulties. In short, to divest itself of authority the Canadian state had to take strong action.

The federal state also maintains an important role because it continues to nurture some vestiges of the embedded liberalism that characterized the Keynesian welfare state. Part of the Chrétien Liberals' rationale for deficit elimination has been to ensure that their government can continue to play a role in social policy. In this regard they maintain the paradigm that prevailed under the Pearson and Trudeau governments. While some may not approve of its ungenerous way of life, reports of the federal state's demise are greatly exaggerated.

Provincial Governments

As a rule, federal devolution has increased both the de facto and the de jure jurisdiction of the provinces, which have welcomed the extra power when the financial implications were neutral but have had mixed reactions when it has had uneven fiscal effects. When downloading has been accompanied by general cuts in transfer payments, all provinces have protested. When these cuts in transfer payments have disproportionately favoured the equalization-receiving, have-not provinces, their otherwise-better-off 'cousins' have objected vociferously.

Since the Canadian government negotiates trade treaties but can implement them only in areas of its own constitutional jurisdiction, provincial involvement has been necessary to realize what are understood to be the benefits of liberalized trade. For this reason, Ottawa has encouraged increased provincial participation since the 1970s, when the Tokyo Round first brought non-tariff barriers to the trade negotiating table.[8] Paradoxically, an increased provincial role in trade policy–making has resulted in decreased provincial capacity for industrial policy, because trading principles such as national treatment or the right of establishment diminish a sub-national government's ability to foster the competitiveness of its home-owned enterprises. While provincial influence over trade policy has increased, Canada's trade initiatives have been driven by the federal government.[9] The growing authority of global and continental governance over areas of provincial jurisdiction suggests that increased provincial interest in trade policy is the result more of federal initiatives and federal uploading than of federal downloading or independent province-building.

The provinces' increasing fiscal weight since the 1970s has given them greater authority in what used to be the federal preserve of macroeconomic management, but their use of this authority has been strongly influenced by the federal state. For example, the federal government's 1990 transfer cuts precipitated choleric criticism in the provincial capitals, which then proceeded to bring down just the kind of tough, deficit-cutting budgets that Ottawa had sought to provoke.[10] Monetary policy is a matter of federal jurisdiction and has also been used, particularly via the Bank of Canada's price stability policy, to influence provincial fiscal policy. All those attempting to swim against this monetary-policy tide eventually fell into line, particularly Ontario.[11] In sum, while provinces have acquired increased capacity and authority, they have done so in a neo-liberal context that has been largely shaped by the federal state.

The Municipal Level

One consequence of the strain on provincial budgets caused by federal devolution has been the domino effect of further sub-national downloading to municipal governments. The great concentration of power in provincial executives jealously guarding their bailiwick has meant that Ottawa's relations with municipal governments are far weaker than Washington's role in U.S. cities, even though in both countries local governments are constitutionally the creatures of their states or provinces.[12] Provincial restraint on municipalities has drastically curtailed their limited powers, again especially in Ontario, whose principal city, Toronto, has suffered a virtual putsch at the hands of the provincial government at that Queen's Park.

Their constitutional orphan status does not mean that Canadian cities are cut off from the international political economy. Indeed, a principal mechanism through which the global and continental orders operationalize themselves is a network of international cities that act as growth nodes and connectors to other cities and their regional hinterlands.[13] The Canadian federal government has helped shape this global–local interface, captured by the notions of 'glocalization' and 'glurbanization,' insofar as it has promoted or resisted globalization. In promoting globalization – for example, by subsidizing infrastructure investments designed to support a World's Fair or Olympic bid – Ottawa has enhanced the position of its international cities through which trade is organized – particularly Montreal, Calgary, and Vancouver – at the expense of other urban areas.

The Continental Regime

The uneven projection abroad of governmental, societal, or entrepreneurial actors characterizes the development of governance at the continental level. If an integrated North American market is being forged by corporations operating continentally thanks to the North American Free Trade Agreement's (NAFTA's) new rules on investment and trade,[14] and if a halting evolution of continental norms can be detected in the work of dozens of NAFTA's working groups beavering away on specialized issues such as the cross-border transportation of dangerous chemicals,[15] one might think that the Canadian state was on the road to irrelevance. But NAFTA was designed by its progenitors to prevent any supranational form of continental governance from developing. Far from encouraging greater political integration, its two northern member states are carefully monitoring their borders to obstruct immigration from Mexico and restrict general labour mobility. In the name of their national autonomy, the three governments have already taken steps to hobble NAFTA's putatively autonomous Commission for Environmental Cooperation. In the interests of buttressing this autonomy, they are also resisting the creation of a North American monetary authority that might clone Europe's European Monetary Union.[16]

Notwithstanding its lack of supranationality, the new continental governance has had a reconstitutionalizing effect on the Canadian state. Most debated have been the strictures on the range of permissible government action imposed by NAFTA and its forbear, the Canada–United States Free Trade Agreement (FTA) on many policy areas formerly considered to be at the sovereign discretion of the federal or provincial states. The problem is not just that NAFTA establishes specific constraints on Canada's industrial, energy, and cultural policy. It is that these policy capacities are altered as if they were being entrenched in constitutional form: they cannot be changed back in response to a democratic mandate being won by a political party dedicated to revising them. Although these inhibitions parallel the negative integration that characterizes the European Union's market-centred and state-limiting processes,[17] their actual effects on Canadian governments have been hard to measure.

A contemporaneous shift in the managerial philosophy of both elected and bureaucratic policy makers away from a big-is-better activism in favour of a small-is-best disengagement makes it difficult to determine whether a reduction in interventionist practices by federal and provincial governments resulted from officials' fear of falling afoul of the new continental rules or from their own conversion to minimum-government neoliberalism. Non–decision making is famously resistant to scholarly observation: analysts can rarely tell to what extent NAFTA has prevented state actions that might have been taken in its absence. Furthermore, Canadian decision makers may have renounced industrial policies that support national enterprises because of their compulsion to eliminate budget deficits or because they no longer believe that they should be trying to pick winning national champions, not because of NAFTA's principle of national treatment.

The Global Order

The evolution of a global level of governance further diminishes the freedom to run its own affairs formerly enjoyed by the sovereign state. Whether global economic commitments have been adopted willingly or reluctantly, the post-national state has tied its own hands. Its loss of internal sovereignty may be partially offset by a corollary capacity to exercise external sovereignty through participation in intergovernmental decision making at the global level. This enhanced deliberative capacity may mean little if it only establishes the autonomy-limiting norms, regulations, and disciplines that it subsequently imposes on itself.[18] But if these rules make it easier for a country to achieve its international objectives, then this external sovereignty delivers a pay-off at the national and sub-national levels. In 1990, half way through the long Uruguay Round, it was Canada that proposed introducing the more authoritative institutional structure that transformed the ineffectual General Agreement on Tariffs and Trade (GATT) into the more substantial World Trade Organization (WTO).[19] The same round of trade talks also yielded what had eluded the grasp of the Canadian government when negotiating the FTA and NAFTA. The WTO's comprehensive subsidy code, combined with its strong dispute-settlement body, promised to reduce the vulnerability of Canada's exports to the kind of U.S. harassment that can unilaterally allege unfair subsidies and impose stiff countervailing duties.

In principle, Ottawa believed that a mid-sized state was better off in a rules-based system with a dispute-settlement mechanism strong enough to enforce the rules, if the alternative was a power-based system in which the most powerful states imposed their will arbitrarily. In practice the logic of the GATT process was itself based on power: the strongest states dominated the Uruguay Round negotiations, so that the new global rules tended to incorporate the norms advocated primarily by the United States on behalf of its giant multinational corporations (MNCs). For this reason, globalism does not necessarily present Canada with a real escape from continentalism. Much of the constraint that the WTO has imposed on Canada in the few years of its existence has been an application of U.S.-inspired rules uploaded from the national and continental levels and entrenched in the global regime. Policies established years and even decades ago to support a modest Canadian magazine economy have been declared invalid, exposing that part of the Canadian cultural system to annihilation. None the less, such global institutions give federal – and, on occasion, even provincial – government officials legitimate platforms on which they can attempt to build coalitions with the like-minded to defend their state interests.

Thus the interplay of exogenous and endogenous forces over several decades has decentred the Canadian state, redistributing power along the federal–provincial–municipal jurisdictional spectrum. Such internal adjustments were not thought to be life threatening to the state. More problematic for its primacy was the superimposing on it of new international centres for rule making and adjudication at the continental and global levels. To see what this five-level architecture of stateness means for Canadian governance, we need to look at how the

Canadian state is carrying out its traditional activities – both in economic policy (in the next section) and in its role as 'civil state' (in the section after that).

Economic Functions in a Decentred State

Having located stateness on five levels, we need now to reconsider some of the chief functions performed by the Canadian state. We can examine how its traditional responsibilities have been reconfigured both under external pressures of globalization and under internal forces pressing for political change. Pride of place goes to the state's role as macroeconomic manager. Then comes its familiar guise as industrial promoter, as trade-rule negotiator, and as regulator of banking and telephone systems.

The State as Economic Manager

It is in the state's capacity to direct the economy that neoliberalism's impact has been greatest, whether out of ideological preference or as a response to global or technological 'necessity.' Over two decades the reigning philosophy applied to budgetary governance in Canada has shifted from the language of John Maynard Keynes to that of Milton Friedman. Concern for short-run fine-tuning so characteristic of the Keynesian approach has been set aside in favour of a longer-term structural approach to macroeconomic policy. The earlier priority of reducing the level of unemployment has been displaced by the fight against inflation, just as a Trudeau-era focus on maintaining consumer demand has given way to the Mulroney/Chrétien commitment to making the 'supply side' of the economy more efficient. Deficits, of which ministers of finance once boasted in their stimulative zeal, have become the cause for ministerial apologies. Actively intervening in specific sectors of the economy in order to promote national enterprise has ceded its place to a more generalized concern to get the fundamentals right and less interest in firms' performance at the micro-level. The desire to control foreign investment lest it do more harm than good has been replaced by an almost-desperate quest to attract foreign investment as a means to and an indicator of global competitiveness.

Since its origin as a resource periphery of more powerful imperial centres, Canada's staple-based economy has always had to take its cues from the the global marketplace.[20] It was in no way breaking with tradition, therefore, when Canadian neoliberalism in the late 1980s began taking its cue, from the discourse of globalization. Recently deregulated global financial markets would not tolerate – on pain of exchange rate crises induced by currency speculators – signs of uncontrolled inflation in a national economy. The Bank of Canada used this external threat to justify imposing on the economy a tight monetary policy – commonly known as 'zero inflation.'[21] Canadian economists, who are not generally renowned for social-democratic leanings, wrung their hands at the made-in-Canada recession precipitated by the Bank of Canada's obdurate governor, who demonstrated his de facto autonomy from the Canadian government as a power centre by pushing up interest rates unmercifully and, along with them, the unemployment lines.

A radical reduction of the country's fiscal deficit was a second manifestation of recent macroeconomic responses to globalization pressures. For neoliberalism's first ten years, deficit reduction was a mantra observed more in the breach than in practice. Tight money raised interest rates and aggravated the recession of the early 1990s. Free trade caused sectoral dislocation and severe job losses, provoking increased government spending on social assistance. Both shifts caused the public deficit to swell under the Mulroney phase of neoliberalism. It was only when public faith in Keynesian nostrums about a munificent state had been sufficiently shattered that the federal government (returned in 1993, after nine years of Progressive Conservative rule, to the hands of the same Liberal Party that had constructed the Keynesian welfare state) was able to launch an open and unflinching attack on the budget deficit. Whereas Mulroney's government had made many reductions of government spending by stealth, Chrétien's launched a concerted campaign of program slashing in order to reduce the deficit to zero – a target that it reached in 1998.

Although many saw the restricting of government programs as the Canadian state amputating its own limbs, such actions, along with the zero-inflation policy, perhaps allowed it to retain its central function. The neoliberal state might have shed some tasks, but it had clung to its role of economic policeman.

The State as Industrial Promoter

Beyond policies that target the general economic environment, those aimed at improving the functioning of specific economic sectors also distinguish the Pearson/Trudeau state from its Mulroney/Chrétien incarnation.

Under the earlier regime, both the federal and provincial governments were deemed responsible for intervening to save troubled industries and protect national economic players. In the Fordist, post–Second World War compromise between labour and capital, wages rose as productivity increased – thanks to government-sanctioned collective bargaining that gave trade unions the legal right to claim their share of rising revenues. Resulting high wages for workers in assembly-line industries made possible the mass consumption that generated enough demand to keep these manufacturing processes growing. This regime of accumulation shattered in part because it failed to develop complete linkages between the extraction of natural resources and their processing into finished products for local consumption or export. Instead, resources went mostly to the U.S. market, in massive quantities and at nominal prices, while manufacturing for the national economy was undertaken by branch plants of U.S. transnational corporations, which typically imported high-cost components for local assembly. In the process, Canada received minimal rents for its resources and contributed to higher returns in the United States. At the same time, the branch-plant economy led to a rising financial drain of management charges, royalties, and dividend payments to the U.S. head-office economy.

The 1970s crisis of Canada's macroeconomic management was linked to this fractured regime of accumulation. With tax revenues from Canada's truncated economic system kept low, the welfare aspect of the federal state never reached European levels in protecting citizens from the vicissitudes of industrialism. Dependence on U.S. capital limited the development of too generous a state. A relatively low level of workers' mobilization meant that government was not pushed very hard 'from below.' National unity and nation-building, rather than class struggle, provided the dominant axis along which social conflict was organized.

As GATT-negotiated declines in Canada's tariffs steadily reduced protection for territorially based manufacturing through the 1970s, and as the federal government's efforts at developing a post-Keynesian interventionist practice failed by the early 1980s, the logic justifying a century-old industrialization strategy of import substitution collapsed. The Canada Development Corporation, the Foreign Investment Review Agency, the National Energy Program, and Petro Canada had expressed the faith that the government should control developments within its own territory, particularly for the benefit of the industrial heartland in Ontario. But with new Canadian direct investment abroad having exceeded the entry of new foreign direct investment since 1975, Canada's continentally oriented regime of accumulation could no longer sanction a national mode of regulation that had become intolerable to those, such as the western provinces, that felt that they had never been its beneficiaries.[22]

The neoliberal view of industrial policy was based on the perceived failure of social-democratic efforts to build national champions based in Canada and able to compete in global markets. The shift from importing to exporting direct investment and the resistance of resource-based provinces to subsidy-based policies favouring the industrial heartland helped discredit activist industrial strategies. A traditionally weak state[23] and management's distrust of a labour force that was highly fragmented had also impeded the development of a market economy organized along the lines of the continental European model. For proponents of a liberal market economy whose voices informed the neoliberal consensus by the mid-1980s, industrial strategies were not needed because they did not work.[24] Government should not try to pick winning sectors or firms. Rather, it should let the 'invisible hand' of the market carry out this function. The government's industrial role shifted to getting the fundamentals right, responding to business signals about the kind of tax regime (as low as possible), labour market (as flexible as possible), and infrastructure, whether physical (as high tech as possible) or human (as high quality as possible), that it needed.

Intervention in the national market under the guise of an industrial strategy became unacceptable. Instead, the government took pride in negotiating international rules that were to replace and even prohibit the old ways of shaping the economic game. The federal withdrawal from industrial policy accelerated during the Chrétien Liberals' attack on their inherited deficit. To this end NAFTA's facilitation of enterprise mobility to the United States or Mexico put heavy pressure on trade unions to make wage concessions and to provide the greater 'labour flexibility' that business in Canada was demanding. Supporting this competitive imperative, the Canadian state whittled down the social wage, reducing unemployment insurance benefits, cutting assistance to people on welfare, and generally doing less to protect citizens from the destabilizing economic circumstances that it was itself fostering.

The squeezing out of Keynesian dogma by neoclassical economic dogma was not the only factor transforming microeconomic management. Astonishing advances in information technology, resulting from breakthroughs in both computers and communication, shifted thinking on innovation from manufacturing and productivity to a knowledge-intensive approach. In this new techno-economic paradigm, microeconomic, firm-, or sector-centred industrial policy gave way to a focus on investing in education for skills development and in communication infrastructure for attracting footloose investment to locate in Canada.[25] In this optic, government should be no longer a hierarchically superior organization connected through a vertical relationship with the market, but rather a heterarchically articulated agency nourishing a horizontal, information-sharing, and morale-boosting relationship with the private sector. Such rethinking of government's proper role preached moving away from Fordist mass-production assembly plants towards more specialized, more dynamic clusterings of flexible, knowledge-based firms with a less permanent, less structured workforce.

If government at any level could assure business a supply of highly skilled, well-trained labour, and could absorb the costs of health and disability insurance, if road and rail connections could guarantee the conditions for just-in-time delivery, if the latest, ultra-fast telecommunication infrastructures could be installed, then investors – no matter whether foreign or national – would surely come to locate, innovate, and germinate.

Under this decentring approach, sub-national regions become more logical loci of action than the federal tier for the needed public-sector encouragement of private-sector partnerships and alliances. In a huge country containing geographically distinct economic centres, the federal system has difficulty developing a co-ordinated economic activity that satisfies all regions. One national policy configuration does not fit all needs. As a consequence, the provinces may constitute the preferable administrative tier for establishing innovative systems that galvanize private-sector initiatives within a techno-economic, knowledge-based, lean production mission.[26]

The disengagement of the central government could be seen in falling levels of federal funding for industrial programs. The re-empowerment of provincial governments appeared in their taking on the new vocabulary of competitiveness and skills training even when displaying their formal acceptance of neoliberalism. Ontario provides a delicious example of this phenomenon. A new Liberal government in 1985 officially converted to the doctrine of the non-protectionist, knowledge-based economy. In 1990 a social-democratic government pursued this path by establishing partnership programs bringing labour and management together to work out new forms of co-operation, sector by sector. Most recently in 1995 a neoconservative government started off by demolishing these programmatic innovations, only to bring them back in when it came to understand the logic of its new role of business promoter in the information-technology age.[27]

Manifesting the reality of 'glocalization,' municipalities conscious of their vulnerability in the face of footloose capital have attempted to generate attractive local conditions such as industrial parks located adjacent to university campuses that are conducive to clusterings of knowledge-intensive innovators. The sharp distinctions that previously characterized municipal, provincial, and federal governments' approaches to industrial development are increasingly blurring. So is the distinction between initiatives undertaken by the public and private sectors, since governments, universities, business associations, and private firms are implementing similar types of incubator policies in the quest for the pot of gold called innovation. The decentred state is also an interconnected state.

Disregarding the nationality of capital and welcoming investors, whatever the colour of their money, have characterized Canadian politicians' attitudes for over a century. Patriotic concerns about foreign domination and the resulting nationalist policies to favour indigenous enterprise have been historically exceptional and significant only in certain key sectors. Recent industrial policies appear more to be variations of hybrid approaches. Favouring national champions (otherwise known as picking winners) may have been officially discarded as an approach, but Ottawa found money to put into 'technology partnerships' funds that are targeted to the efforts of home-based corporations – whether domestically (Bombardier) or foreign-owned (Pratt and Whitney) – to compete in high-tech markets.

Efforts to screen foreign direct investment in order to extract greater benefits from incoming capital (particularly takeovers of existing corporations) were never very effective, even though the Foreign Investment Review Agency generated disproportionate amounts of antagonism among American and European investors. Performance requirements on foreign investment have been cut back both by the federal government, which wants to make the economy more welcoming, and by continental and global trade agreements, which have outlawed such governmental devices as improper barriers to economic liberalization.

The end result is that Canada's approach to encouraging enterprise can be compared to pollywog breeding. A generous tax regime to favour research and development, universal public health insurance, high-quality public education, excellent infrastructure: these are the conditions put in place to promote entrepreneurial breeding. Beyond this, government does little to manage the growth process and protect the successful progeny. The frogs' eggs hatch into pollywogs. The pollywogs evolve into frogs. But there is virtually nothing that Canadian governments do to prevent predators from swallowing the frogs as they mature.

The Canadian software industry graphically illustrates this problem. Existing on the periphery of the world-dominant American software sector, Canadian software entrepreneurs have difficulty even getting access to the U.S.-controlled distribution system within their own country's market. Those micro-firm tadpoles that do make it to the medium-sized frog stage tend rapidly to be swallowed by the Microsofts or Disneys or IBMs. Even for a national champion such as Northern Telecom, which owes its success to a long incubation within the protected monopoly of Bell Telephone, the need to survive and grow in the global marketplace has pushed it to locate its major research and manufacturing operations in the United States of America.

Canada's National Research Council still uses its dwindling allocation of public funding to support both pure research and adoption of its findings by the market through co-operative venture programs. Ottawa still provides selected corporations with discretionary subsidies under its Technological Partnerships program and proffers what it claims to be the world's richest tax credits for research and developments, which provincial governments complement with their own subsidies and incentives for high-tech skills training. Both levels of government admit their impotence in securing home-based corporations from takeover or emigration and have become hesitant, even reluctant, sponsors of corporate clients. In sharp contrast, the trade-policy function under neoliberalism has become bold to the point of brash.

The State as Trade Negotiator

Both macroeconomic and industrial-policy changes were decided internally in response to exogenous pressures. Trade policy manifests the opposite phenomenon: demands from within the Canadian political system led to an externally moulded policy regime. The ideological pressures for free trade came from a number of sources, especially the perceived weakness of Canadian capital, thought to be flabby because of tariffs and governmental protection.[28] What better way to force entrepreneurs to be free than by pushing them under the cold shower of unprotected global competition? How better to compel protectionist provincial governments to disarm than to face them with an international agreement presenting no alternative and no recourse? In this sense, the misleadingly labelled policy of 'free trade' was Canadian neoliberalism's actual industrial strategy.

In the rationale offered by its proponents, Canadian–American free trade meant not just increased Canadian access to U.S. markets (lower U.S. tariffs) but secure access (exemption from the uncertainty-creating harassment of anti-dumping and countervailing duties that U.S. trade remedy law empowered American competitors to trigger against Canadian exporters).

In the event, the FTA failed to achieve Canada's goal of secure access. It did, however, incorporate the principal elements on the U.S. negotiating agenda, which was integral to a broader American trade strategy. The United States believed that foreign governments unfairly subsidized their exporting producers. While Washington was hardly afraid of the Canadian state, it wanted to use the FTA as a precedent in its dealings with those states whose competitive powers it did fear. Hence any policies regulating foreign investment or subsidizing Canadian enterprises had to be declared unacceptable. Accordingly, once it signed the FTA, Canada could no longer use its comparative advantage in petroleum or hydroelectric resources to give its own enterprises lower input costs for energy. The principle of national treatment when extended from imported goods to foreign investment forbade governments from favouring their own domestically owned enterprises unless they gave the same grants or incentives to foreign-controlled firms. However 'grandfathered' existing cultural policies might be, any new initiatives to favour Canadian culture at the expense of U.S. entertainment corporations would make any sector of the Canadian economy vulnerable to U.S. retaliation.

Free trade generated an unprecedented polarization in the Canadian political system. The Conservative government's free trade agreement was attacked in the 1988 election by both opposition parties. If the opposition's broad coalition of labour unions and social movements, native peoples and cultural groups, the poor and the pensioned feared anything, it was that the FTA would sabotage the state's economic policy capacity.

Powerful popular resistance to free trade did not stop the Mulroney government from joining with the United States and Mexico to negotiate the FTA's expansion. NAFTA deepened the disciplines that it imposed on government action, particularly in adding tough intellectual property rights to the new continental rulebook. Nothing daunted by the extra commitments that it had made, Ottawa simultaneously supported the final push of the Uruguay Round negotiations to create the World Trade Organization (WTO).

The combination of neoliberal macroeconomic policies with reduced industrial policies and enhanced trade liberalization has created a decentred political economy characterized by at least five elements:

- blocked continentalism
- denationalized industry
- labour-market fragmentation
- corporate restructuring
- U.S. corporate empowerment
- privatization

Blocked integration. That the Canadian political economy has not become more centralized around the de facto continental capital of Washington is paradoxically ensured by those U.S. interests that do indeed fear the Canadian state and the unfair competition that they allege it promotes. Anti-dumping and countervailing duty actions sponsored by the U.S. government have targeted those Canadian exports that put American producers under uncomfortably high degrees of competitive pressure. The softwood lumber industry induced Congress to change its trade law's definition of subsidy in such a way as to prevent competitive Canadian exports from expanding their share of the U.S. market. Farmers along the forty-ninth parallel in the midwest states have blocked the highways bringing Canadian grain to U.S. markets. Blocking Canadian exports may not be entirely consistent with the spirit of trade liberalization, but, as has so often been the case in the past, it is such manifestations of U.S. economic nationalism that push Canadians to retain their separate political and economic institutions, preventing them from merging in the continental U.S. system more completely.

Denationalized industry. When U.S. protectionism prevents Canadian producers from exporting their goods, it may force them to export their capital, inducing a forced integration of the smaller Canadian sector in the larger U.S. system. Because U.S. anti-dumping policy has been applied ruthlessly to their exports, Canadian steel companies have been compelled to locate their new, highest-technology smelters in the United States, ipso facto weakening this once superior and autonomous Canadian sector and melding it into the ranks of its former competitor.

Labour-market fragmentation. Increased competition from the U.S. southwest's right-to-work states as well as from Mexico's maquiladora region has induced Canadian corporations to press labour unions into accepting cutbacks in wages and fringe benefits or face plant closures. The extent of concessionary bargaining varies by sector, region, and gender, with its major incidence falling on low-skilled males in unionized environments and on part-time females who are reduced to piecework and remain unprotected by union-negotiated benefits. Exceptionally, within the automobile sector, which has become decisively integrated on a North American basis following NAFTA, the independent Canadian Auto Workers have managed to extract from the prospering major car and truck assemblers generous settlements that increased both wages and fringe benefits.

Corporate restructuring. Overall, the FTA and then NAFTA have created a regulatory regime to facilitate a continentalized system of production. Having gained new freedoms from governmental intervention, medium- and large-scale corporations have been able to close down branch plants in Canada or restructure their operations for what in many sectors has become a single, continental market.[29] Foreign-owned branch plants evolved into hollowed out subsidiaries or warehouses for their parent firm.[30] Canadian-owned national champions, which once served the domestic market, have restructured themselves to serve the continental market – variously moving their headquarters to the United States, expanding by buying out U.S. firms, or being swallowed up completely by their former American competitors. Corporations in some major sectors such as the auto industry have been continentally specialized for several decades.

U.S. corporate empowerment. The main thrust of the new continental and global trade rules has been to disempower the state by forbidding former practices that directed the activity of both national and foreign corporations within its territory. An ancillary effect of an apparently innocuous rule in NAFTA is actually to give substantial new powers to American (and in principle to Mexican) corporations to prevent Canadian governments from taking regulatory measures that might impinge on these firms' profitability. This provision is lodged in a set of clauses innocently known as chapter 11 in NAFTA. The innocence has to do with the chapter's protection of a company based in one North American country from 'expropriation' by a government in another. Understood in Canadian parlance, this protection had to do with compensation in the case of the nationalization of a firm's property. Understood in American administrative law, expropriation and measures 'tantamount to expropriation' include what are known as 'regulatory takings' – any governmental measure that negatively affects a company's earnings.

As Canadians have discovered in practice, chapter 11 has given American corporations the power to overturn regulatory measures taken to protect the health of Canadians against putatively dangerous substances such as the gasoline additive MMT. The legal reality of NAFTA is stark: foreign corporations have greater rights against the Canadian government than national corporations enjoy, and these rights mean that foreign corporations can overturn the actions taken by democratically elected executives and legislatures.

Privatization. The sale of crown corporations represents another significant rupture in Canadian state practice, expanding the private sector into the construction, operation, and ownership of what used to be considered sacrosanct components of the public domain: highways, municipal water systems, power utilities. The transportation industry has been particularly affected. Once sold off, Canadian National Railways has fallen under majority American ownership and undertaken a corporate expansion program to position itself as the dominant rail carrier from central Canada down the Mississippi Valley to Mexico. Its previous private-sector counterpart, Canadian Pacific Railways, had long since gone 'continental.'

In the airline industry a similar phenomenon has occurred. Air Canada, a now-privatized crown corporation, has taken on U.S. management and, aggressively responding to the Canada–United States 'open skies' agreement, has moved into the medium-distance routes that link Canadian cities more intensively with American airports to the south.

Meanwhile Air Canada's private-sector counterpart, Canadian Airlines (formerly Canadian Pacific Airlines), became a minor partner with American Airlines, which in 1999 came close to getting monopoly control of the entire Canadian air system. Air Canada beat off American's attempted hostile takeover to emerge as the country's new monopolist of the airways.

Whether they be of airways or airwaves, monopolies call for governments to regulate. Air Canada's takeover of Canadian Airlines has caused Ottawa to reactivate its regulatory role in the airways, where its formula for ensuring competition in the face of monopoly may well be to open the door to foreign airlines. As for Canada's airwaves, they have shifted from stable regional monopolies to much more volatile, transnational competitive partnerships because of a shift in the Canadian state's regulatory behaviour.

The State as Regulator

In telecommunication, a complex set of changes has empowered the federal level of government to disempower itself. Following the Supreme Court of Canada's attribution of exclusive jurisdiction over telecommunications to the federal level and the inclusion of telecommunication liberalization in the FTA, NAFTA, and the WTO, the Canadian Radio-television and Telecommunications Commission (CRTC) proceeded to reverse Canada's long tradition of establishing regional telephone monopolies in exchange for imposing considerable price regulation. In its place, the CRTC introduced a phased program of deregulation, which is permitting two linked processes: first, the convergence of formerly separated functions such as cable television, telephone, voice, images, computers, and Internet communication; and second, the introduction of competition into these services, including the gradual takeover of the Canadian telephone and cable companies by their larger American and European counterparts. As a result, the formerly dominant regional monopolies, Bell Canada and Rogers Cablevision, have entered strategic alliances with far more powerful global telecommunication companies, Ameritech and ATT, respectively. At the same time, consumers, whether citizens or corporations, are being wooed with the most up-to-date services, putatively making them globally competitive.

Banking is another area where the federal government has traditionally played a decisive role – one that it may be on the point of abandoning – in maintaining Canadian control of a key economic sector. Having established a national banking system of extraordinary stability, it gradually let foreign competitors enter on a second-class basis. The highly profitable retail market had been effectively reserved for half a dozen Canadian-controlled 'chartered banks,' which have also been allowed in recent years to expand their activities into the formerly restricted domains of stock brokerage, trust companies, and even insurance. Now that financial services have also been brought under the aegis of bilateral (FTA), trilateral (NAFTA), and multilateral (WTO) trade agreements, Ottawa's capacity to maintain the national content of its banking system is at risk.

Recent efforts to consolidate the major Canadian banks has triggered a vigorous debate about the contradictory imperatives of achieving competitiveness or efficiency within the global system (which argues for allowing a couple of national champions to consolidate) and securing competition or equity within the national system (which suggests maintaining a large number of banks). The victory of equity over efficiency in the recent showdown over bank mergers suggests that proponents of a 'civil state' were far from powerless. Indeed, however beleaguered they may be, continuing social and cultural policies reveal that the neoliberal, decentred state still has a social-democratic touch.

The Civil State

In his last mandate as prime minister (1980–4), Pierre Trudeau and his cabinet fought to maintain the welfare state as intended by its Keynesian architects. Established in the Pearson and Trudeau years, universal health care delivered payments through social insurance grants to individuals according to universalistic standards rationalized as rights of equal citizenship. The passage of the Canada Health Act (CHA) of 1984, which prohibited user fees and extra-billing, embodied the Trudeauites' last, perhaps quixotic effort to shore up a social security system undergoing financial stress In this section we consider the federal government's actions in social policy, cultural policy, national unity, and foreign policy.

Social Policies

Policy activists have been insistent about the damage caused both to health care and to the more general social safety net by the severe deficit-cutting measures taken by the federal government and imposed as a consequence on the provincial governments through the mechanism of jointly funded programs. Although Canadians continue to see theirs as a generous welfare state, their social security system has been cut back over the last quarter-century.

After their 1984 federal victory, the Progressive Conservatives began by limiting through stealth the growth of social spending.[31] By the time of their re-election in 1988, social programs were overtly retrenched. Following its 1993 victory, the Liberal Party replaced the social framework – the CHA, the Canada Assistance Plan (CAP), and Established Programs Funding (EPF) – with the less comprehensive and generous Canada Health and Social Transfer (CHST). Anti-poverty advocates argue that the creation of the CHST 'unleashed the most destructive chain reaction of government domino downloading and government cost-cutting of welfare and social spending that has ever been inflicted on Canada's poor and marginalized populations.'[32] The Mulroney/Chrétien years have seen welfare payments income-tested, targeted, and increasingly made conditional on the recipient's engaging in work or training.[33] The level of public support for the poorest, the oldest and the least employed has fallen markedly. Cuts have affected funding for public education and for public health, the crisis in which has become a national concern, focused on long waiting periods for hospital emergency services. A sharp increase in homelessness, affecting not just single men but entire families, has become the centre of another national debate. All this evidence of a deterioration in social cohesion notwithstanding, data continue to confirm that, while income inequalities have increased with the rich getting richer and the poor getting poorer, actual levels of after tax income inequality have remained constant during the neoliberal years if one factors in redistributive measures in the tax regime.

By the 1980s and continuing into the 1990s, the Canadian social system was threatening to implode. The weakening of national standards accelerated when Ottawa cut back its social policy transfers to the provinces. Under the CAP, provincial receipt of federal funds required that welfare be available to everybody in need, that there be an appeals process, that the provinces provide certain basic information about their program performance to the federal government, and that no provincial residency requirements be imposed on recipients. The sole surviving condition in the CHST is the prohibition of residency requirements. The CHA's principles are still operative, but erosion in the comprehensiveness of coverage has occurred as funding has declined.

This provincialization of social policy, whose costs can in turn be off-loaded to municipalities, has a further disintegrating impact on the federation's cohesion. Since equalization has been built into such programs as the 'cap on CAP' and employment insurance, which discriminate in favour of the less prosperous provinces at the expense of the richer, the divergence of interests between the equalization-receiving and the equalization-contributing provinces has risen.

If sustaining social cohesion is the political rationale for social policies, promoting national cohesion is the political rationale for most cultural policies. But the state's capacity to maintain a vibrant made-in-Canada cultural life is increasingly jeopardized by budget constraints, trade liberalizing agreements, and a deregulated telecommunication system that is powerless to resist the public's bombardment by the U.S. entertainment industry.

Cultural Policies

Cultural policies comprise another area that has been subject to severe cuts in government support. This contraction extends from the Canada Council's patronage in the arts, through public funding for the Canadian Broadcasting Corporation (CBC), to support for university research. Nevertheless, all these areas of activity have maintained their operations, if with less generous levels of funding and lower levels of staffing. The CRTC, created in 1968 to supervise and control not just the telephone industry but the public and private broadcasting systems by making regulations and issuing broadcasting licences, has become an important proxy for the state in all of its broadcasting activities. It has been regarded as both pariah and messiah – with private interests deeming its policies commercially restrictive and nationalist groups viewing it as a cultural saviour with insufficient commitment to their cause.

In the private sector, where government regulation has intervened to create a Canadian industry out of what would otherwise have been a simple extension of the American market, signs of life vary from marginal to vibrant. In the film industry most of the very considerable commercial action amounts to producing material competitively priced in low Canadian dollars for Hollywood to market through its global distribution oligopoly.

Despite Canada's need to strengthen the sense of nationhood motivating it to engage in protecting and promoting a distinctive Canadian cultural identity, cultural policy has consistently been challenged by U.S. power and by the neoliberal economic agenda. A good example can be found in recorded music. In the shadow of U.S. cultural hegemony, Canada's recorded music industry has become a vibrant cultural activity, having been fostered by a collection of talent rivalled only by Canada's endless supply of comedians. But while Canadian comedians continue to venture south of the border in search of greater success, the majority of Canada's recording artists now elect to maintain an identity with Canada as their musical heartland.[34]

Canada's recorded music industry owes its development to an import tariff imposed in the 1920s by the federal government on all finished foreign recordings. This typical strategy for an infant industry created a domestic market for records. Once importing U.S.-made records became unprofitable, branch plants were established in Canada to supply the domestic market from within. Canada's recording business became a miniature replica of the U.S. industry: each major U.S. multinational firm established record-pressing operations in Canada, with coast-to-coast sales networks to market their products.[35]

While the tariff contributed to the development of a Canadian market for recorded music in general, it did not create a market for *Canadian* music.[36] In the 1960s, Canadian music accounted for 4 to 7 per cent of all music played on the airwaves.[37] Further federal legislation induced the market to feature home-grown music. Declaring that domestic talent should have the chance to be heard on Canadian airwaves, the Broadcasting Act of 1968 empowered the CRTC to establish minimum levels of Canadian music for radio.[38] Assuming the role of cultural protector, the CRTC regulations established minimum levels of Canadian content in AM and FM radio broadcasting. In effect, Ottawa made radio the promotional springboard, sending into the nation's homes music that listeners would not have otherwise wanted to purchase. By 1986, 'Cancon' levels had risen to 30 per cent for AM stations and between 10 and 30 per cent for FM.

With such a significant increase in requirements for Canadian music, radio broadcasters began to demand a greater variety of Canadian artists to play. Accordingly, the record labels began to produce more albums by Canadian acts. The increase in airtime gave Canadian artists more exposure, stimulated rising record sales for this local talent, and further strengthened the country's music industry. Ottawa's import tariff and regulatory policy had created a virtuous, but tenuous, circle of viability for Canadian music.

The healthy market for Canadian music has been seriously challenged in the Mulroney/Chrétien period. On the one hand, the FTA eliminated the import tariff, causing the multinational corporations to meld their east–west distribution networks into single continental systems operating on a north–south basis. This continentalization of the dominant players deprived the smaller Canadian-owned recording businesses of their national distribution channels. Offsetting this threat is the easier access to U.S. audiences now enjoyed by Canadian musicians who have been signed by American 'labels.'

From the 1960s to the 1980s, a division of labour characterized the Canadian industry. Domestic record labels signed bands and recorded music, while multinational branch operations produced and distributed their recordings. In this process, the domestic record labels retained their ownership of copyright to the music. Canadian content rules ensured these companies cash from broadcasting royalties. Beginning in the late 1970s, major multinational labels began taking a stronger interest in Canada's music in order to offset a general decline in sales experienced throughout the industry. By the 1980s, when copyright revenues displaced record sales as the main source of revenue in the industry,[39] the multinationals' share of the Canadian industry was growing to the detriment of local firms.

The negotiation of the FTA and NAFTA gave the U.S. multinationals a chance to change the rules of the game by enhancing the scope of intellectual property rights. After initial resistance, Ottawa accepted Washington's position on intellectual property once it had been incorporated into the Uruguay Round's version of the GATT, which ultimately provided the substance for NAFTA's chapter 17. Article 1706 of NAFTA states: 'Sound recording producers shall have similar rights to those of a copyright holder.'[40] Under this innocent-sounding wording, if Canadian labels merely record the music, leaving manufacturing/production and distribution to a multinational firm, they lose their claim to its copyright. With most firms now relying on the revenues generated from the exploitation of copyrights, article 1706 threatens the survival of many Canadian firms. By the same logic, this provision now grants the multinationals greater distribution and production power, as their own claim to copyright enables them to exploit intellectual property without fear of infringing someone else's rights. Additionally, although NAFTA's provisions on intellectual property rights empowered only the U.S. multinational record labels,[41] the WTO's TRIPS granted similar privileges to all multinational labels, further squeezing the independent national record labels from the Canadian market.

Before NAFTA and TRIPS, the federal government was free to alter intellectual property provisions to advance the goals of the domestic industry. Now its power to change policy is also marginalized, nullifying its ability to protect this part of Canadian culture. The new intellectual property rights are arguably neoliberalism's greatest victory in the cultural sphere.

Television broadcasting is a further area under overall American domination but containing a smaller, poorer Canadian component, whose very existence is the result of state regulation. First the CBC and then Canadian-content regulations produced a minimal level of domestic production of entertainment and documentary TV programming. Francophone radio and television industries are healthier and more vital, benefiting as they do not only from the federal and provincial governments' subsidy and regulatory protection, but also from the added stimulus afforded by their distinct language.

The threat of U.S. trade retaliation is now a strong *external* limitation to state policy favouring cultural activities. Americans generally consider that Canadian cultural policies are covert protectionist actions that discriminate against the U.S. entertainment industry in order to take a slice from its export earnings. The FTA, NAFTA, and the WTO have given the United States a set of rules that decree culturally protectionist policies to be in contravention of Canada's international obligations – or at least the American interpretation of these obligations.

The new continental and global trade regime will continue to challenge Canadian practices so long as they try to secure a national culture, but it is not the only force threatening to eliminate the state's cultural role. The internet, along with the convergence of computer and mass media delivery systems, threatens to make laws restricting foreign ownership and content ineffective even before the WTO declares them illegal.

It is characteristic of the contradictory nature of the neoliberal state that the same government both implements policies to protect Canadian culture and signs agreements that put it in danger. While the federal government displays a continued commitment to the ideals of intervention in cultural policy, trade liberalization pulls the carpet from under its feet. Some policy-making powers that were formally held at the federal level have ascended to the continental and global levels. What remains in federal hands has shifted, so that the efficacy of policy has waned. Much of the cultural protection generated in the Pearson and Trudeau years still existed on paper in the Mulroney/Chrétien era, but many of these policies are currently in danger of becoming irrelevant or illegal. While Ottawa may continue to sing embedded liberalism's tune in the sphere of cultural policy, neoliberalism continues both to mute the federal government and to overpower its melody with a song of its own.

National Unity

The danger inherent in any claim that a sea change has occurred in Canada's state forms is to ignore the features of continuity that persist from the formally discarded paradigm. Consider, for example, those characteristics of the Canadian polity that Trudeauphiles claim to be his lasting legacy, and which continue to shape the Canadian polity:[42] the Charter of Rights and Freedoms; the impact of multiculturalism and bilingualism; and the long struggle to establish native land claims, which was launched in the Trudeau years.

Various pan-Canadian aspects of the Trudeau era's policies remain intact and substantial. Bilingualism may not be the most prominent feature of federal policy, but it remained a touchstone both of the Mulroney and Chrétien governments. Multiculturalism, based on high levels of immigration from all continents of the world, becomes every year more entrenched as a central component of the Canadian identity. Most powerful of all the evidence of continuing centripetal tendencies is the cumulating judgment made by the court system – the Supreme Court in particular – in interpreting the Charter of Rights and Freedoms that was introduced into the Canadian constitution in 1982. However neoliberal Canadian politicians may become, Supreme Court judges have retained the liberal spirit in which the Charter was written. Rights of women's groups, of gays and lesbians, and in particular of native peoples have been advanced over this period in a pattern showing convincing levels of consistency. The deepening of these Charter-based rights boosts federal power because they are defined as pan-Canadian norms.

Foreign Policy

One of the great paradoxes of continental trade liberalization for Canada has been the increased autonomy of a civil Canadian foreign policy – a result thought to be impossible by opponents of free trade ten years ago. In the event, it is the end of the Cold War that has proven the decisive factor. With the East–West nuclear standoff no longer requiring complete solidarity among the NATO powers, Canada has found itself able to take some distance from Washington's positions, whether this be in relations with Cuba (strong opposition to the Helms–Burton Act), peace-making (the landmines treaty), or international law (an International Criminal Court). Ottawa has resisted the temptation of disagreeing with the United States as a matter of principle, joining the NATO campaign to end ethnic cleansing in Kosovo. To a surprising degree, then, Canada's foreign policy under free trade has taken back power from the continental level. The old formula – maintain good relations with the United States but form multilateral coalitions to pursue other objectives when possible – holds; but the balance between subservience and autonomy has shifted.

Conclusion

This review confirms that substantial changes have taken place in the functions and structures of the Canadian state from the activist, generous practices of the Pearson and Trudeau governments to the leaner and, yes, meaner stances of neoliberal politics. State shapes have shifted in response to a changing global system and have in turn helped to shape that system. The federal and provincial states are different from their modernist predecessors both because of their neoliberal traits and because they have become so tightly interconnected with governance above and below that they each now constitute just one tier in an evolving and nested multi-level state structure. While there has been change, its nature is not always obvious, and its consequences are not always consistent. Continuities with earlier eras also exist – notably, a civil service rooted in traditions of respect for the values of the democratically elected government of the day, with bureaucrats guaranteed tenure so that they can serve parties of any ideology with equal and competent devotion. There is some evidence of a return to a more active federal state, as surpluses replace deficits on the public agenda and as the insufficiency of the neoliberal model itself creates the basis for further evolution.

In drawing conclusions, we must guard against nostalgia. Twenty-five years ago those on the left bitterly criticized the inadequate social provision of a state then thought to be reactionary. Now the Trudeau state appears to be decidedly social-democratic by comparison with the Chrétien state. Sovereignty is now divisible. Identities are multiple. Governance is deconstructible. As federal and provincial negotiations with native nations are showing, self-government can take many forms, involving diverse geographical and sectoral components, with various types of 'stakeholders' wielding powers of different weights.

The boundaries between state, market, and society have become more porous. It does not follow that the state is declining just because airlines administer immigration procedures at their check-in counters or because advertisers take on the job of policing their own practices. These developments could simply be an indicator of sensible delegation. Similarly, the transnational activity of social movements, epistemic communities, and NGOs may complicate intergovernmental relations but may not ipso facto threaten the raison d'être of sovereign states.[43] While strong states may lose some of their monopoly control over foreign affairs, weaker, more decentralized states such as Canada may gain by co-opting their NGOs' transnational energies to project the national interest abroad.

Even if we have developed a sufficient synthesis to allow an understanding of the Canadian state's evolving nature, we have not answered the normative question about how to regain the quality of the social and political life achieved under the welfare state of the first post-1945 decades. To be sure, the phenomenon of globalization may be a process through which capitalism is liberating itself from political control and engendering ever-increasing disparities between rich and poor both within and among countries.[44] Although a decline in the level of social services for the citizenry, a weakening of trade union powers to defend workers, and a diminished capacity to redistribute wealth on egalitarian principles seem to be indicators of social regression inherent in neoliberalism, they do not appear to be necessary concomitants of the emerging multilevel state. Even though the shapes of governance are shifting, the world of federal states may not be as global as both proponents and critics of globalization assume.[45]

If some variant of the proposed 'Tobin tax' on international capital flows were instituted, redistribution of a capital rent in favour of the poor might become possible precisely through a variant of global governance formerly talked about only by dreamy-eyed world federalists. A citizens' version of the Multilateral Agreement on Investment is being proposed by the Council of Canadians, an NGO that has developed an international coalition to demand that rights given to transnational corporations in the global order be balanced by obligations on foreign investors to create jobs with high labour standards, maintain satisfactory levels of environmental performance, and protect national cultural distinctiveness.[46] The European Union has shown that social welfare and workers' rights can be defended in principle – though very imperfectly in practice – at the continental level. Asian capitalism offers an alternative, less individualistic political model for achieving economic competitiveness and social solidarity.[47] In short, capitalisms vary, as do popular responses to them. The postmodern, multi-level state is far from synonymous with a reprise of pre-modern, Dickensian practices.

Ottawa remains potentially capable of restoring the Canadian welfare system but is fiscally constrained. The public knows that social spending lags considerably behind that enjoyed in the Trudeau era, and renewed flexing of federal muscle can be anticipated as budget surpluses swells. Another factor that may result in a different, but reinvigorated role for the Canadian state is the new federal–provincial Social Union Framework Agreement of 1999. It could generate a new species of co-operative federalism, in which Ottawa reclaims some of its earlier functions by enriching its transfer payments and working in tandem with the provinces, although Quebec is again not a signatory.[48] While the rhetoric of consensus around the talks leading to the Social Union Agreement disguises inevitable political and jurisdictional disagreements, the Child Tax Benefit, which was their first product, indicates that some movement has taken place. However, since the Social Union has freed the provinces and territories from what they considered the tyranny of federal standards, it would cost Ottawa hefty amounts to regain sufficient clout for it to re-establish these norms.A final danger dogs those who would declare the Keynesian paradigm dead and buried. With substantial resistance to neoliberalism gaining expression both at home (with the distress of hospital services and the scandal of E. coli pollution in munucipal water supplies brought on by cutting back of the state) and abroad (with the crisis of the globalized financial market system in 1997–98 and dramatic protests lodged against the WTO and the IMF in 1999–2000), no new point of equilibrium has been reached. The neoliberal model leaves the state without an obvious role to play as a buffer against the short-run economic vicissitudes that characterize capitalist economies. In abdicating this function, the federal state exists with a lacuna at its centre.

The neoliberal model has clearly been the winning approach since the Mulroney government took office in 1984, but the silence at its heart renders it incomplete. It is unable to be both true to itself and responsive to the social needs to which governments may feel compelled to respond. Nor does a less regulated global market provide more optimal distributional results on an inter-state basis. Because politicians have deprived themselves of the tools and the rationales for discretionary intervention, citizens demanding a more activist state must speak from outside the neoliberal ideological loop. Over time the neoliberal vision is subject to contestation, against which it has only weak arguments. Indeed, considerable authority and legitimacy having located elsewhere, the federal government may try to reassert itself in ways that it had earlier abandoned and reclaim some of the authority and legitimacy that it had previously alienated. Given the inability of the neoliberal model to respond to some of these concerns, the pendulum may even be poised to swing back towards a state less reluctant to exercise its power to regulate the market and to provide society with the services that it desires. New money for health and other provisions in its 1999 and 2000 budgets suggested the re-emergence of a more socially engaged federal government. Automatic stabilizers and measures to maintain aggregate demand remain in the policy arsenal. Calls for government action to improve physical and human infrastructure are continually heard. Proposals keep emerging from the legal community to create a genuinely supranational dispute- settlement order for NAFTA. Suggestions for government action to re-establish order in the world's financial markets imply enhanced roles for states co-operatively to achieve some variant of global Keynesianism. Municipal elites are rallying behind the notion of a constituional charter for cities. As a result, the potential for contestation and further change remains at each level of the five-tier system of state power.

What characterized the postwar consensus so celebrated by its analysts was its long period of relative stability. At the turn of the millennium a prime characteristic of the Canadian state is the level of its flux. If it suffers from chronic instability, this is largely because the citizenry, which has borne the brunt of neoliberalism's 'reforms,' is now clamouring for their attenuation. But it is also because the corporate sector, in its endless efforts to merge and acquire to protect itself from the vicissitudes of the global market, never stands still. What makes future shapes even more difficult to foretell is the proliferation of the sites where policy is made and norms are set. The postmodern state wears a distinctly multi-centred mask.

NOTES

I wrote a precursor of this analysis with Tim Lewis as 'The Contested State: Canada in the Post–Cold War, Post-Keynesian, Post-Fordist, Post-National Era,' in Leslie Pal, ed., *How Ottawa Spends: 2000* (Toronto: Oxford University Press, 1999). The present text was deepened thanks to the research contributed in 1999 by my students Sara Boyne, Paola Cifelli, Trevor deBoer, Franca Fargione, Daniela Follegot, Chris Giggey, Michael Hong, Monica Misra, Ambrese Montagu, Karis Rae, Angela van Damme, and Brian Zeiler.

1 Anton L. Allahar and E.C. James, *Richer and Poorer: The Structure of Inequality in Canada* (Toronto: Lorimer, 1998).

2 Tony Clarke, *Silent Coup: Confronting the Big Business Takeover of Canada* (Toronto: Lorimer, 1997).

3 Stephen McBride and John Shields, *Dismantling a Nation: The Transition to Corporate Rule in Canada*, second edition (Halifax: Fernwood, 1997).

4 John Shields and B. Mitchell Evans, *Shrinking the State: Globalization and Public Administration Reform* (Halifax: Fernwood, 1998).

5 In this chapter, 'regional' applies to sub-national jurisdictions, 'continental' to groupings of several sovereign states that encompass most of a continental landmass.

6 In this text 'state' refers to the enduring – if evolving – ensemble of political, judicial, administrative, and coercive institutions, and 'government,' to the executive, legislature and bureaucracy that enjoys the current electoral mandate.

7 McBride and Shields, *Dismantling a Nation.*

8 On the role of provinces in trade issues, see Douglas M. Brown, 'The Federal–Provincial Consultation Process,' and 'Canadian Federalism and Trade Policy: The Uruguay Round Agenda,' in Peter M. Leslie and Ronald L. Watts, eds., *Canada: The State of the Federation 1987–88*, (Kingston: Institute of Intergovernmental Relations, Queen's University, 1988); 'Canadian Federalism and Trade Policy: The Uruguay Round Agenda,' in Ronald L. Watts and Douglas M. Brown, eds., *Canada: The State of the Federation 1989*, (Kingston: Institute of Intergovernmental Relations, Queen's University, 1989); and 'The Evolving Role of the Provinces in Canadian Trade Policy,' in Douglas M. Brown and Murray G. Smith, eds., *Canadian Federalism: Meeting Global Economic Challenges?* (Kingston: Institute of Intergovernmental Relations, Queen's University, 1991).

9 Ian Robinson argues that the FTA and NAFTA are centralizing in their effects. See 'NAFTA, the Side-Deals, and Canadian Federalism: Constitutional Reform by Other Means?' in Ronald L. Watts and Douglas M. Brown,

eds., *Canada: The State of the Federation 1993*, (Kingston: Institute of Intergovernmental Relations, Queen's University, 1993); and 'Trade Policy, Globalization, and the Future of Canadian Federalism,' in François Rocher and Miriam Smith, eds., *New Trends in Canadian Federalism* (Peterborough: Broadview Press, 1995).

10 Robert M. Campbell, 'Federalism and Economic Policy,' in Rocher and Smith, eds., *New Trends in Canadian Federalism*, 200.

11 The major exceptions are British Columbia and Nova Scotia. British Columbia was not hit very hard by the recession in the early 1990s, but its economy struggled in the late 1990s, and its fiscal position does not seem to be tending towards balance. Nova Scotia's position, like that of the other Atlantic provinces, improved because of ballooning equalization payments, which originated in the strength of Ontario's economy.

12 Richard Simeon, 'Canada and the United States: Lessons from the North American Experience,' in Karen Knop, Sylvia Ostry, Richard Simeon, and Katherine Swinton, eds., *Rethinking Federalism: Citizens, Markets, and Governments in a Changing World*, (Vancouver: University of British Columbia Press, 1995), 251.

13 Thomas J. Courchene, 'Glocalization: The Regional/International Interface,' *Canadian Journal of Regional Science* 18, no. 1 (Spring 1995), 1–20.

14 Stephen Blank, Stephen Krajewski, and Henry S. Yu, 'U.S. Firms in North America: Redefining Structure and Strategy,' *North American Outlook* 5, no. 2 (February 1995).

15 Commission for Environmental Cooperation, *NAFTA's Institutions: The Environmental Potential and Performance of the NAFTA Free Trade Commission and Related Bodies* (Montreal: CEC, 1997).

16 Stephen Clarkson, 'The Joy of Flux: What the European Monetary Union Can Learn from North America's Experience with National Currency Autonomy,' in Colin Crouch, ed., *After the Euro: Shaping Institutions for Governance in the Wake of European Monetary Union* (Oxford: Oxford University Press, 1999).

17 Fritz W. Scharpf, *Negative and Positive Integration in the Political Economy of European Welfare States* (Florence: European University Institute, 1995).

18 Wolfgang Streeck has suggested a similar hypothesis for the member states of the European Union, arguing that they have compensated for what they have lost in internal sovereignty by what they have retained in their intergovernmental bargaining in the EU's various institutions – although decision-making deadlocks and democratic deficits at the continental level of governance are high prices to pay for this exchange. See Wolfgang Streeck, 'Public Power beyond the Nation-State: The Case of the European Commu-

nity,' in Robert Boyer and Daniel Drache, eds., *States against Markets: The Limits of Globalization* (London: Routledge, 1996), 299–315.

19 Michael Hart, *Fifty Years of Canadian Tradecraft: Canada at the GATT, 1947–1997* (Ottawa: Centre for Trade Policy and Law, 1998), 191.

20 Daniel Drache, ed., *Staples, Markets and Cultural Change: Selected Essays by Harold A. Innis* (Montreal: McGill-Queen's University Press, 1995).

21 Observers often describe this policy as one of 'zero inflation.' In fact, it was directed to price stability, which may or may not constitute zero inflation. For example, if prices rise in one year, but not the next, inflation in the second year would be zero, but prices would not have been stable. See proceedings of a conference held by the Bank of Canada, May 1997, *Price Stability, Inflation Targets, and Monetary Policy* (Ottawa: Bank of Canada, February 1998).

22 Stephen Clarkson, 'Disjunctions: Free Trade and the Paradox of Canadian Development,' in Daniel Drache and Meric S. Gertler, eds., *The New Era of Global Competition: State Policy and Market Power* (Montreal: McGill-Queen's University Press, 1991), 103–26.

23 Michael M. Atkinson and William D. Coleman, *The State, Business, and Industrial Change in Canada* (Toronto: University of Toronto Press, 1989).

24 Macdonald Commission, *Report of the Royal Commission on the Economic Union and Development Prospects for Canada into the 21st Century* (Ottawa: Minister of Supply and Services, 1985).

25 An example of government investment in education is Ontario's Access to Opportunity Program to promote postsecondary enrolment in engineering and computer science programs. Under this program, the government would match private-sector contributions dollar for dollar. Nortel has already pledged $20 million to the program, because 9,000 employees from its worldwide labour force of 75,000 are engaged in research and development in Ontario. See David Crane, 'Nortel Sets Example by Tackling Skills Gap,' *Toronto Star*, (3 March 1999), E2.

26 David Wolfe, 'The Emergence of the Region State,' in Thomas J. Courchene, ed., *The Nation State in a Global/Information Era: Policy Challenges*, (Kingston: John Deutsch Institute for the Study of Economic Policy (1997), 205–40.

27 Ontario Jobs and Investment Board, *A Road Map to Prosperity: An Economic Plan for Jobs in the 21st Century* (Toronto: OJIB, March 1999).

28 Macdonald Commission, *Report*, vol. 1 (Ottawa: Minister of Supply and Services, 1985).

29 Blank, Krajewski, and Yu, 'U.S. Firms in North America.'

30 Harry Arthurs, 'The Hollowing Out of Corporate Canada,' in J. Jenson and B. Santos, eds., *Globalizing Institutions: Case Studies in Social Regulation and Innovation* (London: Ashgate, 2000).

31 A noteworthy exception to the fiscal trends outlined has been funding for disabled persons, which has been substantially increased by the federal Liberal government and many provincial governments, including Mike Harris's Tory government, in Ontario.

32 Loren Fried, director of North York Harvest Food Bank, quoted in 'Ottawa Urged to Take Lead on Poverty Issues,' *Globe and Mail* (6 December 1997), A16.

33 Keith Banting, 'The Internationalization of the Social Contract,' in Thomas J. Courehene, ed., *The Nation State in a Global/Information Era: Policy Challenges* (Kingston: John Deutsch Institute for the Study of Economic Policy, 1997), 255–86.

34 While musical acts such as the Guess Who, Gordon Lightfoot, and Anne Murray are often regarded as some of Canada's early musical exports, it is often forgotten that Canada has always had a successful stream of artists, although they may not have always achieved success while in Canada. Examples include Neil Young and Joni Mitchell; both are highly regarded and have had international recognition, although they were once regarded as non-Canadian simply because of their success in the United States. Present-day Canadian-born international artists such as Shania Twain, Alanis Morisette, Céline Dion, and Sarah MacLachlan publicly express their Canadian pride, although the first two currently reside in the United States.

35 In the music industry, the activity of writing music is considered not 'production' per se but rather 'creation' or 'recording.' 'Production' refers to the industrial process whereby vinyl records, tapes, CDs, and the like are manufactured. See Tim Straw, 'Sound Recording,' in Michael Dorland, ed., *Canada's Cultural Industries* (Scarborough, Ont.: Carswell, 1996), 102.

36 Canadian music is defined as any piece that satisfies at least two requirements of the MAPL: the *music* composed entirely by a Canadian; the *artist* principally performing the music and/or lyrics is Canadian; *production* recorded wholly in Canada or performed wholly and broadcast live in Canada; and *lyrics* written entirely by a Canadian.

37 Tim Straw, 'Sound Recording,' 132.

38 CRTC website http://www.crtc.gc.ca/eng/info_sht/g11e.htm

39 Line Grenier, 'Cultural Exemptionalism Revisited: Quebec Music Industries in the Face of Free Trade,' *Mass Media and Free Trade* (Austin: University of Texas Press, 1996), 317.

40 Department of External Affairs and International Trade Canada, *NAFTA: What's It All About?* (Ottawa: Queen's Printer, 1993), 80.

41 Steve Jones, 'Mass Communication, Intellectual Property Rights, International Trade and the Popular Music Industry,' in Emile G. McAnany and

Kenton T. Wilkinson, eds., *Mass Media and Free Trade: NAFTA and the Cultural Industries,* (Austin: University of Texas Press, 1996), 331.

42 Andrew Cohen and J.L. Granatstein, eds., *Trudeau's Shadow* (Toronto: Random House, 1998).

43 Thomas Risse-Kappen, *Bringing Transnational Relations Back In: Non-state Actors, Domestic Structures, and International Institutions* (New York: Cambridge University Press, 1995).

44 Stephen Gill, 'Globalisation, Market Civilisation, and Disciplinary Neoliberalism,' *Millennium: Journal of International Studies* (Tokyo: United Nations University, 1994): 399–423.

45 On the argument that the world is not as global as is often thought, and that even if it is, downward policy harmonization does not follow, see William Watson, *Globalization and the Meaning of Canadian Life* (Toronto: University of Toronto Press, 1998); and Paul Hirst, 'The Global Economy: Myths and Realities,' *International Affairs* 73, no. 3 (1997): 409–25.

46 Heather Scoffield, 'Groups Pitch Alternative to MAI,' *Globe and Mail* (8 July 1998), B4.

47 Richard Stubbs, 'ASEAN's Distinctive Capitalism: Implications for International Trade Rules,' in William D. Coleman and Geoffrey R.O. Underhill, eds., *Regionalism and Global Economic Integration: Europe, Asia and America,* (London: Routledge, 1997).

48 'A Framework to Improve the Social Union for Canadians: An Agreement between the Government of Canada and the Governments of the Provinces and Territories,' 4 February 1999.

Part Three

The International System and Multiple Centres of Power

6. The Emergence of International Parliamentary Institutions: New Networks of Influence in World Society

Robert M. Cutler

Democratization and transnationalization are two fundamental trends in the evolution of international affairs today. They come together in the neglected phenomenon of international parliaments and inter-parliamentary associations, which, for the sake of brevity, I group together as international parliamentary institutions (IPIs). The academic literature pays almost no attention to IPIs. Some recent research confirms that the European Parliament (EP) is significant not only for the political and economic life of citizens of its member states, but also for the conduct of international affairs in Europe at large.[1] To demonstrate this point, one need only mention the EP's forcing of the resignation of Jacques Santer and the entire European Commission in March 1999. The European Commission's attention to environmental questions as an aspect of international security in Central and Eastern Europe derives from an impulse first provided by the EP and embodied in its legislation. To observers, it is obvious that the EP has affected important choices along the road of the European Union's development. It has even constructed a good number of the road signs. For example, the Treaty of Maastricht developed out of a series of proposals presented to the EP by a caucus of its members in 1984.

The significance of IPIs is wide-ranging and growing. The EP is only the best-known example. There are nearly two dozen such international institutions in the world today, with varying scopes and responsibilities. Scepticism over the efficacy of IPIs is no longer justified; a blanket dismissal cannot be defended. IPIs introduce national elites from countries that are not yet fully democratized to ranges of views and perspectives, particularly from democratic oppositions in other regimes. IPIs have also given birth to a new form of diplomacy called parliamentary diplomacy.[2] This represents today, from both an analytical and a practical standpoint, an important middle ground between the traditional level of interstate diplomacy and the new level of transnational co-operation among grassroots non-governmental organizations (NGOs). IPIs are developing into an important societal mechanism for oversight on traditional executive-based diplomacy. IPIs also establish ongoing transnational relationships that restrain old power politics where civil society and NGOs are underdeveloped and politically constrained. In such a manner they prepare a middle ground for interstate co-operation.

This chapter analyses the emergence of IPIs – a type of institution that has been in existence for half a century but has recently started to proliferate. The chapter uses IPIs as a vehicle for discussing the nature of the emerging international system and how this affects the institutions structuring the current international order. The first section of the chapter offers a brief explanation of why neither 'world public opinion' nor 'global civil society' adequately describes the impact of world society on world politics. The second section explains why the intersection of the concepts 'complexity' and 'world society' accurately characterizes the new international environment. It also outlines briefly what this means for the level, scope, and scale of analysis of international affairs. The third section surveys parliamentary and quasi-parliamentary institutions in world politics as well as defining and offering a typology of IPIs. The fourth section discusses how to assess their institutional development. For this purpose, it synthesizes two seemingly contradictory frameworks (functional and epigenetic), showing them to be complementary. It traces the development of the EP according to this framework in order to illustrate its aptness. Finally, the conclusion reflects on the implications of IPIs for the evolution and design of future international orders.

Neither World Public Opinion nor Global Civil Society

Two concepts that have in the past helped us understand the impact of transnational social life and action on international politics are world public opinion and global civil society. However, neither of them is adequate for either theoretical conceptualization or policy guidance in the twenty-first century.

World Public Opinion

The concept of 'world public opinion' was an early and crude term designed to help us assess the impact of public opinion on the conduct of international affairs. The term was poorly defined. It often referred to the expressed opinion of governments, either capitalist or communist, without reference to the populations of the states concerned. Other times it referred to the collective opinion of editorial writers of leading newspapers. In the eyes of some observers, especially during the heyday of the Nonaligned Movement, resolutions of the UN General Assembly became a referent for world public opinion.

This ambiguity reproduces the same misconceptions that were characteristic of early attempts, a century ago, to study domestic public opinion. Those projects used what was then the most obvious source of expression from the public – the journalistic press. Newspapers, it was understood, revealed the opinions of social classes and estates. However, the dominant social and political philosophy of the time assumed that these classes and estates were created by the state. Even this school of thought was marked by an absence of any theory of the press that integrated the media system analytically with the political system or with society at large.

The meaning of the concept of 'public opinion' depends on how one defines the political community and how that community is represented.[3] A systematic theory of the press finally emerged not in Western Europe but rather in Central Europe, where the nationality question revealed the poverty of such distinctions as the simple dichotomy, in nineteenth-century France, between *le pouvoir* and *l'opinion*. In nineteenth-century central Europe, accelerated social mobilization, accompanied by rapid urbanization and a jump in literacy rates, impelled the creation of parliamentary regimes and the extension of suffrage in conditions where the tension between republicanism and monarchical principles did not have the luxury of time to be resolved. The rise of the nationality question in central Europe forced the issue of state–society relations. In social science, this development was formulated analytically as the question of the influence of public opinion on government policy.

In response, German social scientists attempted to establish a science that they called *Zeitungswissenschaft*, about newspapers and other journalistic media. The German sociologist Max Weber, the first person to treat the press as a component of the social system, made the previously unknown distinction between 'newspaper opinion' and 'public opinion.' In the first decade of the twentieth century, and against the dominant view, he argued that public opinion is not a given and that the study of its formation was legitimate.[4] Indeed, Vladimir Lenin's conviction that publishing his party-revolutionary newspaper *Iskra* was equivalent to creating public opinion, rather than influencing it, merely reflects the era's general lack of knowledge about public opinion. Only in the 1920s was the historian Wilhelm Mommsen able to conclude that the press of any era represents only a portion of public opinion.[5]

Today, there is still no comprehensive theory of how the press is related to society, and the growth of electronic communication complicates systematic analysis. The rapidity and proliferation of messages today gives much mass communication the quality of rumour.[6] Communication strategies today run the risk of being seen as no more than propaganda. The notion of world public opinion has become so problematic that one rarely hears it invoked anymore. References to 'global civil society' are the heritage left to us by the passing of world public opinion.

Global Civil Society

The concept of 'global civil society' is equally problematic. For Hegel, civil society mediated the relations that the family had with the state and hence referred to, among other things, economic exchanges and the market. Given this history of the concept, it is remarkable that many references today to global civil society ignore economic activity, whether of individuals or of multinational corporations.[7] This contemporary connotation of 'global civil society' is a result of the way in which 'civil society' was reintroduced in the 1980s to analyse political transitions from authoritarian rule. It referred to the power arising from the political association of people living in societies that were undergoing political transformation in South America, South Africa, Southern and Eastern Europe, and the Soviet Union, without reference to economic activity.

Thus the dominant conception of civil society refers to the ensemble of political associations mediating between the individual and the state. Evident shortcomings in this concept nevertheless encourage us to consider alternatives. The term 'NGO' seems inappropriate because many NGOs in transitional countries have been fronts for, or sponsored by, governments. The term 'private voluntary organization' has entered into currency, but these organizations have often been sponsored by individuals pursuing private agendas and private economic interests. The term 'third sector' has evolved to reflect activity that falls under the aegis neither of the state nor of private enterprise (including criminal organizations and the Mafia).

Some writers have argued that the definition of global civil society ought to include economic activity, as it did when the term first developed.[8] They see civil society as an overarching social form that dominates both states and individuals; they emphasize transnational economic activity as the principal characteristic of this social form. Yet if the former view of global civil society ignores transnational economic activity, then this latter view tends too much to ignore and minimize transnational political activity. However, recent speculations about and explorations of 'transnational democracy' make it clear that such considerations are non-trivial.[9] An Archimedean point is necessary, capable of equilibrating these two overemphases. This is provided by a new approach called 'complex world society.'

International Parliamentary Institutions in Complex World Society

The idea of complex world society combines the world society approach with the insights of complexity science. Complexity science is a new way of looking at physical, biological, and social phenomena. A complex system is a system having multiple interacting components, the overall behaviour of which cannot be inferred from the behaviour of its components. Complexity is not complicatedness, or overdetermination, or a multiplication of explanatory variables.[10] Complexity science offers an innovative perspective on the evolution of the international system and on the behaviours of actors within it.

The Complexity of World Society and Its Politics

The emergence today of an interconnected global civilization and multiple centres of power in world politics manifests complexity. Recent developments in international relations theory have sought to take this complexity into account.[11] Much complexity-based work recently has been in the field of agent-based modelling, and this is insightful. However, complexity is not merely a set of new implements to be added to existing theoretical toolkits. Using its insights does not require computer programming or even quantitative analysis. The complexity of present-day international politics has implications for the level, for the scope, and for the scale of analysis. The phenomenon of IPIs illustrates how current developments in world politics manifest complexity in all three of these aspects.

The Level of Analysis

Complexity science offers us a means of understanding levels of analysis and helps us to reconstruct analytically the international political system. Questions about the level of analysis draw attention to the issue of emergence. Emergence is the evolution of new (qualitative) phenomena through a system's interaction with its environment. IPIs are an example of such emergent phenomena. The multiplication of issue-areas in international politics and security manifests such emergence. The whole growth of questions about deterritorialized aspects of international politics does so as well. Emergence invokes questions about the dependence of a system on its parts and the interdependence and specialization of these parts. Studying the parts in isolation no longer works. Changes in one part may affect other parts and the behaviour of the system as a whole. Increased academic interest in 'counterfactuals' demonstrates how important this aspect of complexity is.[12]

The Scope of Analysis

Issues about the scope of the analysis draw attention to a category of questions concerning stability and change. This category subsumes adaptation, pattern formation, and evolution. As such, it draws attention to issues of learning, including organizational learning. It also balances issues of emergence, such as transnational networks concerned with non-territorial issues, with equally important territorial aspects of the post–Cold War world, such as establishment of regional international systems. While such systems today are more autonomous of the global political system than they were during the Cold War, they have grown stronger and more interrelated. These include not only regional international subsystems (for example, Europe and Southeast Asia), but also international littoral subsystems (such as the Pacific Rim, the Baltic, and the Caspian). The proliferation of regional IPIs is an aspect of this phenomenon. The territorial aspects of world politics today thereby lead us to treat the global political system and its components as complex adaptive systems.[13]

The Scale of Analysis

Scale of analysis draws attention to self-organization, which arises from the fact that under conditions of complexity fine scales influence large-scale behaviour. To understand complex systems therefore requires multi-scale descriptions. The degree of complexity that is apparent to an observer also depends on the scale at which the system is described. For example, one requirement of complexity is to establish correlation between large and small scales. This reduces the overall smaller-scale complexity. This is happening every day in world politics. International regions that self-organize as emergent multilateral networks are an example. Among other things, they produce IPIs. Self-organizing regions are characteristic of the current international transition and the new system to which it will give way. This provides the ground to introduce the complexity concept of self-organized criticality.[14]

A Taxonomy of Institutions in Complex World Society

I use the term 'institution' here, as clarified by Sidney Tarrow, to mean 'established and routinized relations among states and non-state actors in the international system whose competence in recognized sectors of activity is governed by agreed-upon norms and regulations.' Tarrow also sees a hierarchy of international institutions, 'starting at the lowest level [with] occasional contacts between states, succeeded by conventions, treaties, and regimes, and capped by sustained international institutions.'[15]

On this basis, three categories of international institutions attract attention – societal, executive, and parliamentary. We can designate transnational advocacy networks[16] and transnational social movements as part of a category of international societal institutions. On that basis, we may consider traditional international organizations such as the Organization for Economic Cooperation and Development (OECD) as international executive institutions, since it is the executives of national governments that are signatories and members.

The notion of international parliamentary institutions (IPIs) as a phenomenon to be analysed appears natural in this context. Indeed, to these three categories we may further add hybrid types of parliamentary-societal, parliamentary-executive, and executive-societal international institutions.[17] The following discussion summarizes these reflections.

Pure Types

International executive institutions. Traditional international executive organizations are mostly of this category, with national political executives determining national representation and policy. Cox and Jacobson differentiate them according to their membership and purpose[18] – specifically, by whether their membership is restricted or universal and by whether they were created for a specific issue or for a general purpose.

International parliamentary institutions. This category is the focus of the present chapter. Its scope is clarified below.

International societal institutions. Restricted-membership specific-purpose institutions of this category include NGOs and transnational advocacy networks. Restricted-membership general-purpose organizations of this category are theoretically possible, but none exists. The recent UN initiative for a Millennium People's Assembly attempted to convoke such a universal general-purpose body for a single meeting. Its logistical and political problems make evident the associated questions of representation.

Hybrid Types

Mixed international executive-societal institutions. A universal organization of this type does not exist. Theoretically, restricted-membership organizations of this type may be created ad hoc; in practice, they mainly exist indirectly through IPIs, set up to address issues of representation.

Mixed international parliamentary-executive institutions. The universal general-purpose organization in this category would be an institution bringing together the UN General Assembly and the Inter-Parliamentary Union (IPU). Universal specific-purpose organizations here are theoretically possible, but their function is assumed by implementation of the series of co-operation agreements signed in the last several years by the IPU with many of the UN family's specialized agencies. Restricted-membership general-purpose organizations of this type exist as formations incorporating IPI participation. One example is the system uniting the Nordic Council with the Nordic Council of Ministers. Another is the Baltic Council, which unites the Baltic Assembly with the national executives of its member states. Restricted-membership specific-purpose organizations of this type are usually components of organizations such as the Baltic Council.

Mixed international parliamentary-societal institutions. Technically, the parliamentary component here must be IPI-based. In practice, if the parliamentary components are national, then the parliamentary–societal institution is transnational rather than international, although the embedded inter-parliamentary component is still transgovernmental.[19]

IPIs Defined: Distribution and Types

Approaches to international studies that were developed over the past fifty years are now limited by the concerns of the Cold War: bilateralism, crisis bargaining, and territorialized national security. These traditional approaches are not necessarily the best vehicles to carry one across the terrain of post–Cold War world politics. New approaches that treat non-state actors and non-traditional security issues as central have proliferated. Although distinctions among superpowers, great powers, and regional powers have not disappeared, middle-range and lower-level phenomena have become objects of study, increasingly seen as dominant forces in an international system that now self-organizes. IPIs reflect the importance of international regions that are today enjoying greater autonomy, having been relieved of Cold War superpower conflict.

What Is and Is Not an IPI

A working definition of an IPI may consider it as an international institution:

- that is of a parliamentary nature, whether legislative or consultative, and has three or more member states
- of which the parliamentarians are either selected from national legislatures in a manner that they determine or popularly elected by the electorates of the member states
- that is a regular forum for multilateral deliberations on an established basis, either attached to an international organization or itself constituting one

Different IPIs come from varying political origins, and their respective founding documents establish them as having different demarcations of authority. For example, the Parliamentary Assembly of the North Atlantic Treaty Organization (NATO-PA, until recently called the North Atlantic Assembly, or NAA) has no formal statutory relations with NATO. It was created to assist harmonization of legislation across member states and to facilitate opinion formation among parliamentarians and their constituents. The NATO-PA example also demonstrates how the authority of IPIs is often limited: its founding documents explicitly exclude any possibility of supranationality.

The development of the Baltic Assembly provides a contrast to that of the former NAA. In 1989 people living in the Baltic republics in the old Soviet Union, inspired by the Baltic Entente of the interwar period, formed a transnational social organization that they called a new Baltic Entente. This body found itself represented among established political parties in the region as well as among the new political parties that sprang up at the time. When these parties became governing and opposition parties as the Soviet Union collapsed, the Baltic Entente social organization found itself represented in new national parliaments.

In due course the parliaments of Estonia, Latvia, and Lithuania institutionalized an interparliamentary Baltic Assembly. Today that body has formal powers to make recommendations to member governments on a whole range of issues. It also has the responsibility to determine whether recommendations are followed, although it cannot enforce compliance. The Baltic Assembly is not unique in its origins and responsibilities; the Central American Parliament and the Andean Parliament are comparable. The Central American Parliament is already directly elected, and the Andean Parliament will soon be.

IPI Distribution and Typology

Distribution

There are many types of international parliamentary formations on the international scene. A gradation of parliamentariness is useful in analysing the range of such organizations. In descending order of parliamentariness, one can identify the following types of international parliamentary formations (*formations*, because not all of them are institutions).

1 semi-formal parliamentary caucuses in the European Parliament associated with different factions

2 factions in the European regional assemblies such as the Rainbow Coalition, and still less formal groupings on the political right and left
3 bodies not composed exclusively of parliamentarians, including members of political executives and / or ex-parliamentarians (for example, Interaction Council, Bilberberg Group, Trilateral Commission)
4 other mixed organizations of a special historical character such as the Socialist International
5 the UN General Assembly
6 other international organizations having deliberative assemblies where representation comes not from parliaments but from executives
7 such groups such as the G77, G10, and G8

The foregoing list serves to demonstrate the problems inherent in analysing such a diverse phenomenon as IPIs in world society. It is still useful to draw on distinctions between general and specific purpose and between universal and restricted membership.[20] This chapter focuses on regionally based, general-purpose, restricted-membership IPIs. Their experience points to their eventual role in developing a broader regional participation in global governance. In Europe, a large number of IPIs have been formed in the last decade. The Baltic Assembly, the Central European Initiative, and the Organization for Black Sea Economic Cooperation all provide for regular institutionalized interparliamentary co-operation. Initiatives to establish and promote IPIs have been under way for some time in Asia and Africa, where several already exist. Today, there are nearly two dozen IPIs throughout the world, of which half were formed in the last twelve years.

Figure 6.1 provides a more comprehensive view, outlining a classification of existing international parliamentary formations, including IPIs. Among restricted-membership, general-purpose international parliamentary formations it distinguishes between regional and linguistic bases. The shaded box meets the definition of IPIs.

The brevity of this analysis, and the policy concern with global governance that informs the conclusions below, make it necessary to exclude IPIs that are not geographically based (see Figure 6.1). Thus this analysis does not include the Inter-Parliamentary Union, the Commonwealth Parliamentary Association, or the Association internation-

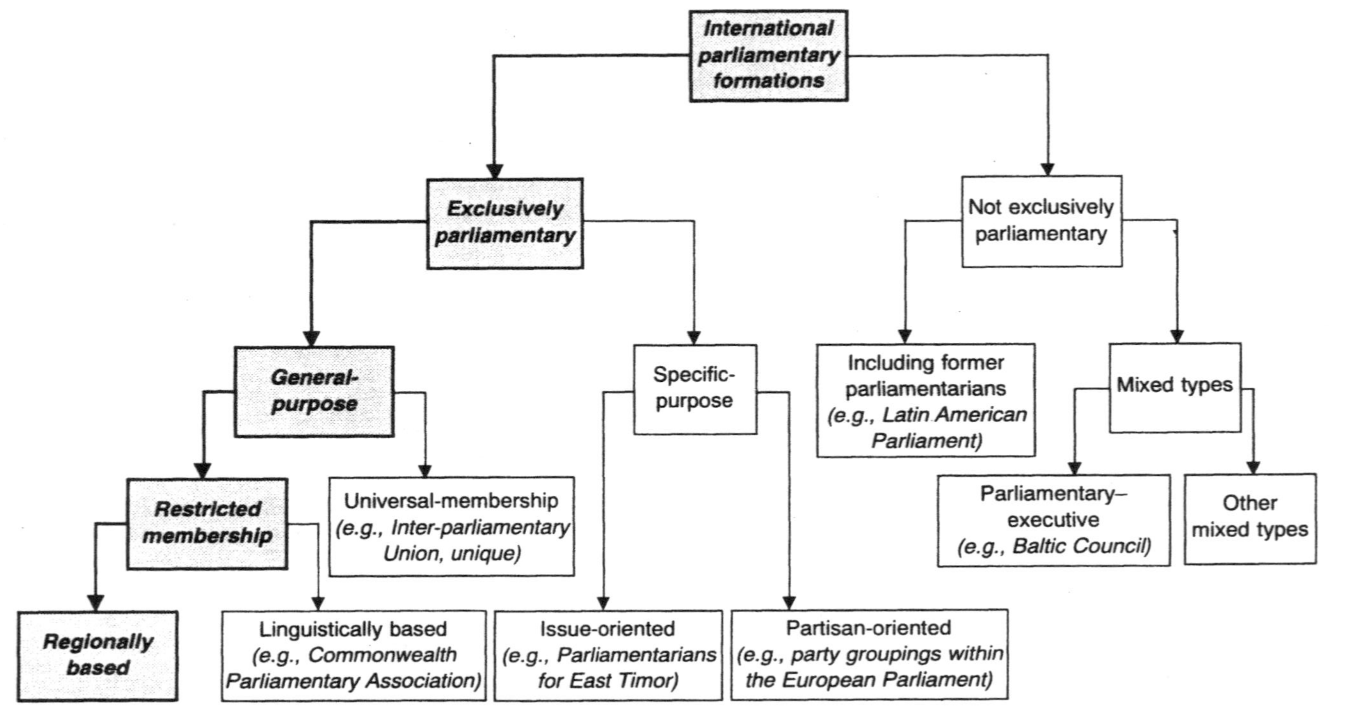

Figure 6.1 Types of international parliamentary formations. Heavy boxes at left indicate subjects of this study.

TABLE 6.1
Growth of IPIs, 1950–2000

Year	Number of IPIs	Number of states belonging to at least one IPI	Number of state-memberships of IPIs (including multiple memberships)
1950	1	13	13
1955	4	15	40
1960	6	16	51
1965	7	23	59
1970	9	46	78
1975	11	50	118
1980	12	52	122
1985	12	90	143
1990	15	97	172
1995	22	139	290
2000	23	150	328

Figures are for end of year. Those for 2000 were projected in 1999.

ale des Parlementaires de Langue française. For the same reason it omits the new Islamic Inter-Parliamentary Union (more formally, Parliamentary Union of the Organization of the Islamic Conference), which has yet to hold its first regular meeting. This analysis also excludes dormant IPIs such as the Nordic Inter-Parliamentary Union, formed in 1907 but inactive since 1957. Table 6.1 shows that IPIs have become a regular fixture in international politics. It also reports the total number of country memberships, confirming the increasing trend in participation.

Table 6.2 illustrates how the rates of formation of IPIs have varied across regions and systems. It is convenient to distinguish three international systems – the Cold War system, from 1947 until 1973; the system of multilateral interdependence, from 1974 to 1991; and the current international transition, beginning in 1992. Table 6.2 also illustrates an increase in number of IPIs formed under each of the three systems. There is an apparent acceleration in the rate of IPI formation: about one every four and a half years during the Cold War; one every three years under multilateral interdependence; and more than one a year under the international transition. Also it is clear that, during the Cold War, IPIs formed principally in the Atlantic and/or European regions, whereas in the current period most have formed in either Latin American or Eurasia.

TABLE 6.2
Formation of IPIs across international regions and systems, 1948–1998

By region	By international system Cold War system (1947–73)	Multilateral interdependence (1974–91)	International transition (1992–)	Totals by region
European	3	1	2	6
EurAtlantic	2	–	–	2
Asian	1	1	–	2
Latin American	–	3	2	5
African	–	1	1	2
Asian–African	–	1	–	1
EurAsian	–	–	3	3
EurAtlAsian	–	–	1	1
Totals by system	6	7	9	22

Typology
We can identify four types of IPIs: Congress, Assembly, Parliament, and Legislature. These types refer to stages of institutional development, not to the specific names that individual IPIs may have. The three transitions between succeeding pairs of types may be referred to as initiation, takeoff, and spillover. After we examine the types, we consider the details of the transition phases.

Congress. When various national parliaments, or members of them, come together in a meeting, we call this a Congress. A Congress does not require a permanent secretariat. For a Congress to move to the next level of development means passing through stage of *initiation.*

Assembly. The next level of development is Assembly. An Assembly is not merely a single gathering, as is a Congress, but rather represents its participants' recognition of a common situation that motivates them to meet so on a regular, even if uninstitutionalized, basis. Having come together more than once, they are able to take common decisions and perhaps move in a common direction. An Assembly may function quite well with a limited secretariat or some form of informal institutional continuity. On that basis, the nascent institution may choose to enter the *takeoff* stage of development. However, a simple series of conferences that has not established an autonomous secretariat is less likely to have the momentum and drive to succeed in developing itself further.

Parliament. The etymological root of the word parliament signifies 'a place where there is talk.' Historically, a national parliament did not necessarily enjoy the right, obligation, or power to propose laws, let alone discuss or ratify them. Similarly, the Russian Duma derives its name from the Russian verb 'to think.' The regular functioning of a Parliament sets the foundation for possible, but not inevitable, creation of a Legislature. The path by which a Parliament evolves into a Legislature is called *spillover.*

Legislature. The Latin root of the word 'legislature' means not *to make* laws, but *to carry* laws. The distinction is important. The Roman Senate legislated when it carried or placed a law that it had approved before the people in the Forum for their approval. In a representative democracy today, people have delegated this task of approval to their national political executives. An IPI of the Legislature type deliberates with some juridical or statutory authority, proposes laws for approval by member states, and may assist in implementation and oversight, should member states adopt recommended laws.

There is a simple way to conceive of the progression of an IPI through these levels, using the standard structural-functional typology of domestic interest groups.[21] Before the level of Congress, there is no organized interest group at all, or what is called an anomic interest group. The Congress level is a non-associational interest group: the membership of a potential IPI is defined by geography (or other categorical attribute). The level of Assembly is like an associational group, the sort of voluntary social or political organization typical of domestic society. The levels of Parliament and Legislature are both institutional groups; the difference is that the latter has relative international juridical autonomy.

Assessing IPI Development

It is useful to develop a comprehensive framework for evaluating the growth and decline of IPIs. Such a framework may contribute to an understanding of the evolving arrangements of global governance by helping to determine what leads some IPIs to respond to demands

TABLE 6.3
Elements for an epigenetic analysis of IPI development

Explanation			Understanding
Stage of development	Locus of power	Performance	Sequences of integration
(explanans or 'independent variable')	(explanans and explanandum, or 'intervening variable'):	(explanandum, or 'dependent variable'):	('interpretation')
1 Initiation 2 Takeoff 3 Spillover	1 Degree of elitism 2 Degree of internalization 3 Responsiveness to demands/feedback	1 Information 2 Communications 3 Control	1 Nature of merging units 2 Nature of emerging units 3 Nature of functional statements versus 'real sequences'

imposed on them by the international environment and why others do not. The skeleton of four developmental levels sketched above is epigenetically inspired. This means that it recognizes that subsequent levels of development are conditioned by the accumulated experience of earlier levels.

Two Taxonomies in Search of a Typology

Functional and Epigenetic Taxonomies

The four-level typology focuses not on established functions of IPIs, but rather on new functions for growth. It draws on a framework sketched by Amitai Etzioni, a sociologist who criticized the structural-functional perspective that was popular among social scientists thirty years ago.[22] Etzioni adopted what he called an epigenetic approach, treating institutions, and international communities in particular, in an organic, almost biological, fashion. ('Epigenesis' refers to emergence into existence through successive stages of maturation.) His key concepts, as they may be applied to IPIs and other international institutions, are set out in Table 6.3.

Thus the four-level typology indicates how IPIs grow from one phase of development to another. We can deepen it by taking into account (following the complexity-based need for multi-scale analysis) not just an epigenetic account of how they grow but also a functional account of how they survive. Klaus Hüfner and Jens Naumann furnish

TABLE 6.4
Internal and external functions of an international organization

Internal functions	External functions
Informational activities	Interactions with other organizations
Normative activities	Adaptation
Rule-creating actities	Normative Integration
Rule-supervisory activities	Cultural issues
Operational activities	

a functional taxonomy of the activities of international organizations,[23] which was further elaborated by Harold Jacobson.[24] It emphasizes the creation of structures designed to accomplish two kinds of functions – internal and external. Table 6.4 summarizes the distinctions between them. This chapter focuses on internal functions, because success in performing them is crucial to an organization's survival through its initial stages of development.

Setting epigenetic and functional taxonomies against one another helps us bring forth questions for empirical investigation and helps us analyse information concerning the development of international institutions, specifically IPIs. This chapter lays out the conceptual framework for that exercise, which allows us to analyse the internal functions of an international institution as they relate to the three stages of development as identified in the epigenetic taxonomy. Moreover, it allows us to investigate the correlation between the external functions of an international institution and the locus of power and performance categories identified in the epigenetic taxonomy.

From the Functional Taxonomy to an IPI Typology

The functional taxonomy distinguishes between internal and external functions. The multiplication of internal functions can be seen as responses to challenges in the growth of an IPI. Success in meeting such challenges represents a passing from one level of evolution to another. IPIs establish internal functions in the following sequence:

- informational activities
- normative activities
- rule-creating activities
- rule-supervisory activities
- operational activities

Thus only IPIs that successfully perform initial internal functions have an opportunity to move on to later ones. Historically, IPIs must first evolve internal functions that allow them stable instutional relationships with their constituent member states. They then may engage the external environment. The last of these functions, operational activities, is autonomously undertaken with reference to the physical and institutional environment. In this idealized sequence, operational activities represent the spillover from the development of internal functions to the fulfilment of external ones.

From the IPI Taxonomy to a Ladder of Institutional Development

The first phase in the development of an IPI is the establishment of a Congress. The completion of the initiation phase transforms a Congress into an Assembly. During this stage the IPI takes on informational and normative activities, both of which are internal functions. Once these two internal functions have developed, an Assembly has the opportunity to enter takeoff. Takeoff and the development of a Parliament require the successful establishment of rule-creating and rule-supervisory activities. A Parliament may acquire international juridical autonomy and evolve into a Legislature by completing the transitional spillover phase. During spillover, IPIs take on operational activities, specifically in reference to their interaction with other international organizations. The following scheme expands this logic in detail.

Initiation: from Congress to Assembly. A Congress does not need a permanent secretariat. However, if a permanent secretariat is set up, its initial activities generally are informational and normative. *Informational activities* involve the distribution of information to member states and to other international organizations. *Normative activities* involve the setting of meeting agendas, fixing the legal status of the secretariat under domestic or international law, determining the distribution of budgetary contributions, and answering questions of employment and the nationality of employees. Institutionalizing normative activities by an emergent secretariat creates the potential for a further deepening of the activities of the secretariat and of the IPI overall. *Initiation* is accomplished when an IPI has regularized the internal functions of informational and normative activities.

Takeoff: from Assembly to Parliament. Following the initiation phase, an assembly may face new challenges. Its newly institutionalized secretariat may feel the need to engage in *rule-creating activities.* These may involve no more than devising parliamentary rules of order so as to provide a means of orderly conduct in the Assembly during its meetings. However, these rule-creating activities are sufficient to produce a qualitative evolution in the IPI. Rule creation involves and builds on the regularization of the normative activities that began during initiation. Such activities become possible only following the establishment of the IPI's juridical personality under international law, the definition of its status in the country where its seat is located, and the confirmation of any relevant founding documents of the IPI itself. An IPI that undertakes rule-creating activities enters the phase of takeoff. Once such rules are created, it becomes necessary to administer and verify their execution as well as to evaluate their appropriateness. Administering, verifying, and evaluating involve *rule-supervisory activities.* Just as engaging in normative activities is required to move from congress to assembly, so undertaking rule-supervisory activities opens the way to the establishment of a parliament.

Spillover: from Parliament to Legislature. When a Parliament engages in operational activities, then the IPI can be said to have entered the spillover transition phase. Operational activities of IPI secretariats include not only programmatic activities arising from rule creation and supervision but also other undertakings generated from the deliberations of parliament. These activities often stem from demands arising from both the IPI's internal and its external environments. When the IPI begins to propose laws for adoption by member states, the transformation to a Legislature is completed.

Table 6.5 depicts the foregoing framework. The typology is a template for the possible evolution of IPIs and demonstrates the utility of combining the functionalist and epigenetic frameworks. When combined, the two approaches point the way towards a systematic comparative taxonomy of the stages of IPI development. This discussion does not suggest that all IPIs have the means of becoming a Legislature, or even that they would seek to do so. Some, such as the NATO-PA, are limited by their founding documents, which explicitly prohibit them from taking on certain internal and external functions.

TABLE 6.5
Ladder of development in the potential life of an IPI (read from the bottom up)

Exercise of compellent legislative authority over IGO bodies (or members) with which the IPI may be affiliated or over similar other-directed authority if there is no such IGO	[Leading to] 'Legislature' Type of world-societal group: Institutionalized supranational-authoritative
Operational activities	*Spillover*
Exercise of not advisory but deterrent oversight over IGO bodies (or members) with which the IPI may be affiliated or over similar other-directed oversight if there is no such IGO	[Leading to] 'Parliament' Type of world-societal group: Institutionalized transnational-deliberative
Rule-supervisory activities *Rule-creating activities*	*Takeoff (2nd Stage)* *Takeoff (1st Stage)*
First regularized meeting following establishment of secretariat a requisite for acquisition of international juridical personality permitting autonomous proactive initiative	[Leading to] 'Assembly' Type of world-societal group: Associational
Normative activities *Informational activities*	*Initiation (2nd Stage)* *Initiation (1st Stage)*
First actual meeting where members come together for the purpose of establishing an IPI, or an organization later becoming an IPI, whether affiliated with any antecedent IGO or not	Congress Type of world-societal group: Nonassociational
First preliminary or preparatory meeting that generates the organization later evolving into the IPI or foundation of an antecedent regional IGO with which it may (eventually) be affiliated	[Pre-Congress] Type of world-societal group: Anomic

The European Parliament: Its Example and Normative Significance

The framework in Table 6.5 makes sense of the chronology of the institutional development of the European parliament. If we use it to track the European parliament's epigenesis, we observe the following:

Pre-Congress and Congress. The pre-Congress event of the European parliament's development is the first meeting of the Parliamentary Assembly of the European Coal and Steel Community (ECSC) in September 1952. The Treaty of Rome established the European Parliament's status as a Congress in March 1957, following the creation of the European Economic Community (EEC).

The initiation to Assembly. At this stage the demands and supports from the European Parliament's environment were fairly routine, so the development to the level of Assembly passed easily. The inaugural meeting in March 1957 was quickly followed by informational and normative activities, which sparked the stage of initiation. The European Parliament, having acquired a secretariat and a nominal international juridical personality, reached the level of Assembly by 1958.

The takeoff to Parliament. The EP proceeded swiftly to establish rule-creating and supervising activities. However, with respect to rule-supervisory activities, it encountered significant resistance from other institutions of the regional integration organization. It easily supervised the rules that it had created to govern its own activities, but it was not until 1970 that the EP achieved regular consultation with member states concerning budgetary matters for the whole of the EEC. This institutional performance was, however, eventually successful, and a new equilibrium emerged between the European Parliament and its institutional environment. Anticipation of the first wave of the EEC's enlargement provided the necessary jolt to help break the logjam that inhibited the European Parliament's institutional development. Still it did not attain the level of Parliament until nearly a decade later. Although the Treaty of Rome provided in 1957 for the EP to oversee the organization's executive, this did not actually begin happening in an effective way until after the first direct election of the European Parliament by the member states' electorates in June 1979. Until then, members of the European Parliament had been chosen by member states' own national parliaments. The European Parliament's willingness and ability to oversee other institutions mark its attainment of the level of Parliament.

The spillover to Legislature. Operational activities at this level refer not only to the European Parliament's relations with external bodies that were part of the European communities system, but also to its participation in Europe's foreign affairs. The European Parliament began to participate in an operational way following the elaboration of the Common Foreign and Security Policy in 1983. This event sparked the stage of spillover. A fully fledged Legislature finally emerged with the legitimization of the European Parliament's authority over other bodies of the integration organization, following the signing of the European Parliament's Single European Act of 1986, which improved procedures and introduced regular legislative co-operation between the European Parliament and the European Council.

It is the European Parliament's trail-blazing that encourages other IPIs to emulate it or to learn the lessons of its experience. IPIs from around the world arise from different political and social needs, have different demarcations of authority as spelled out in their founding documents, and have different statuses under international law. The European Parliament was motivated and set into place by states working together first within a nascent integration organization, the European Coal and Steel Community (ECSC). The European Parliament's qualities derive from its origin as an ECSC body. Its capacity to force the resignation in 1999 of the European Commission headed by Jacques Santer has its origins in the desire of the national governments that formed the ECSC to be able to oust that organization's administration. The ECSC in turn was unique because it was a manifestation of sector-specific international integration, which subsequently became illegal under the rules of the General Agreement on Tariffs and Trade (GATT). So while the development of the European Parliament to its present stage is the result of idiosyncratic factors, its uniqueness is almost an accident.

The European Parliament's experience nevertheless lends itself as a template from which other IPIs at various stages of development can learn. It is fair to say that there is no issue or task that any IPI will confront that does not have some strong if not direct analogy with some aspect of the European Parliament's experience. This is not to suggest that other IPIs will follow the same path. If IPIs are a part of regional integration organizations, their relations with the executive of those organizations and with member states will influence their evolution. Most Latin American IPIs seek to provide a forum for co-operation among members of national parliaments. These IPIs remain unrelated to international security organizations, although the Organization of American States, just in 2000, created an associated IPI, and also they are part of regional economic integration organizations. Even so, regional organizations have begun to expand into such issue-areas as conflict resolution and biodiversity.

Conclusion: IPI and International Order

Let me begin to conclude this chapter by offering a remark on the designation 'multiple centres of power,' which has lately animated much thinking. The opposite of a state-centric system may be not a multicentric system but rather, properly speaking, a state-eccentric system. This term aptly describes the present-day situation. States have been dethroned from their centrality, yet they retain considerable significance. It is difficult to designate the international system except by reference to what we no longer have. Complexity science tells us that states that attempt to function in the old way, that refuse to learn lessons from their new environment, and that continue to act like institutions instead of transmuting their diplomatic activity into a networked form are in for a hard time.

IPIs as Both Institutions and Networks

The arrival of new information technologies has changed the international environment. As recently as two decades ago, the exchange of information required face-to-face meetings in order to ensure follow-through. The distribution of information often required a secretariat; and the supervision of joint action required the establishment of a separate office. Today this activity can be done via the internet, where the only co-ordinating institutions would be the shared software through which participants exchange information and a network of data transmissions. As a result, it has become more problematic to identify international institutions. Today we may ask whether an electronic mailing list is an institution. After all, it has an archive physically located on a computer drive and a nominal secretariat of at least one person.

None of this should be surprising, given the tenets of complexity science. Moreover, the activity of a formal international institution today is more likely to be underestimated than overestimated. Traditional research methods cannot account for all the transactions and flows among participants in an IPI. Thus we may attribute states' divergent policy outputs to conflicting interests, when in fact they may result from an undetected yet co-ordinated division of labour.

IPIs catalyse the self-generation of NGOs and inter-NGO networks. Not only have IPIs launched initiatives that have created NGO networks, but more than one IPI has been launched by NGO networks. NGO networks include many non-IPI parliamentary formations: semi-formal parliamentary groupings in the EP associated with different factions; interest groups in which parliamentarians from more than one country participate; and transnational advocacy groups that focus their activity on IPIs. Recent research identifies the European Union as a catalyst for the formation and aggregation of transnational interests by institutions in complex world society.[25]

The implication of all this for global governance, accountability, and the management of transnational problems is that institutional design by itself will provide no final answers. That is the case because what must be managed is no longer institutions but instead networks. This is not to say that attempts at the design of international institutions should be abandoned, but only to suggest that their subsequent redesign will become necessary sooner than we think. In such an environment, the more an institution acts like a network, the more successful it will be. Consequently we should think about international order not in static terms of security and co-operation, but rather in dynamic terms of co-operative security, which seeks to make change predictable and to keep change transparent so as to build confidence and minimize perceived threat.[26]

What IPIs Can Do

Events of late in Kosovo and East Timor are only the most recent reminders that countries care about what is happening in their regions. This being so, it becomes realistic after the end of the Cold War to foresee the participation of regional integration organizations in global governance. In present circumstances, the difficult part is to figure out how to link regional concerns with a global structure, because chapter 8 of the UN Charter is too rigid for contemporary purposes. So, what might be the role of IPIs in a global governance system that integrates and co-ordinates the activities of regional organizations with one another yet does so without imposing imperative mandates?

IPIs and the Democratic Deficit

One thing that IPIs can do is to decrease the 'democratic deficit.' Representative bodies are a forum for ensuring democratic accountability. Traditionally, they can do so in at least three ways. First, they may secure comments from social and interest groups about issues under consideration. Second, they may perform investigative studies. Third, the representatives may be decision makers chosen and dismissed by the people. In the developmental typology elaborated above, Assemblies can perform the first of these tasks; Parliaments, the first two; and Legislatures, all three.

IPIs can do still more than that. Let us adopt Albert Hirschman's now-classic distinction among exit, voice, and loyalty.[27] An Assembly can promote moves towards regional confidence building, leading to cooperative security. Specifically, it discourages exit. This is also important for the initiation stage. A Parliament can bring new issues onto the international agenda and influence how that agenda is set. In other words, it not only discourages exit but also encourages voice. This is also crucial for the takeoff stage. Finally, a Legislature is able not only to prevent things from happening but also to make things happen. As such, it not only encourages voice but also engenders loyalty. This is also essential if the spillover stage is to be successful.

IPIs and Cooperative Security

The second purpose that IPIs can serve, even at the Assembly stage, is to promote co-operative security. From a communication standpoint, IPIs have a record of being a useful forum for discussing regional issues and the linkages between these issues and global affairs on the one hand and national affairs on the other.

Again, the example of Europe is instructive. In addition to the EP, the Benelux countries have had a trilateral interparliamentary body since the 1950s to address questions of their own separate trilateral integration organization. The Nordic Council existed for years before any of the Scandinavian countries became members of the European Union, and it continues to operate on its own regional level today. Add to this complex network a pre-existing Assembly of the West European Union and the NATO-PA. It should be evident that there are enough spheres of responsibility in complex world society to justify a proliferation of integration organizations with overlapping memberships and interparliamentary bodies.

Already one sees instances where regional IPIs co-ordinate interregional consultation and consolidate interregional co-operation. A forerunner is the established relationship between the Baltic Assembly and the Nordic Council. The remarkable aspect of this inter-IPI co-operation is that the regional integration organization has a mixed parliamentary–executive makeup, which increases the efficacy of transgovernmental co-ordination on environmental and educational issues. Increasing education encourages deeper exchanges at all levels of society, enhancing cross-border understanding and working constructively with differences.

The Future of IPIs

It is important that the emergence of a global network of IPIs not be regarded as representing a geographical division of labour, in which one IPI is associated with a specific regional integration organization. This would risk establishment of segmented pillars encompassing regional groupings that have no contact with one another and where interaction occurs only at the level of the executives that manage affairs on behalf of their regions. Any notion of a design for global governance that includes regional integration organizations and their IPIs should not divide the world into regions, each to be administered by a designated single institution.

It is no longer the case that all IPIs have an origin in co-operation among national elites. The history of the Baltic Assembly and the Central American Parliament illustrate the roots of IPIs in transnational social movements. There are, and will be, many different types of successful IPIs, at different levels of development, with different origins and different paths to different kinds of success. IPIs in the future will be able to establish co-operation more easily with other IPIs and with other international organizations. In a complex world society that is more networked than hierarchical, new types of IPIs may accumulate more functions and encourage the creation of new international structures that mediate relations between member states and themselves. The networked nature of the emerging international order will facilitate this.

NOTES

This chapter draws on papers presented not only to the Multiple Centres of Power team in Victoria, BC, in May 1999, but also to the 94th Annual Meeting of the American Political Science Association Boston in, September 1998 and to the Fourth Conference of the European Sociological Association in Amsterdam in August 1999. In addition to acknowledging the members of the team, especially Gordon Smith and Daniel Wolfish, I wish to thank Karen Shepard, Ivaylo Grouev, Ramine Shaw and the World Society Foundation; as well as Chadwick Alger, Zachary Irwin, Harold Jacobson, Anthony Judge, Deborah Larson, Robert Miller, David O'Brien, M.J. Peterson, Anne-Marie Slaughter, Sidney Tarrow, and R.B.J. Walker.

1 George Tsebelis, 'The Power of the European Parliament as a Conditional Agenda Setter,' *American Political Science Review* 88, no. 1 (1994): 128–42; George Tsebelis and Amie Kreppel, 'The History of Conditional Agenda Setting in European Integration,' *European Journal of Political Research* 33, no. 1 (1998): 41–71.

2 Victor-Yves Ghébali, *The Conference of the Inter-Parliamentary Union on European Cooperation and Security, 1973–1991: The Contribution of Parliamentary Diplomacy to East-West Détente* (Aldershot: Dartmouth, 1993); 'Parliamentary Diplomacy,' special issue of *Romanian Journal of International Affairs*, 1, no. 3 (1995).

3 See Jürgen Habermas's 1962 view, 'On the Concept of Public Opinion,' in Habermas, *The Structural Transformation of the Public Sphere: An Inquiry into a Category of Bourgeois Society*, trans. Thomas Burger with Frederick Lawrence (Cambridge, Mass.: MIT Press, 1989), 236–50.

4 Hanno Hardt, *Social Theories of the Press: Early German and American Perspectives* (Beverly Hills, Calif.: Sage, 1979), 171–73.

5 Ibid., 155.

6 There are four characteristics of rumour: it is topical, it almost always deals with events or personalities, it has a well-identified protagonist, and it is circulated in an environment lacking standards of evidence. Gordon Allport and Leo Postman, *The Psychology of Rumor* (New York: Henry Holt & Co., 1947), ix–xi.

7 For example, see Michael Walzer, ed., *Toward a Global Civil Society* (New York: Berghahn Book, 1997); compare Jean L. Cohen and Andrew Arato, *Civil Society and Political Theory* (Cambridge, Mass.: MIT Press, 1994).

8 Justin Rosenberg, *The Empire of Civil Society: A Critique of the Realist Theory of International Relations* (London: Verso, 1994). Compare Niklas Luhmann, 'Globalization or World Society: How to Conceive of Modern Society?' *International Review of Sociology* 7, no. 1 (March 1997): 67–80.

9 Daniele Archibugi and David Held, eds., *Cosmopolitan Democracy: An Agenda for a New World Order* (Cambridge: Polity Press, 1995); Daniele Archibugi, David Held, and Martin Köhler, eds., *Re-Imagining Political Community: Studies in Cosmopolitan Democracy* (Stanford, Calif.: Stanford University Press, 1999); John S. Dryzek, 'Transnational Democracy,' *Journal of Political Philosophy* 7, no. 1 (March 1999): 30–51; David Held, *Democracy and the Global Order: From the Modern State to Cosmopolitan Governance* (Stanford, Calif.: Stanford University Press, 1996).

10 Paul Cilliers, *Complexity and Postmodernism: Understanding Complex Systems* (London: Routledge, 1998).

11 For example, James N. Rosenau, *Along the Domestic–Foreign Frontier: Explor-*

ing Governance in a Turbulent World (Cambridge: Cambridge University Press, 1997).

12 Philip E. Tetlock and Aaron Belkin, eds., *Counterfactual Thought Experiments in World Politics: Logical, Methodological, and Psychological Perspectives* (Princeton, NJ: Princeton University Press, 1996).

13 John Holland, *Hidden Order: How Adaptation Builds Complexity* (New York: Perseus Books, 1996).

14 Per Bak, *How Nature Works: The Science of Self-organized Complexity* (New York: Copernicus, 1996).

15 Sidney Tarrow, 'Does Internationalization Make Agents Freer – or Weaker?,' paper presented to the American Sociological Association, August 1999. Cited by permission.

16 Margaret E. Keck and Kathryn Sikkink, *Activists beyond Borders: Advocacy Networks in International Politics* (Ithaca, NY: Cornell University Press, 1998); Thomas Risse-Kappen, ed., *Bringing Transnational Relations Back In: Non-State Actors, Domestic Structures and International Institutions* (Cambridge: Cambridge University Press, 1995); Peter Waterman, *Globalisation, Social Movements and the New Internationalisms* (London: Cassell, 1998).

17 In fact, to be exhaustive, we should include a further category of 'international juridical organizations,' as well as its three two-way mixed types. As none of these involves IPIs, however, for present purposes these are pursued no further. (Here, the three-way and four-way mixed types are assimilated to the hybrid IPI types.) On international co-operation among courts, see, among others, Lawrence R. Helfer and Anne-Marie Slaughter, 'Toward a Theory of Effective Supranational Adjudication,' *Yale Law Journal* 107, no. 2 (November 1997): 273–391; and Anne-Marie Slaughter, 'A Typology of Transjudicial Communication,' *University of Richmond Law Review* 29, no. 1 (1995), reprinted in Thomas M. Franck and Gregory H. Fox eds., *International Law Decisions in National Courts* (Irvington, NY: Transnational Publishers, 1996).

18 Robert Cox and Harold K. Jacobson, eds., *The Anatomy of Influence: Decision-making in International Organization* (New Haven, Conn.: Yale University Press, 1973).

19 For the transnational–international distinction, see Samuel P. Huntington, 'Transnational Organization in World Politics,' *World Politics* 25, no. 3 (April 1973): 333–68. For transgovernmentalism, see Anne-Marie Slaughter, 'The Real New World Order,' *Foreign Affairs* 76, no. 5 (September/October 1997): 183–97.

20 Cox and Jacobson, eds., *The Anatomy of Influence.*

21 Gabriel A. Almond and G. Bingham Powell Jr, *Comparative Politics: A Developmental Approach* (Boston: Little, Brown, 1966), 75–8.

22 Amitai Etzioni, 'The Epigenesis of Political Communities at the International Level,' *American Journal of Sociology,* 68 (1963): 407–21, reprinted in James N. Rosenau, ed., *International Politics and Foreign Policy,* revised edition. (New York: Free Press, 1969), 346–58.

23 Klaus Hüfner and Jens Naumann, eds., *The United Nations System: International Bibliography* (Munich: Verlag Dokumentation, 1976–present). This publication began in 1976 and continues with regular instalments.

24 Harold K. Jacobson, *Networks of Interdependence: International Organizations and the Global Political System,* second edition (New York: Alfred A. Knopf, 1984).

25 Tanja A. Börzel, 'What's So Special about Policy Networks? An Exploration of the Concept and Its Usefulness in Studying European Governance,' *European Integration online Papers* 1, no. 16: <http://eiop.or.at/eiop/texte/1997-016a.htm>, accessed 9 April 2000; Doug Imig and Sidney Tarrow, 'From Strike to Eurostrike: The Europeanization of Social Movements and the Development of a Euro-Polity,' Working Paper No. 97-10 (Cambridge, Mass.: Center for International Affairs, Harvard University, 1997).

26 For an elaboration of the distinction, see Robert M. Cutler, 'Cooperative Energy Security in the Caspian Region: A New Paradigm for Sustainable Development?' *Global Governance* 5, no. 2 (April–June 1999): 252–3; also available by permission of the publisher at <http://www.robertcutler.org/ar99gg1a.htm>, accessed 9 April 2000.

27 Albert O. Hirschman, *Exit, Voice, and Loyalty: Responses to Decline in Firms, Organizations, and States* (Cambridge, Mass.: Harvard University Press, 1970).

7. International Convention Secretariats and Canada's Role in Future Environmental Governance

Philippe Le Prestre

With the advent of interdependence, global interconnectedness, and the signing of global environmental conventions, the past decade has seen the emergence of several international environmental organizations. Each major international environmental agreement today provides for the establishment of a secretariat to oversee treaty implementation. The role and significance of convention secretariats are neither well defined nor well understood.

Although convention secretariats are not new, their recent proliferation raises questions regarding modes of global governance and the factors that determine the effectiveness of international environmental regimes. Are these secretariats different both from their older prototypes and from traditional larger intergovernmental organizations (IGOs)? Are they better suited than other IGOs to promote international co-operation on environmental issues and to fulfil the goals of the international conventions that they serve? Should Canada encourage the growth of an international governance structure centred around conventions? If so, under what conditions should it do so? This chapter describes several dimensions of the convention governance system and convention secretariats, identifies major issues and trends, and speculates about their significance for Canadian international and public policy.

While convention secretariats have existed for a long time, international lawyers and political scientists have tended to ignore them in studies of international politics. Poor analysis of the resulting system has resulted from a conflation of traditional IGOs with convention secretariats proper – a problem that arose from the oversized and broad mandate of the UN secretariat. Many treaties have created secretariats to co-ordinate the activities of governments and to facilitate their fulfilment of their treaty obligations. These secretariats have tended to be small and play only a passive role.[1] Except for Oran Young and Konrad von Moltke, most institutional studies of international relations fail to recognize or pay scant attention to the potential of convention secretariats for treaty effectiveness.[2] Leading texts on international politics and environmental law often overlook them altogether. Lawrence Susskind and Edith Brown Weiss give only a few pages on the attributes and significance of secretariats.[3] Detailed studies on convention secretariats that do exist tend to focus on the United Nations, the largest and best-known secretariat, but one that is quite different from the environmental convention secretariats formed in the past ten years.

The available literature on convention governance and convention secretariats addresses two questions. By examining how secretariats influence treaty making and how this role can be strengthened, some authors invoke questions of regime formation.[4] Others are interested more in understanding how convention secretariats contribute to regime implementation and effectiveness.[5] These approaches consider secretariats to be a new type of international organization that can play a vital role in furthering interstate co-operation. However, they also assume a trade-off between the efficacy of convention secretariats and state autonomy. I do not share this assumption.

Rosemary Sandford was first to undertake a comparative analysis of environmental secretariats.[6] She focused on the secretariats of the Basel Convention on International Trade in Hazardous Wastes, the Convention on International Trade in Endangered Species (CITES), the Montreal Protocol on Substances that Deplete the Ozone Layer, the Ramsar Convention on the Protection of Wetlands, and the World Heritage Convention. Weiss's study overlaps with Sandford's by providing data on the secretariats associated with CITES, the International Tropical Timber Organizations (ITTO), the London Ocean Dumping Convention, the Montreal Protocol, and the World Heritage Convention.[7] Neither of these two studies, however, examines the secretariats of the three Rio conventions.

This chapter addresses that gap by examining the three conventions that resulted from the UN Conference on the Environment and Development held in Rio de Janeiro in 1992 – the Convention on Biological Diversity (CBD), the Convention to Combat Desertification (CCD), and the UN Framework Convention on Climate Change (UNFCCC) – as well as the Montreal Protocol on the Ozone Layer. These are the four major global conven-tions on the environment. This chapter refers to other environmental conventions and secretariats when necessary.

Available studies often assume that while the international context may be evolving, IGOs and convention secretariats will be able to continue to perform their traditional roles and perhaps reinforce them by fulfilling the hopes of World Federalists. These studies presuppose not only that the trends that they have noted will endure, but that new opportunities will arise to consolidate them. This analysis is flawed. Existing IGOs may benefit, but may also suffer, from this evolution. As international politics changes, what seemed important in the old context may appear less so as new concerns arise. Secretariats may thus represent an adaptation by the state to the complexity and turbulence of international politics.

Several convention secretariats, such as the International Maritime Organization, have recently reconsidered their functions and responsibilities.[8] Others, such as the CCD and the Persistent Organic Pollutants Convention, are in the process of defining and negotiating, respectively, their mandates. Thus it is an appropriate time to reflect on the characteristics and the factors that shape convention secretariats and systems of convention governance. What role do they play in international environmental co-operation and in the pursuit of state interests? To help answer these environmental questions, in this chapter I look first at the emergence of environmental secretariats; second, at their functions; and third, at their role in global environmental governance.

The Emergence of Environmental Secretariats

The term secretariat is ambiguous. The traditional meaning refers to the structure, administrative body, staff, and offices of an international institution directed by an executive secretary. Examples range from the expansive UN secretariat to the limited administrative support of regional sea programs or fisheries conventions. A second meaning refers to the convention governance system and the statutory bodies created by an international convention, including the secretariat proper and the conference of the parties (CoP), along with its subsidiary committees.

The academic literature refers to both definitions, fostering confusion about the respective powers of the secretariat vis-à-vis the governance system. Typical analyses often examine only the administrative secretariat in an effort to note the properties of the governance system and the functions delivered. We must, however, distinguish between the convention secretariat and the larger system of governance. It is possible that a secretariat could be institutionally weak and the governance system quite influential.

In this chapter, the first two sections address the administrative body, or convention secretariat, and the third section examines the governance system. My main conclusions pertain more to the system than to the secretariat. However, the effectiveness of the secretariat and that of the system are ultimately linked. In this section I outline the history of secretariats; their legal context; and their size, status, and location.

History

Environmental convention secretariats first appeared in the early 1970s and have proliferated ever since. Many international environmental regimes have a secretariat, either instituted by treaty or evolved from the need for administrative co-ordination (see Table 7.1). The four global conventions under consideration in this chapter, plus the Basel Convention on Trade of Hazardous Wastes (1989), the Convention on Migratory Fish Stocks (1995), and the Regional Seas Programs, all include specific provisions for secretariats. But the Antarctic Treaty of 1959 and the International Tropical Timber Agreement of 1983 are silent on this topic.[9]

With the notable exception of CITES, recent treaties have provided more detailed instruction on the establishment of secretariats.[10] They outline the responsibilities of the secretariat and assign functions, sometimes enabling a secretariat to take an activist role. Three factors have influenced their growing importance.

First, the nature of the global issue being addressed has affected the structure and role of secretariats. The system of convention governance is the UN's answer to the complex web of conventions signed by states that face difficult challenges in implementation and compliance. In some conventions, states have negotiated distinct mechanisms to meet these challenges. Such procedures work both to prevent non-compliance by, for example, funding technical assistance and training programs and to resolve problems with compliance by using flexible mechanisms that encourage sanction instead of legal reparation.[11] Some of these secretariats therefore have assumed a mediating and

TABLE 7.1
Selected environmental secretariats*

Convention†	Signature/ ratification	Location	Host organization
Basel Convention on International Trade in Hazardous Wastes	1989/1992	Bonn	UNEP
Convention on Biological Diversity (CBD)	1992/1993	Montreal	UNEP
Convention on International Trade in Endangered Species (CITES)	1973/1975	Gland	IUCN (to 1984) UNEP (since 1984)
Convention on Migratory Species (CMS)	1979/1983	Bonn	UNEP
Convention to Combat Desertification (CBD)	1994/1996	Bonn	UN
Montreal Protocol on Substances that Deplete the Ozone Layer	1987	Nairobi	UNEP
Montreal Protocol Fund	1991	Montreal	UNEP
Ramsar Convention on the Protection of Wetlands	1971/1975	Gland	IUCN
United Nations Framework Convention on Climate Change (UNFCCC)	1992/1994	Bonn	UN
World Heritage Convention (WHC)	1972/1975	Paris	UNESCO‡

*Excludes LRTAP and regional seas programs
†**Bold**: global conventions
‡Since 1992, WHC has had a separate budget line under the UNESCO general budget.

negotiating role. These negotiations involve a variety of actors who no longer remain in the background.[12] Secretariats have to respond to various demands from actors who have acquired a legitimate role in the maintenance and evolution of the regime.

Second, new approaches to negotiation have affected the influence and capacity of secretariats. Use of the framework treaty–protocol model of negotiation and incorporation of financial mechanisms into treaties have made the secretariats' operation and role more important.[13]

Third, the preference of states for a decentralized form of international governance enhances the role of convention secretariats and of the governance system as a whole. It is difficult, however, to provide incontestable evidence of state's desire to regain control over the international agenda from IGOs. None the less, the role given to the CoPs testifies to states' concern with controlling the pace of policy change.

The Legal Context

All framework treaties institute a CoP that meets periodically and provides a forum where the principles, norms, decision procedures, and implementation of the convention are continuously negotiated and worked out.[14] CoPs are the governing body of each of the four global conventions. In each case the CoP's role is similar; it

- oversees the operation of the convention secretariat
- adopts the procedures governing the exchange of information mandated by the convention
- assesses the scientific information received from subsidiary bodies
- ensures the coherence of adopted policies
- negotiates convention protocols, amendments, and appendices
- creates subsidiary bodies
- oversees implementation of the convention[15]

CoPs determines the frequency of meetings, and decisions are usually arrived at through consensus.[16]

While convention secretariats are under the control of the CoPs, their relationship with states varies. Some secretariats, as in the case of the Ramsar Convention on Wetlands, enjoy significant independence because CoPs seldom convene.[17] In others, such as CITES, CoPs play an active role in directing the secretariat and in the evolution and implementation of the convention.

By being administratively attached to the United Nations, the four global secretariats enjoy the legal status of that organization. The question then arises as to the extent to which they can call on this status. For example, subject to the specific agreements that link it to the United Nations, could a secretariat claim the right to negotiate and sign treaties, be a party to an internal legal dispute, or have diplomatic relations with states?

Size, Status, and Location

Environmental secretariats are typically small. Their budgets increased markedly after Rio de Janeiro's UN Conference on the Environment and Development of 1992, but they are still dwarfed by the budgets of traditional international IGOs. Secretariats also make considerable use of temporary staff and external consultants. For example, the largest, the UNFCCC's, employed about 150 people in early 1999, although regular staff members number far fewer.

Since the early 1970s, the administrative relationship that secretariats have with host organizations has varied (see Table 7.2). It can be a major source of tensions. Six models can be identified:

- *Independent*. For example, the 1946 whaling convention establishes a commission authorized to appoint its own secretary and staff.[18] The ITTO secretariat is independent of any other international organization.
- *Loosely attached to the UN secretariat*. The UNFCCC and the CCD are attached directly to the UN secretariat in New York. Special arrangements gives them quasi-independent status, although they use resources of the UN Environment Program (UNEP) for administrative purposes;
- *Hosted by an agency of the UN system*. UNEP has the responsibility to provide secretariat services for the Basel Convention, the CBD, CITES, and the Montreal Protocol. On the basis of article 24 of the CBD, CoP-1 designated UNEP as administrator of its secretariat. In 1998 the two bodies negotiated a memorandum of understanding that sought to define their relationship better.[19] UNEP's executive director names the SCBD's executive secretary on the recommendation of the CoP's bureau. Although the secretariat has its budget approved by the CoP and made up of contributions by the parties, 'the financial and common support services of the CBD secretariat will be provided by UNEP, UN Office in Nairobi or any other UN entity, as appropriate, and as agreed by the Executive Director of UNEP, in full cooperation with the Executive Secretary of the convention.'[20] The executive secretary must have UNEP's approval before proceeding with proposed expenditures and personnel appointments.
- *Hosted by an NGO*. The Ramsar Convention on Wetlands of 1971 specifies that the World Conservation Union (IUCN) will provide secretariat services for the convention; CITES was also administered by the IUCN until 1984. Admittedly, the IUCN is a special kind of organization, since its membership includes NGOs, as well as government agencies.

TABLE 7.2
Administrative arrangements of the four global conventions

Elements	Convention on Biological Diversity (CBD)	Convention to Combat Desertification (CCD)	Montreal Protocol (ozone)	UNFCCC (climate change)
Structure	Secretariat; CoP; SBSTTA; financial mechanism	Secretariat; CoP; STC	MoP; scientific and technical committees	Secretariat; CoP; SBSTA; SBI; financial mechanism
Budget	• Prepared by secretarial • First approved by UNEP and them submitted to CoP • Administered by UNEP's Global Environmental Facility, responsible for interim financing mechanism	• Prepared by secretariat and approved unanimously by CoP • Funds (general supplementary, special) established by UN secretary general approves • CoP approves scale of contributions • Funds administered by secretariat • CoP can abolish any fund	• Operating budget prepared by secretariat, approved by UNEP's executive director and then by MoP • Fund created in 1991, in accordance with the financial rules of the UN and following operational procedures of the UN Fund for the Environment	• Prepared by secretariat and approved by CoP • UN ensures contractual obligations fulfilled • Secretariat exempted from budgetary restrictions imposed on UN for operational expenses • Fund also exempt from requirement of maintaining a reserve for day-to-day operations
Personnel	Recruited jointly by UNEP and secretariat	Recruited by secretariat; currently provided by UN.	UNEP personnel	Secretariat has complete authority over recruitment, promotion, task description, and discipline.
Executive secretary and officers	Executive secretary named by UNEP after consultation with parties. United Nations must approve officers.	Executive secretary named by UN secretary general	Designated by UNEP	Executive secretary is named by CoP and in turn selects all officers.

MoP: Meeting of the parties; SBI: Subsidiary Body on Implementation (UNFCCC); SBSTA: Subsidiary Body for Scientific, Technical Advice (UNFCCC); SBSTTA: Subsidiary Body for Scientific, Technical, and Technological Advice (CBD); STC: Science and Technology Committee (CCD)

- *Embedded*. The secretariat's functions are assumed by an existing IGO; it has no independent legal status, such as an independent budget. For example, the Geneva Convention on Long Range Transport of Air Pollutants (LRTAP) of 1979 calls on the UN Economic Commission of Europe to provide secretariat services.[21]
- *Rotating*. Secretariat functions are assumed by the regular civil service of the parties on a rotating basis; there is no independent international civil service, budget, or legal status.[22] These arrangements are the product of several factors – first, willingness to link a secretariat with an organization that will provide it with technical expertise; second, the historical involvement of some of these organizations in the formation of the regime; and third, the lessons learned by CoPs and their desire to reduce uncertainties and control the initiatives of IGOs. In the last stages of the negotiation of the CBD, discussions over the relative role of CoP versus UNEP were prominent. The emphasis given to the CoP reflects parties' misgivings about UNEP's executive director and about giving it a large controlling role. There also was an attempt to assert control over the direction of the CBD.[23]

Location will also greatly affect the relationship of a secretariat to its host organization, preventing it from acquiring much autonomy if it is in the same building and dependent on the host for administrative support. Some secretariats, such as those associated with the Ramsar Convention and the World Heritage Convention, are located with their hosts; others are in different cities. For example, secretariats for the CCD, CITES, the UNFCCC, and the Convention on Migratory Species are in Bonn, and Montreal is home to the secretariat for the CBD and the Montreal Protocol Fund.

Locating secretariats away from their host organization is becoming more common. One material reason stems from the bidding competition among cities and governments to host them. The meetings that they generate, their links with the local community, their power to attract organizations that are part of the network, and the prestige that they bring are attractive to governments. Many governments do not hesitate to commit significant long-term resources to support a secretariat. Some governments also want to prevent the secretariat from being captured by the host. For example, the CCD's CoP decided that, in order to ensure its administrative and financial autonomy, the secretariat should not be linked to a particular UN structure or program.[24]

The Functions of Secretariats

Current Practices and Future Hopes

This section outlines, first, the current and possible future functions of the secretariats administering environmental conventions – especially the four global ones – and, second, factors likely to shape their future evolution.

Environmental conventions, regardless of whether they are limited or global in scope, specify the mandate of the secretariat that they establish. This mandate is subject to change only by the CoP. Some secretariats are restricted to serving the CoP, while others oversee and promote implementation of the convention (see Table 7.3). Their domain of activities can also be limited (for example, protecting the ozone layer or certain habitats) or expansive and touch on many different and sensitive areas (desertification, biodiversity).

Because secretariats are small, their reach and ambitions are limited. Yet they can fulfil a variety of functions, depending on the nature of the issue, the provisions contained in the convention, and the practices that have evolved. Signatories may debate functions continuously. For example, because a separate secretariat was created for the Montreal Protocol Fund, the functions of the main secretariat remain limited. In contrast, the CCD and UNFCCC secretariats have claimed extensive responsibilities. Finally, the CBD secretariat is still defining its role so as to be commensurate with the scope of the convention.

Unlike traditional IGOs, secretariats are first and foremost service organizations and do not have specific regulatory or decision-making powers. All perform core tasks such as arranging and servicing the CoP and its subsidiary bodies, preparing reports on implementation of the convention, co-ordinating activities with relevant IGOs and NGOs, and compiling and analysing information on request of parties.[25] Additional tasks will vary, depending on treaty provisions, mandates, and the existence of specific regulatory protocols.

Secretariats have also developed new tasks. For example, in interviews with staff members of the Ozone secretariat, some individuals identified the following additional tasks: training, promotion of the treaty to non-parties and public relations, and technical assistance to developing countries.[26] Over time, the CITES, ITTO, and World Heritage Convention secretariats have acquired new functions, including training and administering special projects, and hence have become more powerful, although their staffs remain small.[27]

TABLE 7.3
The formal convention mandates and functions of the four global secretariats

CBD	CCD	Montreal Protocol	UNFCCC
• **Basis: article 24** • Arrange for and service meetings of CoP • Perform functions assigned to it by any protocol • Prepare reports on execution of its functions • Co-ordinate with other IGOs • Perform other functions determined by CoP	• **Basis: article 23** • Arrange for and service meetings of the CoP • Compile and transmit reports • Facilitate assistance to parties in compiling and communicating information required • Co-ordinate with other IGOs • Enter, under guidance of CoP, into administrative and contractual arrangements required for discharge of its functions • Prepare reports on execution of its functions • Perform other secretariat functions determined by CoP	• **Basis: article 12 (plus article 7 of the Vienna Convention)** • Arrange for and service CoPs and MoPs • Receive and make available data provided (**article 7**) • Prepare and distribute reports based on information received (**articles 7 and 9**) • Notify parties of requests for technical assistance received (**article 10**) • Encourage non-parties to act in accordance with provisions of protocol • Provide information to non-party observers • Perform other functions assigned by parties	• **Basis: article 8** • Arrange for and service meetings of the CoP • Compile and transmit reports • Facilitate assistance to the parties in compiling and communicating information required • Prepare reports on its activities • Co-ordinate with other IGOs • Enter, under guidance of CoP, into administrative and contractual arrangements required for discharge of its functions • Perform other secretariat functions specified in the convention and any protocol and other functions determined by CoP

Some observers have argued that secretariats should be strong and independent. They reason that effective oversight of, implementation requires the ability to gather and verify data, assess implementation, engage in capacity building, transfer funds, and promote regime adaptation and development.[28] These tasks, however, remain highly controversial. Other observers would entrust secretariats with the collection and appraisal of scientific and technical information. This implies a diversification of information sources and can lead to the legitimization of specific ideas and practices.[29]

Following this logic, the CCD's secretariat has proposed a set of tasks that would make it central to a co-ordinated system of governance on desertification matters and that may transform it into a quasi-operational organization. The secretariat proposes to become a locus of expertise and scientific and technical assessment for countries through provision of legal expertise, co-ordination of studies analysing and evaluating national programs, and development of a clearing-house mechanism. On the model of university research, the secretariat would then aim to become a kind of center of excellence, albeit one whose role combines the advancement of basic knowledge with the promotion of specific policies.[30]

The CCD secretariat interprets its role as one of 'guarantor of the sound implementation of the convention.' This role involves activities designed to publicize the convention, to disseminate information about its national implementation, to evaluate the impact of the convention, and to ensure timeliness of available knowledge on the ecological risks linked to desertification and drought. The target of these consciousness-raising activities would be not only government decision makers but also the general public.

The Group of 77 is officially in favour of such a broad definition of tasks for the CCD secretariat, seeing that institution as a means of mobilizing resources and knowledge.[31] OECD countries, however, find that this set of tasks goes beyond the CCD's mandate and believe that expansion of functions would duplicate the activities and missions of other bodies. They also fear a gradual transfer of power from the CoP to the secretariat, which, in their eyes, must remain a service organization. It should not be an independent source of expertise entrusted with synthesizing available knowledge or promoting a specific methodology.[32]

Of course, one could see in scientific subsidiary bodies a way to meet these concerns and deliver this function. Again, this evolution will depend on the nature of the issue and of the existing governance structure. It may be much easier to develop this role for a new issue (such as ozone or climate change), where knowledge is limited and scattered and where no other national or international institutions holds a competing claim on this role. It will prove much more difficult if governments already rely on well-established institutions as sources of expertise and operational programs. Further, some issue-areas lend themselves easily to the emergence of indicators and the construction of 'objective' knowledge, and others far less so, which then makes this knowledge more politically sensitive.

'Scientific information,' Young and von Moltke remind us, 'is rarely available in a form that lends itself directly to policy application. The questions asked by policy makers and scientists are rarely identical. Thus, the interpretation of often incomplete, contradictory or indeterminate scientific information is a critical task, but it is necessarily coloured by the culture of both science and policy. No internationally agreed rules exist for the conduct of science assessment.'[33] Since, accordingly, countries are reluctant to entrust the assessment function to independent scientific bodies,[34] Young and von Moltke see secretariats as playing 'a critical function in organizing the science assessment by framing questions, by selecting participants and by providing secretariat services to a process that is fundamentally indeterminate.'

Yet in so doing, a secretariat may raise suspicions of promoting either one particular member's positions or its own. The alternative to building in-house expertise is to develop more proactive subsidiary scientific bodies serviced by the secretariat – that is, to build a system of convention governance, not just a secretariat. Of course, this assumes that experts staff these bodies, whereas often most participants are de facto dependent on one or two delegations that possess it. But if secretariats develop successful clearing-house mechanisms, this problem of dependence could be circumvented. Contracting out expert knowledge, provided that these sources are diversified, may help avoid the intellectual sclerosis that often accompanies the buildup of in-house expertise. Under article 25 of the CCD,[35] the subsidiary scientific bodies could themselves help set up expert networks and commissions to assert the credibility of the information provided by the secretariat.

What Factors Will Affect the Definition of Secretariats' Tasks?

Weiss identifies three sources of influence of the convention secretariat: first, the staff may be the only people with comprehensive knowledge of whether states and other actors are complying with the treaty; second, they know what kinds of problems have arisen at the national level; and third, they communicate, in their official capacity, not only with government officials but with a whole array of interested parties – private-sector officials, NGOs, and interested individuals – who seek information and advice or who have usable knowledge on which to claim a role in the process of implementing the convention.[36]

The roles that secretariats will be able to claim for themselves will depend on four major factors, involving resources that they must have and obstacles that they must overcome. First, significant administrative challenges have to be faced, starting with the quality of the staff. Obviously a knowledgeable, impartial, and responsive staff will have greater credibility and thus greater legitimacy. Building this credibility takes time. However, the annual contract requirements that are imposed on secretariat personnel or the comparatively unattractive professional conditions offered them in some cases impede that process. In CITES and the World Heritage Convention, unfortunately, there has been an increased trend to short-term contracts (one to six months), which may reflect budgetary uncertainty and funding constraints in the UN system as well as rocky relations with host organizations.

Chronic underfunding is often mentioned, but its significance is unclear, since it also reflects disagreements about the role of the organization. Asking for their budget to come in part from the United Nations to avoid secretariats being 'perceived as narrowly beholden to the parties to the treaties who are paying the bill'[37] assumes that only financially independent organizations may be able to pursue the collective good. Being beholden to the UN budget in many cases means being beholden to a specific UN agency, which is no guarantee of far-sightedness. As well, secretariats cannot hope to go further than the more advanced of their members. Additionally, being financially beholden to states does not mean that secretariats are dependent on them for all the resources that they need. Multiple dependencies can create room for manoeuvre.

Second, what may pose greater difficulties is the relationship with the host organization. The challenge is how to pool administrative capacities so as to promote procedural coherence and avoid wasting resources and at the same time prevent the host organization from trying to influence policy. Such disputes have in some cases paralysed a secretariat or prevented it from realizing its mandate. Links with UNEP, for example, have triggered significant conflicts with several secretariats that it hosted. This experience informed later models.[38]

Third, ever since Cox and Jacobson's classic study, we know that executive heads do matter. The attitude of governments towards the secretariat and the roles that it plays is often rooted in their opinion of the administrative and diplomatic abilities of its executive head. This seems to be very significant in the case of global secretariats. At a minimum, the executive secretary should be empowered to speak for the regime.

This leadership should be entrepreneurial, structural, or intellectual. The executive secretary must prevent capture of the secretariat by a coalition of states or stakeholders. He or she must protect 'the secretariat's mandate from cannibalisation by national interests ... [and] build a constituency among members who ultimately hold the power of decision on substantive issues of the regime as well as the power of appointment (or reappointment).' He or she must demonstrate excellent administrative skills – running a mission-oriented organization requires different skills than those needed for an organization that mainly manages programs. The effectiveness of the executive secretary will also lie in that person's ability to build bridges between stakeholders, to develop an issue network, and to steer the regime forward while remaining sensitive to the diversity of views of the parties regarding the nature, scope, and evolution of the regime.[39] 'This is a delicate task requiring the development of strong informal relations of trust with some members without jeopardizing the overall impartiality of the secretariat and attention to issues that are likely to become defining in the relationship between executive head and members.'[40]

Fourth, and linked to the preceding, is legitimacy. In some ways, secretariats can hope to develop greater legitimacy than any other actor in an issue-area. One of the bases of that legitimacy is rooted in norms that lie at the heart of governance structures. How those norms are identified, interpreted, operationalized, and promoted is key to the success of secretariats and convention systems as units of governance.

'Institutions that lack legitimacy are seldom effective over the long run.'[41] Constructivists in international relations have resurrected legitimacy (following the lawyers and the practitioners) and insisted on its relationship with the effectiveness of a norm or institution. On what does this legitimacy depend? How is one to achieve convergent intersubjective understandings of institutional legitimacy by agents comprising the issue network that systems of convention governance may help build?

Secretariats must be perceived by other actors as operating according to the principles on which they claim a role and according to procedures widely understood as right. Legitimacy depends on the secretariats' ability to provide good governance acting in accordance with the principles of transparency, accountability, and participation. There will be no regime effectiveness without some key role coming from society, and that has to be enabled through transparency. Compared with secretariats, traditional IGOs and NGOs may suffer from a lack of procedural legitimacy, being viewed as much less democratic than some individual states. Here convention governance systems may have an advantage if they open up not only to organized interests but also to networks of researchers. Participation does not have to be defined the same way for every secretariat.[42] It is in their ability to marshal relevant expertise and clarify issues (rather than impose them) that secretariats exercise influence. Moreover, secretariats are mission-oriented institutions rather than primarily managers of interests.

Secretariats and Global Environmental Governance

This section suggests areas for research to ascertain the degree to which secretariats and the convention governance system could become key governance units and why therefore they should be both carefully studied and cautiously supported. In an anarchical international system, where actors have multiplied and claim a legitimate role in defining and solving collective problems and where information is borderless (but not stateless), systems of convention governance may be well suited to pursuing limited but essential goals alongside traditional IGOs. To expand on the idea, I look in this section at the possible advantages that they may offer to member states and to regimes.

The Advantages of Secretariats for Member States

Systems of convention governance, rather than secretariats, may become more prominent because they help states maintain their influence, reflect the new features of the international system, and, through issue networks, help co-ordinate collective action. Systems of global convention governance are focused, accountable, and flexible – three characteristics valued by states: focused, because their concerns lie far more with convention implementation than with management of an organization; accountable to states through CoPs and because states do not have multiple interests within the organization; and flexible, because they can quickly change their mission, tasks, and priorities. CoPs are forums where implementation is negotiated; they provide rapid recognition and formalization of new developments and represent new and more effective instruments of advancing convention aims. The CoP is potentially a more flexible and more powerful body than a traditional IGO governing council. This power does not always rest on clear legal foundations. In practice, states see themselves bound by CoPs decisions even when those decisions change their original obligations.[43]

Government officials may yet believe that a centralized authority would be preferable to the existing governance[44] structure or to the greater fragmentation that, in their eyes, an expansion of secretariats would embody. The *Canada 2005* report, for example, fears 'the proliferation of separate issue-specific international agreements, leading to organizational inefficiencies, as well as to a potential lack of coordination.'[45] These fears reflect concerns with the waste of resources, contradictory policies advocated by member governments in different settings, and inter-organization competition. Greater coherence and co-ordination involves, for proponents of centralization, an allocation of tasks and responsibilities across issues under a central co-ordinating authority. For some, this authority should be the UNEP.[46] Others would prefer a new Earth Trusteeship Council or a World Environmental Organisation.[47] The executive director of the WTO in March 1999 explicitly advocated this solution as a way to reconcile commercial and environmental objectives. The authors of the chapter 'Environmental Sustainability' in *Canada 2005* make a similar comment: 'International environmental institutions have also failed to keep up with international economic institutions, and with developments such as global free trade and globalisation in general. While progress has been made in addressing specific environmental issues, there is increasing interest in the question of international environmental standards which would respond to the governance challenges posed by international trade rules as well as competitiveness pressures. The creation of a single multilateral body on international environmental and sustainable development issues ... could potentially provide an umbrella for a range of such activities and could facilitate access to markets for Canadian firms.'[48]

Leaving aside the vague link between a world environmental organization and the market power of Canadian firms, how can a country such as Canada hope to be able to promote its interests better within such a multifaceted and unwieldy body and avoid being a policytaker? *Canada 2005* continues in somewhat-contradictory fashion, 'If Canada is not a policy maker it will, by default, be a policy taker, adapting to the consequences of the decisions made by others. The best strategy is therefore a proactive one in which Canada seeks to exert its influence to the extent possible into the international arena. A proactive strategy is required for environmental reasons (to ensure international outcomes meet our environmental needs) and for economic reasons (to ensure approaches taken internationally do not harm our economic and trade interests).'

Canada's influence might be far more modest in a global environmental Organization than in individual secretariats. The first would facilitate issue linkages that might encourage successful bargaining over some issues; but that could also work both ways, to advance and to delay Canada's preferences. Further, nothing suggests that such an organization could demonstrate the needed adaptability and escape the ills of other large (and this one would be even larger) similar organizations: uncertain legitimacy, waste of resources, internal paralysis, incoherence of activities, and competition with other institutions. As the chapter 'Governance' in *Canada 2005* stresses,

> The key to optimising Canada's influence will be to focus our efforts on issue-based alliances, where we change the company we keep according to the issues we are negotiating. This will involve identifying Canada's comparative advantages on certain issues, establishing which international organizations and coalitions of like-minded states should have priority on which issues, and working to reform those institutions so as to optimize their effectiveness both in terms of cost and impact ... The complex and overlapping network of international organizations has been criticized as inefficient. However, overlapping institutional structures can actually work to our advantage by allowing flexible responses to changing political circumstances and problems of membership.

In that context, it may be more advantageous for Canada to achieve greater coherence through convention governance systems and an issue-based comprehensive governance system 'composed of collective actors at multiple levels, with overlapping authority, linked together through various kinds of networks.'[49]

The emphasis here on the system of convention governance is important. The debate, as we saw above for the CCD's secretariat, is between those who would like secretariats to be engaged in furthering compliance and in the implementation and effectiveness of conventions and those who would like them to be primarily service organizations. Again, there is confusion between the secretariat and the governance system. For government representatives, the secretariat is just that: the staff entrusted with implementing CoP decisions. Thus, as with the CCD, they have been reluctant to grant it a role that they see as the prerogative of the CoP or its subsidiary bodies. Opposition to a given secretariat performing a certain role is not opposition to the role itself. Parties may oppose a strong secretariat but not a strong governance system.[50]

In other cases, however, the opposition to a strong convention governance system and secretariat and to some of their functions may stem from fears that they will supplant other organizations (national or international) that deliver them. For example, national aid agencies might be much more in favour of secretariats with functions limited to basic services than of other agencies. National scientific units will often bemoan the lack of internal scientific expertise but be loath to leave secretariats the task of co-ordinating the process of scientific consensus building that scientific and technical subsidiary bodies could perform.

The Advantages of Convention Governance System for the Regime

Apart from the service functions that define their core tasks, secretariats and systems of convention governance have a particular contribution to make in areas that are often neglected but may prove crucial to the effectiveness of international environmental agreements.

Information and Capacity Building

Secretariats are the focal point for communication on regime-related matters; this is their core co-ordination function. In that sense, they can develop and maintain issue-networks that may eventually define the governance structure within a given issue-area (more on that aspect below). Secretariats will not supersede existing agencies but complement them. Thus capacity building should be limited to encouraging regime-oriented capacity-building initiatives by traditional IGOs as well as national agencies. Secretariats could, however, perform the useful function of building a coherent knowledge set that harmonizes the various ways in which existing national and international agencies approach a given problem and the solutions that they offer; or they could point out these agencies' differences, assumptions, strengths, and weaknesses so as to enable recipient countries to make informed choices. This function, then, would be very different from the current fashion favoured by states and IGOs alike – drawing sets of 'lessons' from widely disparate cases and disseminating them as current wisdom.

Reducing Competitive Pressures among UN Organizations

This concept may sound paradoxical, since secretariats have themselves been victims of such pressures, but this function stems from the role of building issue networks (see below). Competitive pressures have in the past encouraged duplication as organizations try to capture a new issue, have limited co-ordination, and have stymied leadership, as in the UNEP's early attempts to co-ordinate the environmental activities of other agencies or its current efforts to claim a similar role. As Young and von Moltke have pointed out, 'the tendency of the UN system to competitive behavior actually inhibits efforts at more effective interaction among international organizations ... A more positive goal, might be to integrate activities of different agencies in the same field so that they reinforce each other rather than get in each others' way.'[51] Issue networks can be the instruments of such integration.

Linking the Local and the Global

The capacity of regimes to manage environmental problems, as Oran Young observes, depends largely on the convergence between arrangements that come from above – the treaties – and those that come from below – local practices. Secretariats may be as well placed as if not better placed than, other organizations to perform that role, because that link is legitimate, and so is participation by other stakeholders. The CCD governance system for fighting disertification is directly charged with this task. Moreover, states in some cases will seek to involve other stakeholders in the governance process.[52] One should not confuse influence with control. That states retain the power to prevent the imposition of any decision that they have not collectively adopted is natural, since they ultimately are responsible for carrying them out. Linking the local to the global does not have to take place at the expense of the state.

Mediating between Governments

Secretariats work directly with national agencies, and individual officials who seek their assistance may induce secretariat staff to float ideas and test their acceptability by other governments.[53] Susskind insists on this potential role as mediator or facilitator in the context of the management of environmental conflicts and dispute resolution,[54] but this idea seems to be better suited for the convention governance system; it also assumes that the secretariat has built significant legitimacy and credibility.

Learning

Regime effectiveness implies the ability to adapt institutions, rules, and procedures to new balances of power, new interests, and new needs. The difficulties experienced by traditional IGOs have been attributed variously to the structure of interests that dominate their operations (a coalition of states and other stakeholders), to their size and operation, to the ideology that they and their staffs embody, or to staff training and expertise. Convention governance systems, in contrast, can be construed as learning devices, more open to the development of new consensual knowledge that leads to the adoption of new values and new problem definitions.[55]

- They are more capable of correcting their errors – that is, of improving their performance in the light of the purpose of the convention.
- The secretariats' staffs are typically small.
- The convention governance system and secretariats are more mission- than management-oriented.
- They can easily modify their internal structure by creating committees or subsidiary bodies in order to integrate new knowledge into their operations and respond more quickly to new demands and to new information.
- They can play with innovative forms of governance.

Issue-Based Networks of Governance

Thus, in a world characterized by interdependence and turbulence, convention governance systems and their secretariats can be the ideal decentralized authority for at least six reasons:

- They reflect the real distribution of power across one issue and thus overcome the gap between the structure of institutions and the real balance of power.[56]
- They can be the locus for striking limited (thus more acceptable) bargains between modern and postmodern states;

- They can accommodate a multiplicity of actors.
- They can provide a way to experiment with a range of group processes so as to improve the effectiveness of the regime.[57]
- They can provide a means of experimenting with new institutional arrangements or value allocation and thereby foster the evolution of the regime. The technical committees of the Montreal Protocol are a good example of a co-operative process with industry that has worked to foster voluntary compliance and map the evolution of the regime.
- They can foster coalitions of like-minded states and advance a particular issue through the negotiations of protocols.

Several of these attributes reflect the potential of secretariats and convention governance systems to serve as hubs of an extensive network linking parties, NGOs, and, for most treaties, the private sector. Effective co-ordination does not require a centre or an enforcer. Complex systems, for example, have positive feedbacks that reinforce behaviour of mutual benefit. The proliferation of international convention governance systems does not imply inefficiencies, provided that they can share experience and expertise. Such systems in environmental matters have already established this type of link.

Such a model of decentralized governance is not unique. For example, one could institute a division of labour among existing UN agencies, to which secretariats would be subordinate. Agencies, not convention governance systems, would be the units of governance. One would then create inter-agency task forces according to a division of labour among particular agencies responsible for specific aspects of the regime. A loosely connected network of IGOs co-ordinated by the International Forum on Forests and the Interagency Taskforce on Forests includes the Food and Agriculture Organization, the Intergovernmental Panel on Forests, the ITTO, the SCBD, the UN Development Program, the UNEP, and the World Bank secretariat as lead agencies for various elements of the regime – national plans, causes of deforestation, traditional uses, evaluation trade, institutions and instruments.[58] This model, however, responds to the need for coordinating the activities of international agencies in an issue-area; it does not have the mandate that secretariats possess of serving the needs of parties to a convention or promoting the goals of the regime and its implementation. It may be a model best suited to a phase prior to the signing of a convention and the creation of a secretariat.

As key, focused players in issue networks, secretariats and convention governance systems in collaboration with other actors in the network can do more than try to reconcile divergent interests. They can help share knowledge, promote norms, ideas, and interpretations, and ultimately shape an international understanding of an issue that will lead to change. Convention governance systems can play a key role in structuring advocacy coalitions, identifying and empowering actors, and shaping a community of ideas that will lead to policy change. The Ozone experience is a good illustration of these dynamics.[59]

Among others, Wolfgang Reinicke believes in the importance of global policy networks, which can function as instruments of governance as well as fostering the development of an international community.[60] A possible response to globalization would be to 'take public policy out of its territorial context,' – that is, separate governance from a structure of government. Other authors, such as Rosenau and Czempiel, have raised similar ideas.[61] Reinicke sees this occurring in specific issue areas through co-operation with IGOs as well as elements of civil society, including business. He bases his reasoning on the greater adaptive capacities of both groups (resulting from their dynamism and ability to respond to changes in knowledge bases). Better than traditional IGOs, secretariats would seem particularly well suited for this role and could even constitute the core of such issue networks. Putting segments of society in charge of some aspects of global policy would promote accountability, increase the legitimacy of such networks, and ensure that all interests are represented. Rather than being adversaries (for example, NGOs versus the World Bank), IGOs and NGOs become partners. These policy networks, to which state agencies would also belong, would encourage mutual learning and openness to change. The structure of the IUCN and the International Labour Organization already provides an example of this idea.

In a turbulent and interdependent system, global public policy networks may be a collective way for states to regain a sense of control. Secretariats are particularly well suited to nurturing these networks, for they are smaller and more mission-oriented than traditional IGOs (their mission is not to protect the environment, for example, but to ensure that certain commitments are fulfilled and principles operationalized). Through society, they can co-ordinate rather than perform research and actions on the ground. They can encourage change in traditional IGOs and state agencies, provide access, and encourage transparency.

The operationalization of this model, however, needs further elaboration. On what basis, for example, does an organization become a member of the network, and who decides? How can one ensure accountability and avoid the creation of what has been termed 'complexes' in other settings – organizations that seek only to protect their mutual interests? In particular, can NGOs be both inside – participate in the development and implementation of policies and programs – and outside – function as watchdogs? How will states isolate those organizations in the network from influences that they do not find legitimate? And what is the democratic impact of institutionalizing actual epistemic communities?

Further research is required regarding the capacity of issue networks really to learn and change. Constructivist approaches may explain the rise and maintenance of norms and issue networks better than they can explain change.[62] If perceived illegitimacy is a scope condition for change, would issue networks be better prepared to adapt to those changing norms? Composed of different stakeholders, and characterized by transparency and access, these networks could indeed evolve as soon as some stakeholders perceive them as illegitimate.

Conclusion

Rather than thinking only about secretariats, we should focus on the unit of governance that they serve and represent – that is, not just the personnel appointed to administer a convention, but also the general mode of governance of a convention, including the CoP and its subsidiary bodies and the secretariat. It is this system, and the networks associated with it, that are worth investigating. Nevertheless, convention governance systems and their secretariats have been largely overlooked by academics interested in the implementation and effectiveness of environmental regimes. Reflection on the nature, origins, and effects of their roles is absent, even though the context of their action is changing rapidly.

Since global convention secretariats are young, it is to be expected that their role will evolve with practice and the signing of protocols. Proposals for expanding this role share a similar perspective – namely, the wish to set up strong international institutions, with independent power that can effectively move states along the path towards solving environmental problems. It would be a mistake, however, to project onto secretariats preconceived ideas of what they should be able to do in the context of a desired evolution of the system towards a greater supranational role for IGOs. Rosemary Sandford, Lawrence Susskind, and others wonder how secretariats could become like traditional IGOs, albeit more activist. In effect, that would entail distancing them from states.

This is a misguided and anachronistic approach. The emergence of international environmental secretariats has occurred at a time of pronounced state hostility, at least on the part of developed states, towards most IGOs. This is not a coincidence. The question is not whether secretariats should or will fulfil the hopes of international integration. They will not. Governments are weary of being presented with *faits accomplis*. And the UNEP has come out weaker than stronger from its own activist period in the 1980s. Rather, the issue at hand is to ascertain to what extent they could be the embryo of new forms of governance that give states the feeling of being in control while allowing other parties a significant role in regime governance and evolution and helping focus energies towards the goals of the convention.

Secretariats are an attempt by states to regain control of the role and functions of IGOs. But they are also more than that, in that they are also conceived as mission-oriented organizations more responsive to the needs of the states and to the requirements of the regimes. A common approach that underlies current thinking on global governance is often to speculate that global norms and structures – a new system of authority – could eventually supplant the state system and move it from anarchy to organized governance. This chapter has suggested that such an evolution need not occur at the expense of states. Indeed, states can be key players in the development of new modes of governance. Secretariats represent alternatives to IGOs that may in some circumstances be better adapted to pursuing specific environmental objectives in a new international context characterized by three factors – the need to include multiple stakeholders in governance, overlapping issues, and states' attempts to regain some autonomy.

Yet, in practice, states' official position towards secretariats is ambivalent, largely, we believe, because they fear a return to the old model. Secretariats and convention governance systems, however, could become the engine of a new model of decentralized governance if kept within a mission-oriented mandate. If, as Young and von Moltke claim, 'it is not too much to say that the effectiveness of the secretariat is a necessary condition for the effectiveness of the regime,'[63] then states cannot ignore them.

International agreements or processes increasingly drive Canada's environmental agenda. Secretariats embody that trend. But the direction that trends take is not inevitable. One can choose strategies that resist them, favour them, or shape them, so as to further the maintenance or strengthening of the fundamental prerequisites of effective state action while facilitating progress towards international collective goals.

NOTES

1 Lawrence Susskind, *Environmental Diplomacy: Negotiating More Effective Global Agreements* (New York: Oxford University Press, 1994).
2 For example, see Peter M. Haas, Robert O. Keohane, and Marc A. Levy, eds., *Institutions for the Earth: Sources of Effective International Environmental Action* (Boston: MIT Press, 1993); Patricia W. Birnie and Alan E. Boyle, *International Law and the Environment* (Oxford: Oxford University Press, 1992); Oran Young and Konrad von Moltke, 'International Secretariats,' Background Paper for the Workshop at the Rockefeller Brothers Conference Center, Pocantico, NY, 15–18 June 1995.
3 Susskind, *Environmental Diplomacy*; Edith Brown Weiss, 'The Five International Treaties: A Living History,' in Edith Brown Weiss and Harold K. Jacobson, eds., *Engaging Countries: Strengthening Compliance with International Environmental Accords*, (Cambridge, Mass.: MIT Press, 1998), 89–172.
4 Susskind, *Environmental Diplomacy*; Rosemary Sandford, 'International Environmental Treaty Secretariats: Stage-Hands or Actors?' in Helge Ole Bergesen and Georg Parmann, eds., *Green Globe Yearbook of International Cooperation on Environment and Development* 1994 (London: Oxford University Press, 1994), 17–29.
5 For example, Young and von Moltke, 'International Secretariats.'
6 Rosemary Sandford, 'Secretariats and International Environmental Negotiations,' in Lawrence E. Susskind, Eric Jay Dolin, and J. William Breslin, eds., *International Environmental Treatymaking* (Cambridge, Mass: Program on Negotiation at Harvard Law School); Rosemary Sandford, 'International Environmental Treaty Secretariats.'
7 Weiss, 'The Five International Treaties.'
8 The International Maritime Organization, which acts as the secretariat of the London Convention of 1972, asked for guidance in defining the secretariat's role at the consultative meeting of its members in 1993, focusing on its roles as compliance facilitator and enforcer, provider of assistance to parties, and fund manager. See Weiss, 'The Five International Treaties.'

9 Young and von Moltke, 'International Secretariats.'
10 Sandford, 'International Environmental Treaty Secretariats.'
11 P.M. Dupuy, *Droit international public* (Paris: Dalloz, 1992), 893–6.
12 Susskind, *Environmental Diplomacy.*
13 Sandford, 'International Environmental Treaty Secretariats.'
14 Alexandre Kiss, 'Les traités-cadres: Une technique juridique caractéristique du droit international de l'environnement,' *Annuaire français de droit international*, 39 (1993).
15 On dispute resolution by the CoP, see Winfried Lang, 'Diplomacy and Environmental Law Making: Some Observations,' *Yearbook of International Environmental Law*, 3 (1992): 108–62.
16 Thomas Gehring, 'International Environmental Regimes: Dynamic Sectoral Legal Systems,' *Yearbook of International Environmental Law* 1, no. 35–56 (1990): 37.
17 Possible causes include the non-controversial aspect of the convention implementation and the lack of prospects that the reach of the convention will be expanded.
18 Young and von Moltke, 'International Secretariats.'
19 Administrative Arrangement between the United Nations Environment Programme (UNEP) and the secretariat of the convention on Biological Diversity (CBD), signed 3 April 1998 (UNEP/CBD/CoP/4/24).
20 Ibid., note 41, para. 22.
21 Young and von Moltke, 'International Secretariats.'
22 Ibid.
23 This attitude also manifested itself several years later as the bureau of the CBD-CoP asserted its role regarding the appointment of the executive director of the convention.
24 Report of the CCD–CoP on its First Session, Rome (29 September–10 October 1997), ICCD/CoP(1)/11/Add.1, Decision 3/CoP./, paras. 4–5.
25 Sandford, 'International Environmental Treaty Secretariats.'
26 Ibid.
27 Weiss, 'The Five International Treaties.'
28 Young and Konrad von Moltke, 'International Secretariats.'
29 Andreas Obser, 'Institutional Choice in International Secretariats: Nested Governance Arrangements in the Administration of Global Change,' paper presented at the International Studies Association Annual Meeting, Washington, DC, 1999.
30 ICCD/CoP(2)/6 (15 September 1998).
31 Especially African countries, which the convention singles out and which placed one of their own citizens at the head of the secretariat.
32 Interviews, April 1999.

33 Young and von Moltke, 'International Secretariats.'

34 As evidenced by the hesitation to use the International Council of Scientific Unions and its related bodies for this purpose, the creation of the Intergovernmental Panel on Climate Change, and the Scientific and Technical Advisory Panel (STAP) of the Global Environment Facility (see ibid.).

35 Article 25 of the CCD states, 'The Committee on Science and Technology shall, under the supervision of the CoP, make provision for the undertaking of a survey and evaluation of the relevant existing networks, institutions, agencies and bodies willing to become units of a network. Such a network shall support the implementation of the convention.'

36 Weiss, 'The Five International Treaties.'

37 Susskind, *Environmental Diplomacy,* 59.

38 According to some accounts, the experience of the CBD's secretariat induced parties to link the CCD's secretariat directly to the UN secretariat in New York rather than to UNEP or FAO (interviews, April 1999).

39 M.J. Peterson, 'Organising for Effective Environmental Cooperation,' *Global Governance* 4 (1998): 415–38.

40 Both quotes from Young and von Moltke, 'International Secretariats,' 15.

41 Commission on Global Governance, *Our Global Neighborhood: The Report of the Commission on Global Governance* (New York: Oxford University Press, 1995), 66.

42 For example, participation through near-universal membership and a governing structure that reflects states' pre-eminence through the CoPs, through subsidiary organs and committees that give access to other stakeholders, and through workshops and dialogues with interested parties; transparency through specific procedures, documentation, electronic communication, and staff access; accountability through the CoP and its bureau.

43 My thanks to Jutta Brunnée for pointing this out.

44 'Governance' refers here to the capacity to co-ordinate interdependent activities and induce change in the absence of the authority to require it. This perspective combines definitions from B. Jessop, 'The Rise of Governance and the Risks of Failure: The Case of Economic Development,' I.S.S.J., 155 (1998), and Ernst-Otto Czempiel, 'Governance and Democratization,' in James N. Rosenau and Ernst-Otto Czempiel, eds., *Governance without Government: Order and Change in World Politics* (Cambridge: Cambridge University Press, 1992), 250–71.

45 Assistant Deputy Ministers' Sub-committee for Global Challenges and Opportunities, *Canada 2005: Draft Interim Report on Global Challenges and Opportunities* (Ottawa, 25 February 1997), chap. 11, 'Governance.'

46 See the *Report of the UN Secretary-General's Task Force on Environment and Human Settlements*, June 1998 (A/53/463, 6 October 1998).

47 In favour of the Trusteeship Council, see Commission on Global Governance, *Our Global Neighbourhood*. For a global environmental organization, see Daniel Esty, *Greening the GATT: Trade, Environment, and the Future* (Washington, DC: Institute for Environmental Economics, 1994); Julie Ayling, 'Serving Many Voices: Progressing Calls for an International Environmental Organization,' *Journal of Environmental Law*, 9 (1997): 343–70.

48 ADM Sub-committee, *Canada 2005*; chap. 13.

49 Matthias Finger and Ludivine Tamiotti, 'Comprehensive Governance in Biodiversity Protection,' paper presented at the Annual Meeting of the International Association, Washington, DC, 1999.

50 A similar confusion appears in the academic literature, for academics also seem to share a view of the functions of secretariats that sometimes includes the subsidiary bodies or even the CoP. Thus, whereas an implementation committee will not be seen by parties as part of the secretariat (and properly so), scholars tend to define for the secretariat functions that belong to the committees or to the CoP's subsidiary bodies.

51 Young and von Moltke, 'International Secretariats,' 14.

52 NAFTA's Commission for Environmental Cooperation may exemplify such a trend.

53 Susskind, *Environmental Diplomacy*; Weiss, 'The Five International Treaties.'

54 Susskind, *Environmental Diplomacy*, 59.

55 This reflects Ernst Haas's general perspective on organizational learning. See Ernst Haas, *When Knowledge Is Power: Three Models of Change in International Organizations* (Berkeley: University of California Press, 1990).

56 Peter Padbury, 'The Future of the United Nations System. Assumptions, Policy Issues, and Knowledge Gaps,' *Global Challenges and Opportunity Network, Research Report* 2 (Ottawa: Policy Research Secretariat, 1998).

57 This is another concern raised in Padbury, 'The Future of the United Nations System.'

58 Obser, 'Institutional Choice in International Secretariats.'

59 Philippe Le Prestre, John R. Reid, and E. Thomas Morehouse, eds., *Protecting the Ozone Layer: Lessons, Models, and Prospects* (Boston: Kluwer, 1998).

60 Wolfgang Reinicke, *Global Public Policy: Governing without Government* (Washington, DC: Brookings Institution, 1998), 40.

61 Rosenau and Czempiel, eds., *Governance without Government*.

62 Steven Weber, 'Institutions and Change,' in Michael W. Doyle and G. John Ikenberry, eds., *New Thinking in International Relations Theory* (Boulder, Col.: Westview, 1997), 229–65.

63 Young and von Moltke, 'International Secretariats,' 1.

8. Rendering unto Caesar: How Legal Pluralism and Regime Theory Help in Understanding Multiple Centres of Power

Robert Wolfe

Introduction

To think of *multiple centres of power* is a paradox, for how can power be divided, or centres be multiple? How can any person be subject to more than one sovereign at the same time? This paradox is not new. When asked in the original trick question whether it was lawful to pay taxes, Jesus said 'Render to Caesar what is Caesar's, and to God the things that are God's.'[1] The Pharisees marvelled at this answer, for it seems to recognize Caesar's authority, and they had no conception of God. We see the same paradox in the current system of states, named for the Peace of Westphalia of 1648. This system of states began as an attempt to organize all normative orders, including those governing religion, property, and civil rights, on territorial boundaries. The attempt never went unchallenged. Today we know that many supposedly *private* or *international* orders (meaning sources of order other than the central institutions of the territorial state) are engaged in the regulation of large domains of collective life. For example, the rules affecting the telephones in our homes are affected not only by the state and its regulatory agencies but by the rules of the World Trade Organization (WTO) and the International Telecommunications Union; the internal operations of giant telecommunications firms; and the evolving practices of the internet, including norms emerging through the new forms of contract established by international law firms and participants in electronic commerce. Our challenge in this project is to craft new analytic frameworks in which to consider the policy implications of living in such a world.

If we think with the Pharisees that world power is organized hierarchically, as implied by theories of imperialism or hegemony, then the mechanism for resolving conflicts between competing claims to authority is relatively clear, even when we introduce ambiguous democratic refinements such as federalism or subsidiarity. In contrast, if we think that collective life is subject to multiple overlapping normative orders within the same social, territorial, or economic space, then we need a more complex understanding of world politics, one in which the state is not seen as the apex of a normative pyramid. Using trade examples, I first suggest how we might think about *multiple centres of power* and then how policy can accommodate such a world. My answer is based on a metaphor: rhythm beats harmony.

How do we imagine a world where the state is important, yet not of central importance? Think of an orchestra. Public servants have their own kind of black humour. A couple of decades ago, something called 'Extracts from a "Management Survey" of a Symphony Orchestra' circulated in Ottawa. The bean counters supposedly observed that 'For considerable periods the four oboe players have nothing to do. Their number should be reduced and the work spread more evenly over the whole of the concert thus eliminating peaks of activity. All the twelve first violins were playing identical notes, an unnecessary duplication. Much effort was absorbed in the playing of semi-quavers, which seems an excessive refinement. No useful purpose is served by repeating on the horns a passage, which has already been played on the strings. It is estimated that if all redundant passages were eliminated, the whole concert time of two hours could be reduced to twenty minutes.' Some of the implications of such an analysis were obvious. The bean counters observed that 'The conductor agrees generally with these recommendations, but expresses the opinion that there might be some falling off in attendance allowing sections of the auditorium to be closed entirely.'

If we substitute the supposed imperatives of globalization for the demands of efficiency, what would a humorist write today? We might be told that multiple national regulations are redundant – better to have one set of regulations spread over many countries. Much time could be saved in managing the world economy if minor differences between legal systems were eliminated, if different authorities within countries did not see the need to say the same thing using different instruments. We would respond as did the conductor that multiple voices can combine to make a whole, that eliminating complexity can mean eliminating the point of the exercise, and that one of the sections of the auditorium that could be closed would be Canada.

Canadian officials are long accustomed to thinking of multiple centres of power, of which Ottawa was but one, authoritative in some domains but not others. Take an example that is familiar, but not in this context, because of the convention that domestic and international politics are different. In his famous report, Thomas Berger framed the Mackenzie Valley pipeline as simultaneously an adventure into Canada's last frontier, and an expansion of the alien industrial system into the homeland of the Aboriginal peoples; an engineering marvel built on tundra, and a risk to the local migration of tens of thousands of caribou. Berger listened to Aboriginal elders, biologists, economists, and oil company engineers. More than mediating between competing interest groups, he legitimated alternative normative orders. The title of Berger's report, *Northern Frontier, Northern Homeland,*[2] reminds us that we can never survey the entire landscape from a single point. We can never reduce a policy problem to one dimension. And we must ask where sovereignty resides – with the people of Old Crow, with the caribou, or in Ottawa? Berger helped everyone see the full complexity of building a pipeline. He understood that his role was constituted by the state, but he did not place the formal authority of the state at the centre of his analytic framework, and he did not claim that it would be possible to harmonize the diverse interests and perspectives into one single structure of authority.

Berger's framing of the pipeline issue is similar to the perspective adopted by the Canadian officials who helped create postwar international order. William Lyon Mackenzie King's *functional principle*[3] was an adaptation to Canada's circumstances of Mitrany's conception of international order.[4] Mitrany's argument that politics should not dominate function in the management of collective problems also influenced the scholars who developed the neofunctional approach to thinking about European integration, and it influenced early theorists of international regimes. The latter idea implies that regimes are partial orders suited to specific administrative domains; that they are embedded in a broader international order. Each issue-area can have a different, if analogous, governance structure – a regime – that is the result of the endogenous interaction of the interests and power at stake. Regimes are organized on the basis of the activities to be regulated not the characteristics of the actors or the territory they inhabit.[5] This idea informed the Canadian insistence on a role commensurate with our contribution, rather than our population, in specified domains of international life.

Fashionable depictions of a *shrinking state* owe little to these older ideas about Canada in the world, but they do have much in common with current thinking about European integration. The old European debate was whether the end-point of the integration process would be an intergovernmental organization or a supranational state. Within this frame of reference, the European Union (EU) after Maastricht looked chaotic, and traditional concepts seemed irrelevant. Responsibility for some issues, for some states, is in varying degree still national, or European Union, or local. So many local issues now go through Brussels that dozens of European regions have offices (not quite embassies) in Brussels.[6] Some call this process *multi-level governance*[7] while others call the European Union a *multi-perspectival polity*.[8] This way of thinking about multiple centres of power is misleading with respect to Canada, in part because neofunctionalist assumptions about European integration do not easily accommodate Canada's experience in North America.

My benchmark for this enquiry, therefore, is not European integration but the WTO. International organizations like the WTO are not part of a world government. How then should we understand multiple sets of public and private, national and international rules contributing to an integrated and orderly trading system? That is both a policy problem and a problem of general theoretical interest for international relations. The policy theme is the problems associated with new negotiations. What should the WTO try to achieve? What objectives should be on the agenda? What modalities should it use? The theoretical theme is the WTO as a problem in social theory. What sort of entity is it? How should we understand what it does? What implications does it have for our understanding of the state? The two themes are linked because particular conceptualizations of the nature of the trading system drive approaches to negotiations.

To anticipate the discussion below, how does my picture differ from the standard view? One of the things trade economists envisage is a world of free trade, and they think that the WTO of their dreams would mandate such a world. I take a different view. I think that the well-known distinction between the WTO as a rules-based system as opposed to a system based on power is misleading. My protagonists are those scholars who think that the state has no or should have no autonomy, who think that harmonization and deep integration are achievable, whether good or bad. I challenge the views of people who think that the WTO can be given coercive capacity to move codified law from the national to the global sphere, who want to reify the trading system in the form of the WTO, who want the WTO Agreements to be an authoritative text with definitive rulings from the dispute settlement system that govern all trade. The obvious deviations from this model are taken as proof that the WTO as an international organization either needs to be strengthened or put out of its misery. The people who want to strengthen the WTO include boosters of globalization, who think that the dispute settlement system should have more enforcement capacity, and civil society groups, who think it should use that enhanced power in the service of the environment and workers.[9]

In contrast, I am not troubled by a world trading system comprised of a number of diverse institutions competing for authority. The policy implication of my approach is that gaps in formal global rules may not be a problem, if autonomous or decentralized rules are adequate. Rules are discovered not made by the WTO, and it often acts best by showing deference to rules that emerge in other international organizations, or from the behaviour of firms in the market, or in daily life. The term *trade regime* is a particular conceptualization of how all these things fit together. It does not assume bargaining away, but does try to place that small part of the regime process in a larger context.

This chapter is an exercise in political economy, although it differs from the standard approaches to markets and the state. One common debate is about whether markets can be self-regulating – either the state is seen as the apex of a normative pyramid, or, in contrast, it is seen as an obstacle to the proper functioning of the market. Both of the standard approaches are centralist; mine is plural: I try to make the state one of many sources of normative order. I use the word *constructivist* to describe my approach. Such labels can be weapons in our discipline, serving too often as little more than the focus for inward doctrinal debate.[10] I use the term only as a signpost for theoretically inclined readers. I would distinguish myself from the dominant tendency in North American international relations scholarship towards rationalist or utilitarian approaches that use ideas borrowed from economics about how individual rationality can explain political behaviour. I have more in common with that group of scholars who use an approach that borrows from sociology and jurisprudence to consider the role of norms and institutions.

The multiple centres of power project is an attempt to develop a new theoretical framework in which to incorporate a host of apparently new, or newly significant actors. If we try to do that while maintaining Westphalian assumptions about the role of the state, then we see a fragmentation of power and authority. The political problem, however, may not be a changing world but our assumptions, now exposed as fictions. The actors of interest today are not new, but we literally could not see them within a Westphalian world view. I try to suggest ways in which we can rethink power, the state, sovereignty, and the law. I do so by trying to incorporate ideas from the field of jurisprudence called legal pluralism in regime theory. Legal pluralism, which differs from liberal pluralism, does not accept the centrality of the state, as if law is only what the sovereign wills; it lets us see the state as only one of the sources of order. Much of international life can be law-governed without being state-governed.

In the next section (1) I lay the basis for a different understanding of international order and the source of authority by discussing the concepts of power and sovereignty. In the following section (2) I briefly review the literature on international regimes as a structure of governance and then show (3) how it can be enriched by concepts borrowed from the literature on legal pluralism. These ideas are brought together (4) in a suggested way of thinking about how the state should orient itself in an increasingly complex international architecture. The conclusion (5) asks where we might find Caesar.

On the Meaning of Multiple Centres of Power

The origin of this project was that part of the *Canada 2005* project that dealt with 'Global Challenges and Opportunities.'[11] The authors of the section on 'Governance' observed what seemed to be a fragmentation of power in Canada and the world. Who are our partners now, they wondered, and what are the implications of these changes for global governance, democracy, and accountability? Have states lost some part of their freedom to act to cities, provinces, regional bodies, global organizations, multinational firms, or civil society? They worried that 'Intergovernmental structures were based on the centrality of the sovereign state and, although states will continue to be the prime actors in international organizations, to retain their legitimacy those organizations will have to respond to demands for increased participation by subnational actors.' They were especially worried about something they called *the rule of law,* which they saw as endangered by 'overlapping and conflicting international obligations and standards,' which created 'a risk that governments will be forced into a position [of] choosing to ignore their commitments to certain international law regimes while respecting other standards.' They concluded that 'Over the next decade, work will be needed on the harmonization of different international law regimes.' Canadians certainly live in a world of multiple normative orders, and knowing how to think about what is Caesar's is one of our central policy challenges, but this statement of the issues modernizes the original trick question. We need to resist the temptation to see globalization as Caesar, an imperious force that requires us to bend to its will. Jesus was being ironic: what we owe the emperor is nothing. What we owe to God, or the rule of law, is everything.[12]

One of my tasks in this chapter is to attempt an explanation of why the *Canada 2005* characterization of the problems facing the Canadian state is as unhelpful for policy as it is for theory. It misunderstands the state, which has neither transferred nor relinquished any of its power, authority, or sovereignty, though the state never was as capable as the authors seem to assume. Intergovernmental structures by definition are based on the centrality of the state, but other actors have always been with us, and have always been important. I begin by discussing power and sovereignty.

Many authors think the world has changed profoundly. In one widely cited account, Mathews speaks of a 'power shift,' arguing that 'The end of the Cold War has brought not mere adjustment among states but a novel redistribution of power among states, markets, and civil society. National governments are not simply losing autonomy in a globalizing economy, they are sharing powers – including political, social and security roles at the core of sovereignty – with businesses, with international organizations, and with a multitude of citizens groups, known as non-governmental organizations (NGOs).'[13] Some authors, following a suggestion of Hedley Bull, have gone so far as to see a return to the Middle Ages, an era of overlapping and divided loyalties.[14] Hirst wonders how we can hold together and integrate a series of levels of governance, from the city-region to the trade bloc? He observes that 'The notion of a New Middle Ages seems superficially plausible, but the problem is that governance cannot function effectively today unless there is a minimally coherent architecture of institutions and a division of labour between them that avoids significant gaps in governance.' He thinks that only the state can act as a 'political lynchpin [*sic*]' holding the different levels together by its practices of scrutiny and constitutional ordering. If the state does not do it, he thinks, it does not get done.[15] Other authors are sceptical. This type of liberal pluralist or neofunctionalist thinking about fragmentation, the diminished state, rising interdependence, and transnationalism is not new.[16] Slaughter explicitly dismisses Mathews, arguing that the state continues, even if other actors gain power.[17] The right way to think of fragmentation, she argues, is as transgovernmentalism, which we observe in the thousands of lower level meetings of all sorts of officials.

The role of the state is not diminished when non-state actors assume increasing importance. The importance of firms has long been recognized – the 'sovereignty at bay' argument of the 1970s was based on the growing power of multinationals. Stopford and Strange observed, for another example, how events in one domain (say firm–firm) can be disrupted by events in another (either firm–government or government–government).[18] Firms should not be seen either as creatures of government or competitors of the state. Indeed globalization, or the increasing salience of international life, may by its very centrality attract more actors, and create a wider arena for their action. Raustiala argues that, 'The dramatic change in NGO activity in the last fifteen years thus reflects the equally dramatic increase in the scope and strength of international environmental law. That NGOs are more pervasive in environmental diplomacy illustrates the expansion, not the retreat, of the state in addressing global environmental problems.'[19] Or as Stairs argues, 'NGOs are public interest groups with a transnational twist. Far from rivalling the state and the state system, they must live in it.'[20]

Other critics of the power shift argument note that it is misleading to think of a fixed quantum of power, or what I call the *lump of power fallacy.*[21] This lump of power fallacy assumes that power is a finite resource, that there is only so much sovereignty, authority, or jurisdiction to go around, and that it can be sliced up and assigned to different levels. These fictions are necessary when we assume that hierarchy determines jurisdiction, or that we need *conflicts of laws doctrine* to resolve the obvious contradictions of a Westphalian system. Federalism is one approach to this problem; subsidiarity is another.[22] All such ideas assume that somebody has to have jurisdiction – the authority the WTO or any international organization gains must come from somewhere, implying a loss of sovereignty or a sharing of powers. But if we understand that this modernist lump of jurisdiction fallacy comes from single point perspective, then we can see that jurisdiction is not necessarily the right question. It asks who has the right to rule; it does not ask who does rule. It does not understand that power can have multiple centres. When we deny the centralist claim, we see that power and authority can multiply as people come together for various purposes.

We also see the fallacy in the belief that a greater role for markets implies that governments have lost power. One of the domains where globalization is thought to have wreaked the greatest such havoc is money, and electronic money is supposed to be the most revolutionary form in its impact. But global capital markets may have been more integrated and fluid at the end of the nineteenth century than they are now, and the new technologies, Helleiner argues, have not caused a shift in power and authority over money. States have never had complete control over money, especially cash which is completely anonymous, while e-money often leaves a trace.[23] Since the state can use information technology too, the spread of e-money may even enhance the state's regulatory capacity. Financial centres have physical location (for example, London and New York) which gives regulatory purchase, but money is in fact a bundle of legal and institutional relationships, e-money more than, for example, gold. That is, a trader can assay gold for purity independently of any knowledge of counterparties or states, but e-money depends on a socially constructed understanding of what it is and on the institutions that allow traders to have confidence in each other. By being more ephemeral, therefore, e-money might be more institutionalized, and more subject to regulatory control.

Power in its variety of forms is a common means of accounting for the shape of the international system. In the Gramscian conception, based on Marxist ideas about the relations of production, this power is exercised by constellations of social forces called historic blocs;[24] the structure of postwar international organization in the Atlantic or 'Free World' order can be linked in this way to a particular constellation of social and industrial forces.[25] The creation of the Bretton Woods system, the shorthand name for this new international economic order, can also be attributed to a different kind of hegemony based on the material power (military or economic) exercised by the most powerful state. The theory that stability in the postwar era was provided by U.S. dominance is a formalization of Kindleberger's famous dictum that 'for the world economy to be stabilized, there has to be a stabilizer – one stabilizer.'[26] This 'theory of hegemonic stability' assumes that the Bretton Woods system and its associated international regimes were created and sustained by U.S. power,[27] whether or not that system could endure without U.S. dominance.[28] The theory has had many critics, and is now discredited.[29] I stress this familiar point because to speak of 'multiple centres of power' is to reject all such hierarchical notions of power.[30]

When we define the international system by power, we cannot account for the sources of law or authority. The other common way to understand the international system is on the basis of *sovereignty,* the name we apply to the apparent source of order. Sovereignty seems to be understood as a natural or inherent characteristic of all states, something solid and immutable, at least until it was undermined by globalization. But does sovereignty lie with some overarching power (a personal sovereign), or with the people? Is the basis of sovereignty in supreme power, or political authority? Fuller in his critique of legal positivism argues that sovereignty is a device to introduce unity in the legal order, but the device assumes an identification of the law, the state, and sovereignty in a kind of holy trinity. We can no longer believe in a personal sovereign, yet 'He, or it, is intended to introduce into governmental phenomena a unifying principle which will make possible at least a formal answer to the question, "What is the law?" The answer is, of course, "That which the sovereign adopts as its will."'[31] The difficulties with sovereignty cause real problems for international relations, because we have no other constitutive organizing principle of world politics.[32]

Mainstream international relations theory takes a centralist view of sovereignty. States are all thought to have like responsibilities within an established territory – the state as a sovereign is closely allied with notions of territory as property. *Property* as a concept is a claim to ultimate authority over whatever is defined as property, be it land, a wife, or an idea. Sovereign states are understood to have like authority for certain domains. States are constituted by the international system, and are constitutive of that system; states are also constituted by, and constitutive of, society. States are alike only in that they are responsible for like functions within their territory. They define themselves and they extend each other recognition on this basis.[33] More formally, *sovereignty* can be provisionally defined as 'a political authority's externally recognized right to exercise final authority over its affairs.'[34] Most international relations theorists would accept the corollary of this view of sovereignty, the anarchy assumption.

Anarchy is said by realists, and some constructivists, to define international politics,[35] although the term has a variety of meanings.[36] It can be a synonym for disorder or chaos; or, for a lack of centralized government or common authority. The latter embodies an assumption from Hobbes that the role of government is either enforcement or coercion, and that the only source of order is obedience to a common government. Since there is no state above the state in the Hobbesian or centralist conception, international politics is to be understood as the interactions of such sovereigns with each other. What is not part of the state, in other words, is assumed not to exist at all. Collective life is either governed by a state, or is not governed.[37] International anarchy, in other words, is counterposed to domestic hierarchy. Legal pluralists deny both accounts on the grounds that central authority is not the source of law or order in either domestic or international life.

I want to stress this last point by observing that it is entirely consistent with Weber's definition of the *state*. Weber argued that states cannot be defined by their tasks, since anything they do is not their *exclusive* task – other forms of association could also do it. Therefore, 'In the last analysis the modern state can only be defined sociologically in terms of a specific *means* which is peculiar to the state, ... namely physical violence ... A state is that human community which (successfully) lays claim to the *monopoly of legitimate physical violence* within a certain territory, this "territory" being another of the defining characteristics of the state.'[38] But violence is only a descriptive characteristic of the state, and the violence must be held to be legitimate. Yet such a state clearly is only good for some things. Control of violence is good for control of physical territory and good for coercion, but we know that some things are not closely linked to territory, and we know that coercion has limits.[39] That is, social order certainly depends on freedom from violence, yet violence must not be met with violence.[40] The state must monopolize violence not to use it, but to safeguard us from it. Force, then, is not the source of law, or sovereignty.

Walker says that sovereignty is first a spatial principle: it 'fixes a clear demarcation between life inside and outside a centred political community.'[41] Sovereignty is 'an expression of a politics that works both inside states and outside states, indeed as a principle that tells us why we must put up with a politics that is split between statist political communities and relations between such communities.'[42] Walker concludes that it is the state's ability to mediate between the local and the global that is called into question by globalization. Sovereignty is not shared or divided, it erodes.[43]

For Fuller, the question about who is inside is a question about who counts as a member of the moral community, 'the community within which men owe duties to one another and can meaningfully share their aspirations.'[44] We cannot find the answer in the morality of duty, the morality of the in-group, but only in the morality of aspiration. The parable of the Good Samaritan shows, he argues, that our neighbours in the moral community are defined not by a territorial principle (those are the two so-called neighbours who passed by the man who had been beset by thieves) but by practice. We must always seek to enlarge the moral community to be inclusive of all men of good will. Sovereignty is a useful fiction, therefore, a social construction of the relevant actors who do or do not extend each other recognition – but they do so on the basis of some characteristic of the actors. The state claims sovereignty on the basis of where we live, where a church might claim sovereignty in a different domain on the basis of what we believe. Sovereignty is a metaphor for telling us who is in and who is out. The sovereign is neither absolute nor the source of order in all domains.

Globalization does not create a new situation, it merely exposes the fiction that the world could be parcelled up into territorial states whose formal official law had absolute regulatory control. This mythology of modernism took hold in part because of the idea that some domains are *private* and others *public*. The fact that the sovereign can only command in the sphere agreed to be public is thereby naturalized rather than properly being seen as undermining the centralist understanding of sovereignty. If we assume that such an absolutist state never existed, then its supposed loss of control looks less serious. We might then recognize that the state is not the only source of law, and that maintaining the rule of law does not require the creation of a uniform supranational order, although in a world of overlapping sovereignty, we might well expect to find sources of law that exist outside or beside states.

An Approach to Regime Theory

One way to think of a plurality of legal orders, or multiple centres of power, operative within the same social space is to think of *international regimes*. Such regimes arise wherever there are underlying cross-border transaction flows. Not surprisingly, therefore, they develop first in shipping (for example on the Danube), telegraph (the International Telecommunications Union), railways (standard gauge in Europe), and trade (when the General Agreement on Tariffs and Trade [GATT] was drafted in 1947, it codified a regime that was already at least a century old). This classic role for international co-ordination arises when firms, often in response to technological change that makes new things tradeable, find themselves operating in markets that have outgrown existing regulatory boundaries.[45] Theories of international regimes typically assume that global governance cannot be explained either by the power of the largest states or by the actions of formal international organizations. The IMF and the World Bank are part of but not identical with the money regime. The focus of regime analysis is often on international organizations of states such as the GATT or the IMF.[46] It is harder to see the pattern of transactions in non-economic regimes, but they too are likely to arise in situations of social interaction where some sort of reciprocity exists.[47] The regime approach has been used on security issues,[48] on the environment,[49] on communications,[50] and on foreign aid.[51]

International regimes are consensually defined as 'sets of implicit or explicit principles, norms, rules, and decision-making procedures around which actors' expectations converge in a given area of international relations'[52] (see Table 8.1). The consensus definition of regimes is based on observable behavioural characteristics, not on what a regime does; it contains no information about where they come from or why they matter. Regime theory is often equated with its rationalist or utilitarian proponents, notably Keohane and his neoliberal followers, for whom regimes are a form of decentralized co-operation under anarchy, or quickly dismissed on the basis of Strange's critique of the concept as a fuzzy fad.[53] But as Gale argues, the approach can serve critical purposes,[54] and its lineage is arguably constructivist.[55] Indeed all regime theories are sub-sets of bigger theories about world politics or international relations, about politics in general, and about social life – the debate between rationalists (neorealism and neoliberalism) and constructivists, or between theories of politics with links to economics or sociology, has deep roots. Regime theories embody ontological and epistemological assumptions about: the nature of the world beyond the state (is it an international system or society; do we observe international cooperation or global governance?); the appropriate explanation of public policy change (do we look for international compulsion, policy convergence, or learning?); the basis for why people do anything (do we expect people to be motivated by force, norms, or incentives?); and finally, by how we evaluate empirical claims (do we know the political world by observation of behaviour, by what people say, or by interpretation?).[56]

When theorists look for regimes, some look for explicit rules, some for implicit practices, and others for evidence of intersubjective communication among state actors.[57] The creation of such regimes can be explained as a response to asymmetries of power (neorealism), asymmetries of information (neoliberalism), or asymmetries of knowledge. When theorists try to explain whether regimes make a difference in collective life, they ask if a given regime has been effective or robust, they ask whether it achieved its stated objectives, or helped participants to do things they could not do before, or whether it has shaped their understanding of themselves as actors in this domain.

The two rationalist or utilitarian theories, neorealism and neoliberalism, treat actor preferences and identity as exogenous, they think in terms of an international system, rather than a society of states, and both discount learning. The epistemic communities literature[58] is a variant of this utilitarian approach that looks to learning as the source of preferences. Neorealists assume that states know what to do, but have to be coerced. Neoliberals assume that states know what to do, but lack information about each other. Their epistemic variant assumes that states lack information about reality and policy choices. Constructivists, in contrast, believe that actors lack information about each other and about reality. Regime theorists divide, therefore, on distinguishing between the origins of rational actors' understandings of the world, and of social actors' self-understandings.[59] These theorists tend to share an assumption that the only regime *actors* are states, an assumption not shared by legal pluralism.

The first major part of the regime definition, norms and principles, is the normative framework, which is hard to observe (see Table 8.1). It does not necessarily stand in a hierarchical relation with the second part, nor do the elements of the first part need to be consistent with each other.[60] This normative framework is not subject to direct negotiation. Organizations reflect the normative framework, 'but they do not create principles and norms.'[61] The trade regime structures the questions states ask about a commercial conflict; these questions structure the answers that the WTO can provide. Trade negotiators may fret over how to express the non-discrimination norm in rules, but they do not challenge it.

The second major part of the definition is its instrumental form, its rules and decision-making procedures. The most important source of instrumental change in a regime is change in the nature of interdependence, or 'dynamic density', which can bring countries closer together or push them farther apart, thereby increasing or decreasing the level of (potential) conflict, and altering the need for rules and procedures to help states manage their current interactions.[62] (See also Figure 8.1, below.) This sort of change alters the problem of surveillance and compliance, without altering the collective purposes of states: an enduring policy objective may require new policy instruments. It follows that institutional economics and neoliberal institutionalism can show how rational self-interested actors can generate institutions in order to minimize transactions costs, institutions that will be understood as rules and procedures.[63] Constructivists, in contrast, will emphasize how norms and principles based on consensual knowledge shape rules.

Regimes occur in 'a given area of international relations'; all regime theories depend in consequence on the notion that world politics can be subdivided. In a plural society, all individuals find their lives encompassed by many overlapping *issue-areas.* Some line up on narrow bases; others are larger and more integrative. Any one issue or state can be found in many issue-areas, in different combinations and using differing, even conflicting or contradictory principles. This pluralist understanding of issue-areas assumes that states can have multiple interests rather than a single hierarchy of interests dominated by 'security.' Each issue-area is thought to have a different, if analogous, governance structure that is the result of the endogenous interaction of the interests and power at stake. Power and interdependence are assumed to vary, and to vary asymmetrically, by issue-area. Power in the trade issue-area, for example, is not consistent with an elite theory model: the largest traders tend to have the greatest influence, while countries important in other domains (such as Russia) have little influence.

As used in the early 1980s regime literature, *issue-area* is an amalgam of the ideas of Haas, Ruggie, and Keohane and Nye, all scholars in the neofunctionalist tradition for whom interdependence is an important force.[64] They see the state not as the realist's unitary rational actor but as 'a fragmented institutional ensemble overseeing multiple policy-making arenas which are increasingly permeated by both domestic and transnational forces.'[65] Onuf notes that such theorists see 'issues/arenas and actors as interdependent' without worrying about whether actors are public or private. 'Indeed, this distinction borders on the meaningless, for states as organizations are implicated in most distributive matters, but cannot exclude other putatively private organizations from also being involved.'[66]

Why then do we bother with the WTO, or any international organization? On the one hand, its existence would be pointless if states felt free to do as they please, or if small states (willingly) followed rules announced by large states. On the other hand, the WTO as a formal organization is not the sole source of order in the global trading system. Regime theory is an attempt to describe the complexity of the forces at work in a given domain. It copes well with a claim that a world of multiple centres of power means that global governance involves a shifting mix of states and organizations. Its weakness is that it lacks a view of supposedly *private* or non-state actors, and of *law*. Legal pluralism can enrich regime theory as a metaphor of *multiplicity*[67] or multiple centres of power.

'Regimes can be defined as sets of implicit or explicit principles, norms, rules, and decision-making procedures around which actors' expectations converge in a given area of international relations.'[68] The normative framework is the 'social' arm of the double movement.[69] Table 8.1 shows the conceptual elements of regime theory.

Legal Pluralism and International Regimes

Legal pluralism is far from the mainstream approach to legal theory. It is easier to begin, therefore, by describing what it is not. Legal pluralism should not be confused with pluralism in political science,[70] nor is it the same as the rational literature on decentralized cooperation exemplified in the transactions cost approach in law and economics.[71] It is not a way to understand how *interest groups* compete for control of the state nor is it a way to think of the possibility of governance as if the state did not exist. It is a way to move the state out of the centre of the frame. It is a way for regime theory to develop an overview of world politics that can accommodate the different and competing forms of power or law that we face as members of families, workers, consumers, participants in our community, citizens, and as nation-states interacting with others.[72] Critical legal pluralism goes farther, denying the homogeneity of any normative order.[73] The import of the idea is obvious within a federal state, where national, provincial, and municipal governments claim authority. It should also be obvious within the administrative state, where legislatures, tribunals, courts, administrative agencies, and even political parties have degrees of legitimate authority.

It is not my task here to outline a full theory of legal pluralism.[74] I accept the definition of legal pluralism as 'a contemporary image of law that has been advanced by sociolegal scholars in response to the dominant monist image of law as derivative of the political state and

TABLE 8.1
The conceptual elements of regime theory

Regime element	Meaning of term/source of change
Sets	• Regimes are not one 'thing,' and they can be embodied in more than one instrumental form.
Implicit or explicit	• This term modifies the other elements. • Typically, norms/principles are implicit/inferential, while rules/procedures are explicit/formulaic.
Normative framework	• The sources of order do not have to be explicit to be real; regimes need not be formal to have influence on the practices of states.
Principles	• When social purposes change, it affects the normative framework of a regime (cf. boxes 1 and 2 in Figure 8.1).
Norms	• Norms form the social dimension.
Instrumental form	
Rules	• A regime's formal and visible instruments are its written rules, and its procedures for monitoring compliance and adjudicating disputes. Its surveillance mechanisms are often the instrumental form of a normative consensus.
Decision-making procedure	• Instruments respond to changes in power, material forces, interests – that is, to change in interdependence or dynamic density (cf. boxes 3 and 4 in Figure 8.1) or to change in the 'market' arm of the double movement. They also respond to the social arm, in the sense that instruments can also be an outcome of a regime's normative framework.
Actors	• Actors in the original definition were generally understood to be states, but this restriction is not well-founded.
Expectations converge	• Refers in part to state practices, but also to the intersubjective basis of regimes. • States need not have the same expectations, only a desire to seek an accommodation.
Given area of international relations	• This term was used as a reference to issue-areas, which are intersubjective creations.

its progeny.'[75] Scholars have found empirical counterfactuals to this dominant view in the observation of more than one *law* operative in a territory. Early studies of non-state legal ordering focused on either the exotic or the pathological – colonialism, folkways, and urban sub-cultures. Since the early 1980s, however, legal pluralists have also sought to explore and analyse the diverse nonpathological manifestations of non-state law in modern, Western, multicultural, and polyethnic societies. So, for example, many scholars still look at the response of colonial administrations to indigenous African law; others explore the autonomy of, for example, gypsy law within modern societies,[76] or the way hegemonic ideas transform national practice.[77] And we see something similar in international regimes.

More important for my purposes are the theoretical counterfactuals to the mainstream view. Law is 'plural,' Macdonald argues, when counterposed to alternatives that 'presuppose a formalized, institutional, definitional criterion for law that is located in State action (centralism). [That] conceive of law in terms of systems of normative ordering that have impermeable territorial and intellectual boundaries (positivism). And [that] posit a singular distinction between law and society as if one were measuring the relationship of two, and only two, separate commensurables (monism).'[78] Legal pluralism suggests in contrast that the state is not the fount of all law, law need not be explicit, and no institution has a normative monopoly within its domain.

Feudal society was marked by radical legal pluralism, by the overlapping authority of canon law, feudal or seigniorial law, royal law, manorial law, urban law, and *lex mercatoria*.[79] Roman law supplanted the plural feudal law beginning in the late eleventh century, but it was only in the nineteenth century that Roman law had been codified and had become the formal state law that now seems to be the legal universe. This single, state-managed legal system was a relatively late development, was not necessarily the end-point of legal evolution, and in fact was never as all pervasive as the dominant discourse imagines.[80] Santos writes: 'Rather than being ordered by a single legal order, modern societies are ordered by a plurality of legal orders, interrelated and socially distributed in different ways. ... Legal pluralism concerns the idea that more than one legal system operates in a single political unit. It originated at the turn of the century in the European antipositivistic legal philosophy as a reaction against the reduction of law to state law carried out by the codification movement and elaborated upon by legal positivism. It was a reaction against state legal centralism or exclusivism.'[81]

When legal centralism became dominant, and lined up on territorial boundaries, it immediately caused problems, and not simply with what Santos calls the other 'intrastate' forms of social order that continued to exist, because many domains have never respected territorial boundaries. The supposedly 'international' aspects of the law increasingly came within the purview of international regimes in a process that accelerated after the Second World War when states attempted to restore international order while maintaining space for domestic policy.

We can now see Polanyi's paradox in another way. Stability and freedom are only possible if governments work together, which requires abandoning what he called the nineteenth-century belief in anarchistic sovereignty, but the point of their working together is to allow national governments to shape domestic institutions.[82] That is, the only way in which governments can preserve some of the *content* of sovereignty is to abandon any insistence on its *form*. Ruggie extended this idea with the notion of the compromise of embedded liberalism.[83] The welfare state, an expression of sovereignty, is only possible when combined with international openness; but free trade can only be stable if combined with the domestic redistribution of the welfare state.

Postwar international organizations embody this paradox of embedded liberalism but it is now harder to maintain this social rapprochement between states and markets, especially in the domain of domestic regulation. Pressures for what is called 'deeper integration' originate with multinational firms whose operations span more than one territorial market. Such firms find it simpler to face common regulatory systems, common labour policies, common intellectual property regimes and common standards throughout their operations. In this sense, Macdonald argues, 'deeper interstate and international integration is the late twentieth century equivalent of the move to national law in the nineteenth century.' In the earlier period it was the culmination of a long effort 'to break the non-official regulatory control of feudal lords, local custom, local markets and fairs, workers guilds, crofters, fishermen and highwaymen.' Now it is a new centralist and monist attempt to create a single body of law for at least some sorts of entities and transactions. Centralists who desire such a global rule of law do not understand that a global rule of law divorced from political authority, which remains local, would be tyranny. Legal pluralism suggests that the WTO can be valuable for enhancing the rule of law without moving formal state-made law to the international level, or centralizing it in one place. Legal pluralism can value rule of law rather than the hierarchical power to announce law.[84]

If law is not the expression of the sovereign's will,[85] what is it? Fuller defines law as 'the enterprise of subjecting human conduct to the governance of rules.'[86] He rejects defining law by its tools (such as courts), or by its results (such as order). 'Unlike most modern theories of law,' he says, 'this view treats law as activity and regards a legal system as the product of a sustained purposive effort.' It is also unlike those theories of law that 'explicitly assert, or tacitly assume, that a distinguishing mark of law consists in the use of coercion or force.' This conception seems useful for regimes, which cannot be coercive, unless we attribute coercive effect to the presence of a hegemon or, in Fuller's terms, a 'formal hierarchy of command or authority.' Note that if we do not define law by the presence of formal hierarchy, then we cannot define it by opposition to the absence of such authority, or anarchy. Fuller's definition is opposed to legal positivism, understood as that direction of legal thought which insists on drawing a sharp distinction between the law *that is* and the law *that ought to be*. The difficulty for positivists lies in separating the text of an agreement from the purpose sought by the parties, which may or may not have been well expressed in the text, and which may or may not be consistent over time.[87] The law of the WTO, therefore, is not separable from the objectives of the officials who read the law, in Geneva or a capital. Positivists distrust such ideas because they want reform to be codified in the legislation of a sovereign power.[88] Reform through practice or negotiation is not favoured. When a rule is announced by the legislature, they think, we know what it is. The most obvious difficulty in calling something 'law' because it comes from an established law making authority is 'the fact that the established authority which tells us what is law is itself the product of law.'[89] That is, it is not enough to say that a rule is legal because the WTO says so if we have no way to explain why the WTO is legal. Is the WTO authoritative because the largest states say so, or because it is somehow part of an 'enterprise of subjecting human conduct to the governance of rules'?

The Fuller criterion for *law* makes all attempts at explicit definitional criteria suspect. To paraphrase a recent speech on implicit law by the president of the Law Commission of Canada,[90] the typical focus of work on trade policy is traditional legal documents – that is, with self-consciously normative writings such as treaties, WTO panel decisions, national statutes, and on their supporting literary material such as institutional archives, government administrative decisions, and newspapers. What would happen, Macdonald asks, if we directed our attention to the *lex non scripta*, or implicit law? By implicit law, he writes,

> I do not mean just the implicit law of the State legal order that sustains and nourishes the legislative and judicial endeavours of the official legal order. Nor do I only mean the unenacted general principles, custom and usages that may from time to time recognized by courts. Most of all, I mean to signal the normativity flowing from the reciprocal adjustment of expectations arising out of human interaction in the myriad social locations where this interaction occurs, quite independently of whether any official legal institution picks it up, and of whether any such institution even acknowledges its existence ... The constructive endeavours I have in mind take place every day in numerous sites and through numerous practices – some of which attach themselves as appendices to an existing text, some of which ultimately generate their own written deposits, and some of which remain tacit.

My research agenda cannot go so far as to look directly at implicit law, yet it depends on a recognition that implicit law exists. Part of what I want to say is that individuals, firms, associations, states, international (non)governmental organizations – all are grappling with the effects of globalization every day. Because it is in the nature of being human to do so, and because some order and predictability is essential, this grappling produces law. It is in our nature to try to write those rules down, to publish them and make them general. It is not the fact that they are promoted by states or incorporated in a WTO treaty that makes them law, however, nor are areas not explicitly mentioned by the WTO areas where there is no law at all, even if it is inherent in the process that people will wish to keep filling such gaps as they become apparent. Such gaps are only apparent, however. What we actually observe is the emergence of law that has yet to be written down. The WTO is now grappling, for example, with the law of the internet as it affects something called *electronic commerce*. The WTO can only add this issue to its negotiating agenda, however, because internet law is already taking shape, not because a gap was waiting to be filled. It is in this sense that the WTO 'discovers' rather than makes rules.[91]

The concept of *international regimes* is an attempt to capture this notion that normativity in a given domain comes from something more diffuse than the concrete organization that may or may not seem to be at its heart. The study of such regimes was blown off course by the importation of ideas about decentralized co-operation from transactions cost economics. This (re)turn to jurisprudence suggests the true realm of regime theory, since our starting assumption is that the study of formal treaties and organizations does not tell us all we need to know about life in a specific issue-area. While it may be impractical to look in detail at much other than WTO documents, when we do read such texts we should see them not as things in themselves but as emanations of the richer normative universe that comprises the global trading system.

A Sketch of the Architecture

The regime literature began as a reaction to the descriptive focus of work on formal organizations and treaties. Authors, as discussed above, can be interested in explaining the existence of a regime or in why the regime matters. The latter work often looks at concrete outcomes or at the informal types of co-operation facilitated by regimes. What we lose is a sense of the complexity of individual organizations. We also lose any sense of the interactions among multiple centres of power. In this section I try to sketch how this interaction might work using the concepts developed in my discussion of regime theory and of legal pluralism. We want to be able to see the formal organizations embedded in a complex net of social interactions, and we should be able to develop ideas on when to expect one or another sort of normative order to be dominant.

I see two principal dimensions of regime activity, one material, the other ideal: as *interdependence* or *dynamic density* (see above) increases within an issue-area, actors perceive an increasing *need* for collective action; and as the salient dimension of an issue changes from developing an intellectual consensus on improving *allocative efficiency,* to resolving *distributive conflict,* the site and form of action will change. This dynamic is represented in Figure 8.1. It is harder to see and understand multiple sources of normative order if we focus in Figure 8.1 on the processes of box 4 alone since they tend to be centralist, positivist, and monist. The boxes describe what we expect to see as the nature of the situation facing social actors, or their understanding of that situation, changes. The relation between the level of interdependence and

	Allocation Implicit norms	Distribution Explicit rules
Low interdependence	BOX 1 Little interaction Discussion of comparable policy problems Surveillance: create transparency.	BOX 3 Increasing conflict Bargaining: **co-ordination** of policies or **negative integration** (remove barriers) Surveillance: promote compliance with agreed norms.
High interdependence	BOX 2 Moderate conflict 'Negotiations' aimed at definitions and norms. Surveillance: peer review of good practice	BOX 4 Greatest risk of conflict Bargaining: **collaboration** on joint action or reciprocal agreements; or **positive integration** (common policies). Dispute settlement bodies essential for enforcement

Figure 8.1 Regime roles

the problem to be solved can affect the level of conflict or engagement between actors.

Regime theory should allow us to see not just formal or concrete organizations but the underlying human associations, the 'enterprise of subjecting human conduct to the governance of rules.' The matrix in Figure 8.1 tries to hold two principles of human association in tension.[92] The first principle of association is the legal principle, which is based on association by common goal (ends), or by duty or entitlement. It tends to be a centralist notion, and it leads to rules that are explicit, for example in the form of government legislation. The second is the principle of association by reciprocity, a voluntary form of association based on shared commitment. Its rules or norms will be implicit, and it recognizes autonomous or decentralized order.

The first form of association is vertical, or hierarchical while the second is horizontal, or autonomous. The first is based on seeing oneself and others in terms of what we share or as a set of beliefs about our common enterprise, while the second is based on what distinguishes us, on reciprocal rights and obligations. The matrix embodies the contradictory assumptions that we work together because we think we want to (left side; second principle) and because we think we have to (right side; first principle). The right side can overemphasize agency; the left side can overemphasize structure. The one sort of explanation might be oversocialized; but the other is undersocialized. The one sees actors as fully constrained by society, the other as atomized individuals. In this context, institutions like international regimes can be seen as merely solving transactions cost problems (Keohane, on the right side), or as part of the social structure of collective life (Ruggie, on the left side).

Unlike rational choice institutionalists, I do not see all world politics as strategic calculation in the presence of collective action problems, or what March and Olsen would call 'a logic of anticipated consequences and prior preferences.'[93] This group includes theorists of decentralized co-operation, including Ellickson.[94] March and Olsen see the alternative as 'a logic of appropriateness and a sense of identity.' Fuller makes this a distinction between a morality of duty and a morality of aspiration. 'Where the morality of aspiration starts at the top of human achievement,' he writes, 'the morality of duty starts at the bottom. It lays down the basic rules without which an ordered society is impossible, or without which an ordered society directed toward certain specific goals must fail of its mark. It is the morality of the Old Testament and the Ten Commandments. It speaks in terms of "thou shalt not," and, less frequently, of "thou shalt." It does not condemn men for failing to embrace opportunities for the fullest realization of their powers. Instead, it condemns them for failing to respect the basic requirements of social living.'[95] The morality of duty is based on notions of reciprocity – the Golden Rule, for example, expresses our duties to each other in terms of our mutual expectations of good behaviour.[96] In Keohane's terms, this is specific reciprocity. The principle of association by reciprocity is based on notions that Keohane would call diffuse reciprocity.[97]

In box 1, common problems can motivate developing a consensus on good policy. Discussion of *norms* and *principles* is central, but consensus is left implicit. As interdependence increases, an understanding of good policy depends on some consensus on abstract distributive issues, on the location of the contract curve.[98] The assumption is that as interdependence increases, and the nature of the problem changes, negotiations shift from *consensual* organizations like OECD or APEC to organizations equipped for distributive negotiations, like the WTO. When *shared commitment* (diffuse reciprocity) is necessary, co-operation within regimes or international organizations can be aimed at pooling information, aiding states to do things they could not do themselves, and co-ordinating their individual actions. When *duty and entitlement* (specific reciprocity) are the basis, then we see the most ambitious type of regime, one aimed at regulating state behaviour.[99] The *form* of co-operation will shift from definitional problems (such as property rights) through *co-ordination* of national policies, to *collaboration* on joint inter-state action.[100] Collaboration, in the sense of joint action, is harder than coordination,[101] just as negative integration (the removal of barriers) is easier than positive integration (the creation of common policies).[102] When officials act in box 4, they assume that we can structure the incentives actors face, but the very idea of 'incentives' assumes atomized rational self-interested actors. It also assumes that the provider of the incentive knows first the right course of action and second how to induce the necessary behaviour, something we only learn through action in the other boxes. Shifting from box 1 to 4 increases the salience of theories that assume rationality, because we know what is at stake, but even in box 4, dispute settlement is an intersubjective process. The key will be how actors perceive the social milieu and the tasks to be performed. The character of an issue-area will have some influence on the kind of co-operation desired by states, even if the form of the regime is given by the institution of multilateralism.

The figure can also be read in terms not of phases of co-operation but of different levels of institutionalization. Here the dynamic moves along an axis from tacit to explicit.[103] The shift through the boxes of Figure 8.1 is from relatively informal or even implicit institutions whose injunctions may be tacit or unarticulated to formal institutions whose explicit formulaic injunctions have the character of written law.[104] The source of normativity is at the beginning of this axis. As we move along it, understandings become regularized and institutions become more formal. This process can also be seen as one where learning takes place, where actors gradually articulate shared interpretations of events, where these interpretations come to define the identity of the actors, the shape of the institutions, and the possibility of 'co-operation.' When states come to capture a normative order in written rules in box 4, they are recognizing understandings generated in one of the other boxes.

The need for *surveillance* in this context will change from informal mechanisms aimed at transparency, to peer review of good practice, to more formal mechanisms aimed at settling disputes. Similarly, deci-

Exporting country \ Importing country	Does not regulate	Regulates
Does not regulate	Regulatory exemption	Regulation at destination
Regulates	Regulation at origin	Regulatory duplication

Figure 8.2 Who regulates?

sion-making rules change from consensus to weighted voting. Where both the expression and the commitment itself are tacit, informal consensual institutions work well. Surveillance and compliance mechanisms can be relatively unobtrusive, like the notification process in WTO committees, or the TPRM process. When we have explicit commitments, formal voting and dispute settlement mechanisms are needed to manage this association by the legal principle.

Illustration: Who Regulates?

We can see how this architecture works by considering the problem of reconciling domestic regulations.[105] I begin by asserting Macdonald's constant, or the law of the conservation of regulation: the amount of regulation does not vary. We never see real deregulation and as discussed above, gaps in regulation are often only apparent. What changes in regulatory reform projects is the form of regulation. Figure 8.2 uses the same implicit format as Figure 8.1 to illustrate the question a centralist faces when domestic regulations overlap: who regulates? Regulation can be carried out by the importing or the exporting state, by neither, or by both.

Roessler uses the presentation of Figure 8.2 to illustrate what he calls the WTO's border adjustment principle, since the rules of the GATT and the GATS do not inherently require a member to have any particular domestic policy.[106] He discusses the table in terms of food inspection, where members could agree to accept the exporting country's inspection, to use an inspector in the importing countries, to require inspection twice, or to have no inspection at all.

The next layer of complexity is: which rule is to be used by the inspectors? It could be a national standard of one of the countries, or an international standard. In the bottom left box, the exporting country could use any one of those three standards, as long as the importing country recognized the testing procedures. In the top right box, the importing country could also use any one of the standards, as long as it applied the MFN and national treatment principles, and as long as the testing agency was not in itself a monopoly that favoured domestic suppliers. In the lower right box, we could have both countries using the same or different standards, and recognizing, or not, each other's process.

Roessler's approach minimally respects the law of the conservation of regulation, but it is positivist and state-centric, and does not consider what the WTO does if regulation is not carried out by a state agency under the control of the trade minister. Box 1, in other words, is not regulatory exemption, it is just not state regulation. In the other boxes, regulation could be carried out by a variety of non-state actors. Written state law does not cover all human interaction, Fuller says, but only those areas where the parties do not know how to get on by reference to other normative orders, or to tacit understandings of what is proper. What he calls 'autonomous' law is pervasive.

The possibilities for dealing with regulation under discussion in the trading system include voluntary or unilateral action, perhaps on the basis of guidelines co-ordinated at the OECD, multilateral standard setting, as in the International Organization for Standardization (ISO), mutual recognition (or regulatory competition), and harmonization.

Figure 8.3 is a first attempt to combine Figures 8.1 and 8.2 as a means of sorting out this complexity. In a situation of low interdependence, where states are still trying to understand the issues, law emerges through practice. At the other extreme, both states might wish to regulate, and the only option would be having a single policy for both, or

	Allocation Implicit norms	Distribution Explicit rules
Low interdependence	BOX 1 Emulation of best practices/voluntary standards.	BOX 3 National treatment (host country acts)/ mutual recognition (host or home country acts)
High interdependence	BOX 2 Multilateral standard setting bodies	BOX 4 Harmonization, or 'deep integration'

Figure 8.3 Concepts of regulatory diplomacy

positive integration. Figure 8.4 shows the institutional requirements. Positive (or deep) integration has stringent institutional requirements, and may be undesirable even if it were possible. Most of the action, therefore, is in the lower left and the upper right.

Standards (box 2) are one of the essential institutions of a capitalist economy, and they are not merely a technical matter.[107] Standards can be a site for contestation between firms or between countries – much is a stake when one company's 'technical specifications' first become a 'de facto' standard widely used by an industry, and then are transformed from a voluntary standard to one whose use is mandated by governments. Ensuring compatibility between standards, for example the width of railway tracks, begins in informal consultations among market actors (box 1) but can end in co-ordination and collaboration problems for governments. Standards emerge from practice, but they are also created by standards organizations. Participation in these bodies is expensive, limiting the role of even the governments of smaller rich countries, like Canada. No state can afford to develop all its needed standards and regulations alone. National standards now fre-

	Allocation Implicit norms	Distribution Explicit rules
Inferential reasoning	BOX 1 Everyday practices/ markets	BOX 3 'We feeling'
Formulaic injunctions	BOX 2 Voluntary bodies	BOX 4 Common institutions

Figure 8.4 Forms of regulatory diplomacy

quently follow international standards, which may emerge from a mixed body, or from one in which governments play little role.

The right side can proceed by negative or positive integration. Co-ordination (box 3) can be accomplished by national treatment or mutual recognition, neither of which requires common policies. The mutual recognition technique works when countries (or provinces!) see themselves and their policy choices as similar, and when they are prepared to accept a degree of institutional competition among their policies.[108] Mutual recognition is first a recognition on the part of the entities of each other. It is a familiar idea in political theory and in discussions of religious tolerance. If such basic mutual recognition does not exist, then the more trivial mutual recognition of standards is not possible. It is based on trust, and a belief that the others will regulate as we do – on 'we feeling,' in other words.

Harmonization or deeper integration requires collaboration, putting it in box 4. It will be a rare form of regulatory diplomacy because, as noted in the literature on positive integration, it has demanding political requirements that are rarely met, even within the Atlantic area.

WTO activities are rarely found in box 4 since even the strictest of its rules require only compatible or co-ordinated rather than collaborative or identical policies. The WTO dispute settlement system is ultimately in box 4, but the rest of the surveillance or transparency process is not. We make a major error if we reduce the WTO to box 4 alone.

In the way that all of these figures have been set up, getting to the lower right is always difficult and may not be desirable, while state action in the upper left is always easier and sometimes just as fruitful for minimizing conflict and reducing transactions costs. The closer we get to the lower right, the more rigid policy becomes, the more we are in a one-size-fits-all world. The closer we are to the upper left, the easier it is to accommodate a plurality of normative orders. This formulation applies to the natural history of the Westphalian system of states as well as to that of any particular problem. Globalization does not force a move all the way to the lower right, nor does it make action there any easier. It does increase the need for states not only to learn from each other (left side) but also to find ways to avoid distributive conflicts (right side.)

This sketch of the architecture helps us see that a number of current issues in the trading system need not be seen in a centralist framework – coherence among international organizations, the role of non-state actors, and the rule of law in dispute settlement.

Coherence in International Economic Co-operation

One important issue for the future of the WTO will be improving the accessibility of the WTO to non-state actors and enhancing its relations with other international organizations.[109] The WTO has some form of inter-organization relations with over sixty intergovernmental organizations, including UN specialized agencies, regional bodies, and standards organizations.[110] People worry about the horizontal links between the WTO and other international organizations, and the vertical relations between trade and such 'domestic' policies as those affecting labour and the environment.[111] A long-standing problem in international economic policymaking is coherence between the IMF, the World Bank, and the WTO.[112] The original Bretton Woods institutions have become more alike over the years, but they still differ from each other in their constituencies and objectives, and both are considerably different from the WTO. Yet all three share a common interest in global prosperity and prosperity for their individual members. Should they apply the same rules, or seek to enforce each other's rules? Coherence with regional trade arrangements also poses the same issues of conflict and co-ordination with multilateral objectives. Roessler thinks that 'the rule of law' in international trade requires states to follow the trade rules, but he is simply treating the trade regime as central and denying the importance of other sources of normativity.[113] The answer is not to see each legal domain as free standing, but to think of ways they can each be true to themselves, simultaneously.

Non-State Actors

With few exceptions, regime theorists have not been interested in considering how actors other than states can be understood within a regime framework.[114] Who might be the relevant actors? The ontological difficulty is identifying the relevant entities; the epistemological problem is knowing what they do. One test might be that the actors be engaged in diplomacy, understood in Bull's definition, as 'the conduct of relations between states and *other entities* with standing in world politics by *official agents* and by *peaceful* means.'[115] The added emphasis signifies the traditional restriction of diplomacy to state actors, its definition by opposition to war, and the implication that actors must be recognized as such by other actors. Who then are the entities with recognized standing in world politics? When other entities claim a role in the trade regime, for example, they need not claim to be able to act 'as-if' they were states – they need to claim that they have legitimate authority in their own domain (which could be a claim to expertise not available to the state).

Raustiala develops a neoliberal understanding of the general benefits that make structured NGO–state co-operation in environmental institutions attractive to governments. As international environmental activity has increased, 'NGOs have, in turn, demanded access to the panoply of new international environmental institutions. States have incorporated NGOs because their participation enhances the ability, both in technocratic and political terms, of states to regulate through the treaty process. The terms of that incorporation reflect the resources, skills, and domestic influence of NGOs: NGO participation provides policy advice, helps monitor commitments and delegations, minimizes ratification risk, and facilitates signaling between governments and constituents.'[116] Those activities fit easily in boxes 1 and 2. Simmons puts NGOs in all four boxes, arguing that they 'affect national governments, multilateral institutions, and national and multinational corporations in four ways: setting agendas, negotiating outcomes, conferring legitimacy, and implementing solutions.'[117] Kofi Annan has a similarly expansive view. He argues that 'NGOs and other civil society actors are now perceived not only as disseminators of information or providers of services [or operational partners] but also as shapers of policy, be it in peace and security matters, in development, or in humanitarian affairs, ... In fact, NGOs are often on the ground before the international community gives the UN the mandate to act.'[118]

Haufler goes farther. She agrees with the traditional view that states can build a regime upon the foundation of practices and norms previously laid down by non-state actors, and they can use private sector agencies to implement some of the functions of the regime itself. But she argues that the relationship between states and non-state actors may be reversed. Private sector actors may construct independent international regimes, or play a relatively equal role with states within a regime of mixed 'parentage'.[119] Haufler's argument is consistent with a claim that the structure of normativity – and power? – is neither monist nor centralist. As Porter argues with respect to a different set of private actors, 'regime analysis suggests that the absence of a strong hierarchical regulatory body for finance that controls states and firms from above does not mean that there are no significant institutions for regulating global finance. It means rather that we must take informal arrangements into account when searching for such institutions.'[120]

It follows that Scholte in seeing the WTO as *supranational governance* misunderstands the WTO and what it can do. His views of civil society are also problematic – by reifying the WTO, he thinks it useful, practical, and legitimate for civil society organizations to seek to influence WTO staff.[121] Since the role of the WTO secretariat is merely to support the work of members (WTO staff do not have the autonomous role of, for example, the staff of the IMF), it is not clear what would be gained. To speak of the WTO, in other words, is to speak of the secretariat, WTO bodies, national delegations, and officials in capitals. Civil society organizations have as much access to national officials as a given state thinks appropriate. That access is only useful, of course, if civil society knows what is going on. Current efforts to improve the accessibility and transparency of the WTO are therefore vital.[122]

To think of multiple centres of power does not require that we reduce them to one. If NGOs are not part of the collective life of an institution, and there is no sense in which they are part of the WTO, for example, in its current guise, then making decisions 'transparent' could be futile – the WTO is not equipped to think in public. The WTO has a characteristic mode of operation that was not meant to accommodate non-state actors. To admit them without fundamental re-thinking and then renegotiating of all the agreements might actually make the WTO less democratic (and more rigid) rather than the reverse.

The theoretical and policy message in the boxes is that the source of normativity is at the beginning of the axis. Rules are a means to avoid and to resolve disputes, but the trading system also creates the things we can bargain about. Non-state actors are part of the process, though not necessarily in all the boxes. Citizens are engaged every day in changing the norms of the trading system, the regime, through their practices and customs

The simple task would be to examine the NGOs clamouring for attention, but we risk over-stating both their significance and their legitimacy. If we are interested in the trade regime, we might also look to corporations, transnational social movements, law firms, the big six consulting/accounting firms, and so on. We are interested in how the regime structures the international commercial relations of participants, at how their law and practices change, but not because of any visible compellence or enforcement by the WTO, which is only part of the trade regime. In addition to WTO rules, we might then look to the harmonization effects of commercial instruments such as standard form contracts or stock exchange rules, which are not actually universal, but effectively project themselves beyond jurisdictional boundaries (the same is true of U.S. bankruptcy law, UK insurance contracts, and so on).[123]

Enforcement

Mainstream legal theorists think 'that legal pluralism undermines respect for the Rule of Law. They argue that without a systematic, integrated, unitary set of legal prescriptions, normative conflict is inevitable and official action cannot be subjected to the censure of controlling constitutional and jurisdictional norms.'[124] Many scholars and a great many officials think that the value of the WTO is that it is a 'rules-based' system as opposed to a system based on power. In the mainstream view, it is easy to identify the precise international obligations accepted by a state, and easy to see if the state complies. When it does not, the dispute settlement system exists for enforcement. This thinking is mistaken on many counts, not least because it collapses the four-fold WTO transparency function of committees, trade policy surveillance, publication of reports, and dispute settlement, into one dimension, but mostly because it reifies the rule of law in the trading system into the WTO. Such thinking also animates the NGOs who want to integrate labour and environmental standards into the WTO because they think it has enforcement capacity. NGOs similarly think that their representatives should help WTO dispute panels make the right decisions.

It is important to stress that compliance with regime rules does not depend on enforcement. The Chayes identify a number of circumstances that often underlie apparent violations of treaty requirements. First, treaty language can be ambiguous. Even when precision is attempted, it may simply add detail without resolving in advance questions of interpretation that arise when actors apply legal language to real life. In situations where reasonable people differ, the issue is not 'compliance.' Indeed merely accepting that the issue is legitimately in dispute within the frame of the agreement is a form of compliance with the normative authority it establishes. Second, states may face limitations on their capacity to carry out their undertakings. Treaties are formally between states on matters affecting their own behaviour (for example, in nuclear test ban treaties). When the real object of a treaty is the actions of private entities, states can comply with requirements, for example, to introduce legislation intended to reduce sulphur dioxide (SO_2) emissions by 30 per cent against a certain baseline, yet be unable to implement the policy, or make it effective. The 'state' that signs a treaty may not have any real competence to act, or its actions may not be sufficient for the achievement of the objective. Third, choosing the point at which to evaluate compliance can be complicated when agreements have varying transition periods. Fourth, the participants in a regime can decide among themselves that a certain amount of variance around the central limit is acceptable. It follows, they argue, that coercive 'enforcement' is unlikely to be useful.[125]

The Chayes recommend a compliance strategy that addresses some well-known institutional design issues. One is ensuring transparency, meaning providing reliable information about what the regime requires and who is doing what. When self-reporting is envisaged, it can be improved by technical assistance, and by NGO monitoring. Long before formal adjudication of disputes is needed, regime participants can clarify disputed issues in many of the other bodies established by a regime. The need to report on one's actions, and be subjected to review by the secretariat and one's peers, perhaps even by NGOs and the public generally, can often motivate policy convergence on regime standards. This openness alone can be useful, but it also works, the Chayes argue, 'because modern states are bound in a tightly woven fabric of international agreements, organizations, and institutions that shape their relations with each other and penetrate deeply into their internal economics and politics. The integrity and reliability of this system are of overriding importance for most states, most of the time.' The largest states depend on the willing co-operation of others to achieve their objectives; they conclude, therefore, that 'for all but a few self-isolated nations, sovereignty no longer consists in the freedom of states to act independently, in their perceived self-interest, but in membership in reasonably good standing in the regimes that make up the substance of international life.'[126]

Some lawyers would prefer to see only box 4, which would require a move to a greater emphasis on adjudication of rules by legally trained people and less recourse to diplomatic fudges. But as Fuller notes, 'As lawyers we have a natural inclination to 'judicialize' every function of government. Adjudication is a process with which we are familiar and which enables us to show to advantage our special talents. Yet we must face the plain truth that adjudication is an ineffective instrument for economic management and for governmental participation in the allocation of economic resources.'[127] Similarly, the architectural design of legal institutions and procedures obviously cannot be drawn by adjudicative decision. Some process of discussion is necessary to know where we are going. We need to know what is up for decision before we can make it. Arthurs agrees that adjudication is an 'inappropriate way to debate and decide important issues of public policy.' He worries that 'the logic of litigation is circumstantial, not systemic: wrongs are ascertained, remedies are awarded and rights are declared on the basis of the particular facts and arguments presented on the record, not with a view to comprehensively assessing and reconciling conflicting social needs, institutional possibilities, financial implications and competing public policies.'[128] As Macdonald notes, 'Once we see that the 'national' legal order is plural, we can end the attempt to replicate this domestic order internationally. Creating an international Rule of Law does not require either centralism or monism; it does require efforts to understand the multiple normative orders that might affect individuals, organizations, and states, and it does require us to understand when one normative order is likely to be more influential than another.'[129]

Conclusion: Who Is Caesar?

The notion of 'multiple centres of power' is a metaphor. It incorporates ideas about power, sovereignty, law, and governance. I have tried to show how we can understand these ideas in a different way, one that does not assume that the state was ever central. The challenge for policy is thereby recast from worrying about a diminished state to one of learning from generations of Canadian experience of playing in rather than conducting the orchestra. Globalization is not Caesar, power is diffuse, sovereignty is a fiction, and law is about constructing the world that ought to be. Where then is Caesar?

Legal pluralists direct our attention away from box 4, away from mechanical adjudication by experts and towards the sources of order by which people, or entities within the trading system, live. They stress not normative competition so much as a recognition that pluralism in law is pervasive, even within state law – think of federal systems, or the different roles of courts and administrative agencies. In the international arena we can see the 'choice of law' decision even in such things as a decision on whether a particular dispute should be conducted within NAFTA (for example, softwood lumber) or the WTO (for example, magazines). WTO rules frequently refer to ISO standards or the practices of the ITU. Legislation and adjudication are not the only or even the most important sources of social order. In the WTO, negotiation, discussion in committees, and surveillance in the TPRM are all part of how we discover and interpret the rules. The elements of the WTO do not stand in hierarchical relationship to each other.

Much international trade may be structured by forms of law that are only indirectly or informally linked to the WTO. Legal subjects, participants in global commerce, are 'law inventing' and not merely 'law abiding.' Creating an international rule of law does not require us to see the WTO as having a monopoly of law in its domain, or as standing in hierarchical relation to all other sources of order in the trading system. It does require efforts to understand the multiple normative orders that are both created by and affect individuals, organizations, and states, and it does require us to understand when one normative order is likely to be more influential than another.

The WTO like any treaty can only establish a framework since we lack an international authority capable of command. World trade is U.S.$6.5 trillion a year and growing. A secretariat of 500 staff could not dream of 'enforcing' something called 'international trade law' even if they were directed to try. The WTO operates at the margins, helping states recognize their own interests, and to recognize their obligations to each other. It aims to avoid disputes, not to structure massive conflicts. It is, then, a statement of aspiration. It recognizes that substance and procedure are linked, that it is more important to shape how states understand themselves in this domain than to announce precise rules that all must follow. This idea obviously differs from that of 'cooperation.' It also obviously differs from Ostry's concept of 'system friction'[130] that sees a resolution of conflict between incommensurable legal systems only in enforced 'harmonization.' But it stands in uneasy relation to Arthurs, who sees this process of state identity being shaped through international agreements as a way in which neo-conservatism is constitutionalized.[131] That is, dominant ideas can be a form of hegemony, as Gramsci showed.

To call the trading system rule-based is to say nothing at all. Any system of social interaction is rule-based. Two things are significant about the trading system: a) the continual effort to recognize the rules and to write them down, making what was tacit, explicit; and, b) the attempt to make the process one of multilateral surveillance and negotiation rather than great-power dictate. Since no single 'rule' determines how we accommodate those conflicting values, much of the WTO agreement concerns the mechanisms – from informal discussion in committees to formal dispute settlement – through which states talk to each other about how to reconcile their competing objectives. The challenge for the WTO is always to understand and reconcile differences, ensuring that the players can get on with things with some degree of predictability. They do not need the same law, or a harmonized law, they just need to have a recognizable rule that structures activity in a fair way. Most important, they need transparency, including the ability to be informed about proposed rules, the right to state views, information on the results of any monitoring exercise, and a forum for settling disputes. All of these elements of transparency are central functions performed by international regimes in their efforts to provide global governance, reconciling the actions of welfare states. The weakness of our current thinking about regimes and international organizations is that we have problems seeing how they should work together, and how non-state actors are part of the regime.

I want to conclude for now, however, by considering how we should understand the *convergent expectations* of the regime definition. Constructivists stress that 'expectations' means intersubjective understandings not formal texts. A synonym for convergence is 'lines tending to meet at a point,' but what is the nature of that focal point? Musical metaphors might help us to synthesize regime theory and legal pluralism. One of the places where we can see the tensions of globalization is in domestic regulation. The only way to sustain a centralist and monist conception of the role of regulation in underpinning market institutions in neo-utilitarian approaches centred on outcomes, especially trade theory, is to see 'harmonization' as an inevitable solution to incompatible regulations. Constructivist accounts centred on the process of intersubjective accommodation see the possibility of rhythm, because the *compromise* of embedded liberalism does not require harmonization, or at least not harmonization as typically understood.[132]

The simple dictionary meaning of harmony is *agreement*, which does not tell us much. Boodman defines harmonization as 'a process in which diverse elements are combined or adapted to each other so as to form a coherent whole while retaining their individuality.' He explains this definition by reference to musical concepts. In music, harmony is the vertical integration of notes – the simultaneous sounding of different tones or pitches – while melody is horizontal integration. 'Harmony, therefore, requires diversity and eschews uniformity. ... A second feature of harmony is that its components, while retaining their individuality, form a new and more complex musical sound.'[133] The people who think that harmonization is a solution to diversity obviously have a different understanding of the term (closer to the sense of the common policies found in box 4), which renders it unsuitable for my purposes.

Rhythm, in contrast to harmony, is determined by the duration of notes. We can think of the focal point as the beat. Chernoff in his musical discussion of the pluralist sensibility of Africans says that 'the continuing music consists of many rhythms, and the "beat" emerges from the way these rhythms engage and communicate with each other. While various rhythms may be more important, no single rhythm can provide a complete focus, and in this sense there is no central point of unity, except God. Equanimity with multiple rhythms and the silent beat can and does serve to inform social relations with a cosmopolitan attitude of toleration, rationality and pragmatism.'[134]

Can we articulate precise rules for how multiple sources of normative order relate to each other? No: some players are louder than others, but this world orchestra has no conductor to keep the beat. Is the regime concept then only descriptive, having nothing to say about fairness? Do I tell a story about how the world is, or about how it ought to be? The 'silent beat' comes from the normative framework of the regime (which can be described, in part, as embedded liberalism), the evolving (multilateral) sense of what constitutes appropriate behaviour in this domain, something that can only be determined in the intersubjective process of participants living their collective life together. I see embedded liberalism as a constitutive compromise, one that values both international openness and the welfare state.

In sum, there is no Caesar. Rhythm is something all must discover. Rhythm is a process, a way of thinking about collective life, but it is also an objective. International regimes in the era of globalization need not require any actor to play in harmony, so long as all can find the beat.

NOTES

This is a revised version of a paper presented at the workshop Trends: Multiple Centres of Power Workshop, 13 May 1999. I am grateful for the comments of participants at the workshop, notably Julien Bauer and Claire Cutler, and for the comments of friends and colleagues on the earlier versions of some of these ideas.

1 Luke 20:25.
2 Canada, *Northern Frontier Northern Homeland: The Report of the Mackenzie Valley Pipeline Inquiry*, vol. 1 (Ottawa: Minister of Supply and Services, 1977).
3 A.J. Miller, 'The Functional Principle in Canada's External Relations,' *International Journal* 35, no. 2 (Spring 1980): 309–28.
4 Lucian M. Ashworth and David Long, eds., *New Perspectives on International Functionalism* (London: Macmillan, 1999).
5 David Mitrany, *A Working Peace System: An Argument for the Functional Development of International Organization* (London: Royal Institute of International Affairs, 1943), 18–19.
6 Gary Marks, François Nielsen, Leonard Ray, and Jane Salk, 'Competencies, Cracks and Conflicts: Regional Mobilization in the European Union,' in Gary Marks, Fritz W. Scharpf, Philippe Schmitter and Wolfgang Streeck, eds., *Governance in the European Union* (London: Sage Publications, 1996), 40–59. For a critique of this literature, see Simon Hix, 'The Study of the European Union II: The "New Governance" Agenda and Its Rival,' *Journal of European Public Policy* 51 (March 1998): 38–65.

7 Philippe C. Schmitter, 'Examining the Present Euro-Polity with the Help of Past Theories,' in Gary Marks, Fritz W. Scharpf, Philippe Schmitter, and Wolfgang Streeck, eds., *Governance in the European Union* (London: Sage Publications, 1996), 1–14.

8 John Gerard Ruggie, 'Territoriality and Beyond: Problematizing Modernity in International Relations,' *International Organization* 47, no. 1 (Winter 1993): 139–74.

9 This chapter was completed before the WTO ministerial meeting in December 1999. For an assessment, see John M. Curtis and Robert Wolfe, 'The WTO in the Aftermyth of the Battles in Seattle,' in Maureen Appel Molot and Fen Osler Hampson, eds., *Vanishing Borders? Canada among Nations 2000* (Toronto: Oxford University Press, 2000).

10 With respect to the different tendencies among constructivists, the approach that I am developing here is neither positivist nor postmodern, and it owes much to ideas about rules borrowed from legal theory. On the terms of debate, see Ted Hopf, 'The Promise of Constructivism in International Relations Theory,' *International Security* 23, no. 1 (Summer 1998): 171–200; Peter J. Katzenstein, Robert O. Keohane, and Stephen D. Krasner, 'International Organization and the Study of World Politics,' *International Organization* 52, no. 4 (Fall 1998): 645–85; Nicholas Onuf, 'A Constructivist Manifesto,' in Kurt Burch and Robert A. Denemark, eds., *Constituting International Political Economy* (Boulder, Col.: Lynne Rienner Publishers, 1997), 7–17; and John Gerard Ruggie, *Constructing the World Polity: Essays on International Institutionalization* (London: Routledge, 1998).

11 Assistant Deputy Ministers' Sub-committee for Global Challenges and Opportunities, *Canada 2005: Draft Interim Report on Global Challenges and Opportunities* (Ottawa, 25 February 1997), 'The International Context.'

12 The drafters of Canada's Charter of Rights and Freedoms understood the need to avoid reifying the rule of law. The preamble states that 'Canada is founded upon principles that recognize the supremacy of God and the rule of law.' This claim forces us to recognize that both God and the rule of law are absolutely sovereign. Neither is reducible to the other, and neither is knowable except through interpretation. In this context, both God and rule of law are metaphors. See Brayton Polka, 'The Supremacy of God and the Rule of Law in the Canadian Charter of Rights and Freedoms: A Theologico-Political Analysis,' *McGill Law Journal* 32 (1987): 854–63.

13 Jessica T. Mathews, 'Power Shift,' *Foreign Affairs* 76, no. 1 (January/February 1997): 50.

14 David Held, 'Democracy and Globalization,' *Global Governance* 3, no. 3 (September–December 1997): 262.

15 Paul Hirst, 'Power,' in Tim Dunne, Michael Cox, and Ken Booth, eds., *The Eighty Years' Crisis: International Relations 1919–1999* (Cambridge: Cambridge University Press, 1998), 133–49; for a similar view, see Charles Taylor, 'Globalization and the Future of Canada,' *Queen's Quarterly* 105, no. 3 (Fall 1998): 331–42.

16 Richard Little, 'The Growing Relevance of Pluralism?' in Steve Smith, Ken Booth, and Marysia Zalewski, eds., *International Theory: Positivism and Beyond* (Cambridge: Cambridge University Press, 1996), 66–86.

17 Anne-Marie Slaughter, 'The Real New World Order,' *Foreign Affairs* 76, no. 5 (September/October 1997): 183–97.

18 John Stopford and Susan Strange with John S. Henley, *Rival States, Rival Firms: Competition for World Market Shares* (Cambridge: Cambridge University Press, 1991).

19 Kal Raustiala, 'States, NGOs, and International Environmental Institutions,' *International Studies Quarterly* 41, no. 4 (Fall 1996): 720.

20 Denis Stairs, 'The Policy Process and Dialogues with Demos: Liberal Pluralism with a Transnational Twist,' in Maureen Appel Molot and Fen Osler Hampson, eds., *Leadership and Dialogue: Canada Among Nations* 1998 (Toronto: Oxford University Press, 1998), 48.

21 The familiar 'lump of labour' fallacy assumes that as there is only so much work to go around, unemployment can be reduced if the available work is better distributed by eliminating overtime and cutting working hours.

22 Andrew Adonis and Andrew Tyrie, *Subsidiarity: No Panacea* (London: European Policy Forum, 1993); Joel P. Trachtman, 'International Regulatory Competition, Externalization, and Jurisdiction,' *Harvard International Law Journal* 34, no. 1 (Winter 1993): 47–104.

23 Eric Helleiner, 'Electronic Money: A Challenge to the Sovereign State?' *Journal of International Affairs* 51, no. 2 (Spring 1998): 387–411.

24 Robert W. Cox with Timothy J. Sinclair, *Approaches to World Order* (Cambridge: Cambridge University Press, 1996); Stephen Gill, ed., *Gramsci, Historical Materialism and International Relations* (Cambridge: Cambridge University Press, 1993).

25 Craig N. Murphy, *International Organization and Industrial Change: Global Governance since 1850* (Cambridge: Polity Press, 1994).

26 Charles P. Kindleberger, *The World in Depression, 1929–1939*, revised and enlarged edition (Berkeley: University of California Press, 1986), 304.

27 Robert Gilpin, *War and Change in World Politics* (Cambridge: Cambridge University Press, 1981).

28 Robert O. Keohane, *After Hegemony: Cooperation and Discord in the World Political Economy* (Princeton, NJ: Princeton University Press, 1984).

29 Duncan Snidal, 'International Political Economy Approaches to International Institutions, ' in Jagdeep S. Bhandari and A. O. Sykes, eds., *Economic Dimensions in International Law: Comparative and Empirical Perspectives* (Cambridge: Cambridge University Press, 1997), 477–512.

30 This discussion is focussed on the sites of power; a different issue is thinking about the forms of power. Constructivism stresses the importance of understanding both material and discursive power – the power of knowledge, ideas, culture, ideology, and language. Ted Hopf, 'The Promise of Constructivism in International Relations Theory,' *International Security* 23, no. 1 (Summer 1998): 177. Canada's former foreign minister, Lloyd Axworthy, for example, was bewitched by misleading notions of 'soft power,' for which he was criticized by scholars – see Fen Osler Hampson and Dean F. Oliver, 'Pulpit Diplomacy: A Critical Assessment of the Axworthy Doctrine,' *International Journal* 43, no. 3 (Summer 1998): 379–406. On soft power, see Robert O. Keohane and Joseph S. Nye, Jr, 'Power and Interdependence in the Information Age,' *Foreign Affairs* 77, no. 5 (September/October 1998): 81–94; Joseph S. Nye, Jr, and William A. Owens, 'America's Information Edge,' *Foreign Affairs* 75, no. 2 (March/April 1996): 20–36.

31 Lon L. Fuller, *The Law in Quest of Itself* (Chicago: Foundation Press Inc., 1940), 34, 45. Fuller was an influential American legal scholar – see William J. Witteveen and Wibren van der Burg, eds., *Rediscovering Fuller: Essays on Implicit Law and Institutional Design* (Amsterdam: University of Amsterdam Press, 1999).

32 International law also has trouble with sovereignty. One study of the implications of the creation of the WTO begs the issue, concluding that 'questions of where sovereignty actually resides and where it should be allocated for the most efficient and effective regulation of transnational economic activity (i.e., at the sub-state, regional, state, or supranational level) will become ever more salient.' Susan Hainsworth, 'Sovereignty, Economic Integration, and the World Trade Organization,' *Osgoode Hall Law Journal* 33, no. 3 (Fall 1995): 622.

33 John Gerard Ruggie, 'Continuity and Transformation in the World Polity: Towards a Neorealist Synthesis,' in Robert O. Keohane, ed., *Neorealism and Its Critics* (New York: Columbia University Press, 1986), 131–57; Ruggie, 'Territoriality and Beyond.' Ruggie provides a compelling account of the link between territoriality, single-point perspective, and sovereignty. His image of the 'unbundling' of territoriality is evocative, but his analysis seems to remain state-centric.

34 Thomas J. Biersteker and Cythnia Weber, 'The Social Construction of State Sovereignty,' in Thomas J. Biersteker and Cythnia Weber, eds., *State Sover-*

eignty as Social Construct (Cambridge: Cambridge University Press, 1996), 1–21; on the mutual recognition of sovereign entities, see Barry Buzan, 'From International System to International Society: Structural Realism and Regime Theory meet the English School,' *International Organization* 47, no. 3 (Summer 1993): 327–52.

35 John Gerard Ruggie, 'Political Structure and Dynamic Density,' *Constructing the World Polity: Essays on International Institutionalization* (London and New York: Routledge, 1998), 151.

36 Snidal, 'International Political Economy Approaches to International Institutions,' 487–8. See also Helen Milner, 'The Assumption of Anarchy in International Relations Theory: A Critique,' in David A. Baldwin, ed., *Neorealism and Neoliberalism: The Contemporary Debate* (New York: Columbia University Press, 1993), 143–69.

37 Ellickson observes that economists in the legal centralist tradition overestimate the state's ability to make and enforce rules, not least by missing the implications of their own theories. Information is costly, which implies that actors do not always know what the legal rule might be. Do firms know the GATT? Do officials in environment ministries? He concludes that, contrary to what Coase argues, law (by which he means formal rules) can be less relevant when transaction costs are high. Robert C. Ellickson, *Order without Law: How Neighbors Settle Disputes* (Cambridge: Harvard University Press, 1991), 280. The question is evaded by the rational/economic approach in international relations, which postulates that the source of order is a kind of invisible hand that fosters positive and suppresses negative interactions. International order emerges, by assumption, from self-interested interaction.

38 Max Weber, 'The Profession and Vocation of Politics,' in Peter Lassman and Ronald Speirs, eds., *Weber: Political Writings* (Cambridge: Cambridge University Press, 1994), 310–11.

39 Ian Hurd, 'Legitimacy and Authority in International Politics,' *International Organization* 53, no. 2 (Spring 1999): 379–408.

40 Fuller, *The Law in Quest of Itself*, 118.

41 R.B.J. Walker, *Inside/Outside: International Relations as Political Theory* (Cambridge: Cambridge University Press, 1993), 62.

42 R.B.J. Walker, 'Both Globalization and Sovereignty: Re-imagining the Political' Centre for Global Studies, University of Victoria, internet site: http://www.finearts.uvic.ca/~cgs, Nov. 1998.

43 Sovereignty is in no sense divisible, it cannot be shared, nor can the state as a particular social form divide its power, since sovereignty is about inside/outside, and the state is about violence.

44 Lon L. Fuller, *The Morality of Law,* revised edition (New Haven, Conn.: Yale University Press, 1969), 181.

45 Craig N. Murphy, *International Organization and Industrial Change: Global Governance since 1850* (Cambridge: Polity Press, 1994).

46 Jock A. Finlayson and Mark W. Zacher, 'The GATT and the Regulation of Trade Barriers: Regime Dynamics and Functions,' in Stephen D. Krasner, ed., *International Regimes* (Ithaca, NY: Cornell University Press, 1983), 273–314; Michael C. Webb, 'Canada and the International Monetary Regime,' in Claire Cutler and Mark W. Zacher, eds., *Canadian Foreign Policy and International Economic Regimes* (Vancouver: University of British Columbia Press, 1992), 153–85.

47 Vinod K. Aggarwal, ed., *Institutional Designs for a Complex World: Bargaining, Linkages, and Nesting* (New York: Cornell University Press, 1998).

48 James F. Keeley, 'The IAEA and the Iraqi challenge: roots and responses,' *International Journal* 49, no. 1 (Winter 1993–4): 126–55; Albert Legault, Isabelle Desmarais, Julie Fournier, and Charles Thumerelle, 'The United Nations at Fifty: Regime Theory and Collective Security,' *International Journal,* 50, no. 1 (Winter 1994–5): 71–102; Janice Gross Stein, 'Detection and Defection: Security "Régimes" and the Management of International Conflict,' *International Journal* 40, no. 4 (Autumn 1985): 599–617.

49 Oran R. Young, 'Negotiating a Global Climate Change Regime,' in *International Governance: Protecting the Environment in a Stateless Society* (Ithaca, NY: Cornell University Press, 1994), 12–32.

50 Mark W. Zacher with Brent A. Sutton, *Governing Global Networks: International Regimes for Transportation and Communications* (Cambridge: Cambridge University Press, 1996).

51 Jean Philippe Thérien, 'Le Canada et le regime international de l'aide,' *Études internationales,* 20 (June 1989): 311–40.

52 Stephen D. Krasner, 'Structural Causes and Regime Consequences: Regimes as Intervening Variables,' in Stephen D. Krasner, ed., *International Regimes* (Ithaca, NY: Cornell University Press, 1983), 2.

53 Susan Strange, 'Cave! hic dragones: A Critique of Regime Analysis,' in Stephen D. Krasner, ed., *International Regimes* (Ithaca, NY: Cornell University Press, 1983), 337–54.

54 Fred Gale, '*Cave "Cave! Hic Dragones"*: A Neo-Gramscian Deconstruction and Reconstruction of International Regime Theory,' *Review of International Political Economy* 5, no. 2 (Summer 1998): 252–84.

55 John Gerard Ruggie, 'International Responses to Technology: Concepts and Trends,' *International Organization* 29, no. 3 (Summer 1975): 557–83.

56 Andreas Hasenclever, Peter Mayer, and Volker Rittberger, *Theories of International Regimes* (Cambridge: Cambridge University Press, 1997).

57 The notion of intersubjective communication among states may be confusing. If we assume that states are 'actors,' then we must assume that they have some ability to communicate with each other. In game theory actors can communicate through signalling; other approaches notice what some call transgovernmentalism – state officials talk to each other all the time, at all levels.

58 Peter M. Haas, 'Introduction: Epistemic Communities and International Policy Coordination,' *International Organization* 46, no. 1 (Winter 1992): 1–35.

59 Hasenclever, Mayer, and Rittberger, *Theories of International Regimes*, 137.

60 Friedrich V. Kratochwil, *Rules, Norms and Decisions: On the Conditions of Practical and Legal Reasoning in International Relations and Domestic Affairs* (Cambridge: Cambridge University Press, 1989), 59.

61 Ernst B. Haas, *When Knowledge Is Power: Three Models of Change in International Organizations* (Berkeley: University of California Press, 1990), 173.

62 The term 'dynamic density' comes from Durkheim, who wrote, 'The dynamic density may be defined, the volume being equal, as the function of the number of individuals who are actually having not only commercial but also social relations, i.e., who not only exchange services or compete with one another, but also live a common life.' He added, 'We have shown elsewhere how all growth in the volume and dynamic density of societies modifies profoundly the fundamental conditions of collective existence by rendering social life more intense, by extending the horizon of thought and action of each individual.' Emile Durkheim, *The Rules of Sociological Method* (New York: Free Press, 1895/1964), 114–15. See also Ruggie, 'Political Structure and Dynamic Density,' *Constructing the World Polity*; Alexander Wendt, 'Collective Identity Formation and the International State,' *American Political Science Review* 88, no. 2 (June 1994), 389–90. In Keohane's terms, an increase in interdependence means an increase in the density of policy space – which could also mean an increase in dynamic density. Another way to think about interdependence or dynamic density is Mitrany's notion of action on shared tasks oriented to basic needs as the basis for a working peace. In contemporary trade negotiations jargon, this idea is operationalized as 'critical mass.' The United States added in a footnote that its 1995 offer on basic telecommunications was 'contingent on the agreement by a critical mass of WTO members to provide market access and national treatment for basic telecommunications services, as well as to provide commitments similar to those offered by the United States on pro-competitive regulatory disciplines,' *Financial Times* (20 September 1995), 5. 'Critical mass' meant two things here. It required substantial offers from the largest markets, and offers comparable in form from countries that are

relatively small market participants. In any issue-area the number of participants does not matter as long as they are the right participants (a mix of intellectual leadership and market weight), and MFN, and the single undertaking to hold it all together. Finnemore and Sikkink also employ the concept of critical mass in understanding when a sufficient number of states have adopted a norm to give its diffusion self-sustaining momentum. While numbers of states seem to be important, 'it also matters which states adopt the norm. Some states are critical to a norm's adoption; others are less so.' What constitutes a 'critical state' will vary from issue to issue, but one criterion is that critical states are those without which the achievement of the substantive norm goal is compromised. See Martha Finnemore and Kathryn Sikkink, 'International Norm Dynamics and Political Change,' *International Organization* 52, no. 4 (Autumn 1998): 887–17.

63 Keohane, *After Hegemony;* Duncan Snidal, 'International Political Economy Approaches to International Institutions,' in Jagdeep S. Bhandari and A.O. Sykes, eds., *Economic Dimensions in International Law: Comparative and Empirical Perspectives* (Cambridge: Cambridge University Press, 1997), 477–512.

64 Ernst B. Haas, 'Why Collaborate? Issue-Linkage and International Regimes,' *World Politics* 32, no. 3 (April 1980): 357–405; John Gerard Ruggie, 'International Responses to Technology: Concepts and Trends,' *International Organization* 29, no. 3 (Summer 1975): 557–83; Robert O. Keohane and Joseph S. Nye, *Power and Interdependence,* second edition (Glenview, Ill.: Scott, Foresman and Company, 1989), 64–5.

65 David Held, 'Democracy, the Nation-State and the Global System,' in David Held, ed., *Political Theory Today* (Stanford, Calif.: Stanford University Press, 1991), 280.

66 Nicholas Greenwood Onuf, *World of Our Making: Rules and Rule in Social Theory and International Relations* (Columbia: University of South Carolina Press, 1989), 246.

67 Roderick A. Macdonald, 'Metaphors of Multiplicity: Civil Society, Regimes, and Legal Pluralism,' *Arizona Journal of Comparative and International Law* 15, no. 1 (1998): 69–91.

68 Stephen D. Krasner, 'Structural Causes and Regime Consequences: Regimes as Intervening Variables,' in Stephen D. Krasner, ed., *International Regimes* (Ithaca, NY: Cornell University Press, 1983), 2.

69 See Robert Wolfe, *Farm Wars: The Political Economy of Agriculture and the International Trade Regime* (London and New York: Macmillan and St Martin's Press, 1998).

70 For example, Robert A. Dahl, *Who Governs? Democracy and Power in an American City* (New Haven, Conn.: Yale University Press, 1961).

71 Eirik Grundtvig Furubotn and Rudolf Richter, *Institutions and Economic Theory: The Contribution of the New Institutional Economics* (Ann Arbor: University of Michigan Press, 1997).
72 Boaventura de Sousa Santos, *Toward a New Common Sense: Law, Science and Politics in the Paradigmatic Transition* (New York: Routledge, 1995).
73 R.A. Macdonald, 'Critical Legal Pluralism as a Construction of Normativity and the Emergence of Law,' in A. Lajoie, ed., *Théories et Émergence du Droit* (Montreal: Thémis, 1997).
74 For a survey of approaches to the social diversity of law, see the introduction written for a collection of essays on the topic – Jean-Guy Belley, 'Law as *Terra Incognita*: Constructing Legal Pluralism,' *Canadian Journal of Law and Society* 12, no. 2 (Fall 1997): 1–15.
75 Martha-Marie Kleinhans and Roderick A. Macdonald, 'What, is a *Critical* Legal Pluralism?' *Canadian Journal of Law and Society* 12, no. 2 (Fall 1997): 25–46.
76 Walter Otto Weyrauch and Maureen Ann Bell, 'Autonomous Lawmaking: The Case of the "Gypsies,"' *Yale Law Journal* 103, no. 2 (November 1993): 323–99.
77 H.W. Arthurs, 'Globalization of the Mind: Canadian Elites and the Restructuring of Legal Fields,' *Canadian Journal of Law and Society* 12, no. 2 (1997): 219–46.
78 Macdonald, 'Metaphors of Multiplicity,' 74.
79 Santos, *Toward a New Common Sense*, 58.
80 Macdonald, 'Metaphors of Multiplicity,' 74–5.
81 Santos, *Toward a New Common Sense*, 114-15. The other common critique of legal centralism is found in the work of such transaction costs economists as Williamson and Coase; see Ellickson, *Order without Law*, 138–9.
82 Karl Polanyi, *The Great Transformation: The Political and Economic Origins of Our Time* (Boston: Beacon Press, 1944), 253.
83 John Gerard Ruggie, 'International Regimes, Transactions, and Change: Embedded Liberalism in the Postwar Economic Order,' in Stephen D. Krasner, ed., *International Regimes* (Ithaca, NY: Cornell University Press, 1983), 195–231.
84 Macdonald, 'Metaphors of Multiplicity,' 89, 78.
85 Or the analogous concept from Dicey's conception of the rule of law, a 'bridle' for the state Leviathan. Harry W. Arthurs, "'Mechanical Arts and Merchandise": Canadian Public Administration in the New Economy,' *McGill Law Journal* 42, no. 1 (February 1997): 46.
86 Lon L. Fuller, *The Morality of Law*, Revised Edition (New Haven, Conn.: Yale University Press, 1969), 106.

87 Compare Fuller, *The Law in Quest of Itself*, 10.
88 Fuller, *The Morality of Law*, 131.
89 Ibid., 147–8.
90 Roderick A. Macdonald, 'Perspectives on Informal Legal Relations: Between Languages and Law in Europe,' paper presented at the Colloquium on Harmonization and Dissonance: Languages and the Law in Canada and Europe, May 1999.
91 Harry Arthurs (private communication) observes, however, that to choose where to discover is in fact to make the rule.
92 The concept is found in many places in Fuller's work, notably Lon L. Fuller, 'Two Principles of Human Association,' in Kenneth Winston, ed., *The Principles of Social Order* (Durham, NC: Duke University Press, 1981), 67–85. My understanding of it has evolved through many discussions with Rod Macdonald. For his own most recent attempt to grapple with Fuller and these two principles of human association, see Roderick A. Macdonald, 'Legislation and Governance,' in William J. Witteveen and Wibren van der Burg, eds., *Rediscovering Fuller: Essays on Implicit Law and Institutional Design* (Amsterdam: University of Amsterdam Press, 1999), 279–311.
93 James G. March and Johan P. Olsen, 'The Institutional Dynamics of International Political Orders,' *International Organization* 52, no. 4 (Autumn 1998): 943–69.
94 Ellickson, *Order without Law.*
95 Fuller, *The Morality of Law*, 5–6.
96 Ibid., 20.
97 Robert O. Keohane, 'Reciprocity in International Relations,' *International Institutions and State Power: Essays in International Relations Theory* (Boulder, Col.: Westview Press, 1989), 132–57; see also Polanyi, *The Great Transformation*, chap. 4.
98 Oran R. Young, 'The Politics of International Regime Formation: Managing Natural Resources and the Environment,' *International Organization* 43, no. 3 (Summer 1989): 349–75.
99 Haas, *When Knowledge Is Power*, 198.
100 John Gerard Ruggie, 'Multilateralism at Century's End,' *Constructing the World Polity: Essays on International Institutionalization* (London: Routledge, 1998), 102–30.
101 Arthur A. Stein, 'Coordination and Collaboration: Regimes in an Anarchic World,' in Stephen D. Krasner, ed., *International Regimes* (Ithaca, NY: Cornell University Press, 1983): 115–40.
102 Jan Tinbergen, *International Economic Integration*, second revised edition (Amsterdam: Elsevier Publishing Company, 1965).

103 Friedrich V. Kratochwil, *Rules, Norms and Decisions: On the Conditions of Practical and Legal Reasoning in International Relations and Domestic Affairs* (Cambridge: Cambridge University Press, 1989), 55.

104 Charles Lipson, 'Why Are Some International Agreements Informal?' *International Organization* 45, no. 4 (Fall 1991): 495–538.

105 Robert Wolfe, 'Regulatory Diplomacy: Why Rhythm Beats Harmony in the Trade Regime,' in Thomas J. Courchene, ed., *Room to Manoeuvre? Globalization and Policy Convergence* (Kingston: John Deutsch Institute for the Study of Economic Policy, 1999).

106 Frieder Roessler, 'Increasing Market Access under Regulatory Heterogeneity: The Strategies of the World Trade Organization,' *Regulatory Reform and International Market Openness* (Paris: Organisation for Economic Co-operation and Development, 1996), 117–30.

107 Liora Salter, 'The Housework of Capitalism: Standardization in the Communications and Information Technology Sectors,' *International Journal of Political Economy* 23, no. 4 (Winter 1993–4): 105–13.

108 Miles Kahler, 'Trade and Domestic Differences,' in Suzanne Berger and Ronald Dore, eds., *National Diversity and Global Capitalism* (Ithaca, NY: Cornell University Press, 1996), 331.

109 Curtis and Wolfe, 'The WTO in the Aftermyth of the Battles in Seattle.'

110 WTO, *Annual Report 1998*, vol. 1 (Geneva: World Trade Organization, 1998), 129–36.

111 Kym Anderson, 'Environmental and Labor Standards: What Role for the WTO?' in Anne O. Krueger, ed., *The WTO as an International Organization* (Chicago: University of Chicago Press, 1998).

112 For a discussion of the issues, see Gary P. Sampson, 'Greater Coherence in Global Economic Policyrnaking: A WTO Perspective,' in Krueger, ed., *The WTO as an International Organization*, 257–70. See also Sylvia Ostry, *Reinforcing the WTO* (Washington: Group of Thirty, 1998).

113 Frieder Roessler, 'Domestic Policy Objectives and the Multilateral Trade Order: Lessons from the Past,' in Krueger, ed., *The WTO as an International Organization*, 213–29.

114 Some scholars have begun this work. For a Gramscian approach to the non-state sources of normativity in commercial relations, see Claire Cutler, 'Locating "Authority" in the Global Political Economy,' *International Studies Quarterly* 43, no. 1 (March 1999): 59–81; and Claire Cutler, 'Public Meets Private: The International Unification and Harmonisation of Private International Trade Law,' *Global Society* 13, no. 1 (1999): 25–48. For another extended treatment of *lex mercatoria*, see Santos, *Toward a New Common Sense*. For explorations of private regimes, see Claire Cutler,

'Canada and the Private International Trade Law Regime,' in Claire Cutler and Mark W. Zacher, eds., *Canadian Foreign Policy and International Economic Regimes* (Vancouver: University of British Columbia Press, 1992), 89–109; Virginia Haufler, 'Crossing the Boundary between Public and Private: International Regimes and Non-State Actors,' in Volker Rittberger, ed., *Regime Theory and International Relations* (Oxford: Clarendon Press, 1993), 94–111; Virginia Haufler, *Dangerous Commerce: Insurance and the Management of International Risk* (Ithaca, NY: Cornell University Press, 1997); Tony Porter, *States, Markets and Regimes in Global Finance* (New York: St Martin's Press, 1993); Fred P. Gale, *The Tropical Timber Trade Regime* (New York: St Martin's Press, 1998); David Humphreys, 'Regime Theory and Non-Governmental Organizations: The Case of Forest Conservation,' *Journal of Commonwealth and Comparative Politics* 24 (1996): 90–115; and Claire Cutler, Virginia Haufler and Tony Porter, eds., *Private Authority and International Affairs* (Albany: State University of New York Press, 1999).

115 Hedley Bull, *The Anarchical Society: A Study of Order in World Politics*, second edition (New York: Columbia University Press, 1995), 156.

116 Kal Raustiala, 'States, NGOs, and International Environmental Institutions,' *International Studies Quarterly* 41, no. 4, (1996): 720.

117 P.J. Simmons, 'Learning to Live with NGOs,' *Foreign Policy* no. 112 (Fall 1998).

118 Kofi Annan, 'The Quiet Revolution,' *Global Governance* 4, no. 2 (April–June 1998): 134.

119 Virginia Haufler, 'Crossing the Boundary between Public and Private: International Regimes and Non-State Actors,' in Volker Rittberger, ed., *Regime Theory and International Relations* (Oxford: Clarendon Press, 1993), 94–5.

120 Tony Porter, *States, Markets and Regimes in Global Finance* (New York: St Martin's Press, 1993), 14.

121 Jan Aart Scholte with Robert O'Brien and Marc Williams, 'The WTO and Civil Society,' *Journal of World Trade* 33, no. 1 (1999): 108 and 111.

122 Gabrielle Marceau and Peter N. Pedersen, 'Is the WTO Open and Transparent? A Discussion of the Relationship of the WTO with Non-governmental Organizations and Civil Society Claims for More Transparency and Public Participation,' *Journal of World Trade* 33, no. 1 (1999): 5–49.

123 I owe this suggestion to Harry Arthurs.

124 Macdonald, 'Metaphors of Multiplicity,' 78.

125 Abram Chayes and Antonia Handler Chayes, *The New Sovereignty: Compliance with International Regulatory Norms* (Cambridge, Mass.: Harvard University Press, 1995), 10–22.

126 Ibid., 26–7.
127 Fuller, *The Morality of Law*, 176.
128 H.W. Arthurs, 'Constitutionalizing Neo-conservatism and Regional Economic Integration: TINA x 2,' in Thomas J. Courchene, ed., *Room to Manoeuvre? Globalization and Policy Convergence* (Kingston: Published for the School of Policy Studies by McGill-Queen's University Press, 1999), 17–74.
129 Macdonald, 'Metaphors of Multiplicity,' 80.
130 Sylvia Ostry, *The Postwar International Trading System: Who's on First?* (Chicago: University of Chicago Press, 1997).
131 Arthurs, 'Constitutionalizing Neo-Conservatism and Regional Economic Integration.'
132 For a tentative discussion of why harmonization is not a helpful way to think about globalization and domestic regulation, see Wolfe, 'Regulatory Diplomacy.'
133 Martin Boodman, 'The Myth of the Harmonization of Laws,' *American Journal of Comparative Law* 39 (1991): 701–3.
134 John Miller Chernoff, *African Rhythm and Sensibility: Aesthetics and Social Action in African Musical Idioms* (Chicago: University of Chicago Press, 1979).

9. Conclusion: Implications for Governance and Policy

Gordon Smith and Daniel Wolfish

In *Canada 2005*, the Assistant Deputy Ministers' Sub-Committee on Global Challenges and Opportunities stated, 'Over the past few years most industrialized countries, including Canada, have seen a profound shift in power away from central governments. The once uncontested authority of states and central governments is being challenged by the rise of nongovernmental actors and by the development of international organizations and arrangements that seek to hold all nation-states accountable to certain standards of behaviour.'[1] The assumption underlying this statement is that fundamental changes in the social and institutional location of decision-making power are occurring and that we no longer live in a world where the state is the sole source of authority regulating our social, economic, and political life. The ADMs' sub-committee believes that there is a profound shift under way not only in who is actually making or influencing decisions, but also in generally accepted views about who is a legitimate actor in the policy process.

The purpose of this book is to evaluate the validity of the above statement. While for the most part the contributors agree that the state and locus of decision-making authority may be changing, the tenor of their comments suggests that the conclusions of the ADMs' sub-committee are overstated. Indeed, the current governance and policy-making environment offers the state new opportunities to assume an active and authoritative role. While the state retains an authoritative role, we need to be mindful of the government's responsibility of ensuring the security of its citizens and maintaining accountable and democratic governance.

The arguments contained in this volume contribute to an ongoing debate on governance and the role of the state. First, the authors comment on the authoritative nature of the state. They look into and often disagree with each other on the extent to which the state is the appropriate and authoritative agent to settle disputes, distribute resources, and set policy on behalf of its citizens. This investigation leads the authors to question whether the state has a monopoly on authority or whether it shares authority with political non-governmental organizations or corporations and other regulating mechanisms, such as the market.

Second, the issue of the authoritative nature of state is related to, yet distinguishable from, government capacity – that is, the ability of governments to address substantive issues successfully and to solve substantive problems. As people find fault with the state's performance and as the state gives up some of its activities, its authority can erode.[2]

Lastly, as governments discover new ways to operate effectively in a multicentric world, issues concerning state responsibility, political accountability, and democratic governance arise. Just as governments are engaging in ever more public consultation, some of the authors in this volume question both the extent to which government has lived up to its responsibility to protect the public good and the degree to which it is in fact accessible and accountable. This chapter looks at the world of multiple centres of power, its effect on the role of the state, the challenges to social policy and democracy, the management of transnational issues, and implications for policy makers and potential areas for further research.

Multiple Centres of Power: The Triumph of Ambiguity and the Rule of Law

There can be no doubt that 'politics as usual' today is not like the 'politics as usual' of yesteryear. Even the most cursory of investigations reveals that the number of players interacting with governments in the policy process has grown. Powerful multinational corporations today can mobilize greater resources for their goals than some national governments. Some of these private-sector actors, such as bond-rating agencies, have such a profound impact on government policies that they affect the everyday lives of Canadians.[3] Moreover, many more NGOs now interact with governments, international organizations, and multinational corporations in negotiating and setting agendas, implementing solutions, and conferring legitimacy.[4] In addition, central governments, including Canada's, have devolved more responsibilities to sub-national governments, while at the same time negotiating more international treaties obliging these same sub-national governments to adhere to particular policies and courses of action. In short, proliferation of political actors operating nationally and internationally is the norm.

These political actors engage with one another on a regular basis, often forming temporary coalitions when pursuing common goals and acting in discord when their goals clash. The participants in these relationships often operate from different sets of rules, norms, and traditions. We live in a multicentric world, where power, authority, and influence emanate not only from governments but also from other sources – above all, from actors in the private sector and in society. Some of the contributors to this volume even suggest that it is rarely a simple matter to discern whose rules and practices have the highest degree of legitimacy, who has the authority to make rules, or indeed where the source of legitimacy and authority lies in the first place. While this last statement may seem somewhat exaggerated, varying norms, rules, and standards are invoked in different situations, depending on which actors are engaged and under which circumstances. Today many implicit and explicit laws and norms shape our behaviour and are arrived at through intersubjective consensus – that is, through an implied understanding arising from continual interaction.

Robert Wolfe has noted in chapter 8 that states can build an international regime, or an issue-specific governance system, on the foundation of norms and practices previously laid down by non-state actors, and they can use private-sector agencies to implement some of the functions of the regime itself. Similarly, private-sector actors may also construct independent regimes as well or play a relatively equal role with states within a regime of 'mixed parentage.'[5] As well, the absence of a strong hierarchical regulatory body or regime to control states and firms from above does not mean that there are no significant institutions for regulating behaviour. It means rather that we must take informal arrangements into account. Ambiguity is often the rule.[6]

It could be argued that this ambiguity either undermines, or exists in the absence of, the rule of law. The temptation is to minimize this ambiguity by imposing harmonized rules on all the actors. Wolfe argues that such an undertaking would be futile. Development of a set of harmonized rules meant to have coercive power over a wide range of state and non-state actors might result in something that looked satisfactory on paper, but which would in fact be unworkable. In the absence of an underlying consensus, no amount of legal precision will bring clarity. When consensus exists, rules, whether informal or formal, develop that can in turn pattern behaviour and foster a convergence of expectations. Thus, creating a rule of law, whether international or national, presupposes an understanding of the multiple normative orders affecting individuals, organizations, states, NGOs, and firms, and it requires an assessment of which normative order is likely to be most influential. It need not involve harmonization, argues Wolfe.

Finding Its Role: The State as Linchpin

The fact of more actors participating in the political process does not necessarily mean that the state has become obsolete or that its power and authority have been eclipsed. On the contrary, the studies presented in this volume all indicate that, far from leading to the end of the state, the proliferation of new actors has strengthened it. One common belief revealed in this collection as questionable pertains to the 'upward' transfer of authority and sovereignty to supranational organizations and to supranational norms and standards.[7] Canada has become a party to a growing number of international organizations and conventions requiring it to abide by international obligations, standards, and norms. However, Clarkson, Le Prestre, and Wolfe caution us not to exaggerate the federal government's loss of authority.

Investigating the various sources of authority, Wolfe (chapter 8) introduces us to the lump-of-power fallacy to demonstrate that Ottawa's loss of authority is overstated. People who are guilty of this fallacy assume that there is only a finite source of power, sovereignty, and authority and that it can be sliced up and assigned to different levels in the political system and to different political actors. It follows from this that, when one level is given jurisdiction or authority, another must relinquish it. But if we understand that this misconception comes from a state-centric perspective, then we can see that jurisdiction is not necessarily the right yardstick. Authority can have multiple sources. When we look beyond the state-centric view, Wolfe suggests, we can see that power and authority can spring forth as people come together for various purposes.

Looking at the international level, Le Prestre (chapter 7) notes that, since the UN Conference on the Environment in Rio de Janeiro in 1992, states have attempted to regain control of the international agenda and the management of transnational issues from intergovernmental organizations (IGOs) by promoting the convention governance system. Framework conventions in this type of governance system call for the creation of a conference of parties (CoP) that provides a forum where member states continuously negotiate and work out the norms, principles, decision-making procedures, and implementation of the convention. It is through CoPs, he contends, that states control the pace of policy change and the agenda and deliberate the implementation of collective action in often highly contested issue-areas such as protection of the environment.

Making a comment on Canada's North American trade commitments, Clarkson (chapter 5) points out that it is difficult to know how much the North American Free Trade Agreement (NAFTA) has constrained Canada's sovereignty. NAFTA was accompanied by a shift in the managerial philosophy of both elected and bureaucratic policy makers away from 'big-is-better activism' in favour of a more disengaged and limited government. This philosophical sea change makes it hard to determine whether a reduction in interventionist practices by federal and provincial governments is the result of erosion of state power or of their own conversion to neoliberalism. Moreover, NAFTA, unlike the European Union, does not enjoy continental institutions of governance that could offset the power asymmetry between the U.S. and Canadian governments. Judicial power has not been 'uploaded' to the continental level. Despite the provision for ad hoc bi- and trinational panels to settle disputes between Canada, the United States, and Mexico, the three states have resisted harmonizing their laws on such common procedures as anti-dumping and countervailing duties. Although all three agreed to cede review of trade determinations to this trilateral regime, they conceded little sovereignty because they did not create permanent supranational institutions. The failure of NAFTA mechanisms to resolve disputes expeditiously has ultimately pushed the member governments to settle their disputes through political negotiation in the old-fashioned way, argues Clarkson.

Not only does the state retain considerable power in governing, it also fulfils a unique role in the governance process. The state occupies, Julien Bauer and Philippe Le Prestre argue in chapter 2, a peculiar place as the intermediary or nexus among IGOs, sub-national governments, the private sector, and society at large. As intermediaries, states preserve a real margin of manoeuvre and power of decision to mediate conflicts that arise between these various actors. At the international level, the state links external actors with domestic actors and constructs a space for them to advance their interests and views. The state is the only actor that possesses a general knowledge of the problems and interests of all 'stakeholders' and is capable of identifying, negotiating, and enforcing solutions that may be acceptable to all. The diffusion of power increases the state's capacity to serve as intermediary between domestic and external actors, as we can see in three policy areas – climate change, landmines, and trade.

To illustrate this point, consider, first, the international negotiations surrounding the Kyoto Protocols of 1996 for the reduction of emissions of greenhouse gases. One can identify a multitude of actors having a real stake in the negotiations. Many environmental NGOs sought significant reductions in emissions and other environmental safeguards. These NGOs lobbied national governments as well as international organizations and secretariats. Multinational corporations from the energy industry were also key stakeholders, as they feared losses of revenue or stringent regulations that either could not easily be met or would force a significant reallocation of resources. Sub-national governments, such as Alberta in Canada, depend on high-priced petroleum for the economic health of their regions and for revenue from which they fund social programs and other government services. At the same time, various countries came to the negotiations with different interests, while the secretariat of the UN Framework Convention on Climate Change (UNFCCC) had its mandate to fulfil. This example demonstrates how the state is the only actor that possesses a general knowledge of the problems and has the interest of all stakeholders in its purview. It is the state's responsibility to identify, negotiate, and enforce a solution with which all or most of the participants can live. Then, as Le Prestre argues in chapter 7, the convention governance system reinforces the state's role as primary international actor in negotiation and enforcement of treaties.

Second, the proliferation of NGOs and citizen's groups also offers opportunities for middle powers such as Canada to find new partners in pursuing international policies, and Ottawa's campaign to ban landmines is a case in point.[8] The International Coalition to Ban Landmines (ICBL) proved to be an effective partner for Canada in helping to raise the consciousness of citizens, officials, and politicians throughout the world, particularly in Europe and the United States, to the issue of landmines. It mobilized public opinion and forged political coalitions within and between countries. It lobbied officials and politicians for access to funds, for opportunities for agenda setting, and for participation in international negotiations as observer components of national delegations. Nevertheless, this foreign policy initiative was also pursued through direct state contact and international organizations. Partnering with the ICBL proved ideal for Canada in pursuing an international objective, which would have unfortunately met with failure had Canada lobbied only foreign governments. Partnering with the ICBL, one can thus argue, strengthened Canada.

Third, on the issue of trade, the federal government in Canada, Stephen Clarkson (chapter 5) argues, is likely to remain the key intermediary. To start with, neither provinces nor business can themselves initiate a dispute-resolution process, which is dependent on the discretion of the federal government. Since NAFTA dispute settlement mechanisms remain problematic, Clarkson argues, Ottawa may turn down provincial requests to set up a dispute panel. He suggests that the federal government has the discretion to choose how to settle a trade dispute; it may seek redress through the World Trade Organization (WTO), or it may turn to the NAFTA dispute mechanism, but it may also decide to resolve a high-tension disagreement through political negotiation and sacrifice a local interest for some other advantage.

The examples of climate change, landmines, and trade demonstrate that not only has the state retained significant power, but also that its role as an intermediary or nexus between the multiple centres of power has strengthened the state.

Introducing the concept of transformative capacity, Vincent Della Sala (chapter 4) elaborates on Bauer and Le Prestre's comments on the state as a vital intermediary. Della Sala notes that we should not equate state capacity with a state's intervention in the economy; a common mistake. In fact, advanced industrialized countries value the protection of property rights, which may limit state intervention in the economy. A state's transformative capacity refers to its ability to adapt to external shocks and pressures by generating new means of governing industrial and technological change.[9] Its capacity to generate new means of 'managing change' depends on its ability to co-ordinate productive resources, to be selective, and to enforce rules and modes of behaviour while meeting regime goals. In this light, the success of states in fostering economic growth in an era of globalization is a measure of their tranformative capacity.

In addition to depicting the state as a vital intermediary operating in a political space among the other centres of power, the studies presented in this volume encourage us to see the state not as a unitary actor but as a complex unit capable of pursuing various interests simultaneously. The state consists of a set of institutions that interact with other actors internationally and domestically in the governance and policy process.

Emphasizing this point, Ronald Crelinsten (chapter 3) notes that state officials from the judiciary, bureaucracy, executive, and legislature interact with societal and private-sector actors in a fluid manner at the local, national, and international levels; this behaviour cannot be said to be co-ordinated in a real way. This complex movement back and forth, he argues, results in a convoluted arrangement of feedback loops and hence in contradictions, ambiguities, and uncertainties, helping to blur the distinction between domestic and foreign affairs. This is consistent with Margaret Keck and Kathryn Sikkink's characterization of the state as constituted by 'networked components' that 'bring to international relations identities and goals that are not purely derived from their structural position in a world of states – and that may even be constituted by relationships with citizens of other states.'[10]

Robert Cutler's discussion of international parliamentary institutions (IPIs) in chapter 6 further reminds us that states are not unitary actors. IPIs represent, from an analytical and practical point of view, a valuable middle ground, he argues, between the traditional level of interstate diplomacy and the new level of transnational co-operation among grassroots NGOs. Making the distinction between legislative and executive branches of government, Cutler notes that IPIs also can oversee traditional executive-based diplomacy and executive-based governance in general.

Abdicating Social Responsibility and the Erosion of Democracy

While one may argue that reports of the erosion of state authority are exaggerated, this does not mean that governance in advanced industrialized societies has not undergone significant change. Casting a critical eye on the transfer of authority and responsibilities to IGOs, subnational governments, the private sector, and society in general, some of the contributors suggest that democracies are shirking their responsibilities in the social field and are making their institutions less open to groups that may favour alternative ways of regulating social, political, and economic life.

Some of the authors argue that a change in management philosophies by both bureaucrats and senior elected officials has resulted in the casting off of government functions to non-government actors and hence the shirking of responsibility. Stephen Clarkson (chapter 5) notes that the shift from the social-democratic ideals of Lester Pearson and Pierre Trudeau to the neoliberal orientation of Brian Mulroney and Jean Chrétien encouraged the growth of multiple centres of power.[11] Neoliberal-oriented policy can be identified, he argues, with the 'downloading' of functions to lower levels of government, an 'uploading' of authority to international structures, and an 'offloading' of government functions to society and to the private sector, with concomitant increased reliance on the 'imperatives' of the market.

In particular, there is some cause to be worried about how neoliberalism has encouraged governments to privatize and offload government functions.[12] First, the tension, Ronald Crelinsten (chapter 3) notes, between fiscal and economic policy on the one hand and social goals on the other hand renders problematic the co-ordination of government policy across social and economic domains.[13] Social goals may become subordinate to economic imperatives. Crelinsten asks whether the social policy agenda of governments today is in large part determined by economic considerations. Vincent Della Sala (chapter 4) posits that powerful financial markets monitor many, if not all, aspects of state spending and therefore are able to determine broad policy goals with respect to employment, social welfare policy, and taxation. Second, neoliberalism has helped produce the downsizing of government and has encouraged the contracting out of government services and responsibilities to the private sector. This has produced a situation, Crelinsten suggests, where government services are made into commodities and are marketed as products to be consumed not by citizens but by clients or customers.

Third, Della Sala notes that, as a result of the triumph of neoliberalism, the market, with all its vagaries, is increasingly regulating social and economic life. The effect of bond-rating agencies such as Moody's and Standard's and Poor's on bond markets and the cost of financing public expenditures ensures that decisions in the federal Department of Finance are made with an eye beyond the demands of the public. Of course, the market regulates without any reference to social and public goods such as high employment, environmental protection, crime prevention, or poverty alleviation. In each of these situations, Crelinsten and Della Sala contend, the public good ends up being subordinated either to the demands of the market or to the profit motive of service providers. The role of the state, they note, as protector of citizen's rights and the notion of the public good fall through the cracks.

As the state takes on fewer responsibilities, Della Sala argues, it becomes 'hollowed out.' As the state becomes more hollow, it also becomes less accessible to citizens because governments make it harder for broad sections of society, particularly those that will be hurt by economic liberalization, to obtain access to state structures to resist change.[14] For example, a government is less likely to be receptive to citizens' input on decisions that have significant spending implications as it grows increasingly captive to the demands and expectations of international financial markets.

Even in cases where the state cedes power and responsibility to lower levels of government or NGOs, there are also concerns about lack of access and accountability. The conventional view of downloading of authority to lower levels of government or to entities outside government such as NGOs is that it will increase citizens' access by bringing service delivery closer to the people. Although this may be true in many cases, it should not be taken for granted. An unintended result of downloading may be that sources of authority and responsibility become so diffuse that citizens no longer know where to turn for redress or for communicating their wishes and ideas. Moreover, NGOs do not necessarily adopt democratic governance structures for their own organizations.

One should not overstate the argument that government is growing increasingly inaccessible to its citizens. We must recall that the Canadian federal government is increasingly conducting inclusive, even wide-ranging consultation processes. For example, it has set up an elaborate consultation process through the National Climate Change Secretariat to discuss ways in which Canada can meet its international obligations to reduce greenhouse gas emissions.[15] The governments in Canada, along with other stakeholders, are examining options available to implement the Kyoto Protocols, including the costs and benefits of implementation. The purpose of the consultation process is to ensure that Canadians have the opportunity to take part in the development of Canada's national implementation strategy. Organized groups of stakeholders, called issue tables, are the means for this input. Different issue tables are responsible for consulting with a broad group of Canadians who have an interest in the table's sector or issue. Table members are drawn from positions in the broad community interested in a sector or issue. They include government, industry, environmental NGOs, and other representatives.

The hollow state creates a paradox. On the one hand, the state, from the citizen's perspective, remains the most visible centre in a multicentric world. On the other hand, the diffusion of power and authority across multiple centres means that there are fewer and fewer areas where the responsibility and accountability of the state are unambiguous. Thus, although citizens will continue to turn to the state, expecting it to take responsibility and be held accountable for a variety of economic, social, and political matters, the state no longer has the authority to respond as it once did.

Clarkson (chapter 5) reminds us that the hollowing out of the state is not inevitable. He contends that, just as the predominance of neoliberalism produced a world of multiple centres of power, the ascendance of an alternative philosophy could reverse this trend. He argues that neoliberalism is unresponsive to the social needs to which governments may again feel compelled to respond. Given the inability of the neoliberal model to respond to some of these concerns, the pendulum may be poised to swing back towards a state less reluctant to exercise its power to regulate the market and to provide society directly with the services that it desires. Indeed, considerable authority and legitimacy having shifted elsewhere, the federal government may try to reassert itself in ways that it had earlier abandoned and reclaim some of the authority and legitimacy that it had previously abandoned. As a result, the potential for further change remains.

Managing Transnational Issues in an Era of Global Interconnectedness

Today, questions of democracy and accountability need not be limited to national politics, but can extend to the international arena as well. David Held has observed that regional and global interconnectedness challenges the traditional national orientation of democracy. The processes of governance often escape the reach of the nation-state. National communities by no means exclusively make decisions and determine policies for themselves; governments do not alone determine what is appropriate for their own citizens. The idea of consent through elections and the notion that the relevant constituency of voluntary agreement is the state become problematic as soon as the issue of regional and global interconnectedness is considered and the nature of the relevant community is contested.[16] Moreover, some traditional IGOs and NGOs suffer from a lack of procedural democracy and transparency and so may be viewed as much less legitimate than some individual states. In transnational and global issues such as acid rain and climate change, questions arises: whose consent is required and whose participation is justified in decisions concerning the management of such issues?

Both Cutler and Le Prestre address accountability in an era of regional and global interconnectedness. Cutler (chapter 6) argues that IPIs such as the European parliament are helpful in democratizing transnational relations. IPIs are international institutions of a parliamentary nature, whether legislative or consultative, that meet on a regular basis and in which members are selected either from their national legislatures or popularly elected directly by the citizenries of member-states. As such, IPIs contrast with traditional IGOs, which comprise national political executives determining national representation and policy. Cutler argues that IPIs establish transnational relationships that restrain old power-politics patterns and encourage accountability to society and interaction with NGOs. IPIs also tend not to be issue-specific, but rather deal with the array of transnational issues that arise between member states.

Le Prestre's solution in chapter 7 contrasts with Cutler's. He argues that democratic states need to regain control of the global agenda and the management of transnational problems from traditional IGOs in order to guarantee accountability. To do so, states should promote a convention governance system. Conventions, unlike traditional IGOs and IPIs, are issue-specific. Moreover, convention secretariats are mission-oriented institutions that are answerable to a conference of parties made up of signatory states. Secretariats are not responsible for managing the issue; they are first and foremost service organizations that do not have direct regulatory or decision-making authority. The convention governance system may, Le Prestre argues, have an advantage if it is allowed to open up not only to member states but also to NGOs and to individual networks of researchers. In short, the system of convention governance is a focused, accountable, and flexible way of managing transnational issues.

Implications for Policy Makers and Avenues for Future Research[17]

Although nation-states may be doing less by virtue of having ceded powers and functions to other levels of government, to international organizations, and to NGOs, they remain the place to which citizens turn for redress and to offer input. The growing number of arrangements involving either the contracting out of service delivery to agents outside the public service or partnering arrangements for service delivery among different levels of governments can render accountability complicated and confusing. National governments, therefore, must learn how to remain responsive to citizens even in areas over which they no longer have direct control. Governments must learn how to manage their relationships with citizens in an environment where accountability for designing and delivering public programs is increasingly spread over a variety of actors.

Not all policy areas are equally amenable to citizen's engagement. For example, independent central banks have been established so as to be insulated from public opinion and political demands when setting monetary policy. Policy development in areas such as health and education is, however, a very different matter. Crelinsten (chapter 3) argues that in a world of tightened international constraints, there is a danger that public consultations will heighten, not reduce, cynicism about the responsiveness of political institutions because it could prove to be difficult to reconcile international obligations with public demands when the two diverge. It would be useful to analyse how different policy areas lend themselves to citizens' engagement and the suitability of different models of citizen participation.

We are in a period in Canada of significant rethinking about 'who does what' in terms of the most appropriate responsibilities for municipal, provincial, and federal governments. The emergence of multiple centres of power casts this debate into sharp relief. Governments at all levels must learn how better to conceptualize their own roles and responsibilities, how to communicate this vision to other levels of government, and how to reconcile divergent views about their respective roles and responsibilities when visions differ across the levels of government. Governments are on uncertain ground as they seek to hive off entire areas of responsibility to other centres of power.

The multicentric world means that interconnectedness and ambiguity are everywhere. The reality of the multi-centred world is that fewer and fewer relationships are amenable to being formally codified in law or enshrined in contracts. Governments are traditionally very uneasy about operating with this kind of ambiguity. They will have to acquire competence for managing ambiguity and for developing systems and rules that help different kinds of stakeholders to understand each other's norms and predict each other's behaviour.

NOTES

We would like to thank Mark Schacter, who, on behalf of the Institute on Governance, provided a summary report of the workshop 'Trends: Multiple Centres of Power' held in Victoria, BC, in May 1999. His report helped us prepare this chapter. Thanks also to Michael Carley and Michelle Wingelman for their endless time and support as we prepared this chapter.

1 Assistant Deputy Ministers' Sub-Committee for Global Challenges and Opportunities, *Canada 2005: Draft Interim Report on Global Challenges and Opportunities* (25 February 1997), chap. 11, 'Governance.'

2 James Rosenau, *Along the Domestic–Foreign Frontier: Exploring Governance in a Turbulent World* (Cambridge: Cambridge University Press, 1997), 62.

3 Timothy Sinclair, 'Bond-rating Agencies and Coordination in the Global Political Economy,' in Claire Cutler, ed., *Private Authority and International Affairs* (Albany: State University of New York Press, 1999), 153–168.

4 Thomas Weiss and Leon Gordenker, eds., *NGOs, The UN, and Global Governance* (Boulder, Co.: Lynne Rienner Publishers, 1996); and P.J. Simmons, 'Learning to Live with NGOs,' *Foreign Policy* (Fall 1998): 21–33.

5 Robert Wolfe, chapter 8, above; and Virginia Haufler, 'Crossing the Boundary between Public and Private: International Regimes and Non-State Actors,' in Volker Rittberger, ed., *Regime Theory and International Relations* (Ithaca, NY: Cornell University Press, 1993), 94–95.

6 We would like to thank Mark Schacter for this insight. He developed this idea in his report on the workshop 'Trends: Multiple Centres of Power' prepared in May 1999.

7 See ADM Sub-Committee, *Canada 2005*, chap. 11, 'Governance,' 3.

8 See Ramesh Thakur and William Maley, 'The Ottawa Convention on Landmines,' *Global Governance* 5, no. 3 (July–September 1999): 280–5.

9 In his discussion of transformative capacity, Della Sala refers to Linda Weiss, *The Myth of the Powerless State* (Ithaca, NY: Cornell University Press, 1998), chap. 4.

10 Margaret Keck and Kathryn Sikkink, *Activists beyond Borders: Advocacy Networks in International Politics* (Ithaca, NY: Cornell University Press, 1998).

11 Julien Bauer and Philippe Le Prestre make this argument in a more general fashion in chapter 2, above.

12 See in particular Ronald Crelinsten, chapter 3, above.

13 For this argument, see in particular Crelinsten (chapter 3) and Della Sala (chapter 4), above.

14 See Della Sala, chapter 4, above; and Andrew Gamble, *The Free State and Strong Economy* (Basingstoke: Macmillan, 1994).

15 See the National Climate Change Secretariat's website: http://www.nccp.ca/html/index.htm

16 David Held, *Democracy and the Global Order: From the Modern State to Cosmopolitan Governance* (Stanford, Calif.: Stanford University Press, 1995), 16–28.

17 We thank Mark Schacter for providing advice and illumination on the implications for future research.

References

Adler, Emanuel, and Michael Barnett, eds. *Security Communities.* Cambridge: Cambridge University Press, 1998.

Adonis, Andrew, and Andrew Tyrie. *Subsidiarity: No Panacea.* London: European Policy Forum, 1993.

Aggarwal, Vinod K., ed. *Institutional Designs for a Complex World: Bargaining, Linkages, and Nesting.* Ithaca, NY: Cornell University Press, 1998.

Allport, Gordon W., and Leo Postman. *The Psychology of Rumor.* New York: Henry Holt & Co., 1947.

Amato, Giulio, et al. *Regulazione e garanzia del pluralismo: Le autorita' amministrative indipendenti.* Milan: Giuffre, 1997.

Anderson, Kym. 'Environmental and Labor Standards: What Role for the WTO?' In Anne O. Krueger, ed., *The WTO as an International Organization,* 230–56. Chicago: University of Chicago Press, 1998.

Anderson, Malcolm, Monica der Boer, Peter Cullen, William Gilmore, Charles Roads, and Neil Walker. *Policing the European Union.* Oxford: Clarendon Press, 1995.

Annan, Kofi. 'The Quiet Revolution.' *Global Governance* 4, no. 2 (April–June 1998): 123–39.

Appadurai, Arjun. *Modernity at Large: Cultural Dimensions of Globalization.* Minneapolis: University of Minnesota Press, 1996.

Apter, David. *Pour l'état, contre l'état.* Paris: Economica, 1988.

Archibugi, Daniele. 'The Reform of the UN and Cosmopolitan Democracy: A Critical Review.' *Journal of Peace Research* 30 (1995): 301–15.

Archibugi, Daniele, and David Held, eds. *Cosmopolitan Democracy: An Agenda for a New World Order.* Cambridge: Polity Press, 1995.

Archibugi, Danielle, David Held, nd Martin Kohler, eds., *Re-imagining Political Community: Studies in Cosmopolitan Democracy.* Stanford, Calif.: Stanford University Press, 1999.

Ariès, Paul. *Les fils de McDo: la McDonaldisation du monde.* Paris: L'Harmattan, 1997.

Arnaud, André-Jean. 'De la régulation par le droit a l'heure de la globalisation. Quelques observations critiques.' *Droit et société* 11 (1997): 15–23.

Arthurs, H.W. 'Constitutionalizing Neo-Conservatism and Regional Economic Integration.' In Thomas J. Courchene, ed., *Room to Manoeuvre? Globalization and Policy Convergence*, 17–74. Kingston: Published for the School of Policy Studies by McGill-Queen's University Press, 1999.

– 'Globalization of the Mind: Canadian Elites and the Restructuring of Legal Fields.' *Canadian Journal of Law and Society* 12, no. 2 (1997): 219–46.

– 'The Hollowing Out of Corporate Canada.' Unpublished paper, 1998.

– 'Mechanical Arts and Merchandise: Canadian Public Administration in the New Economy.' *McGill Law Journal* 42, no. 1 (Feb. 1997): 29–62.

Ashworth, Lucian M., and David Long, eds. *New Perspectives on International Functionalism*. London: Macmillan, 1999.

Assistant Deputy Ministers' Sub-committee for Global Challenges and Opportunities. *Canada 2005: Draft Interim Report in Global Challenges and Opportunities* (25 Feb. 1977).

Ayling, Julie. 'Serving Many Voices: Progressing Calls for an International Environmental Organization.' *Journal of Environmental Law* 9 (1997): 343–70.

Babe, Robert E. *Telecommunications in Canada: Technology, Industry, and Government*. Toronto: University of Toronto Press, 1990.

Bak, Per. *How Nature Works: The Science of Self-Organized Complexity.* New York: Copernicus, 1996.

Baker, Don. 'World Religion and National States: Competing Claims in East Asia.' In Rudolf Hoeber and James Piscatori, eds., *Transnational Religion and Fading States*, 16–28. Boulder, Col.: Westview Press, 1997.

Baldwin, David, 'Interdependence and Power: A Conceptual Analysis.' *International Organization* 34 (1989): 471–506.

Balling, Morten, et al., eds. *Corporate Governance, Financial Markets and Global Convergence.* Dordecht: Kluwer, 1998.

Banting, Keith G. 'Social Policy.' In Bruce Doern et al., eds., *Border Crossings: The Internationalization of Canadian Public Policy*, 27–54. Toronto: Oxford University Press, 1996.

Banuri, Tariq. 'The Landscape of Diplomatic Conflict.' In Wolfgang Sachs, ed., *Global Ecology: A New Arena of Political Conflict*, 49–67. London: Zed Books, 1993.

Barkey, Karen, and Mark von Hagen, eds. *After Empire: Multi-Ethnic Societies and Nation-Building.* Boulder, Col.: Westview, 1997.

Bateson, Mary C. 'Beyond Sovereignty: An Emerging Global Civilization.' In R.B.J. Walker and S.H. Mendlovitz, eds., *Contending Sovereignties: Redefining Political Community,* 106–29. Boulder, Col.: Lynne Reinner, 1990.

Bayart, Jean-François. *L'illusion identitaire.* Paris: Fayard, 1996.

Beard, Charles. *An Economic Interpretation of the Constitution of the United States.* New York: Macmillan, 1935.

Bergesen, Helge Ole, and Parmann Georg, eds. 'International Environmental Treaty Secretariats: Stage-Hands or Actors?' *Green Globe Yearbook of International Co-operation on Environment and Development 1994,* 17–29. London: Oxford University Press, 1994.

Belley, Jean-Guy. 'Law as *Terra Incognita*: Constructing Legal Pluralism.' *Canadian Journal of Law and Society* 12, no. 2 (fall 1997): 1–15.

Bemporad, Simone, and Oscar Giannino, 'Storia di un'illusione italiana: Come e perche banche e aziende rimangono di stato.' *Liberal* 16 (July 1998): 11–15.

Best, Joel, ed. *Images of Issues: Typifying Contemporary Social Problems.* Second edition. New York: Aldine de Gruyter, 1995.

Bhalla, A.S., ed. *Globalization, Growth, and Marginalization.* New York: St Martin's Press, 1998.

Biersteker, Thomas J. and Cynthia Weber. 'The Social Construction of State Sovereignty.' In Thomas J. Biersteker and Cythnia Weber, eds., *State Sovereignty as Social Construct,* 1–32. Cambridge: Cambridge University Press, 1996.

Birnie, Patricia W., and Alan E. Boyle. *International Law and the Environment.* Oxford: Oxford University Press, 1992.

Blank, Stephen, Stephen Krajewski, and Henry S. Yu. 'US Firms in North America: Redefining Structure and Strategy.' *North American Outlook* 5, no. 2 (Feb. 1995).

Bodiguel, Jean-Luc, and Luc Rouban. *Le fonctionnaire détrôné, l'état au risque de la modernisation.* Paris: Presses de Sciences Po, 1991,

Boodman, Martin. 'The Myth of the Harmonization of Laws.' *American Journal of Comparative Law* 39 (1991): 699–724.

Börzel, Tanja A. 'What's So Special about Policy Networks? – An Exploration of the Concept and Its Usefulness in Studying European Governance.' *European Integration Online Papers* 1, no. 16. See web site at http://eiop.or.at/eiop/texte/1997-016a.htm, accessed 20 Sept. 1999.

Bourgon, Jocelyn. 'Building a Strong Public Policy Capacity.' Notes for an address to the policy conference 'Policy Research: Creating Linkages.' Ottawa, 1 October 1998.

Boyer, Robert, and Daniel Drache. 'Introduction.' In Boyer and Drache, eds., *States Against Markets: The Limits of Globalization*, 1–13. London: Routledge, 1996.

– 'The Federal–Provincial Consultation Process' In Peter M. Leslie and Ronald L. Watts, eds., *Canada: The State of the Federation 1987–88*, 13–29. Kingston: Institute of Intergovernmental Relations, Queen's University, 1988.

Brown, Douglas M. and Murray G. Smith. 'The Evolving Role of the Provinces in Canadian Trade Policy.' In Douglas M. Brown and Murray G. Smith, eds., *Canadian Federalism: Meeting Global Economic Challenges?* 86–105. Kingston: Institute of Intergovernmental Relations, Queen's University, 1991.

Bull, Hedley. *The Anarchical Society: A Study of Order in World Politics*. London: Macmillan Press, 1977.

Burke, Robert E., and Brian F. Walsh. 'NAFTA Binational Panel Review: Should It Be Continued, Eliminated or Substantially Changed?' *Brooklyn Journal of International Law* 20 (1995): 560–73.

Buzan, Barry. 'From International System to International Society: Structural Realism and Regime Theory Meet the English School.' *International Organization* 47, no. 3 (summer 1993): 327–52.

Buzan, Barry, Ole Waever, and Jaap de Wilde. *Security: A New Framework for Analysis*. Boulder, Col.: Lynne Rienner, 1998.

Campbell, Robert M. 'Federalism and Economic Policy.' In François Rocher and Miriam Smith, eds., *New Trends in Canadian Federalism*, 189–215. Peterborough: Broadview Press, 1995.

Careless, James. 'Law Professor Gets Used to Fame.' University of Ottawa *Gazette*, 4 Dec. 1998.

Cassese, Sabimo. 'Deregulation and Privatization in Italy.' In M. Moran and T. Prosser, eds., *Privatization and Regulatory Change in Europe*, 153–75. Buckingham: Open University Press, 1994.

Cassese, Sabimo, and Vincent Wright. *La recomposition de l'etat en Europe*. Paris: La Découverte, 1996.

Castells, Manual. *The Power of Identity*. Oxford: Blackwell Publishers, 1997.

Chambliss, William J. 'State-Organized Crime: The American Society of Criminology, 1988 Presidential Address.' *Criminology* 27, no. 2 (1989): 183–208.

Chayes, Abram, and Antonia Handler Chayes. *The New Sovereignty: Compliance with International Regulatory Norms*. Cambridge, Mass.: Harvard University Press, 1995.

Checkel, Jeffrey. 'International Norms and Domestic Politics.' *International Relations* 3 (1997): 473–96.

Chernoff, John Miller. *African Rhythm and Sensibility: Aesthetics and Social Action in African Musical Idioms*. Chicago: University of Chicago Press, 1979.

Chesnais, François. *La mondialisation du capital*. Paris: Syros, 1997.

Chossudovsky, Michel. 'La souveraineté des créanciers.' In Sylvie Paquerot, ed., *L'état aux orties? mondialisation de l'économie et rôle de l'état*, 58–74. Montreal: Écosociété, 1996.

Choucri, Nazli, ed. *Global Accord: Environmental Challenges and International Responses*. Cambridge, Mass.: MIT Press, 1993.

Cilliers, Paul. *Complexity and Postmodernism: Understanding Complex Systems*. London: Routledge, 1998.

Clark, Ian. *Globalization and Fragmentation*. Oxford: Oxford University Press, 1997.

Clarkson, Stephen. 'Disjunctions: Free Trade and the Paradox of Canadian Development.' In Daniel Drache and Meric S. Gertler, eds., *The New Era of Global Competition: State Policy and Market Power*, 103–26. Montreal: McGill-Queen's University Press, 1991.

– 'The Joy of Flux: What the European Monetary Union Can Learn from North America's Experience with National Currency Autonomy.' In Colin Crouch, ed., *After the Euro: Shaping Institutions for Governance in the Wake of European Monetary Union*, 163–89. Oxford: Oxford University Press, 1999.

Cohen, Andrew, and Jack Granatstein, eds. *Trudeau's Shadow*. Toronto: Random House, 1998.

Cohen, Élie. *La tentation hexagonale: La souveraineté a l'heure de la mondialisation*. Paris: Fayard, 1996.

Cohen, Jean L., and Andrew Arato. *Civil Society and Political Theory*. Cambridge, Mass.: MIT Press, 1994.

Coleman, William, and Geoffrey Underhill, eds. *Regionalism and Global Economic Integration: Europe, Asia, and the Americas*. New York: Routledge, 1998.

Commission for Environmental Cooperation. *NAFTA's Institutions: The Environmental Potential and Performance of the NAFTA Free Trade Commission and Related Bodies*. Montreal: Commission for Environment Cooperation, 1997.

Commission on Global Governance. *Our Global Neighbourhood*. New York: Oxford University Press, 1995.

Comor, Edward. 'The Department of Communications under the Free Trade Regime.' *Canadian Journal of Communication* 16, no. 2 (1991): 249.

Connell, Ian, and Dauriusz Galasinski. 'Academic Mission Statements: An Exercise in Negotiation.' *Discourse and Society* 9, no. 4 (Oct. 1998): 41–65.

Courchene, Thomas J. 'Globalization: The Regional/International Interface.' *Canadian Journal of Regional Science* 18, no. 1 (spring 1995): 1–20.

Coussy, Jean. 'Les ruses de l'état minimum.' In Jean-François Bayart, ed., *La réinvention du capitalisme*, 22–35. Paris: Karthala, 1994.

Cox, Robert, and Harold K. Jacobson, eds. *The Anatomy of Influence: Decision-*

making in International Organizations. New Haven, Conn.: Yale University Press, 1973.

Cox, Robert, with Timothy Sinclair. *Approaches to World Order*. Cambridge: Cambridge University Press, 1996.

Crane, David. 'Nortel Sets Example by Tackling Skills Gap.' *Toronto Star*, 3 March 1999, E2.

Crelinsten, Ronald. 'The Discourse and Practice of Counter-terrorism in Liberal Democracies.' *Australian Journal of Politics & History* 44, no. 3 (Sept. 1998): 389–413.

– 'The Impact of Television on Terrorism and Crisis Situations: Implications for Public Policy.' *Journal of Contingencies and Crisis Management* 2, no. 2 (1994): 61–72.

– 'Television and Terrorism: Implications for Crisis Management and Policy-Making.' *Terrorism and Political Violence* 9, no. 4 (1997): 8–32.

– 'Terrorism and Counter-terrorism in a Multi-centric World: Challenges and Opportunities.' *Terrorism and Political Violence* 11, no. 4 (1999): 170–96. Also appears in Max Taylor and John Hogan, eds., *The Future of Terrorism* (London: Frank Cass, 2000), 170–96.

– 'Terrorism, Counter-Terrorism and Democracy: The Assessment of National Security Threats.' *Terrorism and Political Violence* 1, no. 2 (1989): 242–69.

– 'Victims' Perspectives.' In David Paletz and Alex Schmid, eds., *Terrorism and the Media: How Researchers, Terrorists, Government, Press, Public, Victims View and Use the Media*, 53–75. Newbury Park, Calif.: Sage, 1992.

Cutler, Claire. 'Canada and the Private International Trade Law Regime.' In Claire Cutler and Mark Zacher, eds., *Canadian Foreign Policy and International Economic Regimes*, 221–38. Vancouver: University of British Columbia Press, 1992.

– 'Locating "Authority" in the Global Political Economy.' *International Studies Quarterly* 43, no. 1 (March 1999): 59–81.

– 'Public Meets Private: The International Unification and Harmonisation of Private International Trade Law.' *Global Society* 13, no. 1 (1999): 25–48.

Cutler, Claire, Virginia Haufler, and Tony Porter, eds., *Private Authority and International Affairs*. Albany: State University of New York Press, 1999.

Cutler, Robert. 'Co-operative Energy Security in the Caspian Region: A New Paradigm for Sustainable Development?' *Global Governance* 5, no. 2 (April–June 1999): 251–71.

– 'Gorbachev as CEO Road Kill.' In Michael Lissack and Hugh Gunz, eds., *Managing Complexity in Organizations: A View in Many Directions*. New York: Quorum, forthcoming.

Czempiel, Ernst-Otto. 'Governance and Democratization.' In James N.

Rosenau and Ernst-Otto Czempiel, eds., *Governance without Government: Order and Change in World Politics*, 250–71. Cambridge: Cambridge University Press, 1992.

Dahl, Robert A. *Who Governs? Democracy and Power in an American City.* New Haven, Conn.: Yale University Press, 1961.

Davey, William. *Pine and Swine.* Ottawa: Centre for Trade Policy and Law, 1996.

D'Crus, Joseph, and A. Rugman. 'Business Network Theory and the Canadian Telecommunications Industry.' In W.T. Standury, ed., *Perspectives on the New Economics and Regulation of Telecommunications*, 86–105. Ottawa: Renouf Publishing Company.

De Senarclens, Pierre. *Mondialisation, souveraineté et théories des relations internationales.* Paris: Armand Colin, 1998.

Deacon, Bob. *Global Social Policy: International Organizations and the Future of Welfare.* London: Sage, 1997.

Della Cara, Ralph, 'Religious Resource Networks: Roman Catholic Philanthropy in Central and East Europe.' In Rudolf Hoeber and James Piscatori, ed., *Transnational Religion and Fading States*, 108–25. Boulder, Col.: Westview Press, 1997.

Della Sala, Vincent. 'Hollowing Out and Hardening the State: European Integration and the Italian Economy.' In Martin Bull and Martin Rhodes, eds., *Crisis and Transition in Italian Politics*, 152–75. London: Frank Cass, 1997.

Dente, Bruno. 'Politica, istituzioni e deficit pubblico.' *Stato e Mercato*, no. 33 (Dec. 1991): 339–70.

Department of External Affairs and International Trade. *NAFTA: What's It All About?.* Ottawa: Queen's Printer, 1993.

Deutsch, Karl. *The Nerves of Government: Models of Political Communication and Control.* New York: Free Press, 1963.

– *Political Community and the North Atlantic Area.* Princeton, NJ: Princeton University Press, 1957.

Devost, Matthew, G. Brian, K. Houghton, and Neal Allan Pollard. 'Information Terrorism: Political Violence in the Information Age.' *Terrorism and Political Violence* 9, no. 1 (1997): 72–83.

Dieckhoff, A. *L'invention d'une nation: Israël et la modernité politique.* Paris: Gallimard, 1993.

Doern, G. Bruce, and Richard W. Phidd. *Canadian Public Policy: Ideas, Structure, Process.* Second edition. Scarborough: Nelson Canada, 1992.

Doern, G. Bruce, Leslie Pal, and Bran Tomlin, eds., *Border Crossings: The Internationalization of Canadian Public Policy.* Toronto: Oxford University Press, 1996.

Dombrowski, Peter. 'Haute Finance and High Theory: Recent Scholarship on Global Financial Relations.' *Mershon International Studies Review* 42 (1998): 1–28.

Donnelly, Jack. 'Human Rights: A New Standard of Civilization?' *International Affairs* 74 (1998): 1–23.

– *International Human Rights.* Boulder, Col.: Westview, 1993.

Doran, Charles. 'Trade Dispute Resolution "On Trial": Softwood Lumber.' *International Journal* 51, no. 4 (autumn 1996).

Drache, Daniel, ed. *Staples, Markets and Cultural Change: Selected Essays by Harold A. Innis.* Montreal: McGill-Queen's University Press, 1995.

Drucker, Peter. 'The Global Economy and the Nation-State.' *Foreign Affairs* 76, no. 5 (Sept.–Oct. 1997): 159–71.

Dryzek, John S. 'Transnational Democracy.' *Journal of Political Philosophy* 7, no. 1 (March 1999): 30–51.

Dunsire, Andrew. 'Modes of Governance.' In Jan Kooiman, ed., *Modern Governance,* 181–202. London: Sage, 1993.

Dupuy, P.M. *Droit international public.* Paris: Dalloz, 1992.

Durkheim, Emile. *The Rules of Sociological Method.* First pub. 1895. New York: Free Press, 1964.

Dyson, Kenneth, and Kevin Featherstone. 'Italy and EMU as a "Vincolo Esterno": Empowering the Technocrats, Transforming the State.' *South European Politics and Society* 1, no. 2 (autumn 1996): 279–99.

Easton, David. *A Framework for Political Analysis.* Englewood Cliffs, NJ: Prentice-Hall, 1965.

Ekiert, Grzegorz. *The State against Society: Political Crises and Their Aftermath in East Central Europe.* Princeton, NJ: Princeton University Press, 1996.

Ellickson, Robert. *Order without Law: How Neighbours Settle Disputes.* Cambridge, Mass.: Harvard University Press, 1991.

Entelis, John P., ed. *Islam, Democracy, and the State in North Africa.* Bloomington: Indiana University Press, 1997.

Erickson, Patricia G., and Jennifer Butters. 'The Emerging Harm Reduction Movement: The De-escalation of the War on Drugs?' In Eric L. Jensen and Jung Gerber, eds., *New War on Drugs: Symbolic Politics and Criminal Justice Policy,* 219–312. Cincinnati: Anderson Publishing, 1998.

Ericson, Richard V., and Kevin D. Haggerty. *Policing the Risk Society.* Toronto: University of Toronto Press, 1997.

Esty, Daniel. *Greening the GATT: Trade, Environment, and the Future.* Washington, DC: Institute for Environmental Economics, 1994.

Etzioni, Amitai. 'The Epigenesis of Political Communities at the International Level.' *American Journal of Sociology* 68 (1963): 407–21. Reprinted in James N.

Roseman, ed., *International Politics and Foreign Policy*, revised edition (New York: Free Press, 1964), 346–58.

Evans, Peter. 'The Eclipse of the State? Reflections on Stateness in an Era of Globalization.' *World Politics* 50, no. 1 (Oct. 1997): 62–87.

Evans, Peter B., Dietrich Reuschemeyer, and Reda Skocpol, eds., *Bringing the State Back In*. New York: Cambridge University Press, 1985.

Fabbrini, Sergio. *Quale democrazia?* Rome: Laterza, 1994.

Falk, Richard. *Communication publique, congrès annuel de l'International Studies Association*. Washington, DC, Feb. 1999.

– *This Endangered Planet*. New York: Random House, 1971.

Fawn, Rick, and Jeremy Larkins, eds. *International Society after the Cold War*. New York: St Martin's Press, 1996.

Feigenbaum, Harvey, and Jeffrey R. Henig. 'Privatization and Political Theory.' *Journal of International Affairs* 50, no. 2 (1997): 338–55.

Ferguson, Yale, and Richard Mansbach. *Polities: Authority, Identities, and Change*. Columbia: University of South Carolina Press, 1996.

Finger, Matthias, and Ludivine Tamiotti. 'Comprehensive Governance in Biodiversity Protection.' Paper presented at the Annual Meeting of the International Studies Association, Washington, DC, 1999.

Finkelkraut, Alain. *La défaite de la pensée*. Paris: Gallimard, 1987.

Finlayson, Jock, and Mark Zacher. 'The GATT and the Regulation of Trade Barriers: Regime Dynamics and Functions.' In Stephen D. Krasner, ed., *International Regimes*, 381–421. Ithaca, NY: Cornell University Press, 1983.

Finnemore, Martha. *National Interests in International Society*. Ithaca, NY: Cornell University Press, 1996.

Finnemore, Martha, and Kathryn Sikkink. 'International Norm Dynamics and Political Change.' *International Organization* 52, no. 4 (autumn 1998): 887–917.

Fischer, Benedikt. 'Prohibition as the Art of Political Diplomacy: The Benign Guises of the "War on Drugs" in Canada.' In Eric L. Jensen and Jurg Gerber, eds., *The New War on Drugs: Symbolic Politics and Criminal Justice Policy*, 157–75. Cincinnati: Anderson Publishing, 1998.

Franklin, Jane, ed., *The Politics of Risk Society*. Cambridge: Polity Press, 1998.

Freeman, John, ed. *Democracy and Markets: The Politics of Mixed Economies*. Ithaca, NY: Cornell University Press, 1989.

Fukuyama, Francis. 'The End of History?' *The National Interest*, 16 (summer 1989): 3–18.

Fuller, Lon. *The Law in Quest of Itself*. Chicago: Foundation Press Inc., 1940.

– *The Morality of Law*. Rev. ed. New Haven, Conn.: Yale University Press, 1969.

– 'Two Principles of Human Association.' In Kenneth Winston, ed., *The Principles of Social Order*, 18–44. Durham, NC: Duke University Press, 1981.

Furubotn, Eirik Grundtvig, and Rudolf Richter. *Institutions and Economic Theory: The Contribution of the New Institutional Economics*. Ann Arbour, Mich.: University of Michigan Press, 1997.

Gale, Fred. 'Cave "Cave! hic dragones": A Neo-Gramscian Deconstruction and Reconstruction of International Regime Theory.' *Review of International Political Economy* 5. no. 2 (summer 1998): 252–84.

– *The Tropical Timber Trade Regime*. New York: St Martin's Press, 1998.

Galtung, Johan. *Human Rights in Another Key*. Cambridge: Polity Press, 1994.

Gamble, Andrew. *The Free State and the Strong Economy*. Basingstoke, England: Macmillan, 1994.

Garland, David. 'The Limits of the Sovereign State: Strategies of Crime Control in Contemporary Society.' *British Journal of Criminology* 36, no. 4 (autumn 1996): 445–7.

Gehring, Thomas. 'International Environmental Regimes: Dynamic Sectoral Legal Systems.' *Yearbook of International Environmental Law* 1 (1990): 35–56.

Geyer, Felix. 'The Challenge of Sociocybernetics.' *Kybernetes* 24, no. 4 (1995): 5–32.

Ghébali, Victor-Yves. *The Conference of the Inter-Parliamentary Union on European Co-operation and Security, 1973–1991: The Contribution of Parliamentary Diplomacy to East-West Détente*. Aldershot, England: Dartmough, 1993.

Gill, Stephen. 'The Emerging World Order and European Change: The Political Economy of European Union.' In Ralph Miliband and Leo Panitch, eds., *Socialist Register*. London, (1992).

– 'Globalisation, Market Civilisation, and Disciplinary Neoliberalism.' *Millennium: Journal of International Studies* (1994): 399–423.

Gill, Stephen, ed. *Gramsci, Historical Materialism and International Relations*. Cambridge: Cambridge University Press, 1993.

Gilpin, Robert. *War and Change in World Politics*. Cambridge: Cambridge University Press, 1981.

Goldmann, Kjell, and Gunnar Sjostedt, eds. *Power, Capabilities, Interdependence: Problems in the Study of International Influence*. New York: Sage, 1979.

Government of Canada. *The Canada–US Free Trade Agreement Synopsis*. Ottawa, 1987.

– *Northern Frontier Northern Homeland: The Report of the Mackenzie Valley Pipeline Inquiry*, Vol. 1. Ottawa: Minister of Supply and Services, 1977.

Government of Canada, Assistant Deputy Ministers' Sub-Committee on Global Challenges and Opportunities, Policy Research Initiative. *Canada 2005, Draft Interim Report: Global Challenges and Opportunities*. Ottawa, 25 Feb. 1998.

Government of Canada, Policy Research Initiative. 'Research Report 5: National Security Implications of Low-Probability, High-Impact Events.' Sept. 1998.

Grenier, Line. 'Cultural Exemptionalism Revisited: Quebec Music Industries in the Face of Free Trade.' *Mass Media and Free Trade*. Austin: University of Texas Press, 1996.

Haas, Ernst. *When Knowledge Is Power: Three Models of Change in International Organizations*. Berkeley: University of California Press, 1990.

– 'Why Collaborate? Issue-Linkage and International Regimes.' *World Politics* 32, no. 3 (April 1980): 357–405.

Haas, Peter. 'Do Regimes Matter? Epistemic Communities and Mediterranean Pollution Control.' *International Organization* 43 (1989): 377–403.

Haas, Peter, Robert Keohane, and Marc Levy, eds. *Institutions for the Earth: Sources of Effective International Environmental Action*. Boston: MIT Press, 1993.

Habermas, Jürgen. 'On the Concept of Public Opinion.' In *The Structural Transformation of the Public Sphere: An Inquiry into a Category of Bourgeois Society*, trans. Thomas Burger, with Frederick Lawrence, 236–50. Cambridge, Mass.: MIT Press, 1989.

Hainsworth, Susan. 'Sovereignty, Economic Integration, and the World Trade Organization.' *Osgoode Hall Law Journal* 33, no. 3 (fall 1995): 583–622.

Hampson, Fen Osler, and Dean F. Oliver. 'Pulpit Diplomacy: A Critical Assessment of the Axworthy Doctrine.' *International Journal* 43, no. 3 (summer 1998): 379–406.

Hardt, Hanno. *Social Theories of the Press: Early German and American Perspectives*. Beverly Hills, Calf.: Sage, 1979.

Hart, Michael. *Fifty Years of Canadian Tradecraft: Canada at the GATT, 1947–1997*. Ottawa: Centre for Trade Policy and Law, 1998.

Harvey, George. 'Benefits of Competition.' In *Canadian Telecommunications: Regulation and Competition*, 71–98. Mississauga, Ont.: Insight, 1989.

Hasenclever, Andreas, Peter Mayer, and Volken Rittburger. *Theories of International Regimes*. Cambridge: Cambridge University Press, 1997.

Haufler, Virginia. 'Crossing the Boundary between Public and Private: International Regimes and Non-state Actors.' In Volken Rittberger, ed., *Regime Theory and International Relations*, 94–111. Oxford: Clarendon Press, 1993.

– *Dangerous Commerce: Insurance and the Management of International Risk*. Ithaca, NY: Cornell University Press, 1997.

Heckman, Gerald. 'Ownership and Control in the Canadian Telecommunications Industry: The Case Of Strategic Alliances.' *Canadian Business Law Journal* 29 (1997): 124–56.

Held, David. 'Democracy and Globalization.' Global Governance 3, no. 3 (Sept.–Dec. 1997): 251–67.

– *Democracy and the Global Order: From the Modern State to Cosmopolitan Governance*. Stanford, Calif.: Stanford University Press, 1995.

– 'Democracy: From City-States to a Cosmopolitan Order?' *Political Studies* 40: (1992): 138–59.

Held, David. 'Democracy, the Nation-State and the Global System.' In Held, ed., *Political Theory Today,* 196–235. Stanford, Calif.: Stanford University Press, 1991.

Held, David, et al. *Global Transformations: Politics, Economics, and Culture.* Stanford, Calif.: Stanford University Press, 1999.

Helleiner, Eric. 'Electronic Money: A Challenge to the Sovereign State?' *Journal of International Affairs* 51, no. 2 (spring 1998): 387–411.

– *States and the Re-emergence of Global Finance: From Bretton Woods to the 1990s.* Ithaca, NY: Cornell University Press, 1994.

Hewson, Martin, and Timothy Sinclair. 'The Emergence of Global Governance Theory.' In Martin Hewson and Timothy Sinclair, eds., *Approaches to Global Governance Theory,* 3–22. Albany: State University of New York Press, 1999.

Hirst, Paul. *Associative Democracy.* Amherst: University of Massachusetts Press, 1994.

– *From Statism to Pluralism.* London: UCL Press, 1997.

– 'The Global Economy: Myths and Realities.' *International Affairs* 73, no. 3 (1997): 409–25.

– 'Power.' In Tim Dunn et al., *The Eighty Years' Crisis: International Relations 1919–1999,* 133–49. Cambridge: Cambridge University Press, 1998.

Hirst, Paul, and Grahame Thompson. *Globalization in Question: The International Economy and The Possibilities of Governance.* Cambridge: Polity Press, 1996.

Hoebing, Joyce, et al., eds. *NAFTA and Sovereignty: Trade-offs for Canada, Mexico, and the United States.* Washington, DC: Center for Strategic and International Studies, 1997.

Holland, John. *Hidden Order: How Adaptation Builds Complexity.* New York: Pegasus Books, 1996.

Holsti, K.J. 'America Meets the English School: State Interests in International Society.' *Mershon International Studies Review* 41, no. 2 (1997): 275–80.

Hopf, Ted. 'The Promise of Constructivism in International Relations Theory.' *International Security* 23, no. 1 (summer 1998): 171–200.

Horlick, Gary, and Amanda DeBusk. 'Dispute Resolution under NAFTA: Building on the US–Canada FTA, GATT and ICSID.' *Journal of International Arbitration* 10 (March 1993).' 62–95.

Howse, Robert. 'Settling Trade Remedy Disputes: When the WTO Forum Is Better than the NAFTA.' *CD Howe Institute Commentary* 111 (June 1998).

Humphreys, David. 'Regime Theory and Non-governmental Organizations: The Case of Forest Conservation.' *Journal of Commonwealth and Comparative Politics* 24 (1996): 90–115.

Huntington, David. 'Settling Disputes under the North American Free Trade Agreement.' *Harvard International Law Journal* 34 (spring 1993): 411–52.

Huntington, Samuel. 'The Clash of Civilizations?' *Foreign Affairs* 72, no. 3 (summer 1993): 22–49.

– 'Transnational Organization in World Politics.' *World Politics* 25, no. 3 (April 1973): 333–68.

Hurd, Ian. 'Legitimacy and Authority in International Politics.' *International Organization* 53, no. 2 (spring 1999): 379–408.

Ikenberry, John. 'The Irony of State Strength: Comparative Responses to the Oil Shocks in the 1970s.' *International Organization* 40, no. 1 (winter 1986): 31–65.

Imig, Doug, and Sidney Tarrow. 'From Strike to Eurostrike: The Europeanization of Social Movements and the Development of a Euro-Polity.' Working Paper No. 97. Cambridge, Mass.: Harvard University Press, 1997.

Jacobson, Harold. *Networks of Interdependence: International Organizations and the Global Political System.* Second edition. New York: Alfred A. Knopf, 1984.

Janisch, Hudson. 'International Influence on Communications Policy in Canada.' In Dale Orr and Thomas A. Wilson, eds., *Electronic Village: Policy Issues of the Information Economy,* 130–52. Toronto: C.D. Howe Institute, 1999.

Jervis, Robert. 'Security Regimes.' In Stephen D. Krasner, ed., *International Regimes,* Ithaca, NY: Cornell University Press, 1983.

Jessop, Robert. 'The Rise of Governance and the Risks of Failure: The Case of Economic Development.' *International Social Science Journal* 155 (March 1998): 18–39.

– 'Towards a Schumpeterian Workfare State?' *Studies in Political Economy* 40 (spring 1993): 7–39.

Jones, Steve. 'Mass Communication, Intellectual Property Rights, International Trade and the Popular Music Industry.' In Emile McAnany and Kenton Wilkinson, eds., *Mass Media and Free Trade: NAFTA and the Cultural Industries,* Austin: University of Texas Press, 1996.

Jurgensmeyer, Marx. *The New Cold War? Religious Nationalism Confronts the Secular State.* Berkeley: University of California Press, 1993.

Kahler, Miles. 'Trade and Domestic Differences.' In Suzanne Berger and Ronald Dore, eds., *National Diversity and Global Capitalism,* 298–332. Ithaca, NY: Cornell University Press, 1996.

Katzenstein, Peter, ed. *Between Power and Plenty: Foreign Economic Policies of Advanced Industrial States.* Madison: University of Wisconsin Press, 1978.

Katzenstein, Peter, Robert O. Keohane, and Stephen D. Krasner, 'International Organization and the Study of World Politics.' *International Organization* 52, no. 4 (autumn 1998): 645–85.

Keck, Margaret E., and Sikkink, Kathryn. *Activists beyond Borders: Advocacy Networks in International Politics.* Ithaca, NY: Cornell University Press, 1998.

Keeley, James. 'The IAEA and the Iraqi Challenge: Roots and Responses.' *International Journal* 49, no. 1 (winter 1993–4): 126–55.

Keohane, Robert. *After Hegemony: Cooperation and Discord in the World Political Economy.* Princeton, NJ: Princeton University Press, 1984.

– 'Reciprocity in International Relations.' In Keohane, ed., *International Institutions and State Power: Essays in International Relations Theory,* 132–57. Boulder, Col.: Westview Press, 1989.

Keohane, Robert, and Joseph Nye. *Power and Interdependence.* Second edition. Glenview, Ill.: Scott, Foresman and Company, 1989.

– 'Power and Interdependence in the Information Age.' *Foreign Affairs* 77, no. 5 (Sept.–Oct. 1998): 81–94.

Kindleberger, Charles. *The World in Depression, 1929–1939.* Revised and enlarged edition. Berkeley: University of California Press, 1986.

Kingdon, John. 'How Do Issues Get on Public Policy Agendas?' In W.J. Wilson, ed., *Sociology and the Public Agenda,* 40–50. Newbury Park, Calif.: Sage, 1993.

Kiss, Alexandre. 'Les traités-cadres: Une technique juridique caractéristique du droit international de l'environnement.' *Annuaire français de droit international* 39 (1993): 102–35.

Kleinhans, Martha-Marie, and Roderick Macdonald. 'What Is a *Critical* Legal Pluralism?' *Canadian Journal of Law and Society* 12, no. 2 (fall 1997): 25–46.

Korten, David. *When Corporations Rule the World.* San Francisco: Kumarian Press, 1995.

Krasner, Stephen. *Defending the National Interest: Raw Materials Investments and US Foreign Policy.* Princeton, NJ: Princeton University Press, 1978.

– 'Regimes and the Limits of Realism: Regimes as Autonomous Variables.' In Krasner, ed., *International Regimes,* 355–68.

– 'Structural Causes and Regime Consequences: Regimes as Intervening Variables.' In Krasner, ed. *International Regimes,* 1–21.

Krasner, Stephen, ed. *International Regimes.* Ithaca, NY: Cornell University Press, 1983.

Kratochwil, Friedrich. *Rules, Norms and Decisions: On the Conditions of Practical and Legal Reasoning in International Relations and Domestic Affairs.* Cambridge: Cambridge University Press, 1989.

Krieger, Joel. *Reagan, Thatcher and the Politics of Economic Adjustment.* New York: Oxford University Press, 1986.

Laïdi, Zaki. *Géopolitique du sens.* Paris: Desclée de Brouwer, 1998.

Lamarche, Lucie. 'L'etat désétatisé et ses fonctions sociales: Éléments de réflexion.' In Sylvie Paquerot, ed., *L'état aux orties? Mondialisation de l'économie et rôle de l'état*, Montreal: Écosociété, 1996.

Lang,Winfried. 'Diplomacy and Environmental Law Making: Some Observations.' *Yearbook of International Environmental Law* 3 (1992): 108–62.

Le Prestre, Philippe. *Ecopolitique internationale.* Montréal: Guérin, 1997.

Le Prestre, Philipe, John R. Reid, and T. Thomas Morehouse, eds. *Protecting the Ozone Layer: Lessons, Models, and Prospects*. Boston: Kluwer, 1998.

Legault, Albert, Isabelle Desmarais, Julie Fournier, and Charles Thumerelle. 'The United Nations at Fifty: Regime Theory and Collective Security.' *International Journal* 50, no. 1 (winter 1994–5): 71–102.

Lipschutz, Ronnie. *Global Civil Society and Global Environmental Governance.* Albany: State University of New York Press, 1996.

– 'Reconstructing World Politics: The Emergence of Global Civil Society.' *Millennium* 21 (winter 1992): 389–420.

Lipson, Charles. 'Why Are Some International Agreements Informal?' *International Organization* 45, no. 4 (autumn 1991): 495–538.

Litfin, Karen. 'Sovereignty in World Ecopolitics.' *Mershon International Studies Review.* 41, no. 2 (1997): 167–204.

Little, Richard. 'The Growing Relevance of Pluralism?' In Steve Smith et al., eds., *International Theory: Positivism and Beyond*, 66–86. Cambridge: Cambridge University Press, 1996.

Luhmann, Niklas. 'Globalization or World Society: How to Conceive of Modern Society?' *International Review of Sociology* 7, no. 1 (March 1997): 67–80.

– *Social Systems (Writing Science)*. Trans. John Bednarz and Dirk Baecker. Stanford, Calif.: Stanford University Press, 1995.

Macdonald, Roderick. 'Critical Legal Pluralism as a Construction of Normativity and the Emergence of Law.' In A. Lajoie, ed., *Théories et emergence du droit*, 65–102. Montreal: Thémis, 1997.

McNeill, William H. 'Territorial States Buried Too Soon.' *Mershon International Studies Review* 41, no. 2 (Nov. 1997): 269–74.

McQuaig, Linda. *Shooting the Hippo: Death by Deficit and Other Canadian Myths.* Toronto: Viking, 1995.

– *Legislation and Governance.* Ottawa: Law Commission of Canada, 1998.

– 'Metaphors of Multiplicity: Civil Society, Regimes, and Legal Pluralism.' *Arizona Journal of International and Comparative Law.* 15, no. 1 (1998): 69–89.

Macey, David. *The Lives of Michel Foucault: A Biography.* New York: Vintage Books, 1995.

Majendie, Paul. 'Divided Anglican Leaders Keep Tough Line on Gays.' *Globe and Mail*, 6 Aug. 1998, A1A.

Mann, Michael. 'Has Globalization Ended the Rise and Rise of the Nation-

State' *Review of International Political Economy* 4, no. 3 (autumn 1997): 472–96.

Marceau, Gabrielle, and Peter N. Pederson. 'Is the WTO Open and Transparent? A Discussion of the Relationship of the WTO with Nongovernmental Organizations and Civil Society Claims for More Transparency and Public Participation.' *Journal of World Trade* 33, no. 1 (1999): 5–49.

March, James G., and Olsen, Johan P. 'The Institutional Dynamics of International Political Orders.' *International Organization* 52, no. 4 (autumn 1998): 943–69.

Marcuse, Herbert. *Reason and Revolution: Hegel and the Rise of Social Theory.* Tenth edition. Buffalo, NY: Prometheus Books, 1999.

Marks, Gary, ed. *Governance in the European Union.* London: Sage Publications, 1996.

Marks, Gary, François Neilsen,Leonard Ray, and Jane Salk. 'Competencies, Cracks and Conflicts: Regional Mobilization in the European Union.' In Gary Marks et al., eds., *Governance in the European Union*, 40–59. London: Sage Publications, 1996.

Marx, Gary T. *Undercover: Police Surveillance in America.* Berkeley: University of California Press, 1988.

Mathews, Jessica Tuchman. 'Power Shift.' *Foreign Affairs* 76, no. 1 (Jan.–Feb. 1997): 50–66.

Mathias, Paul. *La cité internet*. Paris: Presses de Sciences, 1997.

Mayntz, Renat. 'Governing Failures and the Problem of Governability: Some Comments on a Theoretical Framework.' In Jan Kooiman, ed., *Modern Governance*, 1–21. London: Sage Publications, 1993.

Miliband, Ralph. *The State in Capitalist Society.* London: Weidenfeld, 1969.

Miller, A.J. 'The Functional Principle in Canada's External Relations.' *International Journal*, 35, no. 2 (spring 1980): 309–28.

Milner, Helen. 'The Assumption of Anarchy in International Relations Theory: A Critique.' In David Baldwin, ed., *Neorealism and Neoliberalism: The Contemporary Debate*, 143–69. New York: Columbia University Press, 1993.

Mitrany, David. *A Working Peace System: An Argument for the Functional Development of International Organization.* London: Royal Institute of International Affairs, 1943.

Mittlestaed, Martin. 'Clean Air Sooner, NY Asks Ontario.' *Globe and Mail*, 12 May 1999, A6.

Monshipouri, Mahmood. 'State Prerogatives, Civil Society, and Liberalization.' *Ethics and International Affairs* 11 (1997): 233–325.

Morales-Gomez, Daniel, ed. *Transnational Social Policies.* Ottawa: International Development Research Centre, 1999.

Morgan, Philip, ed. *Privatization and the Welfare State: Implications for Consumers and the Workforce.* Aldershot England: Dartmouth, 1995.

Murphy, Craig. *International Organization and Industrial Change: Global Governance since 1850.* Cambridge: Polity Press, 1994.

Nadelmann, Ethan. *Cops across Borders: The Internationalization of U.S. Criminal Law Enforcement.* University Park: Pennsylvania State University Press, 1993.

Nye, Joseph, Jr. 'Soft Power.' *Foreign Policy.* (fall, 1990): 153–71.

Nye, Joseph, Jr, and William Owens. 'America's Information Edge.' *Foreign Affairs* 75, no. 2 (March–April 1996): 20–36.

O'Brien, Richard. *Global Financial Integration: The End of Geography.* London: Royal Institute of International Affairs, 1992.

Obser, Andreas. 'Institutional Choice in International Secretariats: Nested Governance Arrangements in the Administration of Global Change.' Paper presented at the International Studies Association Annual Meeting, Washington, DC, 1999.

Offe, Claus. *Modernity and the State: East, West.* Cambridge, Mass.: MIT Press, 1996.

Oh, Jong-Geun. 'Global Strategic Alliances.' *Telecommunications Policy* 20 (1996): 715.

Ohmae, Kenichi. *The End of the Nation State: The Rise of Regional Economies.* New York: Free Press, 1995.

Onuf, Nicholas. 'A Constructivist Manifesto.' In Kurt Burch and Robert Denemark, ed., *Constituting International Political Economy,* 7–17. Boulder, Col.: Lynne Rienner Publishers, 1997.

– *World of Our Making: Rules and Rule in Social Theory and International Relations.* Columbia: University of South Carolina Press, 1989.

Ostry, Sylvia. *The Postwar International Trading System: Who's on First?* Chicago: University of Chicago Press, 1997.

– *Reinforcing the WTO.* Washington, DC: Group of Thirty, 1998.

Padbury, Peter. 'The Future of the United Nations System. Assumptions, Policy Issues, and Knowledge Gaps.' *Global Challenges and Opportunity Network, Research Report* 2. Ottawa: Policy Research Secretariat, 1998.

Pal, Leslie. *Beyond Policy Analysis: Public Issue Management in Turbulent Times.* Scarborough, Ont.: ITP Nelson, 1997.

Peterson, M.J. 'Organising for Effective Environmental Co-operation.' *Global Governance* 4 (1998): 415–38.

Petrella, Ricardo. *Écueils de la mondialisation: Urgence d'un nouveau contrat social.* Montreal: Fides, 1997.

Polanyi, Karl. *The Great Transformation: The Political and Economic Origins of Our Time.* Boston: Beacon Press, 1944.

Polka, Brayton. 'The Supremacy of God and the Rule of Law in the Canadian Charter of Rights and Freedoms: A Theologico–Political Analysis.' *McGill Law Journal* 32 (1987): 854–63.

Polsby, Nelson. *Community Power and Political Theory.* New Haven, Conn.: Yale University Press, 1963.

Porter, Tony. *States, Markets and Regimes in Global Finance.* New York: St Martin's Press, 1993.

Raustiala, Kal. 'States, NGOs, and International Environmental Institutions.' *International Studies Quarterly* 41, no. 4 (Dec. 1997): 719–41.

Ravetz, Jerome. *Scientific Knowledge and Its Social Problems.* London: Oxford University Press, 1971.

Regini, Marino, and Ida Regalia. 'Italia anni '90: Rinasce la concertazione.' *IRES Lombardia, Collana Discussioni* (Jan. 1996): 1–19.

Reinicke, Wolfgang. *Global Public Policy: Governing without Government.* Washington, DC: Brookings Institution, 1998.

Reviglio, Franco. *Come siamo entrati in Europa.* Milan: UTET, 1998.

Rhodes, R.A.W. 'The Hollowing Out of the British State.' *Political Quarterly* 65, no. 2 (April 1994): 138–51.

Risse-Kappen, Thomas, ed. *Bringing Transnational Relations Back In: Non-State Actors, Domestic Structures and International Institutions.* Cambridge: Cambridge University Press, 1995.

Rocher, François, and Miriam Smith, eds. 'Trade Policy, Globalization, and the Future of Canadian Federalism.' *New Trends in Canadian Federalism.* Peterborough, Ont.: Broadview Press, 1995.

Rodrik, Dani. 'Why Do More Open Economies Have Bigger Governments?' *Journal of Political Economy* 106, no. 5 (1998): 997–1032.

Roessler, Frieder. 'Domestic Policy Objectives and the Multilateral Trade Order: Lessons from the Past.' In Anne Kruger, ed., *The WTO as an International Organization,* 213–29. Chicago: University of Chicago Press, 1998.

– 'Increasing Market Access under Regulatory Heterogeneity: The Strategies of the World Trade Organization.' *Regulatory Reform and International Market Openness,* 117–30. Paris: Organisation for Economic Co-operation and Development, 1996.

Rosenau, James. *Along the Domestic–Foreign Frontier: Exploring Governance in a Turbulent World.* Cambridge: Cambridge University Press, 1997.

– 'Epochal Change and the Dynamics of Globalization.' Center for Studies in Society and Politics conference, Bilkent University, Ankara, Turkey, 5 May 1998.

– 'The Future of Politics.' Presentation to Assembly of the World Academy of Art and Science on the Global Century, Vancouver, 7 Nov. 1998.

– 'Governance, Order, and Change in World Politics.' In James Rosenau and Ernst Otto Czempiel, eds., *Governance without Government: Order and Change in World Politics*, 1–29. Cambridge: Cambridge University Press, 1992.

– 'Toward an Ontology of Global Governance.' In Martin Hewson and Timothy Sinclair, eds., *Approaches to Global Governance Theory*, 287–301. Albany: Statue University of New York, 1999.

– *Turbulence in World Politics: A Theory of Change and Continuity*. Princeton, NJ: Princeton University Press, 1990.

Rosenau, James and Durfee, Mary. 'Postinternationalism in a Turbulent World.' In *Thinking Theory Thoroughly: Coherent Approaches to an Incoherent World*, 31–56. Boulder, Col.: Westview Press, 1995.

Rosenberg, Justin. *The Empire of Civil Society: A Critique of the Realist Theory of International Relations*. London: Verso, 1994.

Ruggie, John Gerard. *Constructing the World Polity: Essays on International Institutionalization*. New York: Routledge, 1998.

– 'Continuity and Transformation in the World Polity: Towards a Neorealist Synthesis.' in Robert O. Keohane, ed., *Neorealism and Its Critics*, 131–57. New York: Columbia University Press, 1986.

– 'International Regimes, Transactions, and Change: Embedded Liberalism in the Postwar Economic Order.' In Stephen D. Krasner, ed., *International Regimes*, 195–231. Ithaca, NY: Cornell University Press, 1983.

– 'International Responses to Technology: Concepts and Trends.' *International Organization* 29, no. 3 (summer 1975): 557–83.

– 'Territoriality and Beyond: Problematizing Modernity in International Relations.' *International Organization* 47, no. 1 (winter 1993): 139–74.

Saint-Étienne, Christian. 'De l'état bureaucratique à l'état incitateur et coordonateur.' In René Lenoir and Jacques, eds., *Ou va l'état ? La souveraineté économique et politique en question*, 321. Paris: Le Monde, 1992.

Salter, Liora. 'The Housework of Capitalism: Standardization in the Communications and Information Technology Sectors.' *International Journal of Political Economy* 23, no. 4 (winter 1993–4): 105–13.

Sampson, Gary P. 'Greater Coherence in Global Economic Policymaking: A WTO Perspective.' In Anne Krueger, ed., *The WTO as an International Organization*, 257–70. Chicago: University of Chicago Press, 1998.

Sampson, Martin. 'The Global Environmental Facility/Black Sea Environmental Program: Part Way into Year 2.' Communication presented to Congress of the International Studies Association, San Diego, April 1996.

Sandford, Rosemary. 'Secretariats and International Environmental Negotiations.' In Lawrence Susskind et al., eds., *International Environmental Treaty-making*, Cambridge, Mass.: Program on Negotiation at Harvard Law School.

Santos, Boaventura de Sousa. *Toward a New Common Sense: Law, Science and Politics in the Paradigmatic Transition.* New York: Routledge, 1995.

Scharpf, Fritz W. *Negative and Positive Integration in the Political Economy of European Welfare States.* Florence: European University Institute, 1995.

Schmitter, Philippe C. 'Examining the Present Euro-polity with the Help of Past Theories.' In Gary Marks et al., eds., *Governance in the European Union,* 1–14. London: Thousand Oaks, Calif.: Sage Publications, 1996.

– 'Still the Century of Corporatism?' *Review of Politics* 36, no. 1 (Jan. 1974): 85–131.

Schnapper, Dominique. *La relation a l'autre. Au cœr de la pensée sociologique.* Paris: Gallimard, 1998.

Scholte, Jan Aart with Robert O'Brien and Marc Williams. 'The WTO and Civil Society.' *Journal of World Trade* 33, no. 1 (1999): 107–23.

Scoffield, Heather. 'Groups Pitch Alternative to MAI.' *Globe and Mail,* 8 July 1998, B4.

Shearer, David. 'Outsourcing War.' *Foreign Policy* (fall 1998): 68–78.

Shields, John, and Stephen McBride. *Dismantling a Nation.* Second edition. Halifax: Fernwood Press, 1997.

Simeon, Richard. 'Canada and the United States: Lessons from the North American Experience.' In Karen Knop et al., *Rethinking Federalism: Citizens, Markets, and Governments in a Changing World,* Vancouver: University of British Columbia Press, 1995.

Simmons, P.J. 'Learning to Live with NGOs.' *Foreign Policy.* (fall 1998): 21–33.

Simon, Hix. 'The Study of the European Union II: The "New Governance" Agenda and Its Rival.' *Journal of European Public Policy* 51 (March 1998): 38–65.

Sinclair, Timothy. 'Bond-Rating Agencies and Co-ordination in the Global Political Economy.' In Claire Cutler et al., eds., *Private Authority and International Affairs* 153–68 Albany, NY: State University of New York Press, 1999.

Slaughter, Anne-Marie. 'The Real New World Order.' *Foreign Affairs* 76, no. 5 (Sept.–Oct. 1997): 183–97.

Snidal, Duncan. 'International Political Economy Approaches to International Institutions.' In Jagdeep S. Bhandari and A.O. Sykes, eds., *Economic Dimensions in International Law: Comparative and Empirical Perspectives,* 477–512. Cambridge: Cambridge University Press, 1997.

Snyder, Richard W., et al. 'Decision-making as an Approach to the Study of International Politics.' In Snyder et al., *Foreign Policy Decision Making: An Approach to the Study of International Politics,* 106–70. New York: Free Press of Glencoe, 1962.

Sprinzak, Ehud. 'The Great Superterrorism Scare.' *Foreign Policy* (fall 1998): 110–24.

Spulber, Nicolas. *Redefining the State: Privatization and Welfare Reform in Industrial and Transitional Economies*. Cambridge: Cambridge University Press, 1997.

Stairs, Denis. 'The Policy Process and Dialogues with Demos: Liberal Pluralism with a Transnational Twist.' In Maureen Appel Molot and Fen Osler Hampson, eds., *Leadership and Dialogue: Canada among Nations 1998*, Toronto: Oxford University Press, 1998.

Stanbury, W.T. 'Chronology of Canadian Telecommunications: January 1992 to January 1996.' In W.T. Stanbury, ed., *Perspectives on the New Economics and Regulation of Telecommunications*, Ottawa: Rebouf Publishers Ltd, 1996.

Stein, Arthur A. 'Coordination and Collaboration: Regimes in an Anarchic World.' In Stephen Krasner, ed., *International Regimes*, 115–40. Ithaca, NY: Cornell University Press, 1983.

Stein, Janice Gross. 'Detection and Defection: Security "Regimes" and the Management of International Conflict.' *International Journal* 40, no. 4 (autumn 1985): 599–617.

Stewart, Phil. 'Brazil's Home for Child Offenders Sparks Anger.' *Globe and Mail*, 9 Sept. 1999, A5A.

Stoker, Gerry. 'Governance as Theory: Five Propositions.' *International Social Science Journal* 155 (March 1998): 1–21.

Stopford, John, and Susan Strange, with John S. Henley. *Rival States, Rival Firms: Competition for World Market Shares*. Cambridge: Cambridge University Press, 1991.

Strange, Susan. 'Cave! hic dragones: A Critique Of Regime Analysis.' In Stephen Krasner, ed., *International Regimes*, 337–54. Ithaca, NY: Cornell University Press, 1983.

– 'The Defective State.' *Daedulus* 124, no. 2 (spring 1995): 55–75.

– *The Retreat of the State: The Diffusion of Power in the World Economy*. Cambridge: Cambridge University Press, 1996.

– 'States, Firms and Diplomacy.' *International Affairs* 68 (1992), 1–15.

Straw, Tim. 'Sound Recording.' In Michael Dorland, ed., *Canada's Cultural Industries*, Scarborough, Ont.: Carswell, 1996.

Streeck, Wolfgang. 'Public Power beyond the Nation-State: The Case of the European Community.' In Robert Boyer and Daniel Drache, eds., *States against Markets: The Limits of Globalization*, 299–315. London: Routledge, 1996.

Stubbs, Richard. 'ASEAN's Distinctive Capitalism: Implications for International Trade Rules.' In William Coleman and Geoffrey Underhill, eds., *Regionalism and Global Economic Integration: Europe, Asia and America*, 68–81. London: Routledge, 1997.

Suganami, Hidemi. 'Overview. A Note on Some Recent Writings on International Relations and Organizations.' *International Affairs* 74, no. 4 (Oct. 1998): 903–10.

Susskind, Lawrence. *Environmental Diplomacy: Negotiating More Effective Global Agreements.* New York: Oxford University Press, 1994.

Taylor, Charles. 'Globalization and the Future of Canada.' *Queen's Quarterly* 105, no. 3 (fall 1998): 331–42.

Tesoro, Ministero del. Le Commissioni di Studi del Ministero del Tesoro. *Pensioni, privatizzazioni e spesa pubblica.* Rome: Istituto Poligrafico dello Stato, 1993.

Tetlock, Philip E., and Aaron Belkin, eds. *Counterfactual Thought Experiments in World Politics: Logical, Methodological, and Psychological Perspectives.* Princeton, NJ: Princeton University Press, 1996.

Thakur, Ramesh, and William Maley. 'The Ottawa Convention on Landmines: A Landmark Humanitarian Treaty in Arms Control?' *Global Governance* 5, no. 3 (July–Sept. 1999): 273–302.

Thérien, Jean Philippe. 'Le Canada et le regime international de l'aide.' *Études internationales* 20 (June 1989): 311–40.

Thiemann, Ronald S. *Religion in Public Life: A Dilemma for Democracy.* Washington, DC: Georgetown University Press, 1996.

Thomson, Janice E. 'Explaining the Regulation of Transnational Practices: A State-Building Approach.' In James N. Rosenau and Ernst-Otto Czempiel, eds., *Governance without Government: Order and Change in World Politics,* 195–218. Cambridge: Cambridge University Press, 1992.

– 'State Sovereignty in International Relations: Bridging the Gap between Theory and Empirical Search.' *International Studies Quaterly* 39 (1995): 213–29.

Tinbergen, Jan. *International Economic Integration.* Second revised edition. Amsterdam: Elsevier Publishing Company, 1965.

Trachtman, Joel P. 'International Regulatory Competition, Externalization, and Jurisdiction.' *Harvard International Law Journal* 34, no. 1 (winter 1993): 47–104.

Tsebelis, George. 'The Power of the European Parliament as a Conditional Agenda Setter.' *American Political Science Review* 88, no. 1 (1994): 128–42.

Tsebelis, George, and Amie Kreppel. 'The History of Conditional Agenda Setting in European Integration.' *European Journal of Political Research* 33, no. 1 (1998): 41–71.

UNDP. *Reconceptualising Governance.* Discussion Paper No. 2. New York: UNDP, 1997.

UNEP. 'Administrative Arrangement between the United Nations Environment Program (UNEP) and the Secretariat of the Convention on Biological Diversity (CBD).' Signed 3 April 1998 (UNEP/CBD/CoP/4/24).

U.S. Government 'Remarks by the President on Keeping America Secure for the 21st Century.' National Academy of Sciences, Washington, DC, 22 Jan. 1999, White House, Office of the Press Secretary, http://www.whitehouse.gov/WH/New/html/19990122-7214.html.

Van Deth, J.W. 'Comparative Politics and the Decline of the Nation-state in Western Europe.' *European Journal of Political Research* 27 (1995).

Vignon, Jérome, 'La cohésion économique et sociale.' In Laïdi. *Géopolitique du sens.*

Vogel, Steven K. *Freer Markets, More Rules: Regulatory Reform in Advanced Industrial Countries.* Ithaca. NY: Cornell University Press, 1996.

Wade, Robert, and Suzanne Berger. *National Diversity and Global Capitalism.* Ithaca, NY: Cornell University Press, 1996.

Waever, Ole. 'Securitization and Desecuritization.' In Ronnie D. Lipschutz, ed., *On Security,* 46–86. New York: Columbia University Press, 1995.

Walker, R.B.J. *Inside/Outside: International Relations as Political Theory.* Cambridge: Cambridge University Press, 1993.

Walter, Andrew. 'Do They Really Rule the World?' *New Political Economy,* 3, no. 2 (July 1998): 288–92.

Waltz, Kenneth. *Theory of International Politics.* Berkeley: University of California Press, 1979.

Walzer, Michael, ed. *Toward a Global Civil Society.* New York: Berghahn Book, 1997.

Wapner, Paul. 'Governance in Global Civil Society.' In Oran Young, ed., *Global Governance: Drawing Insights from the Environmental Experience,* 65–84. Cambridge, Mass.: MIT Press, 1997.

Waterman, Peter. *Globalisation, Social Movements and the New Internationalisms.* London: Cassell, 1998.

Watson, William. *Globalization and the Meaning of Canadian Life.* Toronto: University of Toronto Press, 1998.

Watts, Ronald L., and Douglas M. Brown, eds. *Canada: The State of the Federation 1993.* Kingston: Institute of Intergovernmental Relations, Queen's University, 1993.

– *Canada: The State of the Federation 1989.* Kingston: Institute of Intergovernmental Relations, Queen's University, 1989.

Webb, Michael C. 'Canada and the International Monetary Regime.' In Claire Cutler and Mark W. Zacher, eds., *Canadian Foreign Policy and International Economic Regimes,* 153–85.Vancouver: University of British Columbia Press, 1992.

Weber, Max. 'The Profession and Vocation of Politics.' In Peter Lassman and Ronald Speirs, eds., *Weber: Political Writings,* 309–69. Cambridge: Cambridge University Press, 1994.

– *The Protestant Ethic and the Spirit of Capitalism.* New York: Routledge, 1993.

Weber, Steven. 'Institutions and Change.' In Michael W. Doyle and G. John Ikenberry, eds., *New Thinking in International Relations Theory,* 229–65. Boulder, Col.: Westview, 1997.

Weiner, Antje, and Vincent Della Sala. 'Constitution-Making and Citizenship Practice: Bridging the Democracy Gap in the EU?' *Journal of Common Market Studies* 35, no. 4 (Dec. 1997): 595–614.

Weiss, Edith Brown. 'The Five International Treaties: A Living History.' In Edith Brown Weiss and Harold K. Jacobson, eds., *Engaging Countries: Strengthening Compliance with International Environmental Accords,* 89–172. Cambridge, Mass.: MIT Press, 1998.

Weiss, Linda. *The Myth of the Powerless State.* Ithaca, NY: Cornell University Press, 1998.

Weiss, Thomas, and Leon Gordenker, eds. *NGOs, the UN, and Global Governance.* Bouldner, Col.: Lynne Rienner, 1996.

Weiss, Thomas G., and Girat Chopra. 'Sovereignty Is No Longer Sacrosanct: Codifying Humanitarian Intervention.' *Ethics and International Affairs* 6 (1992): 95–118.

Wendt, Alexander. 'Collective Identity Formation and the International State.' *American Political Science Review* 88, no. 2 (June 1994): 384–96.

Weyrauch, Walter Otto, and Maureen Ann Bell. 'Autonomous Lawmaking: The Case of the "Gypsies."' *Yale Law Journal* 103, no. 2 (Nov. 1993): 323–99.

Wilson, Michael H. *Securing Economic Renewal – the Agenda for Economic Renewal: Principles and Progress.* Ottawa: Department of Finance, 18 Feb. 1987.

Wolfe, David. 'The Emergence of the Region State.' In Thomas J. Courchene, ed.,*The Nation-state in a Global/Information Era: Policy Challenges,* 205–40. Kingston: John Deutsch Institute for the Study of Economic Policy, 1997.

Wolfe, Joel D. 'Reorganizing Interest Representation: A Political Analysis of Privatization in Britain.' In Joel Wolfe and R. Foglesong, eds., *The Politics of Economic Adjustment,* New York: Oxford University press, 1996.

Wolfe, Robert. *Farm Wars: The Political Economy of Agriculture and the International Trade Regime.* London and New York: Macmillan and St Martin's Press, 1998.

Wolfe, Robert. 'Regulatory Diplomacy: Why Rhythm Beats Harmony in the Trade Regime.' In Thomas J. Courchene, ed., *Room to Manoeuvre? Globalization and Policy Convergence,* Kingston: John Deutsch Institute for the Study of Economic Policy, 1999.

WTO. *Annual Report 1998: Volume 1.* Geneva: World Trade Organization, 1998.

Young, Oran. 'Negotiating a Global Climate Change Regime.' In *International*

Governance: Protecting the Environment in a Stateless Society, 12–32. Ithaca, NY: Cornell University Press, 1994.

– 'The Politics of International Regime Formation: Managing Natural Resources and the Environment.' *International Organization* 43, no. 3 (summer 1989): 349–75.

Young, Oran, and Konrad von Moltke. 'International Secretariats.' Background Paper for the Workshop at the Rockefeller Brothers Conference Center, Pocantico, NY, 15–18 June, 1995.

Zacher, Mark. 'The Decaying Pillars of the Westphalian Temple: Implications for International Order and Governance.'In James Rosenau and Ernst-Otto Czempiel, eds., *Governance without Government: Order and Change in World Politics*, 58–101. Cambridge: Cambridge University Press, 1992.

Zacher, Mark, with Brent A. Sutton. *Governing Global Networks: International Regimes for Transportation and Communications*. Cambridge: Cambridge University Press, 1996.

www.ingramcontent.com/pod-product-compliance
Lightning Source LLC
LaVergne TN
LVHW090803070826
844660LV00022B/1065

* 9 7 8 0 8 0 2 0 8 3 8 8 3 *